The Canadian Welfare State

The Canadian Welfare State

EVOLUTION AND TRANSITION

Edited by
Jacqueline S. Ismael

 THE UNIVERSITY OF ALBERTA PRESS

First published by
The University of Alberta Press
Athabasca Hall
Edmonton, Alberta, Canada
1987

ISBN 0-88864-112-5   cloth
       0-88864-113-3   paper

Canadian Cataloguing in Publication Data

Main entry under title:
The Canadian welfare state

Based on papers originally presented at the
Conference on Provincial Social Welfare Policy
held at the University of Calgary, May 1–3, 1985.
ISBN 0-88864-112-5 (bound).—ISBN
0-88864-113-3 (pbk.)

1. Public welfare - Canada. 2. Canada -
Social policy.   I. Ismael, Jacqueline S.
II. Conference on Provincial Social Welfare
Policy (2nd : 1985 : University of Calgary)
HV105.C35 1987   361.6'1'0971   C86-091466-6

Typesetting by Typeworks, Vancouver, British Columbia
Printed by D.W. Friesen & Sons Ltd., Altona, Manitoba, Canada

CONTENTS

Preface   ix

Introduction   xi

Contributors   xxiii

Part I: Evolution and Transition

1   Shadows From the Thirties: The Federal
    Government and Unemployment
    Assistance, 1941–1956   3
    James Struthers

2   Tools For the Job: Canada's Evolution
    from Public Works to Mandated
    Employment   33
    Leslie A. Pal

Part II: Income Security

3   Descriptive Overview of Selected
    Provincial Income Supplementation and
    Work Incentive Initiatives   65
    Gilles Séguin

4   Ideology and Income Supplementation:
    A Comparison of Quebec's Supplément
    au Revenu de Travail and Ontario's
    Work Incentive Program   80
    Andrew F. Johnson

5   Welfare, Work Incentives, and the Single
     Mother: An Interprovincial
     Comparison   101
     Patricia M. Evans and Eilene McIntyre

6   Feeding Canada's Poor: The Rise of the
     Food Banks and the Collapse of the
     Public Safety Net   126
     Graham Riches

Part III: Job Creation

7   Trends and Priorities in Job Creation
     Programs: A Comparative Study of
     Federal and Selected Provincial
     Policies   151
     Stephen McBride

8   Job Creation vs. Development in the
     Atlantic Provinces   171
     Michael Bradfield

9   "Half a Loaf Is Better Than None":
     The Newfoundland Rural Development
     Movement's Adaptation to the Crisis of
     Seasonal Unemployment   192
     Richard P. Fuchs

10   The Bloom Is Off the Lotus: Job Creation
     Policy and Restraint in British
     Columbia   212
     Patrick J. Smith and Laurent Dobuzinskis

Part IV: Policy Process

11   How Ottawa Decides Social Policy:
     Recent Changes in Philosophy,
     Structure, and Process   247
     Michael J. Prince

12   Critical Compromises in Ontario's Child
     Welfare Policy   274
     Gail Aitken

13   Social Policy and Some Aspects of the
Neoconservative Ideology in British
Columbia   300
Chris R. McNiven

14   Public Policy and Social Welfare: The
Ideology and Practice of Restraint in
Ontario   327
Ramesh Mishra

Part V: Perspectives on the Welfare State

15   Canadian Federalism and the Welfare
State: Shifting Responsibilities and
Sharing Costs   349
Frank Strain and Derek Hum

16   Controlling the Deficit and a Private
Sector Led Recovery: Contemporary
Themes of the Welfare State   372
Gordon W. Ternowetsky

PREFACE

This volume was inspired by the second Conference on Provincial Social Welfare Policy, held at The University of Calgary, May 1–3, 1985. Many of the chapters are revised versions of papers presented at the conference. The theme of the Canadian welfare state in transition, one of the central themes of the conference, provided a comparative provincial framework for examining trends across the provinces and identifying common patterns across political, policy, and program boundaries.

I wish to thank the contributors to this volume for their participation, especially Leslie A. Pal who kindly assisted in shepherding the volume through the publication process after my departure for sabbatical. Also, I want to thank Alex Brynen, my research assistant, for her invaluable assistance, Doreen Neville for her patience in typing and correcting the manuscript, and Peggy Raitt for her care in proofing it. Neither the conference nor this volume could have been realized without the support and confidence of Dr. Ray Thomlison, Dean, Faculty of Social Welfare at The University of Calgary, who provided the academic leadership necessary to such endeavours. Finally, I wish to acknowledge The University of Calgary and the Faculty of Social Welfare for their assistance in the publication of this volume.

INTRODUCTION

The theme of this volume is that the welfare state in Canada has evolved and is changing in relation to employment-related social issues. In the evolution of the Canadian welfare state income security policies played the central role in the structure; in the transition of the welfare state job creation programs are beginning to assume this role—suggesting a significant change in the structure of the welfare state itself.

Publication of the Report by the Royal Commission on the Economic Union and Development Prospects for Canada (the Macdonald Commission report) highlights this transition of the welfare state by shifting the developmental thrust from income security to job creation. In effect, the Commission advocates consolidation and containment of social support programs through the Universal Income Security Program proposal, and expansion of human resource deployment programs through the Transitional Adjustment Assistance Program proposal. It is in the context of the Commission's consideration of high unemployment levels as a long-term problem, a "normal" rate of unemployment between six and eight percent, and the problem of youth unemployment, that the shift in focus from issues of social support to issues of human resources deployment is evident. The Commission, however, simply reflects a transition that has been under way for some time by suggesting a policy framework for managing it.

The theme of evolution around income security and transition around job creation is organized in five parts. Part I, Evolution and Transition, focuses on the broad dimension of this process of change. It is introduced by James Struthers's chapter, "Shadows

From the Thirties," which examines the development of unemployment assistance policy between 1941 and 1956. During reconstruction planning in the 1940s, few objectives assumed as much importance within Canadian social work as the reorganization and reform of public assistance. With the memory of the Depression fresh in their minds, Canadian social workers were determined to ensure that social assistance for the jobless should be a right of citizenship, should provide an adequate subsistence minimum, and should be administered by trained personnel. Yet between 1941, when Ottawa terminated its payments to unemployment relief, and the passage of the Unemployment Assistance Act fifteen years later, jobless Canadians not covered by unemployment insurance were ineligible for social assistance in virtually all Canadian provinces and municipalities. During these years, federal government policy oscillated from a declaration of complete responsibility for all the unemployed in the Green Book proposals on social security in 1945, to a denial by 1950 of any obligation to assist the unemployed outside of unemployment insurance. As the last resort for those in need Canada's private charities bore the brunt of caring for this category of the jobless during the 1940s and early 1950s.

Struthers's chapter examines the interaction between the federal government, the Canadian social work profession and the provinces over unemployment assistance during the 1940s and 1950s. Although public pressure by the Canadian Welfare Council between 1950–55 helped to push a reluctant St. Laurent government into implementing the Unemployment Assistance Act this legislation only partially realized longstanding social work goals for the reform of public welfare. The act failed to define a national subsistence minimum to provide a legal right to relief, or to enforce professional standards of public welfare administration. Struthers concludes that, at best, the Unemployment Assistance Act was a transitional piece of social legislation which owed more to the politics of the 1930s than to the changing requirements of social welfare in postwar Canada. Nevertheless, this legislation did contain one ironic and unforeseen outcome. Although premised upon the existence of clear categorical distinctions between the employable and unemployable in need, the Unemployment Assistance Act became one of the principal catalysts for breaking down the categorical approach to poverty in Canada, and establishing expanded eligibility for social assistance to those in need. In this sense, it played a crucial role in paving the way for the Canada Assistance Plan adopted in 1966.

The rapid growth of social programs throughout the fifties and sixties culminated in the Social Security Review launched in the seventies as an effort to improve and expand the system's effectiveness in ameliorating the conditions of poverty, inequality, and inequity in Canada. However, the reform effort represented by the Review dissipated in the restraint and retrenchment programs launched in the second half of the decade. By 1980, it appeared that the welfare state was being dismantled. The demise of the Social Security Review, however, actually signalled the structural shift in the welfare state from income security as its raison d'etre to job creation. Leslie Pal's chapter demonstrates that job creation, in fact, has been an emerging pattern within the welfare state framework from its inception. Whereas the earliest postwar prescriptions for the welfare state called for it to perform a supporting role to the market, it is now conventional to believe that Western governments are responsible for "creating" jobs. Canadian cabinet ministers, at both provincial and federal levels, regardless of political stripe, routinely recite their success on this front. Despite the increase of social spending cuts, monetarist policies, and complaints about the deficit since the demise of the Social Security Review, all Canadian governments have been busily creating jobs through either direct employment, wage subsidies, or affirmative action programs. Their behaviour is indicative of the shift in the welfare state structure. While the expansion of social support programs is being restrained, if not rolled back, job creation programs are growing vigorously.

Canada's record of job creation, until recently, was the best of the industrialized countries and thus makes an interesting case for analysis. Leslie Pal's chapter explores this area of policy from its earliest forms in the notion of public works to its modern manifestation in what he terms "mandated employment," or direct state injunctions concerning hiring, firing, and promotion in private firms. He addresses this evolution within the context of "policy succession"—or the idea that governments typically move through a roughly logical order of policy instruments or tools to achieve their purposes—and demonstrates how the undermining of some of the key supporting ideas of the traditional welfare state, particularly Keynesian aggregate demand management, actually encouraged the use of more, not less, direct policy instruments.

While Part I examines the broad parameters of evolution and transition, Part II focuses on some key aspects of income security policy—particularly on the themes of income security and work incentives that have played counterpoint in the evolution and transition of the welfare state. The federal programs that have been the central pillars of the welfare state—Family Allowance, Child Tax Credit, Old Age Security, Guaranteed Income Supplement, Canada Pension Plan, Unemployment Insurance—constituted its safety net framework. The working poor and unemployed employables, however, fell through the federal safety net. It is in this area that the issues of income support versus work incentives played out the most intense counterpoint. And with the spiralling inflation and unemployment of the great recession initiated in the mid-seventies, increasing numbers of Canadian households fell into these groups. Programs targeted at them fall under provincial jurisdiction. Therefore, this section concentrates on provincial programs.

It is introduced by Gilles Séguin's chapter which provides a descriptive overview of Quebec's Work Income Supplement, Ontario's Work Incentive Program, Manitoba's Child-Related Income Supplement Program, and Saskatchewan's Family Income Plan. It also examines features of provincial social assistance programs which are cost-shareable under the Canada Assistance Plan, with particular emphasis on employment-related assistance granted under these programs.

Andrew F. Johnson's chapter provides an analytic comparison of the Quebec and Ontario programs to identify and explain the similarities and differences between them. Both programs were created in 1979 and, although they were initiated independently of each other, they shared many characteristics. The most striking similarities were that both programs were lightly funded; incentives to work were emphasized within the context of each program; and both were largely perceived as experimental. However, these broad similarities were operationalized in ways that differed significantly.

Johnson concludes that factors which were external to the welfare system account for the similarities. These include fiscal restraint, a general mood of social conservatism as well as electoral competition within each province. However, the different ways in which these similarities were operationalized are largely attributable to the different ideological principles that have been diffused throughout the welfare policy-making system in the two provinces—the principles of Catholic social thought in Quebec compared to the liberal principles in Ontario.

The next chapter, by Patricia M. Evans and Eilene McIntyre, examines the issue of income security versus work incentives, focusing on single mothers—the fastest growing component of social assistance recipients throughout the seventies. Work incentive policies in income maintenance programs mirror with particular clarity the competing demands of social welfare and the labour market. They attempt to resolve the central dilemma of how to provide an "acceptable" standard of living to those in need but not in work, while at the same time ensuring that the perceived need to maintain the incentive to work in the low-wage labour market is not diminished. The current economic recession placed additional but contradictory pressures on these policies: high levels of unemployment severely constrain their effectiveness, yet they receive an increasing emphasis as a possible way to reduce the costs of income maintenance.

Since 1979, most provinces have implicitly redefined sole-support mothers on social assistance as "employable" through introducing new, or strengthening existing, work incentives. Provincial efforts to encourage entry into the labour force are evident in policies which include the imposition of work requirements, attempts to alter the benefit system to increase the rewards of low-paid work, and the provision of a variety of employment-related services. The result may be an erosion of the right to income maintenance for a portion of this group—those deemed able to enter the labour force.

Evans and McIntyre provide a critical analysis of provincial initiatives in work incentive policies, organized in three main sections. First, a discussion of current trends in provincial work incentive policies is organized around the three major work incentive strategies: work requirements, services and efforts to increase the financial rewards of low-paid work. The second part of the chapter examines two central assumptions which underpin these policies: that working and nonworking single mothers represent separate and distinct groups, and that jobs are available which permit a long-term independence from social assistance. The final section concludes with a discussion of future directions.

Graham Riches's chapter concludes this section by focusing on the rise of food banks in Canada as concrete evidence of the breakdown of the public safety net in the early 1980s. The political functions and contradictory roles of food banks are examined from this perspective. Included in the analysis is an examination of the reasons for the rise of the food banks; their origins in the United States, and church, voluntary and labour sectors in Canada; their auspices, funding, and models of organization; their distribution and rationing systems; the people and institutions who use them — both donors and recipients; and their consequences for the public safety net functions of the welfare state in the 1980s. Provincial comparisons in food bank organization are noted as well as the changing demands on federal and provincial systems of social insurance and public relief.

Riches explores the revitalized ethic of voluntarism from a number of perspectives: its potential to accept and condone the breakdown of the system of public welfare in Canada; its capacity to deflect federal, provincial, and municipal political attention away from the issues of hunger, inadequate relief, and the need for reform; and its limitations in providing adequate alternatives. At the same time, food banks are examined as catalysts for promoting public education and advocacy about these issues, particularly with regards to the social rights and legally enforceable claims of all Canadians in need to receive adequate benefits. Policy questions arising from the analysis are examined.

Part III, Job Creation, focuses on the programs emerging in the transition of the welfare state. It is introduced by Stephen McBride's chapter which provides a study of the changing function of job creation policies. Job creation is within a mixed federal-provincial jurisdiction and though the emphasis in McBride's chapter is on the federal level, comparisons are made with the experience of two provinces — Ontario and Manitoba. After a brief historical review of prototypical job creation programs, such as the federal winter works program (1958–68), the chapter shifts to a more detailed analysis of this policy area since 1968. The stated priority attached to the area is gauged through an analysis of the content of throne and budget speeches at the federal level and in the selected provincial jurisdictions. The relationship of the priority accorded job creation to other variables such as increases in the unemployment rate, the political-electoral cycle, changing public policy paradigms, and the ideology of the governing party, receive attention.

From this anaylsis, McBride concludes that, especially in the post-1975 period, a dichotomy exists between the stated and actual priority given job creation. Evidence from the federal level demonstrates that the actual priority of job creation has declined since 1968 despite steadily rising unemployment. This is depicted as the logical result of the adoption, in 1975, of an economic paradigm tolerant of rising unemployment. As a result, the function of job creation has changed, from that of a useful adjunct to a battery of policy instruments aimed at producing relatively full employment, to a means of managing and hence legitimizing unemployment.

Job creation programs, in their origin a subset of overall labour market policies, are becoming a major vehicle for income maintenance for people categorized as employable, reflecting the transcendance of the work incentive ethic over that of social welfare in the transition of the welfare state. The conflict inherent in income security programs in the welfare state's evolution—income security versus work incentives—is also being transcended by a job creation versus economic development conflict inherent in the emerging transition. Michael Bradfield's chapter on the Maritime provinces addresses this directly. By placing federal and Maritime policies in theoretical perspective, Bradfield analyzes the kinds of strategies pursued, focusing on large foreign-owned industrial or processing-oriented projects. The success, strengths, and weaknesses of these strategies are assessed in terms of immediate job creation and long-term development, revealing the contradiction between job creation and development.

The combination of seasonal and structural unemployment has made unemployment an endemic characteristic of the Maritimes. The emphasis on industrial development strategies has intensified rural-urban disparities but not ameliorated structural unemployment. Richard P. Fuchs's chapter examines the problems of seasonal unemployment and rural development in Newfoundland, and how the province's grass-roots Rural Development Movement has met this challenge. He concludes by assessing the potential benefits of a close alliance between Rural Development Associations and the small cooperative credit union system in the province.

The chapter by Patrick J. Smith and Laurent Dobuzinskis concludes this section with an examination of the approach to job creation in British Columbia, where the job creation versus economic development conflict has been most controversial. On March 12, 1984, former Deputy Premier and Minister of Human Resources, Grace McCarthy, addressing a public meeting in Greater Vancouver, stated that "there is no other province in Canada where the Premier could be booed for announcing $200 million of public expenditure for job creation." The Premier simply dismissed his detractors as "bad British Columbians." The event was the announcement of an extension to Advanced Light Rapid Transit, including the building of a bridge across the Fraser River to Surrey, B.C. This public expenditure represented (like B.C. Place/Expo 86, North East Coal and other mega-projects) the province's policy in response to job creation.

In the same month, the Ministries of Labour and of Industry and Small Business Development announced another job creation initiative, the Student Venture Capital Program, 1984. With overall provincial unemployment as the second highest in the country and student/youth unemployment in B.C. at 24.9 percent in February 1984, student grants were eliminated in the February, 1984 budget. The Student Venture Capital Program offered "interest-free loans of up to $2,000 to students who wish to plan to operate their own business." The program represented "a new initiative to provide business experience for students."

Smith and Dobuzinskis argue that these initiatives have been entirely illustrative of the public policy response of the Province of British Columbia to social welfare policy and, specifically, to the question of job creation. At least since the July 7, 1983 budget, the stated policy of the government has been "to downsize" its own operation, "to privatize" much of the current human resource sector, and "to re-establish the risk taker." Their prognosis indicates that as a public policy response to social policy needs in the province, the B.C. approach has failed: in the period since the July, 1983 budget, unemployment has increased, and the expectation that the privatization of social policy, and the idea that self-sufficiency in the midst of a depression would unleash the private sector to create all the necessary jobs, have remained unfulfilled. This failure has occurred at the expense of major public investments to facilitate private development.

Part IV, Policy Process, shifts the focus of attention to the changing nature of the social policy process. It is introduced by Michael J. Prince's chapter on changes at the federal level. The social policy decision-making system in the federal government is in perpetual evolution. To properly understand how Ottawa decides social policy requires a consideration of recent changes in ideas, organizations, and procedures. Accordingly, this chapter examines the social policy philosophy of the Mulroney Government by examining key statements and documents. In addition, new developments in the cabinet system, central agencies, budget system, and other processes are discussed. A central theme of the chapter is that reforms to policy structures and processes always involve choices and trade-offs between values and interests. Assessing the recent changes in this context, Prince concludes that they promote financial restraint and control, ministerial authority and political rationality, and some debureaucratization. All of these changes have significance for how Ottawa will decide social policy.

The subsequent chapters in this section examine the provincial level. Gail Aitken examines the dynamics of change in Ontario's child welfare policies. She compares and contrasts policy processes of the expansionist mid-60s with recent circumstances and events. The first part of the chapter focuses on methods and outcomes of revisions effected through the 1965 Child Welfare Act. Specific attention is directed to changes in adoption policy which were intended to ensure that all crown wards were to be considered adoptable until proven otherwise. The study reveals how weak policies and provincial parsimony compromised the well-being of many of the "hard-to-place," mostly nonwhite or handicapped children beyond infancy. It demonstrates consequences for the rights of children, as well as for their natural, foster, and adoptive parents.

The second part of the chapter compares earlier processes with recent policy trends and developments around the 1985 Child and Family Services Act. It assesses shifts in the dynamics and indicates factors, issues, and events influencing both processes and outcomes. Particular attention is paid to policies concerning adoption disclosure. Clearly evident are the increased "withinputs," that is, policies generated within government, and the decreased responsiveness of government to the input of diverse interest groups. The analysis reflects the fact that the transition of the welfare state has far-reaching implications for the entire field of social policy and its impact on human well-being in Canadian society.

Expanding this theme, the chapter by Chris R. McNiven explores some of the implications for the general direction of social welfare policy in British Columbia resulting from the radical shift to neoconservatism as the ideology of public policy. The development of social policy in different constituencies is influenced not only by economic conditions but by the ideological context within which such development occurs. In British Columbia, the Social Credit and the New Democratic parties hold conflicting but equally strong views about the factors that contribute to socioeconomic welfare and most B.C. residents are affected by the policy choices which the party in power makes on their behalf. In May 1983, a Social Credit government was re-elected for the third time since 1975 and a few weeks later it unveiled a policy of fiscal restraint which turned rapidly into a major plan to develop a B.C. version of neoconservatism. This chapter examines various aspects of what the B.C. government has described as "a challenge to the new economic reality," placing social welfare policy in ideological perspective.

This section concludes with the chapter by Ramesh Mishra which develops a typology of social policy responses to the economic crisis of stagflation. Five different responses are identified with respect to the welfare state: dismantling, retrenching, restraining, maintaining, and transforming. These are conceptualized as broadly corresponding to the politico-economic ideologies extending from the radical right to the radical left. In the Canadian context, the ideology of dismantling has been in action in British Columbia. The ideology of retrenchment, on the other hand, has been at work in the Province of Ontario for many years. While the former, with its drama and visibility, has provoked a strong reaction, the latter has received much less critical attention. Mishra, however, argues that the cumulative impact of retrenchment may prove to be more consequential for social welfare in the long run. This is demonstrated with reference to public policy in Ontario since 1975.

The papers in this section offer a variety of perspectives on the changing social policy process at both federal and provincial levels. They are all focused on social policy as traditionally defined in the evolution of the welfare state and collectively reflect the narrowing scope of the social policy process in the traditional evolutionary welfare state framework. Considered in conjunction with the earlier sections of the volume, the changing policy process reflects a fundamental shift in the structure of the welfare state. Part V, Perspectives on the Welfare State, provides two approaches to the welfare state—one focusing on the process of its evolution, the other on its transition.

The chapter by Frank Strain and Derek Hum examines changes in the Canadian welfare state from an evolutionary perspective. Conceptualizing the welfare state as the assumption by society of the legal and explicit responsibility for the basic well-being of all its members, they examine the way in which political, economic, and constitutional forces have interacted over time to shape the institutions of the welfare state. The chapter begins by considering classical federalism and its relevance today. It then charts selected episodes illustrating Canada's evolution towards a welfare state. This is followed by a description of the common market and public choice models of federalism and a discussion of their weaknesses for understanding the federal welfare state. Finally, Strain and Hum offer an alternative view in which the notion of "primary citizenship" is introduced and document the actual shift of responsibility for financing the federal welfare state activities from provincial societies to the national government. They conclude that primary citizenship is today lodged at the national polity.

The final chapter by Gordon W. Ternowetsky assumes implicitly that the welfare state is not a neutral apparatus serving the interests of society, nor is society a homogeneous body with a common basic standard of well-being. Rather, the structure and functions of the welfare state are subordinate to the primary interests the state itself serves, and these interests are neither neutral, equal, nor complementary in the structure of society. It is from this perspective that the chapter explores selected themes and concepts running through the public economic and policy statements made by the Conservatives in their effort to chart new courses for economic renewal and social policy in Canada. Two key elements in the Conservatives' economic agenda are to lower the deficit and create favourable circumstances for a private sector led recovery. However, their operational definition of the deficit is one-sided, primarily restricted to the impact of direct spending. By turning the deficit debate into a problem of spending, our attention is diverted from the crucial issue of the way the deficit is formed by individual and corporate tax breaks and subsidies. The assumption that the private sector will create jobs once profits are secure is also unfounded among the largest Canadian corporations which are also the main business recipients of public funds. Ternowetsky concludes that it is important to shift the focus of our research and policy concerns from traditional areas of expenditure to those more or less hidden forms of public transfers that go unnoticed, benefit powerful corporations and the rich, and offer little return to the Canadian people.

The contributions in this volume examine the evolution and transition of the Canadian welfare state from a variety of perspectives. Individually, they provide valuable case studies of various dimensions of the welfare state, its relationship to employment related issues, and its changing character. Collectively, the chapters provide insight into the dynamics of change and the direction of transition. The implications of a structural shift within the welfare state from income security to job creation as its raison d'etre are reflected in the changing character of social policy initiatives and processes, as well as the ideology that legitimates them. While the welfare state evolved as a framework for managing short-term unemployment, it is changing into a framework for managing long-term unemployment. Further research is required to understand the significance of this change for the way needs are defined and met in the framework of Canadian society—that is, for understanding the functions of the welfare state itself.

CONTRIBUTORS

Gail Aitken is Professor of the Faculty of Community Services, Ryerson Polytechnical Institute, Toronto. She is continuing research in child welfare policy and conducting research in health-care policy development in Ontario.

Michael Bradfield is Associate Professor of Economics at Dalhousie University. His recent publications include articles on policy analysis and financing development in the Canadian Centre for Policy Alternatives' *The Government's Agenda for Economic Renewal* and *Strategies for Canadian Economic Self-Reliance*, respectively.

Laurent Dobuzinskis is Assistant Professor of Political Science at Simon Fraser University. His current research interests include the function of information and theoretical knowledge in the policy-making process.

Patricia M. Evans is Sessional Assistant Professor in the Department of Social Work at York University. Her article, "Work and Welfare: A Profile of Low-Income Single Mothers" recently appeared in the *Canadian Social Work Review*.

Richard Fuchs is Director of Research and Analysis in the Department of Rural, Agricultural and Northern Development, Government of Newfoundland and Labrador. He also serves as a part-time Lecturer in Sociology at Memorial University of Newfoundland. Among his recent publications is *Steel Island: Rural Residents in the Exploration Phase of the Offshore Oil and Gas Industry, Newfoundland and Labrador*.

Derek Hum is Professor of Economics and Fellow of St. John's College, University of Manitoba. His research interests include social welfare policy, Canadian federalism and quantitative methods. He is the author of *Federalism and the Poor* and co-author of *Experimental Social Programs and Analytic Methods*.

Jacqueline S. Ismael is Professor of Social Welfare, The University of Calgary. Among her recent publications are *Kuwait: Social Change in Historical Perspective, Government and Politics in Islam* (with Tareq Y. Ismael), *Canadian Social Welfare Policy: Federal and Provincial Dimensions, People's Democratic Republic of Yemen: The Politics of Socialist Transformation* (with Tareq Y. Ismael), and *Perspectives on Social Services and Social Issues* (with Ray J. Thomlison).

Andrew F. Johnson is Assistant Professor of Political Science at Bishop's University. He is currently conducting research on the relationship of organized labour to the development of social programs in Canada. He is the author of "Restructuring Family Allowances: 'Good Politics at No Cost'?" in *Canadian Social Welfare Policy: Federal and Provincial Dimensions*.

Stephen McBride is Assistant Professor of Political Studies, Lakehead University. His research interests are in Comparative and Canadian Politics. Recent publications include articles in *Political Studies* and the *Canadian Journal of Political Science*.

Eilene L. McIntyre is Associate Professor of Social Work, University of Toronto. Her current research interests are in the development and testing of mid-range theories of policy formation in Canada, and in methods of policy development.

Chris R. McNiven is Associate Professor of Social Welfare, The University of British Columbia. She is currently conducting research on the purchase of child welfare services from the nongovernmental sector in British Columbia.

Ramesh Mishra teaches social policy at the School of Social Work, McMaster University. His recent publications include *The Welfare State in Crisis: Social Thought and Social Change*.

Leslie A. Pal is Associate Professor of Political Science, The University of Calgary. Among his recent publications are *Public Policy Analysis: An Introduction* and *State, Class, and Bureaucracy: Canadian Unemployment Insurance and Public Policy.*

Michael J. Prince is Associate Professor of Public Administration, Carleton University. His recent publications include *Policy Advice and Organizational Survival, Federal and Provincial Budgeting,* and *How Ottawa Spends 1986–87: Tracking the Tories.*

Graham Riches is Professor of Social Work, University of Regina. Among his recent publications are *Spending is Choosing: Growth and Restraint in Saskatchewan's Personal Social Services, 1966–77,* (with G. W. Maslany) *Social Welfare and the New Democrats: Personal Social Service Spending in Saskatchewan, 1971–81* and *Food Banks and the Welfare Crisis.*

Gilles Séguin is a legislative analyst with the Policy, Planning and Information Branch of Health and Welfare Canada. He is one of the co-authors of the *Inventory of Income Security Programs in Canada.*

Patrick J. Smith is Assistant Professor of Political Science at Simon Fraser University. His current research interests include comparative senior-local government relations and public policy-making in Britain, the U.S., and Canada, and Canadian constitution-making.

Frank Strain is Assistant Professor of Economics, Mount Allison University. His research interests include public finance, the political economy of the welfare state, and Canadian economic history. He is currently working on a book on the Canadian welfare state and federalism.

James Struthers is Associate Professor in the Canadian Studies Programme at Trent University. He is the author of *No Fault of Their Own: Unemployment and the Canadian Welfare State, 1914–1941.*

Gordon W. Ternowetsky is Associate Professor in the Social Administration Research Unit, Faculty of Social Work, University of Regina. His recent publications are in the areas of income inequality and poverty, tax expenditures, and hidden welfare.

PART
I Evolution and Transition

1 Shadows From the Thirties
The Federal Government and Unemployment Assistance, 1941–1956

JAMES STRUTHERS

Between 1941, when Ottawa terminated its contributions to unemployment relief, and the passage of the Unemployment Assistance Act fifteen years later, few social policy questions proved to be as controversial for federal-provincial relations and Canadian social work as the care of the unemployed not covered by unemployment insurance. Certainly on no other issue did Ottawa pursue such a baffling and contradictory set of policy initiatives. During these years, the federal government oscillated between asserting complete responsibility for all the jobless in its Green Book proposals of 1945 to denying any obligation five years later for those not covered by its insurance scheme. Although unemployment remained generally low during the 1940s and early 1950s, the plight of the jobless trapped outside of Canada's insurance framework was bleak. No provincial or municipal government was willing to provide aid to those whom they deemed were a federal responsibility. As a consequence, Canada's private charities were forced to carry a crippling burden of social assistance throughout this period. Only concerted public pressure by Canadian social workers, operating through the Canadian Welfare Council, finally succeeded in pushing a reluctant St. Laurent administration into accepting a measure of responsibility through the Unemployment Assistance Act of 1956.

The tangled history of Ottawa's response to unemployment assistance provides a revealing glimpse into the formation of the postwar welfare state. The 1956 Unemployment Assistance Act was an important and neglected piece of social legislation enacted during a decade otherwise rather barren of social reform. It marked the first permanent federal commitment to social assistance for employables on welfare and provided a crucial bridgehead into the wider welfare reforms of the 1960s. By the time it was phased out in 1966, Ottawa would be spending over $215,000,000 a year on unemployment assistance, or about two-thirds of all payments through unemployment insurance.[1] Clearly unemployment assistance was a major transition on the road to postwar welfare reform.

The process by which the legislation emerged, however, seriously calls into question interpretations of the postwar welfare state which stress the leadership role of bureaucratic elites working within the civil service to round out a social policy agenda first established by the Rowell-Sirois, Marsh, and Green Book proposals of the 1940s.[2] As will be shown, the Unemployment Assistance Act owed very little to bureaucratic reformers, 1940s "blueprints" for social security, or a desire to establish minimum standards in public welfare. Instead, the legacy of war, federal-provincial financial relations, bureaucratic rivalry, and pressure from Canada's social work community combined in unforeseen ways to press a reluctant St. Laurent administration into accepting a responsibility it did not want. Ironically, even this hesitant commitment became a wedge for further reform. Through consequences unforeseen by its sponsors, unemployment assistance, although initially designed to preserve categorical distinctions among those in need, instead played a major role in breaking down the categorical approach towards poverty by paving the way for the Canada Assistance Plan of 1966.

Planning for Depression

When federal policy makers and Canadian social workers began planning for postwar reconstruction in the early 1940s, no issue assumed more importance than unemployment. Most economic fore-

casts predicted substantial levels of joblessness in the immediate
years following the war's end, and for those familiar with its coverage, the 1940 Unemployment Insurance Act was clearly an inadequate policy instrument to cope with any severe economic
downturn. Less than half of the Canadian workforce was protected
under its terms and seasonal and casual workers, who were most
vulnerable to unemployment, were excluded from benefits. As
even federal officials conceded at the start of the war, unemployment insurance "at any one time [was likely to] provide for no
more than one-quarter of the unemployed."[3]

Moreover, because of the 1940 Unemployment Insurance Act
and its broad wartime economic powers, federal officials realized
Ottawa would be held responsible for coping with the plight of *all*
those who found themselves without work upon the war's end. The
postwar jobless would "face unemployment . . . with much greater
resentment—to put it mildly—than displayed during the Depression years," Bank of Canada Governor Graham Towers warned the
federal cabinet. In the "interests of peace, order and good government," Ottawa would have to "assume full responsibility" for the
problem.[4]

Even before the war began, the final report of the National Employment Commission (NEC), in 1938, had reached a similar conclusion. National unemployment assistance, the NEC argued, was
essential both to protect unemployment insurance from assuming
actuarially unsound risks, and to spread the fiscal burden of any
depression evenly across the country, arguments repeated by the
Report of the Royal Commission on Dominion-Provincial Relations in 1941. Consequently, when planning on postwar reconstruction began in earnest during the early months of 1943, a national unemployment assistance plan, as a companion to unemployment insurance, was the guiding principle of federal policy.[5]

Three considerations shaped Ottawa's planning. First, unemployment assistance was politically essential to postwar reconstruction, Alex Skelton of the powerful Economic Advisory Committee (EAC) argued, in order to make possible extensive tax concessions to business. The "generous assistance to private business," necessary to promote full employment, Skelton stressed,
would "intensify demands that the postwar unemployed should
receive an adequate and certain subsistence." Without such aid to

the jobless, the political "atmosphere" would be so uncertain that it would be "difficult to ... [develop] ... a policy of stimulating private enterprise ... on any scale."[6]

Second, unemployment assistance was a more desirable means of meeting this demand than through public works, the favoured strategy of Cyril James's Advisory Committee on Reconstruction. Public works "should not be given too much place in the total picture," W. A. Mackintosh of the EAC argued in criticizing the work of James's committee. They were awkward to implement, useful mainly to skilled workers, and of less importance to reconversion than was aid to private investment. An expanded social security program was a more crucial priority to ensure the maintenance of national income during the "immediate postwar period,"the EAC argued, and "the most urgent [need] is some plan of unemployment assistance to provide for the unemployed who have exhausted insurance benefits or who are not covered by insurance."[7]

Finally, a federal unemployment assistance program formed one of the most essential parts of Ottawa's strategy for securing the provinces' consent in the postwar era to a permanent surrender of their powers to levy personal and corporate income taxes and succession duties. It was the cost of unemployment relief in the 1930s which had driven four of the provinces to the brink of bankruptcy. Removing that uncertainty from their hands formed a powerful argument for expanding Ottawa's postwar taxation powers. Alternatives, such as meeting postwar unemployment through federal grants-in-aid for public works and social welfare were out of the question. "The very magnitude of the transfers ... necessary [would render Ottawa] the puppet of the stronger provincial organizations," Skelton pointed out.[8]

In early 1944 the Department of Labour was handed the task of drafting such a scheme. Although designed for the jobless, unemployment assistance, unlike insurance, could not be governed by any actuarial formula. As a result, the first problem the department faced was to determine who should be eligible for assistance and how much they should receive. Establishing the "employability" of potential applicants appeared to be relatively straightforward. Since the existing network of Unemployment Insurance Commission (UIC) offices would be used to administer the plan, the Commission could apply essentially the same tests as it presently used on insurance claimants to determine fitness for work. More complicated was the question of determining the level of aid. In order not to discriminate "against the poor devils ... paying [insurance] contributions," it was decided that a family "needs" test would determine eligibility for benefits.[9] But social work concerns for an adequate and decent national minimum remained absent from federal planning. The level of assistance provided would bear no relationship to family need. Otherwise, department officials pointed out, work incentives would be severely compromised. As one departmental memo phrased it:

> It might be contended that a Canadian Standard Living Allowance compatible with decency and health in all parts of Canada could be devised which would take account of the actual needs of a family applying for Assistance. Unfortunately, at a rate adequate to meet the needs of the average family, it would exceed earnings in many parts of the country. Those on Assistance could naturally refuse to work at lower levels of income. Employers unable to secure workers and wage-earners who had 'managed' would rebel. Administratively and politically, therefore, a Canadian Standard of Living Allowance is impossible.

Instead, the labour department proposal pegged assistance rates arbitrarily at 85 percent of unemployment insurance benefits. For most of those eligible, this would equal $6.04 a week for single men and $7.04 for those who were married or approximately one-third of the minimum income which the Toronto Welfare Council calculated was necessary to maintain the health and decency of a family of five in most cities. Labour department officials remained unperturbed by this problem. Cases of real hardship could always be "supplemented" by local authorities "after additional investigation."[10]

Nevertheless, the whole idea of federal means-testing, however rudimentary, caused Health and Welfare officials grave concern. Ottawa lacked the "nation-wide machinery" and trained personnel to attempt such a task, that department's deputy minister, George Davidson, warned. If the federal government began assessing need its criteria would have to relate, in some way, to existing provincial and local welfare standards. Once Ottawa was drawn into this morass of "differentials" between provinces, and between rural and urban areas, it would be "subject[ed] . . . to interminable criticism." Yet without a means test, how could federal unemployment assistance be distinguished from a premium-free unemployment insurance plan?

The dilemma was never resolved. With only minor changes, the Labour Department's Unemployment Assistance (UA) scheme was put forward in the federal government's Green Book proposals on social security published on the eve of the Dominion-Provincial Conference on Reconstruction in August 1945. Despite lingering reservations over the difficulties of national means-testing, federal officials consoled themselves with the thought that the scheme was, at best, a transitional measure for the immediate postwar era until unemployment insurance could be "widened to embrace all employed persons." In any event, the alternative seemed worse. As the Green Book argued, in the event of a postwar depression, Ottawa wished to "avoid the make-shift arrangements and controversy with provincial governments which otherwise would be almost certain to recur under the old [conditional grant] methods of providing relief."[11]

In their preparations for the Dominion-Provincial Reconstruction Conference, federal officials were confident that the offer of a nationally administered and financed unemployment assistance scheme would play an important role in convincing the provinces to surrender their right to levy corporate and personal income taxes."The Dominion's assumption of responsibility for unemployment assistance," the Green Book argued, "would relieve provincial and municipal governments of a potential burden which in the past has constituted the most important single threat to real provincial autonomy." At the same time, Mackenzie King warned the premiers that, without such a tax surrender, they could expect no federal aid for unemployment assistance unless their governments were willing to submit themselves "to a means test."[12]

From the provincial perspective, however, Ottawa's unemployment assistance proposal was not very appealing. In the first place, by the time the conference met over the winter of 1945–46, the widespread fears of a postwar depression had mostly evaporated, and, with a national unemployment insurance plan in place, provincial governments were less concerned about the potentially crippling burden of unemployment relief. In any case, the Green Book UA Scheme, in the eyes of many premiers, contained a number of crucial flaws. Self-employed persons and those who could prove only "casual" employment over a two-year period were excluded. In the prairie provinces this was a potentially large portion of the relief load. More importantly, local governments would be held responsible for "supplement[ing] rates of assistance" for families who could not survive on the meagre UA benefits alone. As even a federal government memo conceded, this group might constitute "one-third to one-half of all [assistance] cases."[13] Why, then, should the provinces surrender some of their most lucrative sources of revenue for such an ambiguous federal offer to take over the burden of unemployment relief? Given the vigorous opposition of premiers George Drew and Maurice Duplessis to conceding any provincial taxation powers, agreement at the conference was unlikely in any case, but the framework of Ottawa's unemployment assistance proposal was hardly an incentive to change their minds. As a consequence, in early April 1946, the Reconstruction Conference broke up in failure.

Although the federal government would quickly negotiate separate tax rental settlements with all other provinces except Ontario and Quebec, care of the unemployed not covered by social insurance was left out of the bargain. "It is obvious that the dominion cannot . . . assume responsibility for unemployed employable persons in [some] provinces but not in others," federal Finance Minister J. L. Ilsley told Parliament in June. For the moment, Ottawa's promise to assume responsibility for all the postwar jobless was dead.[14]

Discarding the Green Book

When the postwar depression failed to materialize, unemployment faded from political attention for the remainder of the 1940s. But the problem of responsibility for the more than half of the workforce not covered by unemployment insurance remained. Moreover, as social work professionals pointed out with increasing frequency during the last half of the decade, this was essentially a question of public assistance, not unemployment assistance. When Ottawa pulled out of unemployment relief in 1941, Harry Cassidy noted in a comprehensive 1947 report on social security prepared for the Department of Health and Welfare, "the depression system [of general assistance fell] apart." Outside of British Columbia, Saskatchewan, and parts of Ontario, the rest of Canada had "not advanced beyond the local poor relief stage of public aid for needy persons.... The provisions for general assistance are limited, restrictive, mean, and antiquated.... [T]hey are literally disgraceful and unworthy of a nation of Canada's status."[15]

Other government surveys backed Cassidy's claim. In Manitoba, that province's director of public welfare observed in 1948, "there was really not much more protection against the problem of unemployment relief than was available ten years ago." In other provinces there was less. British Columbia, Alberta, and Ontario all ceased making payments to employables on local relief after Ottawa cut off its support in 1941, and in Saskatchewan such payments were left to the discretion of municipalities. In Quebec, federal officials noted, the jobless were totally at the mercy of private charity. Nova Scotia and New Brunswick still entrusted the indigent to "overseers of the poor" and no aid was given to persons in their own home "if accommodation in the local almshouse was available."[16]

During the winter of 1949–50, this ramshackle system of public assistance was put to its first severe test since the 1930s. Between October and February, the number of jobless registered with the National Employment Service climbed to 375,600, the highest number of unemployed since the Great Depression and an almost 50 percent jump over the previous winter. To make matters worse, at a time when the unemployment insurance fund had accumulated an almost $600,000,000 surplus one-third of the jobless were ineligible for benefits. Provincial and local governments refused to provide them with aid on the grounds than unemployment was a federal responsibility.[17]

In order to provide partial relief for this emergency, the St. Laurent government rushed through changes to the Unemployment Insurance Act in early February, creating thirteen weeks of "supplementary benefits" for those who had exhausted their insurance eligibility between the months of January and March. Although a welcome measure, it was barely generous as benefits were pegged to only 80 percent of the already meagre UI rates. As a subsequent Department of Labour study pointed out, had the 1945 Green Book unemployment assistance proposal been in effect over that winter, Ottawa would have paid out $34,400,000 as opposed to the $4,500,000 distributed through supplementary benefits. Moreover, supplementary benefits were no help to the jobless left uncovered by unemployment insurance.[18]

With spring, unemployment quickly disappeared and, for the next three years under the stimulus of the military spending provoked by the Korean War, the Canadian economy remained extremely buoyant with unemployment rates below 3 percent. Despite this favourable economic climate, memories of the winter of 1949–50 kept the issue of unemployment assistance alive both within Ottawa and in the social work community. As in the 1940s, however, federal government officials and Canadian social workers continued to approach the question from sharply divergent perspectives.

For the St. Laurent administration, the Green Book proposals on unemployment assistance had become an increasing embarrassment. Federal officials conceded that because of the promises made in 1945 provinces, municipalities, and even "the man on the street" assumed that responsibility for all the jobless, including the 45 percent of the workforce not covered by unemployment insurance, belonged in Ottawa's hands. At the same time, because of the changed political and economic circumstances of the 1950s, the government was no longer willing to accept this commitment. The Green Book unemployment assistance proposal, federal officials argued, was based upon "the anticipation of large scale unemployment in the immediate postwar years" as well as provincial "acceptance . . . of the taxation proposals put forward [in 1945] by the Federal Government." Neither development had occurred. Instead a buoyant economy during the early 1950s and favourable tax rental agreements which had been negotiated since the war had left the provinces and municipalities easily capable of handling the relatively small burden of unemployment relief which remained. Moreover, "as long as defence expenditures absorb 50 percent of the national budget and incidentally maintain virtually full employment," Jack Pickersgill, chairman of the influential Privy

Council Office committee on unemployment, told the Prime Minister in 1952, "[I do not think] there is any justification for a demand from local and provincial governments for assistance."[19]

As a result of these views, the St. Laurent administration abandoned Ottawa's commitment to the 1945 Green Book proposal. During 1952, federal government policy returned to a position first put forward by Mackenzie King in 1922. Apart from unemployment insurance, St. Laurent told the Association of Ontario Mayors, "constitutional responsibility for relief and assistance of the unemployed . . . rested with the local authorities." Ottawa was obliged to give financial aid "only when the problem reached emergency proportions."[20]

Provincial governments proved equally stubborn. Ontario had no responsibility to provide aid to employables on relief, W. A. Goodfellow, that province's Minister of Public Welfare, told the Canadian Welfare Council (CWC) in 1952. Through its employment service and unemployment insurance commission, only Ottawa possessed the financial and administrative capacity for dealing with the problem. Consequently, the "maintenance of employable unemployed persons is a responsibility of the Government of Canada."[21]

Private Charities Fight Back

Although the number of jobless without insurance benefits was not large during the prosperity of the early 1950s, their dilemma was acute since no level of government was willing to assume responsibility for their care. By default, the burden fell to the nation's private charities which possessed neither the financial capacity nor the inclination to deal with the problem. As a consequence, no issue had higher priority within the social work profession than resolving the question of responsibility for the jobless with no insurance benefits. Beginning in the autumn of 1950, the Canadian Welfare Council, through its newly formed Public Welfare Division, attempted to break the federal-provincial deadlock on this issue by establishing a "Committee on Public Assistance," chaired by the influential left-of-centre Liberal MP David Croll.

Over the next two years, the Committee struggled to define a social work consensus on public assistance reform which would be acceptable to all levels of government. In the first draft of its report, it suggested a simple but rather sweeping manifesto of welfare rights. All Canadian citizens, the Croll Committee argued, should enjoy a legal right to public assistance, adequate to maintain their health and welfare anywhere in the country. The scope of and eligibility for such assistance should be determined solely by the fact, not the cause, of their need.[22]

Although these principles received praise from social workers in the private welfare sector, government officials were appalled. According to a senior member of Ontario's Department of Public Welfare, the Committee's call for a legal right to relief, without regard to the cause of need, constituted a "doctrinaire formula forming part of the Marxist canon" which could be realized "only in a socialist state." Other government critics denounced the demand for a national minimum as a "pious ejaculation" or attacked the report for "spell[ing] out . . . legislative rights and rates of benefit for an emergency . . . which has not yet happened."[23]

In the face of such criticisms from the very government welfare officials the CWC hoped most to win over, the Croll Committee substantially toned down the recommendations of the final report, "Public Assistance and the Unemployed," which was released in February 1953. As the product of more than two years' work by a group containing many of Canada's most notable social workers and welfare administrators, their report garnered a good deal of attention. Forty-five hundred copies were mailed to newspapers, trade unions, mayors' associations, and citizens' groups across the country. In addition, the CWC arranged a simultaneous presentation of its recommendations to provincial and federal cabinet ministers in every province.[24]

In its final draft, the Croll Committee omitted all references to a "legal right to relief" or a "national minimum." Public assistance rates, it simply noted, "would have to vary in relation to the cost of living in different communities and at different times." Instead of a sweeping call for basic welfare rights, the report focussed specifically upon the problem of the jobless without insurance benefits. For those on UI who exhausted their eligibility, the Committee suggested a new class of "extended benefits," at regular Unemployment Insurance (UI) rates, to be provided without a means test. The jobless not covered by UI should be left to local welfare authorities. However, welfare services for this group would be financed by a federal "purchase of service" from local governments. A basic payment, each year, would cover the cost of administering local public assistance and could be used to develop casework services and the "nucleus of a well-trained staff." A second "variable payment" from Ottawa would fluctuate as the number of employables on relief rose above a statistically determined "normal" welfare caseload. By making federal payment contingent upon an arbitrary mathematical formula, the Committee hoped governments could avoid bickering over whether particular individuals were capable of work.[25]

Despite the optimistic hopes of the Canadian Welfare Council, "Public Assistance and the Unemployed" failed to impress either federal or provincial authorities. George Davidson, the federal deputy minister of health and welfare, and former executive director of the CWC, found the report "confusing and lacking in clarity." The proposal for extended benefits without a means test was simply "an uncontracted handout from the federal treasury" that would undermine the integrity of unemployment insurance. Davidson also rejected the idea that Ottawa should purchase welfare services from the provinces. As he told CWC Director R. G. Davis, the federal government had only a residual responsibility for the jobless outside of UI which depended upon the fiscal need of the provinces, not the number of employables on relief.[26]

Ontario government officials were equally hostile. His province "prefer[red] to have nothing to do with unemployment relief," Deputy Minister of Public Welfare Jimmy Band told the CWC. During the 1930s, this obligation had cost Ontario more than $21,000,000 a year and the government "would not put themselves in a position where they might be called upon to spend such sums again." Band also objected to the administrative burdens flowing from the scheme. Only fourteen of Ontario's 960 municipalities possessed welfare departments. Since this shared-cost plan would be administered by municipalities, "it would mean those who do not have welfare departments would be forced to set [them] up." The provincial cabinet "would hesitate in committing themselves" to such a wholesale reform of local government.[27] So, despite two years of work, close consultation with public welfare administrators, and a sustained effort to arouse public opinion, the CWC's attempt to secure a national reform of public assistance accomplished nothing. With an unemployment rate averaging only 2.5 percent during 1952–53, no government felt pressured to prepare for an economic crisis which had not happened.

The Return of Unemployment

Within a year the picture began to change. By the autumn of 1953 both the Korean War and the massive defence build-up and strategic resource stockpiling which had fuelled the North American boom had come to an end. Unemployment began, once more, to edge steadily upwards. By March 1954, a record 570,000 Canadians were registered as looking for work, an 84 percent increase over the previous winter according to the National Employment Service.[28] To make matters worse, the federal, provincial, and municipal governments continued to refuse responsibility for providing aid to the jobless not covered by UI benefits. From across Canada came reports of acute distress. In Toronto, people were "actually suffering hunger because of unemployment," the local branch of the Canadian Association of Social Workers (CASW) pointed out, because there was "no assistance available from any official source for such families." Vancouver family agencies voiced identical complaints. "Sometimes social workers meeting these . . . persons get quite desperate, especially when there are children involved," CASW branch president Mary Nicholson noted in December. "We have never succeeded in getting municipal or provincial governments to grant assistance."[29]

For the St. Laurent government, this distress was even more embarrassing because the unemployment insurance fund had accumulated an almost one billion dollar surplus, which even Department of Labour officials conceded was 25 percent above estimated contribution requirements. Why could this huge surplus not be used to liberalize UI coverage and benefits beyond the 62 percent of the workforce presently protected by the scheme, Conservative and CCF critics asked in Parliament.[30] From within the federal bureaucracy came conflicting advice. The Department of Labour argued for a liberal extension of supplementary benefits.

Unemployment Insurance and Finance Department representatives vigorously opposed such tampering on the grounds that it would "endanger ... the insurance plan and bring it into disrepute." Payments not justified by acturial criteria were "properly the function of unemployment assistance," the UI Commission argued, and should be administered as such out of a separate fund. This combination of a worsening economy and internal dissent within the federal departments and agencies most involved with the unemployed convinced the St. Laurent government that the time had arrived to "come to some decisions soon on the federal government's role in unemployment assistance." George Davidson was asked by the Privy Council's Committee on Unemployment to re-examine the entire problem and this time to draw up "a plan to deal with it."[31]

By the end of May, Davidson had completed the assignment. In a powerful memorandum, he pointed out that for almost twenty-five years Ottawa's policy on this issue had "fluctuated from one extreme of the pendulum to the other," ranging from a total denial of responsibility in 1930 to promising a complete takeover of the field in 1945. At present, the federal government was pursuing "two alternative lines of policy." On the one hand, by providing nonactuarial "supplementary benefits" to the unemployed, Ottawa was attempting to deal with the problem piecemeal through "an extension of the unemployment insurance system." On the other, federal officials were insisting that the care of those not covered by UI rested with local and provincial authorities unless the cost became "too heavy a financial burden." Clearly Ottawa had "changed its mind [on unemployment assistance] since 1945," Davidson pointed out, but it had "done so in private." In the public eye, the federal government "still remain[ed] committed to the ... Green Book proposals."

Here was the danger. If the St. Laurent administration did not clarify its unemployment policy "while there [was] yet time ... and if a serious unemployment situation should arise ... the federal government could not, at that late date, disentangle itself from the 1945 position."[32]

Davidson's solution was to revive a social work position on unemployment assistance first articulated by Harry Cassidy, Charlotte Whitton, and himself in the 1940s and most recently repeated in the CWC pamphlet, "Public Assistance and the Unemployed." Ottawa should "take the initiative" in devising an unemployment assistance scheme which would be administered and financed primarily by provincial and local governments, but which would involve continuous and permanent federal contributions on a sliding scale varying according to the size of the jobless caseload. Federal participation might range from a one-sixth contribution in normal times (similar to Ottawa's share of payments to the UI fund) to a 50 percent contribution in periods of substantial unemployment. Federal payments might kick in when the number on relief in any province exceeded 1 percent of its total workforce, on the assumption that this figure represented the normal proportion of unemployables on welfare. In this way, Ottawa's insistence that it was only responsible for "employables" could be preserved.

Although a continuous federal presence in unemployment assistance represented a new policy departure, it would save Ottawa money, Davidson argued."The federal government's chances of working out an acceptable 'bargain' with the provinces are much better in normal times than they will be if the unemployment assistance problem mounts to serious proportions." Since the public still held Ottawa responsible for all the unemployed, in the event of a serious crisis public opinion would force the federal government to pick up most of the cost. On the other hand, if an agreement were negotiated now, Davidson argued, "the provinces might be prepared to come in at an early stage and do more for the unemployed than they were now doing and in the long run reduce the financial load on the federal government."[33]

Throughout the summer, the Privy Council Office (PCO) wrestled with conflicting opinions on Davidson's unemployment assistance proposal. Trade and Commerce and Bank of Canada officials were supportive. "[N]ow that the postwar boom has ended," Mitchell Sharp observed, "the country would have to adjust to a new climate over the next few years." During this period of higher unemployment, the federal government "would be in a better position to resist pressure to undertake public works of dubious value if it were already meeting the ... problem through relief assistance." Both the Finance and Labour Departments rejected Davidson's plan, however. Finance officials argued that the recommendation for continuous federal aid in normal times undermined

Ottawa's position that it was concerned only with a province's "fiscal capacity" to assist the unemployed in "emergency situations." Moreover, by accepting partial responsibility for unemployment now Ottawa might compromise its future bargaining position on tax-sharing with the provinces. The Department of Labour continued to cling to the Green Book proposal. National unemployment assistance would permit "uniformity of treatment [for the jobless] across Canada," Labour Department officials stressed, which would not only be "beneficial . . . psychologically," but would also promote a "greater transfer of income in periods of unemployment to those parts of the economy most in need of it."[34]

Outside of the Department of Labour, however, there was no longer support for a completely federal assistance plan and PCO members quickly agreed that "the Green Book proposals should be buried once and for all." Apart from the political difficulties of administering a federal means test and keeping national assistance payments below both unemployment insurance benefits and widely-varying local welfare rates, the Green Book scheme was three times more expensive. As even Labour Department officials conceded, on the basis of the 1954 unemployment rate, Ottawa would have spent $44,000,000 under a nationally-administered assistance program as opposed to an estimated $13,500,000 under the shared-cost proposal put forward by the Department of Health and Welfare.[35]

Despite its apparent low cost, Davidson's plan did not, for the moment, receive PCO or cabinet approval. Instead it was shoved aside by alternative recommendations emanating from the Unemployment Insurance Commission which, in response to cabinet pressure, came forward with a comprehensive reorganization of its system of contributions, eligibility rules, and benefits. Included in these reforms was the addition of ten more weeks of "seasonal benefits," at regular UI rates, to replace the old system of "supplemental benefits," as well as an extension of the minimum benefit period from six to fifteen weeks. For the present, the PCO Committee on Unemployment remained convinced that these changes to UI would "meet more effectively the kind of unemployment problems that now appear likely over the next few years" than the creation of a new unemployment assistance scheme.[36]

The winter of 1955 shattered these expectations. By January the D.B.S. jobless rate stood at 7 percent compared to 5.4 percent in the previous year. Due to a "levelling off in the defence build-up in North America," C. D. Howe conceded, unemployment was "now at the highest level in our postwar experience." In response to this situation, the St. Laurent government quickly introduced its new seasonal benefits scheme in January while promising more substantial reforms to UI in the spring. Beyond this, Ottawa refused to budge. Unemployment was mostly "seasonal," federal cabinet ministers insisted, and the relief burden was "not . . . beyond the capacity of [local] communities."[37]

Newspaper reports from the nation's cities told a different story. In Toronto alone, a municipal delegation informed the St. Laurent cabinet in February, there were 4,000 to 5,000 unemployed "not covered by unemployment insurance." The city would pay relief "only . . . to those who are starving." Out of a total welfare budget of $1,618,000 for 1954, Toronto spent less than $26,000 on aid to employables. As a consequence, "married men [were] deserting their families so that women and children could go on straight relief," soup kitchens had reopened, hostels were full to overflowing, and the city was once again "buy[ing] one-way tickets . . . [to] ship . . . the unemployed to their former homes." In other major cities the story was the same. Vancouver's voluntary welfare organizations, B.C. Premier W. A. C. Bennett told St. Laurent by telegram, "had exhausted their funds." It was a "repetition of . . . the thirties," Opposition critics pointed out in Parliament.[38]

The CWC Intervenes

Forced to pick up the slack as best they could, Canada's voluntary social agencies, as Liberal MP David Croll told Parliament, were soon at "the end of their tether." In response to protests flowing into Ottawa from family agencies across Canada, the Canadian Welfare Council once again decided to launch a national publicity campaign demanding public assistance for the unemployed. In January 9,000 pamphlets outlining the plight of the jobless without insurance were sent to federal and provincial cabinet minis-

ters, members of Parliament and provincial legislatures, newspapers, trade unions, and other large national organizations.[39]

CWC officials were delighted with the "excellent coverage" their
campaign received in the nation's press and their hopes were
raised even further when, a month later, a Council delegation was
granted an emergency meeting with members of the federal cabinet. However, the results were disappointing. Despite CWC arguments that people were "actually going ... hungry because they
are unemployed and not in a category ... to get public assistance,"
St. Laurent's ministers remained unmoved. "[T]he responsibility
lies ... on the provinces," Finance Minister Walter Harris told the
delegation. "Could Ottawa not at least call a conference with the
provinces to discuss the situation?" Council officials asked. Harris
said no. "[I]f the federal government took such an initiative the
other governments would immediately expect it to bear a share of
the cost of any solution." This was something St. Laurent's administration was not prepared to do.[40]

In frustration, the CWC decided to take matters into its own
hands. A week after meeting with the cabinet, the Council issued a
press release announcing its own conference on unemployment for
1 April to which federal and provincial government representatives would be invited. Over the next few weeks, to the chagrin of
federal officials, several provinces signalled their willingness to attend. Realizing that such a conference, coming in the aftermath of
Canada's worst winter of unemployment since the 1930s, could become a public relations disaster for his government, St. Laurent
intervened. In a private meeting with CWC president Lawrence
Freiman on 9 March, the prime minister proposed a face-saving
compromise. He would convene a preliminary meeting of provincial representatives on 26–27 April to plan for the upcoming
federal-provincial conference scheduled for that autumn. At this
first meeting "the subject of unemployment could be placed on the
agenda if the provinces wish to have it discussed." In response to
this proposal, Freiman agreed to cancel the CWC conference. The
following day St. Laurent announced his decision in Parliament.[41]
For Canadian social work this represented perhaps the most significant policy victory the profession had yet achieved in federal
politics. Through adroit publicity by the CWC, Ottawa had finally

been pressured into converting its private and rather indecisive planning on unemployment assistance into public policy.

During early April before the preliminary federal-provincial meeting, George Davidson's proposal for a cost-shared unemployment assistance scheme quickly received cabinet approval. If Ottawa "left [the initiative] to the provinces," Davidson pointed out, "they would want the Green Book proposals." Federal payments would begin when the relief load in any province exceeded 1 percent of its population.[42]

Although the provinces welcomed Ottawa's agreement in principle to participate in unemployment assistance, most objected strenuously to the 1 percent threshold and to Davidson's complicated sliding-scale formula. In response St. Laurent's government agreed to cut the threshold down to 0.45 percent but this did not mollify several premiers. The whole idea of a threshold was a "retrograde step," Ontario Premier Leslie Frost argued. A simple 50–50 split with no minimum threshold was a more "equitable compromise."[43]

St. Laurent wanted no part of this suggestion. A statistical threshold which excluded the unemployable from cost-sharing was essential to uphold existing "constitutional law and practice," or, in other words, Ottawa's categorical distinction that it was only responsible for "employables." Otherwise, the Prime Minister stated, "the Federal government would likely be asked to assist financially in the maintenance of hospitals, old persons' homes, etc., which were clearly a provincial responsibility." Under no circumstances did St. Laurent wish to see a limited commitment to the unemployed become an open-ended responsibility for those in need.[44]

In early January 1956, after six months of negotiations, the federal government finally presented the text of an unemployment assistance agreement to Parliament. Six months later, the Unemployment Assistance Act became law, with four provinces (Ontario, Quebec, Alberta, and Nova Scotia) still refusing to participate in the scheme. In 1958, when the new Conservative government of John Diefenbaker abolished the 0.45 percent threshold and placed the Act on a straight 50–50 cost-shared basis, all provinces except Quebec came under the legislation.

Summary

What did the Unemployment Assistance Act accomplish? Both less and, ironically, more than its sponsors claimed. Although federal Health and Welfare minister Paul Martin initially boasted that the legislation went "much further than the . . . Rowell-Sirois . . . and [Green Book] proposals made in 1945," in fact the 1956 UA scheme, apart from establishing a permanent federal presence in unemployment relief, on the surface did not represent much of an improvement over the old relief acts of the 1930s.[45]

Since the Depression, Canadian social workers had argued passionately that a continuous federal commitment to public welfare was essential to establish national minimum standards in both the levels and administration of social assistance. Judged from this perspective, unemployment assistance was clearly a failure. Conceding that "no attempt would be made to establish uniform standards of social assistance," Ottawa's agreement with the provinces left the determination of welfare rates and eligibility requirements to provincial and local authorities. Even long-detested residency rules, although technically proscribed by the act, continued to "remain part of many provincial welfare statutes," until 1966.

With no definition of minimum standards of subsistence, the assistance granted under the program depended not on federal guidelines but on the varying commitment of provincial and local governments to social welfare. For example, during its first year, the per capita monthly level of support provided by unemployment assistance varied from $11.21 to $32.02 or by as much as 300 percent between Newfoundland and British Columbia. In Ontario only 7 percent of UA cases received supplemental assistance (drugs, medical, optical, dental care, etc.) from the province compared to 95 percent in British Columbia. In New Brunswick, four years after the signing of the UA agreement, Fredericton was the only municipality which possessed a fully-trained welfare administrator and paid relief in cash. In Saint John, UA cases received only food and fuel from the city and were responsible for obtaining their own rent. Clearly, in some provinces life for the needy under unemployment assistance was little better than during the Depression.[46]

Nor did standards of welfare administration improve. Rather

than hiring new trained staff to handle their increased assistance burden, most provinces and municipalities, according to Amy Leigh, British Columbia's assistant director of social welfare, "continued to meet the unemployed problem at the expense of their normal cascload with the result that vast numbers of people were appallingly neglected." Throughout Canada, general assistance remained characterized by "low standards, negative attitudes in determining eligibility, and, inevitably, the choice of second rate personnel for the administration of services," Nova Scotia's Deputy Minister of Welfare pointed out in 1961. To this extent, Canadian social work's long-standing belief that federal conditional grants for unemployment relief would lead to minimum standards in welfare administration and social assistance rates failed to materialize.[47]

This failure is hardly surprising since the reduction of poverty or the establishment of national standards in welfare had never been a conscious objective in federal planning on unemployment assistance. As British historian Pat Thane has recently observed, "In no other area of policy does one expect governments to give primacy to the interests of the weak or to be motivated by single or simple pressures or principles. There is no obvious reason why the making of social policy should differ from other forms of political action." The tangled history of unemployment assistance between 1941–1956 amply confirms Thane's point that to interpret social policy as "simply . . . a manifestation of altruism . . . renders mysterious the fact that much poverty remains."[48]

What pressures did shape federal policy in this field? During the 1940s a completely federal unemployment assistance plan emerged as a means of discharging Ottawa's unquestioned political obligation to those rendered jobless by reconstruction. As a means of dealing with unemployment, an assistance scheme possessed several advantages. Although by no means providing an adequate subsistence, it could nonetheless protect the actuarial integrity of unemployment insurance, which could only cover a small proportion of the anticipated postwar jobless burden. It defused political pressure for more expensive and administratively complicated public works. Most importantly, with the memory of Depression bankruptcy still fresh in premiers' minds, a national unemployment assistance scheme provided federal officials with perhaps their most powerful argument for securing permanent control over lucrative provincial taxation powers at the 1945 reconstruction conference. When the prospect of postwar depression ebbed and Ottawa lost the battle to absorb provincial taxes, it also quickly lost interest in unemployment assistance.

From 1948 onwards, federal policy towards the noninsured jobless was shaped, above all, by the desire, as one cabinet document put it, to "bury the Green Book proposals once and for all." Beyond this, no consensus on this issue existed within the federal bureaucracy. For the Unemployment Insurance Commission, a UA scheme remained an essential means of protecting the actuarial soundness of their own plan from politically-inspired raids on their ever-mounting surplus. Within Trade and Commerce, UA represented a cheaper adjustment to years of anticipated higher unemployment than "dubious public works." Health and Welfare officials argued that a cost-shared scheme, launched in times of prosperity, could save Ottawa from a much more expensive obligation if recession returned. Rising above all these voices was the message from the Finance Department. Under no circumstances should Ottawa unilaterally expand its role in provincial social assistance without similar cooperation from the provinces on tax-sharing arrangements, particularly during an era of high defence spending and low unemployment. The not surprising result of this divided counsel was a commitment to do nothing.

Into this policy vacuum intruded the reality of rising unemployment, the equal stubbornness of fiscally conservative premiers, and the increasingly louder voices of the nation's private charities, forced to pick up a burden which no one else wanted. Through arguably the most effective public relations campaign in its history, the Canadian Welfare Council succeeded in pressuring Ottawa to do something it did not want to do: accept a permanent responsibility for the noninsured unemployed. In the final analysis, as even federal officials conceded, because of national unemployment insurance and their own postwar promises, "the man on the street" did assume that unemployment was Ottawa's responsibility. As a result, the growing distress of the jobless caught in a policy limbo was ultimately a political embarrassment to Ottawa, not the provinces. It was this political reality, symbolized by the

CWC's threatened conference on unemployment, that forced St. Laurent's government to act.

Despite its limitations as an attack on poverty and the grudging nature of its origins, the Unemployment Assistance Act did have two important results. With the availability of new federal money, provinces with long-established social assistance programs (Ontario, Manitoba, Saskatchewan, and British Columbia) were able to improve the range of services and levels of assistance to the unemployed without incurring any significant additional expense. In Quebec and the Maritimes, the mere existence of this legislation sparked the creation of provincial departments of welfare for the first time in order to facilitate the transfer of funds to the municipalities.[49]

More important was an unintended and ironic consequence of the legislation. Once a federal program was in place for sharing the costs of assistance to the employable unemployed in need, provincial governments were handed a powerful incentive to blur existing categorical distinctions between the disabled, dependent mothers with children, and the elderly indigent in their own welfare programs. For these latter clients, federal funding was either nonexistent or subject to fixed ceilings, whereas under unemployment assistance after 1958 Ottawa paid 50 percent of the cost regardless of the number of people or the scale of aid. By shifting other welfare cases into the UA category, provincial governments could realize significant savings.

Ironically, then, the Unemployment Assistance Act contained the seeds of its own demise. Although it was the product of Ottawa's ten-year insistence upon clear categorical distinctions between the unemployable and employable in need, the political impossibility of administering this distinction helped to pave the way for the abolition of the categorical approach to poverty through the Canada Assistance Plan (CAP) of 1966. By the time of its replacement by CAP, the UA scheme had a caseload of almost 800,000 and was expanding incrementally beyond any relationship to the business cycle.[50] From this perspective, then, Ottawa's "war on poverty" in the 1960s can be seen in a different light. The Canadian Assistance Plan, perhaps, emerged as much through the unintended consequences of previous legislation as through a

changed political climate or the benevolent influence of a bureaucratic social policy elite.[51]

Acknowledgements

I would like to thank the SSHRC for a grant supporting the research in this chapter and Leslie A. Pal for his comments on an earlier draft.

Notes

1. Kenneth Buckley and I. Uruquart, *Historical Statistics of Canada*, 2nd
   ed. (Ottawa: 1983), Series C404–16; C248–60.
2. *Report of the Royal Commission on Dominion-Provincial Relations*,
   Book II (Ottawa: 1940); Leonard Marsh, *Report on Social Security for
   Canada* (Toronto: University of Toronto Press, 1975); Dominion-
   Provincial Conference on Reconstruction, *Proposals of the Government
   of Canada* (August 1945). For interpretations of the postwar welfare
   state which stress the role of a bureaucratic reformist elite see Rand
   Dyck, "The Canada Assistance Plan: The Ultimate in Co-operative
   Federalism," *Canadian Public Administration* 19 (Winter 1976): 4; Les-
   lie Bella, "The Provincial Role in the Canadian Welfare State: The In-
   fluence of Provincial Social Policy Initiatives on the Design of the
   Canada Assistance Plan," *Canadian Public Administration* 22 (Fall
   1979): 3; Andrew Armitage, *Social Welfare in Canada: Ideals and
   Realities* (Toronto: McClelland & Stewart, 1975); Richard Splane,
   "Social Policy-Making in the Government of Canada: Reflections of a
   Reformist Bureaucrat," in Shankar A. Yelaja, ed., *Canadian Social
   Policy* (Waterloo: Wilfrid Laurier University Press, 1978); Paul
   Martin, *A Very Public Life, Volume 2: So Many Worlds* (Toronto:
   Deneau, 1985).
3. Queen's University Archives, W. A. Mackintosh Papers, box G, file
   151, memo by Alex Skelton, "The Sirois Report and the War," 24 July
   1940. According to the powerful Economic Advisory Committee, without a billion dollars in federal expenditures at the war's end, unemployment threatened "to develop on a colossal scale," providing Canada with "grave risks of . . . social unrest and a chaotic industrial

situation." PAC, Department of Finance Records, RG 19, vol. 4663, file 187, EAC-47, "Rough Draft of Proposed Report of the Economic Advisory Committee on the Interim Report of the Committee on Reconstruction," n.d. but *circa* November 1942.

4. PAC, W. L. Mackenzie King Papers, MG 26 J1, Graham Towers to King, 15 August 1940.

5. On the work of the National Employment Commission see James Struthers, *No Fault of Their Own: Unemployment and the Canadian Welfare State 1914–1941* (Toronto: University of Toronto Press, 1983), 175–84. The NEC's ideas on unemployment assistance were borrowed from the British Unemployment Act of 1934.

6. RG 19, vol. 3976, file E-3-0, vol 2., memo by Alex Skelton, "Constitutional Problems of Dominion Post-war Policy," May 1943.

7. Ibid., vol. 4663, file 187, EAC-48, memo by W. A. Mackintosh, "Proposed Construction Reserve Commission," 25 November 1942; file 187, EAC-46, "Report of the Economic Advisory Committee on the Report of the Advisory Committee on Reconstruction," 20 November 1943. In its final report, the James Committee had called for the establishment of a National Development Board to coordinate a massive ten-year planning forecast of all public investment. Advisory Committee on Reconstruction, *Report* (Ottawa, 24 September 1943), 27–29.

8. RG 19, vol. 3976, file E-3-0, Alex Skelton, "Dominion Post-war Policy," 13 April 1943. In an aside, Robert Bryce, of the EAC, observed that it was "quite a gamble to make the whole of Canadian postwar plans depend on a constitutional settlement between the Dominion and the Provinces." Skelton's reply is of interest. Ottawa "could not lose by trying since if it did not succeed, it could quickly resort to the system of grants-in-aid," vol. 4662, file 187, EAC-42, "Minutes of the Sub-Committee of the Economic Advisory Committee on Post-war Reconstruction," 31 March 1943.

9. Ibid., vol. 506, file 121-4-7-, memo, R. B. Bryce to Alex Skelton, 5 February 1945. See also, Bryce, "Memorandum for Dr. Clark, *re* Unemployment Assistance Grants," 5 March 1945.

10. PAC, Department of National Health and Welfare Records, RG 29, vol. 23, file 21-2-7, memo by Eric Stangroom, "Notes on a Plan of Non-Contributory Grants to the Employable Unemployed," n.d. but *circa* October 1944; Department of Labour Records, RG 29, vol. 614, memo by Stangroom, "Federal Responsibility," 30 October 1944. According to the Toronto Welfare Council, $35.85 was the minimum weekly income necessary to maintain a family of five in health and decency in a large Canadian city during 1944. RG 29, vol. 1841, Toronto Welfare Council, *The Cost of Living* (Toronto, 1944).

11. RG 29, vol. 23, file 21-2-7, "Minutes of the Committee on Unemployment Assistance," 5 July 1945; W. A. Mackintosh, "Memorandum to the Cabinet Committee on Dominion-Provincial Conference on Unem-

ployment Assistance," n.d. but *circa* July 1945; Dominion-Provincial Conference on Reconstruction, *Proposals of the Government of Canada* (August, 1945), 7, 21–26.

12. *Proposals of the Government of Canada,* 51; RG 19, vol. 537, file 135-0-167(3), "Dominion-Provincial Conference Co-ordinating Committee," statement by the prime minister at the opening session, 28 January 1946.

13. PAC, RG 2, series 18, vol. 76, "Unemployment Assistance: Necessary Requirements of a Dominion Scheme of Unemployment Assistance," Government of Alberta, n.d. but *circa* 1946; vol. 37, *Summary and Proceedings at the Plenary Session: Dominion-Provincial Conference on Reconstruction,* 287, 247. As Ontario officials noted, under the Green Book unemployment assistance proposal, "a large proportion of the cost of unemployment assistance to persons actually employable would fall on the provinces and municipalities." For federal estimates of unemployment assistance coverage see RG 27, vol. 614, "Report of Committee on Unemployment Assistance," 20 April 1946, Appendix "F" and Appendix "G."

14. Canada, House of Commons *Debates,* 27 June 1946, 2913–14. For an excellent recent study of the Reconstruction Conference see Marc J. Gotlieb, "George Drew and the Dominion-Provincial Conference on Reconstruction of 1945–6," *The Canadian Historical Review* 66 (March 1985): 1.

15. RG 29, vol. 1883, file R170/100-1/50 pt. 1, Harry Cassidy, "A Canadian Program of Social Security," vol. 1, 15 November 1947, 121–52.

16. CCSD Records, acc/83, box 60, file "Manitoba Department of Health and Welfare," K. O. MacKenzie to Bessie Touzel, 9 March 1948; RG 29, vol. 918, L. D. Hudson, "The Organization of Unemployment Assistance in the Provinces," 5 December 1949.

17. RG 19, vol. 3442, "The Current Unemployment Situation in Canada," n.d. but *circa* February 1950. On the Unemployment Insurance surplus, see RG 19, vol. 3439, Minutes of the "Interdepartmental Committee on Social Security," 30 December 1949. The level of contributions to UI was based on the average unemployment rate of 10 percent between 1921–1931. As Norman Robertson noted, this represented "an attempt to ensure against a scale of risk that it was politically impossible to countenance ... if it was not politically possible to have unemployment exceed 7 per cent, the difference between that and 10 per cent was room for maneuver in extending coverage [and] increasing the period of benefit." As of 1949 only 67 percent of wage-earners, comprising 46 percent of the total labour-force, were covered by unemployment insurance. Municipalities refused to aid the uninsured jobless, a federal official observed, because "they do not feel ... they would be able to carry the additional financial burden." L. D. Hudon, "The Organization of Unemployment Assistance in the Prairies."

18. RG 19, vol. 3439, Minutes of the Interdepartmental Committee on So-

cial Security, 2 February 1950; House of Commons *Debates,* 23 February 1950, 155–57, 170–71; RG 29, vol. 920, "Reference Paper on Unemployment Aid," n.d. but *circa* 1951. Between January and March 1950, 98,415 people received supplementary benefits. RG 2, 18, vol. 198, file U-11, vol. 1, "Report on Operations of Supplementary Benefits," August 1950.

19. RG 29, vol. 918, "Committee on Unemployment Questions: Draft of a Possible Memorandum to Cabinet on Unemployment Assistance Policy," 15 October 1952. J. W. Pickersgill conceded that the constitutional amendment ceding Ottawa jurisdiction over unemployment insurance provided "a basis in fact for an argument that the federal government is fully responsible for assistance to unemployed employables"; RG 2, series 18, vol. 187, file 50–60(d), "Report of the Working Committee on Unemployment Insurance and Unemployment Aid," 24 November 1950; PAC, Louis St. Laurent Papers, MG26L, vol. 165, file U-11-6, J. W. Pickersgill, "Memorandum for the Prime Minister *re* Unemployment Assistance," 21 October 1952.

20. CCSD Records, acc/83, box 151, file "Public Assistance and the Unemployed," copy of letter from Louis St. Laurent to Seely Eakins, executive secretary of the Association of Ontario Mayors and Municipalities, 23 October 1952.

21. Ibid., W. A. Goodfellow to R. E. G. Davis, 17 September 1952.

22. Ibid., "Minutes of the Second Meeting of the Committee on Public Assistance," 8 December 1950. The Committee members were David Croll (Chairman), Harry Cassidy, John Morgan, R. E. G. Davis, Mrs. Kaspar Fraser, Eugene Forsey, Robena Morris, T. J. Richardson, Harold Shortcliff, Robert Smith, Bessie Touzel, and Elizabeth Govan.

23. PAO, Department of Public Welfare Records, RG 29, Deputy Ministers Correspondence box 399211, file "Canadian Welfare Council, January–April 1951"; D. A. Hogg to B. W. Heise, "Comments on the Interim Report of the Canadian Welfare Council Committee on Public Assistance," 3 April 1951; CCSD Records, acc/83, box 151, file "Public Assistance and the Unemployed," Henry Langford to R. E. G. Davis, 11 January 1952; memo by Elizabeth Govan, "The Processing of the Public Assistance Report," 26 January 1952.

24. CCSD Records, acc/83, box 151, file "Public Assistance and the Unemployed," Phyllis Burns, "Record of Action *re* Public Assistance and the Unemployed 1954–55," 14 June 1955. Members of the CWC's Public Welfare Division who participated in the report included J. S. White, deputy minister of public welfare, Saskatchewan; E. W. Griffith, deputy minister of public welfare, British Columbia; K. O. Mackenzie, deputy minister of public welfare, Manitoba; F. R. Mackinnon, deputy minister of public welfare, Nova Scotia; B. W. Heise, former deputy minister of public welfare, Ontario; and Colonel J. G. Bisson, chief commissioner, Unemployment Insurance Commission.

25. Ibid., *Public Assistance and the Unemployed,* February 1953.

26. Ibid., George Davidson to R. E. G. Davis, 2 February 1953.

27. Ibid., field report by William McGrath on interview with James Band, 10 February 1953.

28. RG 29, vol. 918, file "Interdepartmental Committee on Unemployment Questions," Memorandum on "Extension of Supplementary Benefit Period," 6 April 1954. The Dominion Bureau of Statistics Labourforce Survey reported the unemployment rate at only 6%, compared to 11% according to the N.E.S. The gap between the two figures was a source of considerable embarrassment to the government. See House of Commons *Debates*, 6 April 1954, 3779; 5 April 1955, 2794–95; 15 February 1954, 2086. In either estimate, it was the highest unemployment figure since the 1930s.

29. House of Commons *Debates*, 12 April 1954, 4002; CCSD Records, acc/83, box 151, file "Public Assistance and the Unemployed," Mary Nicholson to Cliff Patrick, 14 December 1953.

30. St. Laurent Papers, vol. 165, file U-11-4, memo from A. McNamara to Milton Gregg, "Re Extension of Unemployment Benefits to Cover Period of Lay-off on Account of Illness," 13 February 1953; House of Commons *Debates*, 23 February 1954, 2359.

31. RG 29, vol. 921, Minutes of the "Interdepartmental Committee on the Unemployment Question," 18 February 1954; vol. 918, memorandum on "Extension of Supplementary Benefit Period," 6 April 1954; Unemployment Insurance Commission, memorandum on "Extension of Unemployment Insurance Benefits," 25 February 1954; Interdepartmental Committee on Unemployment Questions, minutes of meetings, 12 February 1954 and 1 March 1954.

32. Ibid., vol. 918, George Davidson, "Memorandum on Unemployment Assistance," May 1954. Davidson had put forward a similar proposal to cabinet for a federal cost-shared unemployment assistance scheme four years earlier. See RG 2, series 18, vol. 187, file 5–60(d), "Report of the Working Committee on Unemployment Insurance and Unemployment Aid," 24 November 1950; RG 29, vol. 918, "Minutes of the Working Committee on Unemployment Assistance and Relief," 14 November 1950. He had been committed to this approach to unemployment assistance since his years as executive director of the Canadian Welfare Council in the 1940s. See RG 29, vol. 1885, file R170–100-3, George Davidson, *The Future Development of Social Security in Canada* (Ottawa, January 1943), 6–7.

33. RG 29, vol. 918, George Davidson, "Memorandum on Unemployment Assistance," May 1954.

34. Ibid., Minutes of "Interdepartmental Committee on Unemployment Questions," 28 July 1954; vol. 921, J. R. Parkinson, memorandum on "Unemployment Assistance: Proposal to Pay a Minimum Federal Share on a Continuous Basis," 22 July 1954; "The Green Book Proposal on Unemployment Assistance, 1945," 24 July 1954; Paul Martin, *A Very Public Life, Volume II: So Many Worlds* (Toronto: Deneau, 1985), 262. According to Martin, "Ken Taylor of the depart-

ment of finance wanted to . . . hold any federal concession in reserve for the 1955 [federal-provincial] conference. . . . Because the tax-rental negotiations were going to be tough, using unemployment assistance as a sweetener at the conference might [then have meant] accepting 100 percent responsibility. This would have cost the federal government more."

35. Ibid., vol. 918, minutes of the "Interdepartmental Committee on Unemployment Questions," 28 July 1954; "Interdepartmental Committee on Unemployment Questions: Report of Working Group," n.d. but *circa* August 1954; vol. 921, "Estimate of Probable Unemployment Assistance Caseload," 16 August 1954.

36. Ibid., vol. 918, "Interdepartmental Committee on Unemployment Questions," memorandum to cabinet, "Revision of the Unemployment Insurance Act," 27 October 1954.

37. House of Commons *Debates*, 2 March 1955, 1654; 1 March 1955, 1601, 1629–30, 1635.

38. RG 29, vol. 921, "Report of Meeting Between Civic Representatives and Members of the Federal Cabinet *Re:* Unemployment Situation in Toronto"; House of Commons *Debates*, 2 March 1955, 1656–57, 1690–91; CCSD Records, acc/83, box 151, Phyllis Burns, "Record of Action *re* Public Assistance and the Unemployed 1954–55," 14 June 1955; Martin, *A Very Public Life*, 262.

39. RG 29, vol. 920, "Notes of Meeting Between Members of the Cabinet and a Delegation of the Canadian Welfare Council, 3 February 1955.

40. Ibid.

41. CCSD Records, "Record of Action *re* Public Assistance and the Unemployed."

42. RG 29, vol. 918, "Cabinet Committee on Federal-Provincial Conference 1955," 5 April 1955; "Interdepartmental Committee on Unemployment Questions," minutes of meeting, 15 April 1955; "Interdepartmental Committee on the Federal-Provincial Conference 1955," minutes of meeting, 19 April 1955.

43. Ibid., vol. 919, Louis St. Laurent, memorandum for the cabinet, "Unemployment Assistance: Federal-Provincial Sharing Plan," 13 June 1955; vol. 918, minutes, "Federal-Provincial Meeting on Unemployment Assistance," 20 June 1955, Morning Session and Afternoon Session.

44. Ibid., vol. 918, minutes "Federal-Provincial Meeting on Unemployment Assistance," 20 June 1955.

45. House of Commons *Debates*, 29 June 1956, 5476; 11 January 1956, 24–30; 27 June 1956, 5447–73. On the limitations of the Unemployment Assistance Act, see RG 29, vol. 1887, file R170/100 pt 2, Canadian Welfare Council, *Social Security for Canada*, 2 June 1958. Two years after the passage of the UA Act, the CWC was still calling for a federal definition of a "minimum level of health and decency" in local welfare budgets.

46. House of Commons *Debates*, 28 June 1956, 5476; Keith Banting, *The Welfare State and Canadian Federalism* (Montreal: McGill-Queen's, 1982), 96; RG 29, vol. 919, "Statistics of Unemployment and Social Need," n.d. but *circa* January 1959; memo on "Unemployment Assistance," n.d. but *circa* 1959; vol. 921, "Discussion of Unemployment Assistance in New Brunswick," 24–25 February 1960. The province hoped to move to a new food allowance standard of $13.00 a week for a family of five in the near future.

47. Amy Leigh, "The Contribution of the Municipality to the Administration of Public Welfare," *Canadian Public Administration* (June 1964): 152–53; Fred MacKinnon, "Local Government and Welfare," *Canadian Public Administration* (June 1961): 35.

48. Pat Thane, *The Foundations of the Welfare State* (London: Longman, 1982) 289,2.

49. Mackinnon, "Local Government and Welfare." Upon signing the UA agreement in 1958, Nova Scotia, for example, passed a new Social Assistance Act abolishing its 200-year-old poor laws; RG 29, vol. 919, memo on "Unemployment Assistance," n.d. but *circa* 1959.

50. The potential for provincial "shifting" of mothers' allowance, disability, and other categorical welfare recipients onto the open-ended UA caseload had been recognized by federal officials as early as 1955 in the drafting of the Unemployment Assistance Act. See RG 29, vol. 918, "Memorandum to Cabinet *re* Unemployment Assistance," 18 October 1955. In introducing the act in Parliament, Paul Martin also conceded that there was little Ottawa could do if provinces wished to shift disability cases on to UA. House of Commons *Debates*, 27 June 1945, 5453. In 1963 Ontario shifted its dependent fathers with children from Mothers' Allowance to General Assistance in order "quite frankly . . . to obtain the additional financial assistance available under the Unemployment Assistance Agreement." RG 29, vol. 921, "Discussions with Officials of the Province of Ontario on Unemployment Assistance," 4–5 February 1963. Alberta followed British Columbia's lead in merging all welfare cases into a general social assistance category in the early 1960s. Between 1957 and 1965, total federal spending on Unemployment Assistance rose from $11,524,000 to $215,106,000 a year and the number of recipients increased from 123,445 to 789,694 by 1966. Kenneth Buckley and I. Uruquart, *Historical Statistics of Canada*, 2nd ed. (Ottawa, 1983), C404–16, C391–416. This dramatic expansion reflected both the high unemployment of the 1958–63 period and the liberalization of provincial social assistance eligibility because of the Unemployment Assistance Act.

51. For differing interpretations see Dyck, "The Canada Assistance Plan," *Canadian Public Administration* (Winter 1976); Bella, "The Provincial Role in the Canadian Welfare State," *Canadian Public Administration* (Fall 1979); Splane, "Social Policy-Making in the Government of Canada," Yelaja, ed. *Canadian Social Policy*.

2 Tools For the Job
Canada's Evolution From Public Works to Mandated Employment

LESLIE A. PAL

The political prominence of Ronald Reagan and Margaret Thatcher, along with the apparent triumph of neoconservative ideas, has led many observers to conclude that the postwar welfare state, in Canada and elsewhere, is in decline if not complete retreat. Canada's recent political experience would apparently support this view. Though signals are mixed, it seems clear that the Mulroney government continues to contemplate substantial revisions to the Canadian edifice of social and health programs. The 23 May 1985 federal budget highlighted the national debt as the country's main economic problem, and proposed revisions to child benefits, pensions, and transfers to provinces.[1] The 26 February 1986 budget carried these themes forward. With the exception of Ontario's and Quebec's, recent provincial elections have brought Conservative and conservative-minded governments to power, completing a shift to the right begun in British Columbia with Premier Bennett's 1983 restraint package. Indeed, the Bennett program was seen by some observers as only the first salvo in a New Right barrage which would ultimately explode the foundations of the postwar welfare state. Bennettism is only the local variant of Reaganism and Thatcherism, "a frontal attack on government spending and social priorities."[2] A neoconservative drift in national politics seems "unmistakable."[3]

Alternatively, neoconservatism and the New Right may be seen as symptoms, not causes, of a deeper structural crisis in the modern welfare state and advanced capitalism. One recent analysis which is broadly representative of this position argues that the postwar welfare state rested on several assumptions: Keynesianism, post-industrialism, social planning, and supported from the moderate left.[4] These ideas were sustained by prosperity and affluence, at least until the early 1970s. Persistent economic stagnation since then has undermined these ideological supports.

> These changed material conditions have also spelled the breakup of the *de facto* political consensus around the mixed economy and welfare, and revived sharply the somewhat somnolent ideological conflict over the issues of welfare and economic growth.[5]

While welfare capitalism will continue to limp along for the "foreseeable future," its state of crisis makes even such pragmatic predictions risky.[6]

It is not entirely clear, however, that the rubrics of crisis, decay, or decline fully capture the complex restructuring which is undeniably under way among advanced welfare states. Indeed, some observers have even suggested that what appears as a contemporary crisis is really only a historical hiccup. Albert Hirschman proposes that the welfare state is simply passing through a "readjustment" phase after its considerable and rapid expansion.[7] Hugh Heclo concurs in arguing that after passing through phases of experimentation, consolidation and expansion over the last century, the modern welfare state is currently in a fourth phase of retrenchment. The expansion of the 1950s and 1960s made the welfare state a victim of its own success: the Depression's sense of collective deprivation was replaced with isolated pockets of poverty; economic growth generated losers who demanded help; and affluence fragmented the old political coalition supporting welfare. When economic growth stalled, social policy and the welfare state were criticized for high spending, ineffectiveness, and overregulation. In Heclo's view, these criticisms have been met by changed priorities and reduced expectations.

Nowhere is there evidence of major welfare state programs being dismantled. What can be seen here and there among the Western democracies are efforts to slow down some expenditures' growth rates, to institute more cost controls, to refrain from undertaking major new social policy commitments, or to stretch out their implementation over time.[8]

A 1984 Report of the International Labour Office was also cautiously optimistic about current and future trends: "Thus the long-term future which we are assuming is one with substantially higher levels of employment and with a resumption of growth, though not at the rate of the 1950s and 1960s."[9]

This view is not restricted to the liberal centre of social science, but finds endorsement even in neo-Marxist quarters. Claus Offe has argued that the welfare state has become an irreversible achievement, in part because it remains functionally necessary to ameliorate class conflicts, and also because the very process of modernization of which it is a part has undermined or erased alternative arrangements such as extended families or close-knit communities.

> ... I think that although there are many indications that the number of legal claims, services and entitlements organized by the welfare state are being reduced, they have not been *wholly* questioned. In the present period, the typical pattern is that the scope, volume and timing of benefits and services are being reduced and restricted. However, so far there is little evidence that, for example, unemployment benefit programs or rudimentary forms of health insurance and welfare are being considered as unnecessary and therefore in need of outright abandonment.[10]

Casual empirical evidence supports this view, at least for Canada. Total government expenditures amounted to 36.7 percent of GNP for 1969–74. They fluctuated between 40 and 43 percent from 1975 to 1981, jumping to and remaining near 47.3 percent after 1982.[11] The Report of the Royal Commission on the Economic Union and Development Prospects for Canada confirms that current social

policy thinking is not entirely dominated by neoconservative ideas
or a psychology of crisis. The Commission argued that "there is no
strong general case for attacking the deficit by reducing social expenditures." It proposed a reform package which would have included a Transitional Adjustment Assistance Program to support
wage subsidy schemes, mobility grants, training programs, and
early retirement, along with a Universal Income Security Program
which would replace most existing federal tax and transfer programs with a universal guaranteed income.[12] While on balance this
may not represent a substantial expansion of the Canadian welfare
state, it certainly cannot be subsumed under the simplistic formula of "crisis."

The contemporary development of the welfare state, in Canada
and elsewhere, is thus ambiguous. While the dominant theme is
one of retrenchment, cutbacks, and retreat, there are also important counterpoints which suggest that a more complex process is
at work. Unfortunately, none of the available theories of the welfare state, from neo-Marxism to neoconservatism, seems adequate
to the task of describing and explaining the detailed transformation of the welfare state in advanced capitalist democracies.[13] At
this stage, mid-range theory applied to selected areas of social
policy might be more prudent and beneficial.

This chapter examines the postwar evolution of Canadian job
creation strategies as an example of how the welfare state's development is not unidirectional. Even while income security programs have been threatened with cutbacks and restrictions, and
governments have apparently embraced the rhetoric of competition, free enterprise and reduced intervention, there has been increasing emphasis on passive and active job creation by the state.
Indeed, direct job creation has been joined recently by a panoply of
programs designed to give selected groups certain advantages and
protections in the labour market. Together, these policies and programs amount to a strategy of "mandated employment," a
strategy which goes well beyond traditional Keynesian demand
management and represents an intensification, not attenuation, of
state intervention.

Governing Instruments and Policy Succession

A suitable midrange theory is needed to grasp policy developments in this field. Recent work on governing instruments, or the means whereby policies are implemented, offers some insights into the specific ways in which the modern state can and does intervene to manage labour market processes. This section briefly reviews the range of governing instruments and the concept of policy succession, which captures the notion of discernable sequences from one category of instrument to the next.

The most elaborate analysis of governing instruments comes from Christopher C. Hood.[14] Hood argues for a view of government administration as applying a set of "administrative tools, in many different combinations and contexts, to suit a variety of purposes."[15] These tools fall into two broad categories: detectors which tell an agency what is going on in its environment, and effectors which allow it to act upon the environment. Hood then suggests that governments, by virtue of being governments, have four basic resources upon which they can draw for detecting and effecting tools. They are "nodality" (the property of being in the centre of an information or social network), "treasure" (stocks of money), "authority" (the power to officially demand, forbid, guarantee, adjudicate), and "organization" (the possession of personnel and their skills, land, buildings, materials, and equipment).

> In very simple terms it could be said that "nodality" works on your knowledge and attitudes, "treasure" on your bank balance, "authority" on your rights, status and duties, and "organization" on your physical environment or even on your person.[16]

Space does not permit a full discussion of the more than two dozen examples of instruments and devices available to governments using these various resources.[17] It is worth posing a few salient questions about instrument choice, however, assuming that governments do indeed face a "menu" of instruments when considering how to implement a policy or program. The first question is what determines instrument choice. The answer depends on the value being maximized. The two criteria which have been most frequently discussed in the recent literature are technical efficiency and political efficiency. Technical efficiency is usually interpreted to refer to the total social costs (including government and the private sector) of preferring one instrument over another.[18] Hood mentions the size of program or policy clientele as a technical variable encouraging specific choices between active/particular instruments and passive/general ones.[19] Most observers do not feel that considerations of technical efficiency play a major role in the policy process. Doern and Phidd boldly declare that the Canadian literature on governing instruments agrees on one thing: "instruments are not matters of technical efficiency."[20] Political efficiency encompasses policies made to enhance re-election prospects,[21] general popularity, and most broadly, legitimacy.

A second question is whether there is a discernable logic to instrument choice. Do governments move through policy instruments in a particular order, and if so, why? Doern and Wilson hypothesized that "politicians have a strong tendency to respond to policy issues (any issue) by moving successively from the least coercive governing instruments to the most coercive."[22] Hood claimed to find no discernable pattern, either in any logical sense or in the broad sweep of state activity in the postwar period.

Hogwood and Peters have recently developed the concept of "policy succession" which may help address this second question.[23] They define policy succession as one outcome of the policy cycle (the others being policy maintenance and policy termination), "by which a previous policy, program or organization is replaced by a 'new' one directed at the same program and/or clientele."[24] Policy termination is quite rare, as is complete inertia. The reality of policy-making in advanced states is "the replacement of existing policies or programs by new attempts at 'solving' the same problems—or the problems created by previous policies."[25] Policy succession is more prevalent today because of three related phenomena: a crowded policy space, the fact that existing policies themselves create the need for policy change, and resource constraints on policy innovation.[26] Policy succession, according to Hogwood and Peters, is not synonymous with either incremental change or constant, slow expansion. Some types of policy succession resemble maintenance or termination, but "decision-makers wishing to secure a cut-back in a program will have to devote substantially more political resources to securing a cut-back of a given size than to secure an increase of the same size. . . . "[27]

Policy succession, as the product of mid-range theory, seems to accord with the less apocalyptic view of current welfare state restructuring. Pure termination of programs is rare and politically difficult. A more likely strategy is succession or shift to instruments and delivery systems which either achieve roughly the same purpose, or even permit expansion of clientele and purpose at little cost. Hood's concept of tools or instruments of government shows the precise means whereby governments may shift from one delivery mechanism to another.

Our argument is that the modern welfare state is undergoing a complex, fragmented, unsynchronized transition, in which few policies or programs are terminated (in the sense of completely ended, or turned over to the private sector) but where new instruments succeed older ones to achieve roughly the same purpose. The salient feature of this process of policy succession is that it rarely involves a retreat of policy in anything but the modest sense of slightly lowered expenditure or reduced rates of growth. The major consequence of policy succession is the move to cheaper (from the state's view) instruments which are more coercive and impose costs on private actors. The logic of this succession may be determined in part by those broad forces identified in neo-Marxist political economy, but in the modern state it is just as likely that the logic will be insulated from those forces.

It would be impossible to demonstrate this thesis for the entire range of Canadian welfare state programs. This chapter explores these themes by focusing on the policy succession of governing instruments in federal labour market policy, more specifically those programs aimed at "direct employment."

From Public Works to Mandated Employment

LABOUR MARKET POLICY

Labour market policy, as it is generally understood, operates on the supply/demand relationship to ensure that labour is available in sufficient quantities, with sufficient training, to meet demand.

This also includes policies to ensure that labour (as an economic resource) is not wasted or misused. Thus, the labour market policies of modern governments have both supply and demand elements, along with supportive and protective dimensions. Put this broadly, however, virtually every government policy that affects people will affect them as members of the labour force, and so labour market policy might be thought to include everything from elementary school education to medicare. A necessary step in restricting the scope of labour market policy to reasonable limits is to understand that it seeks, first, to address the salient factors of labour market relationships, and second, to do so through direct rather than passive instruments.

In simplest terms, a labour market transaction involves a worker and employer. The worker comes to the exchange with a set of skills and work habits, the employer with tasks that need doing and a fixed amount to pay in wages. Several things can "go wrong" and impede the transactions. On the supply side, workers might not be available in sufficient numbers, might not have the right skills, or might be unaware of job opportunities. Policies to improve information, to assist in training or re-training, and to move labour to areas of high demand can address these problems. On the demand side, employers might not be aware of available labour pools, might be unable to pay prevailing rates of wage, or might not hire from certain qualified groups for noneconomic reasons. Information policies, wage subsidies, and antidiscrimination policies have been developed to attack these problems. These policies are considered direct because they aim at specific and identified elements of the wage relationship. This is in contrast to macroeconomic stabilization policy, which relies on fiscal and monetary levers to act on the economy as a whole, stimulating or reducing demand as necessary and assuming that the appropriate adjustments will follow.

The broad range of Canadian federal manpower policies has been reviewed in several places, and needs no rehearsal here.[28] Instead, this chapter focuses on one important element of labour market policy, that of "direct employment" programs. These may be defined as those programs in which the state is directly responsible for some person's employment. Traditionally, these programs fell into two categories: (i) make-work or job creation schemes in which the state paid all or nearly all of the wages, and (ii) programs with wage subsidies to encourage private employers to hire workers. In the first, the state was the employer; in the second it worked through private employers. The state, of course, is a significant employer in its own right, apart from its labour market strategies. Direct employment policies are distinguished by the fact that they are usually temporary, and that the people they employ are not performing government work *per se*.

In recent years, a third type of direct employment strategy has been increasingly used by government, especially the federal government, in Canada. It may be termed "mandated employment," and involves the use of authoritative sanctions and regulations to improve the employability or the compensation of identified groups. In recent years, these groups have included women, youth, natives, and the handicapped, and policies to assist them have come under the rubrics of affirmative action and workplace equality. Mandated employment policies take job creation or direct employment onto an entirely different terrain, the regulation of private behaviour versus the provision of incentives through subsidy programs.

Mandated employment has a pedigree extending back to the original proposals for public works schemes after World War II. This brief flirtation with job creation was soon dropped as the economy improved and as governments grew to prefer macroeconomic tools such as fiscal and monetary policy. In the 1960s, with the view that a substantial portion of Canadian unemployment was structural and not merely due to deficient demand, federal and provincial governments began to develop manpower and labour market policies. Some of these policies involved direct employment or job creation, but in the fiscal crunch of the 1970s and 1980s may be succeeded by strategies of mandated employment.

FROM PUBLIC WORKS TO JOB CREATION

Government in Canada is the nation's largest employer, and its importance in this regard has grown steadily since World War II.[29] But employment in the public sector as a means for achieving other ends is distinct from employment which is an end in itself. Governments perform a variety of tasks for which they require personnel, but this is not the same as direct employment programs which address the problem of joblessness. In the second case, the tasks performed by the hired personnel are incidental to the use of a direct employment strategy to reduce unemployment. Indeed, the work performed could itself be without purpose or use (e.g., digging ditches); what matters is that a day's work legitimates the payment of a day's wage.

Historically, before and for a short time after World War II, this strategy was known by the rubric of "public works." Canadian governments have a long tradition of direct employment and management of public works projects, going back to the pre-Confederation completion of the St. Lawrence canal system.[30] In this case and others like the national parks system, the work performed was far from useless; it provided essential infrastructure to a developing nation. Public works as a strategy of direct employment were first tried extensively during the interwar years, and especially the Depression. It was in this period that Canada had to face a new kind of unemployment and distress, that of large numbers of able-bodied, working-aged males.[31] Unlike abandoned or widowed mothers, the elderly, or the handicapped, able-bodied males were presumed to be capable of work, and almost always preferred work to the dole. Municipal and provincial relief systems, designed primarily for the former, were unsuited and ill-equipped to deal with the latter. In 1930, Ottawa began to contribute to municipal and provincial relief projects, leaving the design and administration of those projects up to local authorities. Without money to hire competent administrative personnel, these local efforts were chaotic and fragmented.[32] In 1932, work-related relief was largely replaced by the dole, which was less expensive to administer. As a general means of dealing with the unemployment crisis, however, it succeeded in offending both middle-class morality and working-class pride. A new attempt was made with the establishment of federal relief camps in 1932, administered and run by the Canadian army. In exchange for voluntary labour, men would be provided with food, shelter, clothing and medical care, but not wages.[33] These half-hearted measures accomplished little beyond removing transients from overburdened municipalities, and in fact concentrated the discontented, making the camps volatile crucibles of radicalism and unrest.

The 1934 American New Deal example of federally-funded public works as a strategy of dealing with unemployment influenced the Bennett government. The Public Works Construction Act appropriated forty million dollars "for the construction of a series of federal public works such as wharves, post offices, and improvements to existing buildings."[34] Compared to the American effort, this was largely symbolic, and Mackenzie King, after his 1935 election, created the National Employment Commission to find ways of reducing Ottawa's relief expenditures and overseeing provincial relief administration.[35] The Commission's 1938 report in fact recommended expanded federal responsibility for unemployment relief (fully under federal jurisdiction) and a major public works effort. Norman Rogers, the progressive-minded minister of labour at the time, supported these proposals but faced opposition from Mackenzie King and Charles Dunning, the minister of finance. Deepening recession in early 1938 forced consideration of a recovery program of some sort, and the Prime Minister appointed Rogers as chairman of a committee to plan a broad program of public works. The committee's list totalled more than seventy-five million dollars and, much to Mackenzie King's amazement, had Cabinet support. Though King and Dunning opposed these expenditures, which would substantially increase the budgetary deficit, they compromised in order to avoid a Cabinet split and gave Rogers fifty million dollars for the projects he had insisted upon.[36]

Public works as a means of alleviating unemployment had thus become respectable by 1938–39, but were rendered unnecessary by the war boom after 1939. The issue did not languish, however, because of the federal government's need to engage in reconstruction planning. The chaos of World War I demobilization efforts prodded officials to begin planning for the war's end by 1940. The General Advisory Committee on Demobilization and Rehabilitation was appointed that year, with the minister of national defence as its chairman. An interdepartmental committee of officials, the Advisory Committee on Economic Policy (commonly known as the Economic Advisory Committee, or the EAC) was established in 1939, but had its power greatly expanded in 1943. At that point, it became the most powerful player in reconstruction planning, representing as it did the most senior officials from key departments and agencies such as Finance, the Bank of Canada, External Affairs, and the Privy Council Office. Along with three Parliamentary

Special Committees (two in the House of Commons and one in the Senate), the other key advisory body was the Committee on Reconstruction, established in 1941 by Ian Mackenzie, the minister of pensions and national health. Chaired by F. Cyril James, principal of McGill University, the Committee took a broad view of its mandate and prepared reports on social security (the famous Marsh Report) as well as economic affairs. In its first report to Cabinet in 1942, the James Committee recommended that:

> a construction reserve commission should be established to assemble a shelf of public work projects ready for quick implementation, as needed, to counteract the expected postwar depression. This would involve a Dominion advisory council, regional committees, and permanent expert staff, and the ultimate aim was counter-cyclical timing of public work spending throughout the country, led by the federal government.[37]

Federal officials were alarmed at the James Committee's presumption in making such sweeping recommendations, especially since another one of its proposals had been to establish a separate ministry of economic planning. The EAC engineered a bloodless bureaucratic coup and assumed the lead role in reconstruction planning, establishing a sub-committee for that purpose in 1943, the Sub-Committee on Post-war Reconstruction, chaired by W. A. Mackintosh. The Committee's ideas formed a stream which flowed into early postwar budgetary policy, social policy, the 1945 White Paper on Employment and Income, and Ottawa's proposals at the 1945 Dominion-Provincial Conference. The Committee assumed that postwar economic conditions would be characterized by shortages of consumer goods and labour surpluses due to demobilization of the armed forces and war industries. The first tier of government assistance would therefore comprise financial, tax, and commercial incentives, but private industry could not be expected to take up all the economic slack. Like the James Committee, the EAC Sub-Committee supported the idea of a coordinated public works program. Any remaining unemployment would be addressed by a third tier of government social programs.[38]

By the early 1940s, however, public works as a supply-side solution to unemployment was no longer as innovative as it had been even a decade earlier. The war experience had demonstrated that government spending and high levels of economic demand could haul the economy out of the trough of depression into a boom. Moreover, federal Finance officials had experienced their own, special sort of sin—centralized control of the economy and complete occupation of major tax fields. Finance was easily the most influential department in government, and tax instruments were its specialty. Public works, on the other hand, would percolate upwards from the departments of labour, agriculture, and, after 1944, reconstruction. The Department of Reconstruction might have emerged as the champion of direct employment, but under C. D. Howe was more interested in divesting Ottawa of government war industries.[39] Public works did not disappear from the federal agenda, however. Ottawa's 1945 Dominion-Provincial Conference proposals contained a separate section on public works, but it was clear that they were a residual strategy, overshadowed in importance and expense by social programs and fiscal policy. As Louis St. Laurent, minister of justice, put it in outlining Ottawa's proposals: "In the postwar period there will be ample scope for a far-sighted program of public investment."[40] But he also expressed reservations:

> The purpose should not be to find a "cure-all" for unemployment in huge expenditures on public works. The problem is one of devising a sound and consistent program of public improvements which will expand the productive wealth of the community and widen the opportunities for enterprise and employment.[41]

C. D. Howe presented the details of Ottawa's proposed public investment policy. Public works projects would be initiated by all levels of government and would aim at "the conservation and development of mineral, forestry, agricultural and fishery resources, the improvement of transportation facilities, and the construction of public buildings and equipment required for general government services or particular government welfare programs."[42] Beyond providing useful investments, a public works policy should be timed to stimulate employment in an economic downturn. This would require a "shelf" of postponable projects which could be implemented quickly when necessary.

The 1945–46 Dominion-Provincial Conference failed to come to any agreements, and so a jointly-planned federal/provincial public works shelf collapsed. Instead, Ottawa decided to establish its own shelf of $150 million worth of projects.[43] This was also unsuccessful, so that by mid-1947 only $54 million worth of projects had been planned. The "shelf" remained bare largely for three reasons. First, there was a shortage of planning staff. Second, that staff was already overburdened in planning and implementing current projects. Third, the economy enjoyed a boom which few had dared hope or predict in 1944–45. The unemployment rate had increased from 1.6 percent in 1945 to 3.4 percent in 1946, then dropping below 3 percent until the 1949–50 recession, when it reached 3.6 percent. The average rate for the 1946–53 period was 2.8 percent. The rationale of direct employment through public works evaporated, so that in December 1949 the government officially abandoned the idea of a shelf of works projects and "virtually no advanced planning of public works projects was undertaken specifically for stabilization purposes after 1949."[44]

With major social programs such as unemployment insurance, family allowances, and pensions in place, federal economic policy proceeded to ride the coattails of a postwar boom fuelled by renewed consumer spending, the Korean War, and foreign trade. The emphasis in the 1950s was on fiscal policy and, since the prevailing economic context was one of expansion and growth, Ottawa could wed orthodox budgetary practice to Keynesian rhetoric: contra-cyclical policy seemed to call for small surpluses. In these circumstances, with a relatively low unemployment rate, labour market policies and direct employment seemed entirely unnecessary.

The grim grip of recession held Canada once again from 1958 to 1962, with only brief respites. The length and tenacity of the Canadian recession contrasted with the more rapid American recovery, and formed the backdrop to a national debate on the existence of "structural unemployment" and the need for a concerted manpower policy. Though the debate first arose in 1957, its most visible institutional expression was the Senate Special Committee on Manpower and Employment, appointed in 1960. After hearing business, labour, and academic submissions on Canada's economic problems, the Senate Committee recommended a strategy of tax incentives to stimulate secondary manufacturing, and a manpower policy aimed at training for new skills and reducing labour market rigidities.[45]

By this period, the federal government was clearly prepared to mount a broad manpower strategy, focussing at least at the outset on training and education. There had been the wartime precedent of the Vocational Training Coordination Act of 1942, whereby Ottawa subsidized training conducted by the provinces. In 1960, this was replaced with an enriched program, the Technical and Vocational Training Assistance Act, which in turn was followed in 1967 by the Adult Occupational Training Act. A Department of Manpower and Immigration, established in 1966, gave institutional expression to Ottawa's new commitment to dealing with the supply side of the economic equation. Some writers have also included Ottawa's moves to support post-secondary education in a broad manpower strategy.[46]

As Doern and Phidd point out, "direct job creation programs . . . were, relatively speaking, a sidelight in this period,"[47] but their revival signalled the first time since 1949 that Ottawa seriously considered dealing with unemployment through the instrument of either employing people directly or subsidizing their wages. National unemployment levels were rising in 1957 (between 1958 and 1962 they would average 6.7 percent), but the average annual rates masked seasonal fluctuations wherein, during the winter months, unemployment could go as high as 8 or 10 percent. A National Winter Employment Conference in 1958 led to the Municipal Winter Works Incentive Program that same year, whereby Ottawa provided grants for municipally-based construction projects. The Finance Department, keeper of the Keynesian economic keys of aggregate demand management, was unenthused by the program, whose champion had been the Department of Labour. The program lasted until 1968.

The hallmark of fiscal policies aimed at the demand side of the economy had been their generality. It had been assumed that a general tax cut or increase would be sufficiently effective to achieve desired results. Supply side labour market policies compelled a better definition of targets and specific bottlenecks. While

48   L. A. Pal

the first efforts in direct job creation in 1958 aimed at unemployed adult male workers in the construction industry, subsequent programs identified youth as a category of labour market entrants needing special support. The Company of Young Canadians provided jobs for young people in community and social projects they felt had social significance. It was replaced with the more ambitious Opportunities for Youth (OFY) program in 1970, which provided federal grants for local community projects proposed by young people. This program continued until 1976, when it was replaced by the Young Canada Works Program.

In addition to OFY, in 1971 Ottawa announced its Special Employment Plan, comprised of seven related initiatives to directly attack the increasing unemployment levels of that period. The most extensive and expensive ($180 million) was the Local Initiatives Program, which provided grants to private groups and municipalities to finance labour intensive community projects. Another component was the Canadian Manpower Training-on-the-Job Program (CMTJP) under which Ottawa subsidized the wages of each hired unemployed worker by 75 percent. A third major element was the Federal-Provincial Employment Loans Program. It was administered through the Department of Regional Economic Expansion, allowing it to forgive 75 percent of loans for on-site labour costs incurred before 1 June 1972.[48] With these programs, Ottawa nailed its colours to the policy mast: government was now acknowledged to be in the business of directly creating jobs that would not otherwise have been, either by paying formerly unemployed workers directly or through the intermediary of a private employer.

FROM JOB CREATION TO MANDATED EMPLOYMENT

The original rationale of manpower policy in the 1960s was the improvement of information access on employment prospects, and retraining of older workers who needed new skills for a new economy. This was evident in U.S. manpower policy,[49] and in Canadian policy as well.[50] Job creation programs were grafted on to this original purpose for two reasons, political and economic. The economic reasons reflected a growing realization through the late 1960s and 1970s that the incidence of unemployment varied with particular, identifiable groups, such as youth. The political reasons had to do with the ability of these groups to single themselves out for special, remedial treatment because of putative labour market disadvantages. This is why youth and later women were such prominent players in the complex evolution of direct employment policies.[51]

Another contributing factor might have been the somewhat heady—in retrospect—views on the future of work that prevailed in some quarters in the 1960s. Notions of postindustrialism, the social service state, the need to encourage meaningful work experience and socially productive jobs, community development, and participatory decision-making structures, were an accepted part of the policy discourse of that period. They infused labour market and direct employment policies with a vision and progressive purpose that were entirely expressive of the policy atmosphere of the 1960s. Perhaps one of the last flourishes of this conceptual framework can be seen in the 1973 *Working Paper on Social Security in Canada*, with its proposals for a Community Employment Program.[52]

The result of these forces was a surge in manpower programs in the 1970s. Though cautious about making such international comparisons, the 1981 Dodge Report noted that:

> the bulk of the expansion in many European countries took place in the years after 1975, following the major recession of 1974–75. In Canada, where labor force growth had been much stronger than in Europe, the increases in expenditures began somewhat earlier, particularly for job creation programs.[53]

Expenditures on job creation programs, training, and supply/demand adjustment programs (e.g. mobility programs and the employment service) increased substantially in the early 1970s, with the greatest relative increases occurring in job creation or job maintenance programs.[54] In Canada, as noted above, these programs tended to concentrate on the persistence of high unemployment rates among certain target groups and regions. "Governments, as a consequence, paid increasing attention to these equity aspects of social and economic policies."[55]

The concern with equity had always been a part of direct employment programs, but began to emerge in the mid-1970s as the dominant consideration in program design. In 1973, for example, the Department of Manpower and Immigration introduced two new programs "to ensure that manpower services were available to all groups in the population including those unemployed persons considered to be disadvantaged."[56] One new program was the Local Employment Assistance Program (LEAP). LEAP's purpose was "to create worthwhile employment for people who have been unemployed or receiving public assistance and who are not likely to become employed through normal labour market activity during the period of a project (maximum duration of thirty-six months)."[57]

Earlier initiatives such as LIP and OFY had aimed at short-term employment; LEAP shifted attention to chronic or long-term unemployment. By 1976, the Department had consolidated LIP and OFY into the Canada Works and Young Canada Works programs, and had embarked upon the Community Employment Strategy to foster greater intergovernmental and interdepartmental cooperation in alleviating chronic unemployment in specifically targeted areas. By 1976–77, the last year of operation of the Department of Manpower and Immigration, these core job creation programs were complemented by a range of programs for "special needs" clients unlikely to obtain permanent employment even in buoyant times: natives, northern communities, women, ex-inmates of correctional institutions, physically and mentally handicapped, welfare recipients, young workers, and military personnel returning to civilian employment.[58]

In 1976 the federal government began a gradual reorientation of its job creation programs, dramatically symbolized in the amalgamation of the Unemployment Insurance Commissison and the Department of Employment and Immigration into the Canada Employment and Immigration Commission, supported by a special department. The new employment strategy accepted the challenge of further job stimulation, especially over the succeeding four or five years, after which conditions might improve, but it was premised on the rationale of restraint and fiscal discipline which have become synonymous with the current crisis of the welfare state:

We must therefore look toward a strategy that will help to fill the employment gap over the next several years. It must be a

strategy compatible with the restraint of expenditures, moderation in the increase of the money supply, and the avoidance of
massive inflation-stimulating deficits. It must not be a strategy
of major monetary or fiscal stimulation, vast programs of public
construction or public service expansion, or major tax cuts;
these would be incompatible with our need to reduce inflation-
ary forces and to remove wage and price controls.[59]

The five-year employment strategy's centrepiece was the Canada
Works and Young Canada Works programs, which would receive
their incremental funding from savings in the unemployment insurance program. There was greater concern to integrate job creation with private labour markets. Wages, for example, would be
set at the provincial minimum wage; project and selection controls would ensure that "people are not drawn into the labour
market simply to participate in the program."[60] Participants in
Young Canada Works would be discouraged from "doing their own
thing" in favour of projects with "solid community value."[61] In
contrast to earlier policy rationale, there was greater emphasis on
the long-term employment benefits of direct job creation programs. As well, in an atmosphere of restraint, there may have been
growing public pressure to link income support measures with
some kind of work requirement.[62]

The Dodge Report estimated that between the 1971 and 1980 fiscal years, Ottawa had spent approximately $2 billion on direct job
creation programs, exclusive of tax expenditure programs aimed
at private-sector employment. About 260,500 person-years of employment were created,[63] but this did not in itself constitute success. Concurring with earlier assessments made by the Economic
Council of Canada and the OECD,[64] the Dodge Report concluded
that "direct employment projects do not constitute stepping
stones to regular productive employment for most of those employed on the projects or those remaining outside the labour
force."[65] The report did point out that direct job creation was less
expensive than general tax cuts or public expenditures, and recommended a new mix of employment tools as well as a new fit between programs and changing labour market conditions. Using
community-based development as its conceptual framework, it
recommended a shift away from single-project funding on a short-
term basis, to longer term community development. It also em-

phasized the potential of small business and private entrepreneurship.[66] Even though the Dodge Report envisioned the creation of national crown corporations to foster development, it did not advocate the provision of new resources to these initiatives, just a reallocation of existing ones.[67]

While recommending that direct job creation be more cautiously implemented, even to the extent of shifting away from concerns of equity and the disadvantaged as such, the Dodge Report also suggested enhancement of programs and policies aimed at those groups with special employment needs, principally women, native peoples, youth, the elderly and disabled. In this it echoed pledges made in the 1980 Throne Speech to implement improved employment and training programs for these people. Training and job creation programs of the 1970s had, for most of these target groups, only addressed "perceived skill deficiencies of the individual as defined by market requirements instead of barriers in the employment system itself."[68] Problems of systemic discrimination based on institutional patterns and practices had not received adequate attention in the past. The report agreed that further supply-side programs such as training could be useful, but argued that direct employment programs modelled after those in the 1960s and 1970s were inappropriate. It concluded that, along with the more traditional panoply of services, "some form of legislated action may be required to ensure that employers adopt employment practices which make better use of this expanding supply of target group labour."[69]

The Dodge Report's recommendations assumed that Canada was poised on the brink of substantial economic growth, and that current policies had to be re-oriented to facilitate the necessary labour market adjustments. Recession, not transition or adjustment, hit in the latter part of 1981 and undermined the report's impact; nonetheless, subsequent employment policy continued to demonstrate a re-orientation towards special needs groups and away from direct employment of the older variety, all overlaid with a new emphasis on community development and private sector entrepreneurship. This new emphasis was evident in the alphabet soup of programs launched between 1980 and 1982: CCDP (Canada Community Development Projects, 1980) CCSP (Canada Community Services Projects, 1980), LEDA (Local Economic Development Assistance Program, 1980), NTEP (New Technology Employment Program, 1980), PED (Program for the Employment-Disadvantaged, 1981), NEED (New Employment Expansion and Development Program, 1982). In 1983–84, Ottawa decided to consolidate its dozen direct job creation programs into four: Canada Works (incorporated NEED and Unemployment Insurance Job Creation; aimed at UI exhaustees, UI beneficiaries, laid-off workers, and social assistance recipients); Local Employment Assistance and Development (incorporated LEDA and CCDP); Career Access (incorporated NTEP, CSSP, PED); Job Corps (community-based projects to help severely disadvantaged people acquire skills). All of these programs, and especially Career Access which was a wage-subsidy program, made funds available to profit as well as nonprofit organizations. In fiscal 1983–84, the government estimated that it had spent $1.054 billion on these and minor related programs, employing 321,900 individuals for an equivalent of 88,100 person-years.[70]

Two developments dominated 1985–86 on the employment front, suggesting Ottawa's continuing emphasis on new instruments and mandated employment. At the February 14–15 First Ministers Conference, Prime Minister Brian Mulroney announced a $2 billion employment initiative. On 27 June 1985, Employment and Immigration Minister Flora MacDonald released details of the Canadian Jobs Strategy. The Strategy reorganizes the existing training and job development programs into six new categories. The two most important programs are Job Development ($700 million in 1985–86) and Job Entry ($350 million in 1985–86). It is difficult to compare these figures with those of previous programs, but it would appear that the Jobs Strategy increases funding little or not at all for direct employment. While the Jobs Strategy does incorporate some of the Dodge Report recommendations (e.g., community rather than project emphasis; participants may move from one program to another to build up skills), it actually represents little more than procedural housekeeping. Job creation strategies have been in *stasis* since 1980.

The more interesting moves have been on the mandated employment front. As noted earlier, Ottawa repledged itself to affirmative action programs in 1980. In 1982 the adoption of the Charter of Rights and Freedoms as part of the Canadian Constitution included Section 15 on Equality Rights (taking effect on 17 April 1985). Finally, in 1984 and 1985 two Royal Commissions' reports addressed the problem of equity in labour markets, the Royal Commission on Equality in Employment (Abella Commission) and the Royal Commission on the Economic Union and Development Prospects for Canada (Macdonald Commission). The Macdonald Commission's review of equal pay for work of equal value concurred with the recommendations of the Abella Commission, though somewhat cautiously.[71] It supported affirmative action programs, however, more strongly. In echoing the Abella recommendations, the Macdonald Commission expressed concern that "as often before, governmental actions will turn out to be toothless. In order to ensure compliance, these approaches should be firmly legislated rather than merely set out in guidelines. Moreover, the Human Rights Commission should be given more resources so that it can strengthen its monitoring and enforcement activities."[72]

The Abella Commission developed the concept of "employment equity" with respect to equalizing economic opportunities for women, native people, disabled persons, and visible minorities. In its 8 March 1985 statement of response, Ottawa enthusiastically endorsed the concept and measures to achieve it in the federal jurisdiction. Employment equity for women means equal opportunity, affirmative action, equal pay for work of equal value, as well as supportive measures in training and child care; for the disabled new efforts by employers to accommodate incidental handicaps; for natives and visible minorities affirmative action and special recruitment programs. All Crown Corporations (employees: 200,000), federally-regulated business (employees: 450,000), government contractors (employees: 300,000), and the federal government itself come under the scheme. It is up to the companies to develop their own programs, and only reporting is mandatory. Government contractors who fail to meet their commitments will be refused future contracts. The federal government itself will intensify the implementation of its affirmative action programs and in 1986 began the implementation of equal pay for work of equal value. The government emphasized that administrative costs would be kept to a minimum and that a massive enforcement agency would not be needed. Nevertheless, the Minister pledged that this was only the first step in a broader policy offensive.

It would be easy to dismiss these measures as so much policy puffery. No expenditures are involved; the only instrument is mandatory reporting. But placed against the backdrop of the last fifteen years, the context of expenditure restraint, and scepticism over job creation, the shift to mandated employment is clearly discernable and important. Federal policy remains interested in job creation, but direct employment is no longer the centrepiece of supply-side policy. Indeed, mandated employment or employment equity is seen as a demand-side policy insofar as it attacks impediments in hiring, promotion, and compensation practices in the private sector. Job creation had been somewhat uncomfortably situated among other supply-side, labour market policies by claiming that it developed skills and gave experience to the unemployed. As job creation strategies evolved, they paid increasing attention to selected target groups while simultaneously expanding from seasonal programs to full-year, quasi-permanent programs. As well, the focus shifted from the community, nonprofit level to include private businesses and the stimulation of entrepreneurship.

Despite this growth and elaboration, the employment opportunities for key socioeconomic groups like women, youth, and natives remained limited. By the 1980s, despite expenditure restraint, demands for equity had, if anything, intensified, not diminished. It should not be surprising that policy attention shifted to private sector practices. The old job creation policies had assumed that experience and training would be their own advertisement, and that behaviours and practices within firms would automatically respond to economic incentives and competition. Human rights and collective bargaining legislation, worker health and safety regulations and minimum wage laws existed, of course, and served to constrain employer discretion in the private sector, but mandated employment takes a quantum leap beyond these devices. Mandated employment consists of policies which specify that certain groups be favoured with positive discrimination in hiring and promotion (affirmative action) and that compensation levels for these same groups be administratively monitored and set to achieve equality and proportionality. From a

public works shelf of federal building projects to be used in a con-
tracyclical fashion against brief bouts of high unemployment,
direct employment policy has arrived at the threshold of continuous monitoring and state administration of key private market
decisions involving hiring, firing, promotion, compensation—in
fact, every important decision about employment.

Conclusion

The preceding review of postwar Canadian direct employment
policies suggests that the evolution of the welfare state is far from
unidirectional. Even in a period of restraint and apparent fiscal
crisis, Canadian policy has continued to evolve toward more state
control of private market transactions. Even the term "evolution"
may be too strong: it suggests slow incremental change, in which
each step gradually emerges from its predecessors. It may be more
appropriate, if we are to adopt the concept of evolution at all, to
use the notion of punctuated equilibrium.[73] The evolution of direct
employment policies has not been characterized by gradualism;
instead, long periods of relative stability have been punctuated by
brief but intense bouts of change. The dynamics of policy succession are far more complex than the "postwar growth/current
restraint" model would imply.

Direct employment programs went from being a policy pariah in
the 1930s to an important and accepted element of a broad con-
tracyclical economic strategy in 1945. Despite the feverish planning that punctuated the prewar and postwar eras, public works
strategies bore the marks of earlier ancestors in the Depression
such as work camps and construction projects. The shelf of works
was to be activated as economic conditions worsened, presumably
in cyclical and seasonal downturns, and for the traditionally important members of the work force: male heads of households employed in the private sector.

The postwar boom buried the public works approach for almost
a decade, until unemployment began to rise once again in the late
1950s. The winter works programs of that period showed traces of
the community focus which would later emerge as a prominent
aspect of job creation schemes. The 1960 Agricultural and Rural

Development Program was one of the first postwar economic programs to combine regional development concerns with specific sectorial concerns.[74] Regional economic policies were soon twinned with job creation programs for specific target groups. The 1970s, generally considered as an era of restraint and cutbacks, saw an almost verdant growth in job creation programs, and increasing attention to special needs groups such as youth, natives, women, the disabled, and the elderly. The last few years have been another period of rapid change, in which the government's fundamental policy posture has shifted away from direct employment to mandated employment. It may be that expenditure growth in job creation will remain minimal, while the enforcement of employment equity, whereby advantages are conferred on special groups by administrative fiat, will enjoy a boom. Only a myopic identification of the welfare state with spending would consider this a "retreat"; in all important respects it represents an extension of the web of rules and regulations which also mark the welfare state. The state is redistributing rights instead of dollars; different means achieve the same ends.[75]

It would be imprudent, if not foolhardy, to offer an explanation for these contradictory shifts and feints in welfare state evolution. Some of the forces at work can, however, be identified. The first is the quasi-autonomous logic of state policy development. Old programs beget new programs which, to the bureaucratic mind dealing technocratically with policy problems, are "improvements" in the sense of better efficiency or increased impact. It may in fact be true that the billions spent on job creation in the past have not helped special groups or regions, but the bureaucratic instinct is to expand mandates and means to approach a final, effective solution.

Related to this is the development of semi-autonomous branches of government whose mandates and styles of intervention are remarkably insulated from the political pressures usually held responsible for the retreat of the welfare state. Courts and human rights commissions focus on rights, not costs, and will be further encouraged to do so by the Charter of Rights and Freedoms. Women have organized the Legal Education and Assistance Fund (with federal help) to select and pursue Charter-based cases, and other special groups will doubtless follow their lead. Judges are expected to make their decisions in a sort of splendid isolation from the grubby world around them; their eyes fixed on legal principles, it should not be surprising that their decisions may contradict the bottom-line style of thinking peculiar to finance ministers.

Policy succession from direct to mandated employment may, however, also reflect these bottom-line considerations. While regulatory instruments can be more coercive than expenditure-based programs, they are also cheaper. In a fiscal crisis, regulation has a comparative advantage over spending, especially if one assumes that political pressures for new and expanded programs continue unabated. Regulatory instruments shift costs away from government to private sector actors. Rather than spending billions to employ selected target groups, similar results can be achieved by mandating affirmative action programs, attacking systemic discrimination, and enforcing rules on hiring, firing, promotion, and pay. There is some evidence that Canadian policy has gradually shifted over the last decade to a greater reliance on regulatory mechanisms, and fiscal efficiency (from the government's perspective) may be a partial reason.[76]

Should these forces persist, they will clearly propel the welfare state into new directions, but not necessarily ones that imply an attenuation of interventions or programs. As the employment field demonstrates, the "tools for the job" may be refashioned and refined, occasionally left to rust, but never completely abandoned.

Notes

1. Department of Finance Canada, *Budget Papers*, 23 May 1985, 42–58; 71–72.
2. Philip Resnick,"The Ideology of Neo-Conservatism" in Warren Magnusson et al., *The New Reality: The Politics of Restraint in British Columbia* (Vancouver: New Star Books, 1984), 131.
3. Magnusson et al., *The New Reality*, 276.
4. Ramesh Mishra, *The Welfare State in Crisis: Social Thought and Social Change* (London: Harvester Press, 1984), 6–18.
5. Ibid., 161.
6. Ibid., 175 ff. Other examples of this apocalyptic view of the modern welfare state are *The Welfare State in Crisis* (Paris: Organization for

Economic Cooperation and Development, 1981), and M. D. Hanock and G. Sjoberg, eds., *Politics in the Post-Welfare State* (New York: Columbia University Press, 1972).

7. Albert O. Hirschman, "The Welfare State in Trouble," *American Economic Review* 70 (May 1980): 113–16.

8. Hugh Heclo, "Toward a New Welfare State?," in Peter Flora and Arnold J. Heidenheimer, eds., *The Development of Welfare States in Europe and America* (New Brunswick, N.J.: Transaction Books, 1981), 403. For empirical evidence of the different strategies of response to economic crisis, see Manfred G. Schmidt, "The Welfare State and the Economy in Periods of Economic Crisis: A Comparative Study of Twenty-three OECD Nations," *European Journal of Political Research*, 11 (1983): 1–26.

9. *Into the Twenty-First Century: The Development of Social Security* (Geneva: International Labour Office, 1984), 12.

10. Claus Offe, *Contradictions of the Welfare State*, John Keane, ed. (Cambridge, Mass.: The MIT Press, 1984), 287; emphasis in original.

11. Department of Finance Canada, *Economic Review* (Ottawa: Minister of Supply and Services, 1984), Reference Table 46 at 179.

12. Royal Commission on the Economic Union and Development Prospects for Canada, *Report*, Volume 2, (Ottawa: Minister of Supply and Services, 1985), 814–27 (hereinafter cited as Macdonald Commission). Even a recent neoconservative critique of American social policy ends with recommendations supporting unemployment insurance and universal, free education from elementary to graduate school. See Charles Murray, *Losing Ground: American Social Policy, 1950–1980* (New York: Basic Books, 1984).

13. This may seem unfair to works such as James O'Connor, *The Fiscal Crisis of the State* (New York: St. Martin's Press, 1973) and especially Ian Gough, *The Political Economy of the Welfare State* (London: Macmillan, 1979). O'Connor's analysis, however, focuses almost exclusively on American developments, for which it may be accurate, but which resist generalization. See Catherine Jones, *Patterns of Social Policy: An Introduction to Comparative Analysis* (London: Tavistock Publications, 1985), chapter 6. Gough is more careful in this regard, and does try to extract, in his final chapter, specific predictions on crisis response from his more general theory of a capitalist welfare state. But these represent tendencies only, which may or may not be actualized depending on the balance of class forces. Gough also prefers the term "restructuring" to describe what is currently happening to the welfare state and, while his version of neo-Marxist political economy helps explain some general developments and strategic choices, it remains insensitive to all the dimensions of this restructuring, some of which may involve expansion of the welfare state.

14. Christopher C. Hood, *The Tools of Government* (London: Macmillan, 1983). Also see G. Bruce Doern, ed., *The Regulatory Process in Canada*

(Toronto: Macmillan, 1978), chapter 1, and Allan Tupper and G. Bruce Doern, "Public Corporations and Public Policy," in Allan Tupper and G. Bruce Doern, eds., *Public Corporations and Public Policy in Canada* (Montreal: The Institute for Research on Public Policy, 1981), 1–50.

15. Hood, *Tools of Government*, 2.
16. Ibid., 7.
17. For an elaboration of the categories, see Leslie A. Pal, *Public Policy Analysis: An Introduction* (Toronto: Methuen, 1987), chapter 7.
18. Michael J. Trebilcock et al., *The Choice of Governing Instrument* (Ottawa: Minister of Supply and Services, 1982), 22.
19. Hood, *The Tools of Government*, 139.
20. G. Bruce Doern and Richard W. Phidd, *Canadian Public Policy: Ideas, Structure, Process* (Toronto: Methuen, 1983).
21. Trebilcock et al., *The Choice of Governing Instrument*, 33–35; Fred Thompson and W. T. Stanbury, "Looking Out for No. 1: Incumbency and Interest Group Politics," *Canadian Public Policy* 10 (June 1984): 239–44.
22. As quoted in Doern and Phidd, *Canadian Public Policy*, 128.
23. Brian W. Hogwood and B. Guy Peters, *Policy Dynamics* (London: Harvester Press, 1983).
24. Ibid., 17–18.
25. Ibid., 221.
26. Ibid., 2–6.
27. Ibid., 42.
28. Doern and Phidd, *Canadian Public Policy*, chapter 17; Employment and Immigration Canada, *Labour Market Development in the 1980s* (Ottawa: Minister of Supply and Services, 1981); J. Stephan Dupré et al., *Federalism and Policy Development: The Case of Adult Occupational Training in Ontario* (Toronto: University of Toronto Press, 1971); Richard W. Phidd and G. Bruce Doern, *The Politics and Management of Canadian Economic Policy* (Toronto: Macmillan, 1978), chapter 10. For an up-to-date review of these policies, as well as labour market data, see Macdonald Commission, vol. 2, chapter 15.
29. See David K. Foot, ed., *Public Employment and Compensation in Canada: Myths and Realities* (Scarborough: Butterworths, 1978), and David A. Wolfe, "The State and Economic Policy in Canada, 1968–1975," in Leo Panitch, ed., *The Canadian State: Political Economy and Political Power* (Toronto: University of Toronto Press, 1977), 252–88.
30. W. T. Easterbook and Hugh J. Aitken, *Canadian Economic History* (Toronto: Macmillan, 1956), chapter 12.
31. The best account of this issue and its emergence is James Struthers, *No Fault of Their Own: Unemployment and the Canadian Welfare State, 1914–1941* (Toronto: University of Toronto Press, 1983).
32. Struthers, *No Fault of Their Own*, 48–50.
33. Ibid., 81.

34. Ibid., 119–20.
35. H. Blair Neatby, *William Lyon Mackenzie King, 1932–1939: The Prism of Unity* (Toronto: University of Toronto Press, 1976), 155–56.
36. Ibid., chapter 14.
37. Robert A. Young, "Reining in James: The Limits of the Task Force," *Canadian Public Administration* 24 (Winter 1981): 603. For details on the reconstruction planning process, see Leslie A. Pal, "Keynesian Commitment, Keynesian Illusion: The Politics of Canadian Fiscal Policy, 1943–1963" (Ph.D. dissertation, Queen's University, 1981), chapter 3.
38. D. A. Skelton, "Dominion Postwar Policy," 5 April 1943, John Deutsch Papers, Box 106, file 1228, Queen's University.
39. Robert Bothwell and W. Kilbourn, *C. D. Howe: A Biography* (Toronto: McClelland and Stewart, 1979), and David A. Wolfe, "Economic Growth and Foreign Investment: A Perspective on Canadian Economic Policy, 1945–1957," *Journal of Canadian Studies* 12 (1978): 3–20.
40. Dominion-Provincial Conference, *Proceedings* (Ottawa: 1946), 58.
41. Ibid.
42. Ibid., 77.
43. R. M. Will, *Canadian Fiscal Policy, 1945–1963*, Royal Commission on Taxation Study No. 17 (Ottawa: 1966), 9.
44. Ibid., 10.
45. Senate, Special Committee on Manpower and Employment, *Final Report* (Ottawa: 1961), 1–9.
46. Doern and Phidd, *Canadian Public Policy*, 507–8.
47. Ibid., 505.
48. The other Special Employment Plan elements were the Canada Manpower Training Program (Supplemental), the Loan for Multipurpose Exhibition Buildings program, and accelerated CMHC lending. See J. Newark, "Special Employment Plan, Winter 1971–72," *Canada Manpower Review* 3 (1972): 1–7.
49. See Robert Aaron Gordon, ed., *Toward a Manpower Policy* (New York: John Wiley and Son, 1967) and Alan Gartner, Russell A. Nixon, and Frank Riessmen, eds., *Public Service Employment: An Analysis of its History, Problems, and Prospects* (New York: Praeger Publishers, 1973).
50. The Department of Manpower and Immigration's first deputy minister described the essential task of labour market policy to be the provision of "the best possible information about employment opportunities...." As quoted in *Federalism and Policy Development*, 49.
51. On the Opportunities for Youth program, see Robert S. Best, "Youth Policy," in G. Bruce Doern and V. Seymour Wilson, eds., *Issues in Canadian Public Policy* (Toronto: Macmillan, 1974), 137–65.
52. John W. Holland and Michael L. Skolnik, *Public Policy and Manpower Development* (Toronto: The Ontario Institute for Studies in Education, 1975), 70.

53. Employment and Immigration Canada, *Labour Market Development in the 1980s* (Ottawa: Minister of Supply and Services, 1981), 31 (hereinafter cited as Dodge Report).
54. Ibid., 32.
55. Ibid., 33.
56. Department of Manpower and Immigration, *Annual Report 1972–73* (Ottawa: Information Canada, 1974), 8.
57. Ibid., 9.
58. Department of Manpower and Immigration, *Annual Report 1976–77* (Ottawa: Minister of Supply and Services, 1977), 11–15. By contrast, the 1969–70 annual report listed only two special needs groups requiring specific programs: youth and handicapped.
59. Canada, *House of Commons Debates*, 21 October 1976, 340.
60. Ibid., 341.
61. Ibid.
62. Dodge Report, 135.
63. Ibid.
64. Economic Council of Canada, *People and Jobs: A Study of the Canadian Labour Market* (Ottawa: Information Canada, 1976); Organization for Economic Cooperation and Development, *Direct Job Creation in the Public Sector: Evaluation of National Experience in Canada, Denmark, Norway, United Kingdom, United States* (Paris: 1980).
65. Dodge Report, 139.
66. Ibid., 144.
67. Ibid., 141.
68. Ibid., 91.
69. Ibid., 102.
70. Employment and Immigration Canada, *Annual Report 1983–84* (Ottawa: Minister of Supply and Services, 1984), Table 8 at 34.
71. Macdonald Commission, vol. 2, 642.
72. Ibid., 643.
73. Briefly described in G. Ledyard Stebbins and Francisco J. Ayala, "The Evolution of Darwinism," *Scientific American* 253 (July 1985): 72–82.
74. T. N. Brewis, *Regional Economic Policies in Canada* (Toronto: Macmillan, 1969), chapter 6.
75. For the idea of "rights transfers" as part of the function of the welfare state, see Leslie A. Pal, "Federalism, Social Policy and the Constitution," in Jacqueline S. Ismael, ed., *Canadian Social Welfare Policy: Federal and Provincial Dimensions* (Kingston and Montreal: The Institute of Public Administration of Canada and McGill-Queen's University Press, 1985), 1–20.
76. John L. Howard and W. T. Stanbury, "Appendix to Measuring Leviathan: The Size, Scope, and Growth of Governments in Canada" in George Lermer, ed., *Probing Leviathan: An Investigation of Government in the Economy* (Vancouver: Fraser Institute, 1984), 160.

II Income Security

3 Descriptive Overview of Selected Provincial Income Supplementation and Work Incentive Initiatives

GILLES SÉGUIN

Introduction

Much has been written in recent years on the subject of poverty in Canada and the plight of disadvantaged individuals and families by organizations such as the Canadian Council on Social Development, the National Council of Welfare, provincial associations of social workers and various social planning councils, to name but a few. The objective of this paper is not to provide any new insights on the face of poverty in Canada, but rather to examine some recent trends and developments in provincial government social assistance policy concerning two of the larger segments of the poor in Canada—unemployed employables and the working poor.

The first section of this paper will consist of general observations on the evolution of social assistance programs in Canada since the beginning of the current decade. The second section will comprise factual descriptions of four provincial initiatives designed to supplement the incomes of households with insufficient earnings: Quebec's Work Income Supplement Program, Ontario's Work Incentive Program, Manitoba's Child Related Income Support Program, and Saskatchewan's Family Income Plan.

SOCIAL ASSISTANCE IN THE EIGHTIES

The current decade has been marked by record inflation, a stagnant economy and high unemployment, all of which have resulted in a strain on the Canadian income security system, and more particularly on provincial social assistance programs. Welfare rolls increased dramatically in the early- to mid-eighties, swollen by thousands of jobless Canadians whose Unemployment Insurance Commission (UIC) benefits were exhausted and young people leaving the school system with bleak prospects in the job market. Food banks, service clubs and other charitable organizations continued to strive to complement government assistance to persons in need.

In the past five years, provincial government policy concerning social assistance has undergone a number of changes directly related to labour market difficulties. A new spirit of cooperation has developed at the federal level between the Department of National Health and Welfare and Employment and Immigration Canada (EIC); at the working level, provincial social service departments and regional EIC offices cooperate closely on client interface issues. Two provinces—Quebec and Manitoba—have actually integrated their manpower and social assistance programs under the same department; in both provinces, a separate department is responsible for the provision of social services. Collectively, the provinces have implemented and overhauled a wide range of programs providing direct or indirect assistance in such areas as remedial education, retraining, property taxes, home repairs and shelter (including mortgage interest reduction); departments such as Manpower, Education, and Finance, and housing corporations are becoming more directly involved in the field of social welfare.

In the social assistance policy context, program administrators have more than ever since the economic downturn been confronted with the difficult task of stretching their limited budgets to assist a larger number of households. Some of the relevant trends and developments of the past few years in social assistance are noted below.

i) Tighter intake controls: social assistance applications are subject to more stringent screening than ever before (in some provinces, applicants and recipients are required to document any income and all expenses, no matter how minimal); moreover, unemployed employable applicants are subject to

lower asset and income exception criteria than unemployables in the determination of initial eligibility, as well as
lower benefit levels.
ii) Selective rate increases: while certain provinces have legislated social assistance rate indexing provisions, other prov
inces use an "ad hoc" approach which in recent years has
meant selective rate increases, either to specific target groups
(e.g., unemployables) or with respect to specific components
of need (e.g., increased allowances for food or shelter only).
iii) Special considerations for single parents: because of the rise in
family dissolution and the higher incidence of unwed parenthood, many provinces have implemented special programs
offering training, education, and placement opportunities for
the single parent; on the other hand, provinces are also placing more responsibility on single parent applicants to actively pursue the enforcement of maintenance orders or
alimony, or to subrogate that right to the government.
iv) Employment assistance and job creation: all provinces have
established or streamlined their employment support
mechanisms in the past few years, either unilaterally or
jointly with other provincial or federal departments, to offer
their social assistance clients the widest possible range of job
preparation opportunities (e.g., training, counselling, job
placement); moreover, recent provincial job creation efforts
are designed to facilitate the movement of current and potential social assistance recipients to the labour force.
These and other changes in social assistance policy over the past
five years or so have created more incentives for unemployed employables in receipt of or eligible for assistance to join or rejoin the
labour force.

PROVINCIAL INCOME SUPPLEMENTATION INITIATIVES
The four programs described in the following pages are provincial
initiatives implemented between 1974 and 1981 to supplement the
incomes of financially-disadvantaged Canadian households. Although these initiatives preceded the economic difficulties of the
early 1980s, they are nonetheless significant in their common objective of increasing the disposable income of employable persons
receiving social assistance and the working poor. These programs

are similar in concept (benefit levels based on family size and net income), but they differ substantially from one another in terms of their respective provincial contexts and operational definitions. Consequently, each of these programs is examined in its own right; no attempt has been made to compare particular program characteristics interprovincially, nor to comment on the relative merit of any of these initiatives.

Quebec: Work Income Supplement Program

The Act Respecting Work Income Supplement (Ch. 9, 1979) and the related Regulation provide the legislative framework for this program, which was implemented May 30, 1979. The Quebec Ministry of Revenue is responsible for the administration of the supplement; the program is financed out of the Consolidated Revenue Fund of Quebec.

ELIGIBILITY

The objective of the program is to provide cash incentives to low-income earners to remain in the labour force and to motivate employable social aid recipients to join the labour force. The program is open to all families (single-parent or two-parent) with dependent children (i.e., under eighteen years of age *or* over eighteen years attending secondary school) and to single persons and childless couples. The individual or one of the spouses must be at least thirty years of age. Two persons living together as man and wife for at least one full year are considered in the same manner as a married couple. The supplement payable to eligible low-income workers is based on income from work (including self-employment) and other sources specified below, as well as family size. A household is required to submit a new application for the supplement on an annual basis.

To qualify for a supplement in a given year, a household must meet the following eligibility criteria:

   i) the family head (or spouse, or both) or the individual must have received income from wages or self-employment in the previous tax year;

ii) the family or individual must have been residing in Quebec on December 31 of the previous year, and one of the spouses or the individual must have been a resident of Canada since January 1 of that same year;

iii) the gross value of family property on December 31 of the previous tax year must not have exceeded $50,000; "property" does *not* include the family residence and the land on which it is located, furniture and household effects, and one car for personal use.

There are three categories of beneficiaries under the Work Income Supplement Program. To determine which category applies to a particular household, the work income and total income of that household are compared against a reference point ("turning point") which entitles the family or individual to the maximum supplement payable. The "turning point" is the amount of work income beyond which the supplement decreases by one dollar for each additional three dollars of total income. The turning point is equal to the amount of social aid a household of the same size would have received for the calendar year preceding the application for a supplement.

"Work income" is equal to the total of a) gross wages or salaries from work, calculated in accordance with the Quebec Taxation Act and b) net business and self-employment income, calculated in accordance with the Quebec Taxation Act, plus depreciation costs deducted in the calculation of net income.

"Total income" is equal to the aggregate of work income (as above) and taxable and nontaxable government pensions, investment income and private pensions, and any capital cost allowance deducted in the calculation of net income from property rentals. The only exemptions allowed in the computation of total income are the federal Child Tax Credit, federal and provincial Family Allowances, real estate tax refunds, income of any dependent child, and any Availability Allowance received.

BENEFITS

Where an applicant's total income for the year preceding the application is equal to or less than the turning point, the household is considered to be in the first category of beneficiaries; in these

Table 3.1   Quebec Work Income Supplement, 1985

Family Type	Annual Turning Point	Maximum Annual Supplement	Annual Break-Even Point
One person			
— no children	$4815	$1204	$ 8430
— one child	8268	2067	14470
— two or more children	8772	2193	15350
Couple			
— no children	$7650	$1913	$13390
— one child	8268	2067	14470
— two more more children	8772	2193	15350

NOTE: This table provides maximum supplement levels for various family types payable for the 1985 calendar year (with the final installment, if necessary, payable in March 1986) based on 1984 work income and total income. The supplement to which a household is entitled for this benefit period is payable in $550 installments (except where entitlement is less than this amount).

cases, the maximum supplement is equal to 25 percent of work income.

For the second category, total income exceeds the turning point but work income is less than or equal to the same turning point; in these cases, the supplement is equal to 25 percent of work income less an amount equal to total income exceeding the turning point.

For the third category, work income exceeds the turning point, but is less than the "break-even point" (income level where the supplement ceases to be payable). The break-even point is calculated by multiplying the maximum annual supplement by three and adding an amount equal to the turning point. The supplement payable to applicants in the third category is equal to the maximum supplement appearing in Table 3.1 *less* "other" income (total income less work income), from which is deducted one-third of the difference between work income and the turning point.

The supplement is not taxable under the federal and provincial income tax systems; the annual supplement is payable in a maximum of four instalments (in August, September, December, and the following March).

Any amount received under the Work Income Supplement Program is exempted from the calculation of the financial resources of a household in receipt of Social Aid.

STATISTICS
The Work Income Supplement Program caseload since 1979 has fluctuated in the range of 25,000 households per year; program costs have grown from just under $16.7 million in 1979 to over $20.8 million per year in 1983.

Ontario: Work Incentive Program

The Work Incentive (WIN) Program is administered and financed under the authority of The Ministry of Community and Social Services Act by that Ministry. Implemented in October 1979, WIN provides an allowance and health-related benefits for up to two years to recipients leaving regular Family Benefits (FBA) and GAINS-D (both long-term social assistance programs) who wish to become self-supporting through full-time employment for them or their spouses. As of April 1985, however, the province of Ontario has not enforced this two-year time limit.

ELIGIBILITY
Applicants under the WIN Program must meet the following conditions of initial and continuing eligibility:
   i) continuous receipt of social assistance (including short-term municipal General Assistance) for at least three consecutive months prior to WIN participation and receipt of regular FBA or GAINS-D for one full month immediately preceding WIN participation;
  ii) maintenance of eligibility under the regular FBA program or GAINS-D (i.e., no change in the household situation resulting in ineligibility under the appropriate program), except for criteria affecting assets, hours of work, and income;
 iii) engagement in full-time employment as defined in WIN policy (minimum 130 hours of work or $450 per month, with some discretionary flexibility); and

iv) voluntary withdrawal from regular FBA or GAINS-D by signing a WIN application.

Assets are not taken into consideration under the WIN Program.
However, should a WIN participant reapply for regular FBA or
GAINS-D upon termination of employment, all requirements re-
garding property and liquid assets will apply.

WIN allowance levels are based on family size, case category,
and the total income and earnings of the family, excluding casual
earnings of dependent children. For the purposes of this program,
"family income" includes the aggregate sum of gross earnings and
gratuities, room and board income (imputed amounts based on the
age of each roomer and boarder) and net income from property
rental, farm revenue and operation of a business. Family income
docs not include income such as Family Allowances, Child Tax
Credits, and Ontario Tax Credits. Initial WIN entitlement is based
on the estimated income for the first full month of work; the second and subsequent months' entitlement is based on actual income for the previous month.

BENEFITS

A disabled, permanently unemployable or aged client who voluntarily withdraws from regular FBA or GAINS-D to start full-
time WIN employment may receive a maximum WIN allowance
varying from $145 to $275 monthly, depending on the size of the
family. For sole-support mothers, the maximum allowance varies
from $150 to $240 monthly, based on family size. The WIN allowance is not taxable under the federal and provincial income tax
systems. Maximum allowance levels and break-even points appear
in the accompanying table. All maximum allowances are reduced
by $0.50 for each dollar of total family income in excess of $675
monthly ("turning point"). Maximum allowances, break-even
points and the monthly turning point have been in effect since October 1981.

In addition to the monthly incentive allowance, supplementary
benefits include complete coverage of provincial health insurance
premiums, prescription drug costs, dental care, eyeglasses, and
hearing aids; these supplementary benefits are extended for three
months after a participant's eligibility under the Work Incentive
Program is terminated.

Table 3.2   Work Incentive Program, Maximum Monthly
Allowance Levels and Break-even Points, March 1985

| Family Size | Maximum Monthly Allowance[1] | | Monthly Break-Even Point[2] | |
	Sole-Support Mothers	Other FBA and GAINS-D Recipients	Sole-Support Mothers	Other FBA and GAINS-D Recipients
1	N/A	$145	N/A	$ 965
2	$150	185	$ 975	1045
3	180	215	1035	1105
4	200	235	1075	1145
5	220	255	1115	1185
6	240	275	1155	1225

NOTES: 1) The maximum monthly allowance level for any given family size is payable where income from all sources is less than $675 monthly (for *any* size of family).
2) "Break-even point" is the level of income beyond which the allowance ceases to be payable.

A lump sum phase-out allowance of $250 is paid to a person who leaves the regular FBA program or GAINS-D to participate in the WIN Program. Where the person leaves regular FBA or GAINS-D for full-time employment outside of the WIN Program, the same phase-out allowance may be spread over a three-month period to ensure continuous health insurance coverage. Although there is no restriction on the number of times a person may enter the WIN Program over any given period, entitlement to the phase-out allowance is limited to once per year.

If employment ceases, the WIN participant is eligible to return immediately to regular FBA or GAINS-D; the recipient would normally be required to apply for (municipal) General Assistance under the General Welfare Assistance Act, at a lower benefit level than regular FBA and GAINS-D, and await transfer to the Family Benefits Program some three months later. To bridge the time period between the loss of employment and the first FBA or GAINS-D cheque, a special WIN allowance is paid in an amount equal to the client's entitlement under FBA or GAINS-D.

74   G. Séguin

STATISTICS

In March 1985, the active WIN caseload stood at 2,434, comprising 1972 sole-support parents and 462 disabled persons, bringing the number of participants since the program's inception to just under 10,000. WIN program expenditures for 1984–85 are estimated at $2.3 million.

Manitoba: Child Related Income Support Program

The Child Related Income Support Program (CRISP) was implemented in January 1981 under the Social Services Administration Act and the Child Related Income Support Program Regulations. Although the Department of Community Services and Corrections was initially responsible for CRISP administration, the program was transferred during the 1983–84 fiscal year to the newly-created Department of Employment Services and Economic Security. This same department is also responsible for program funding, except that under the Canada Assistance Plan, the federal government cost-shares 50 percent of CRISP benefits paid to families eligible for provincial Social Allowances.

ELIGIBILITY

CRISP is designed to provide monthly cash assistance to low-income families with dependent children under eighteen years of age and eligible for federal Family Allowances. CRISP benefits are not payable to wards of the province or persons in temporary placement under provincial child welfare legislation or to Treaty Indians who are either living on reservation land or receiving social assistance payments from the federal Department of Indian and Northern Affairs. A family must reapply each year to remain eligible for benefits.

CRISP benefits are payable to all Manitoba families who:
  i)   support one child or more under eighteen years of age listed as dependent(s) of the applicant on a valid Manitoba Health Services Card;
  ii) receive federal Family Allowances on behalf of each such child; and
  iii) have a total family income within specified levels.

CRISP benefits are not payable to an applicant who has assets with a total net value (current market value less any debts owed on the asset) greater than $50,000 as of the date when the application for benefits is made. "Assets" includes:
  i)   cash, savings and chequing deposits (including retirement savings plans and annuities);
 ii)   stocks, bonds, shares, and other investments;
iii)   real estate (other than the principal residence and its furnishings);
 iv)   family vehicles other than the one used most often,
  v)   land and buildings used for farm or business purposes;
 vi)   capital equipment and motor vehicles used for farm or business purposes;
vii)   business inventories and accounts receivable.

In determining financial eligibility, calculations are based on family income for the taxation year immediately preceding the benefit year (July 1 to June 30) for which an application is submitted; for example, the family's monthly CRISP benefit for the period from July 1, 1984 to June 30, 1985 is calculated using family income for the 1983 tax year. Estimated income for the current tax year may be used (instead of the previous year's income) where there has been a change in the family's circumstances due to a death, a relatively permanent or long-term disability, a change in marital status, or the recent immigration of the family to Canada.

Gross family income includes:
  i)   income from employment (including commissions and tips);
 ii)   training allowances, student assistance, net research grants;
iii)   retirement pensions and disability allowances (including Workers' Compensation);
 iv)   Family Allowances, Unemployment Insurance benefits;
  v)   interest and dividend income; and
 vi)   support, maintenance, and alimony payments.

In determining *net* family income levels, the following deductions are allowed:
  i)   6 percent of total gross annual family income;
 ii) $685 for each eligible dependent child;
iii)   any maintenance or alimony payments made by the applicant.
Income levels for CRISP eligibility are reviewed annually and updated in accordance with the Consumer Price Index.

Table 3.3   Child Related Income Support Program,
July 1984–June 1985

Number of Eligible Children	Maximum Annual Benefit	Annual Turning Point (*Net* Income)	Annual Turning Point (*Gross* Income)	Annual Break-Even Point (*Gross* Income)
1	$ 360	$9,640	$10,984	$12,516
2	720	9,640	11,713	14,777
3	1,080	9,640	12,441	17,037
4	1,440	9,640	13,170	19,298
5	1,800	9,640	13,899	21,559
6	2,160	9,640	14,628	23,819

NOTES: 1) Turning point and break-even point incomes shown are for the 1983 tax year.
2) "Break-even point" is the level of *gross* family income where CRISP benefits cease to be payable.
3) Where an applicant declares income from self-employment, such as fishing or farming, eligibility is assessed on an individual case basis using approved accounting procedures.

BENEFITS

The maximum CRISP benefit payable from July 1, 1984 to June 30, 1985 is $30 per month per child where *net* family income for the 1983 tax year did not exceed $9,640 (annual "turning point") regardless of family size. Benefits are reduced by $0.25 for each additional dollar of net family income above the annual turning point. For the sake of convenience, annual turning points for various family sizes are also expressed in terms of gross family income in the Table 3.3.

Benefits are paid from the month in which the application is received, but not prior to July 1 of each benefit year. CRISP is not taxable under the federal and provincial income tax systems. CRISP benefits are considered as part of the Social Allowance entitlement of families eligible therefor under the Social Allowances Act and Regulations.

STATISTICS

In March 1985, CRISP benefits were paid to 8,534 families on be-half of 19,390 children; benefit expenditures for the 1984–85 fiscal year were $6.1 million.

Saskatchewan: Family Income Plan

The Family Income Plan (FIP) was established in October 1974 through amendments to the Saskatchewan Assistance Act and Regulations (social assistance legislation), rather than under sepa-rate legislation, in order to facilitate the interface between FIP and the provincial social assistance program. FIP is administered and funded by the Department of Social Services, except that under the Canada Assistance Plan, the federal government cost-shares 50 percent of FIP benefits paid to families eligible for provincial so-cial assistance.

ELIGIBILITY

Family Income Plan benefits may be paid to any Saskatchewan resident (holder of a valid Saskatchewan Health Services Card) whose gross assets are valued at less than $150,000, who is receiv-ing Family Allowance payments on behalf of his/her dependent child or children under eighteen years of age, and whose annual in-come meets FIP requirements. FIP is not payable on behalf of any person living in Saskatchewan on a student visa, nor to a Regis-tered Indian unless s/he has been living off-reserve for over a year and not receiving social assistance from the Department of Indian and Northern Affairs. Where a dependent child earns sufficient in-come to be ineligible for federal Family Allowances, this child is deleted from the family unit for the purposes of calculating FIP eligibility and benefit rates.

The calculation of assets is based on current gross market value and does not include any provision for related liabilities. "Assets" include the following:

i)   cash, savings and chequing deposits, including the value of an RRSP or annuity;
ii) stocks, bonds, shares, and other investments;

iii) property and real estate other than the principal residence and the furnishings therein;
iv) family vehicles other than the one used most often;
v) any debts owed to the family head and/or spouse;
vi) any insurance benefits received as a result of fire, theft, or property damage on unexempted assets;
vii) undepreciated value of business or farm assets.

Entitlement to FIP benefits is based on estimated income of the household, excluding the earnings of any dependent child in receipt of Family Allowances, for the current calendar year. "Income" means gross income of the family (excluding dependent children receiving Family Allowances) less allowable deductions and exemptions, as stipulated in section 26D of the Saskatchewan Assistance Plan Regulations. In the case of farmers and business persons, FIP entitlement is based on net income (as defined by regulation) actually received in the previous calendar year or, in hardship cases, on the current calendar year income estimate. This estimate is included on the application form which all applicants are required to re-submit early each calendar year. The income estimate for a given calendar year is the base figure used for calculating the monthly FIP benefit from April of that year to March of the following year (benefit period). Each FIP household is required to submit a quarterly report (cheque stub or special form) to indicate any change in family size, actual income to date, anticipated income for the remainder of the year, assets, or shelter cost. The purpose of the quarterly report is to allow adjustments to FIP payment levels during the benefit period resulting from income fluctuations or other changes in family circumstances. In addition, the household must submit an annual statement of actual income, assets, family size and shelter costs for a given accounting period (calendar year) at the beginning of the next accounting period. The annual statement serves to reconcile income and family circumstances for the previous accounting period with FIP benefits paid during the first three quarters of the benefit period (from April to December); any adjustments are made to FIP benefits payable for the last quarter (January to March). By overlapping the accounting and benefit periods in this manner, the Department may recover any overpayments incurred before the end of the benefit period in cases where the household ceases to be eligible for FIP.

BENEFITS

Maximum FIP benefits payable since April 1984 are $100 per month for each of the first three children and $90 per month for the fourth and each subsequent child. The maximum benefit levels apply to families whose income does not exceed the total of $8,200 per year and annual Family Allowance payments; benefits are reduced by one dollar for every two dollars of family income exceeding this level. FIP benefits are not taxable under the federal and provincial income tax systems. FIP benefits are considered as part of the social assistance entitlement of families eligible therefor under the Saskatchewan Assistance Act and Regulations.

STATISTICS

In March 1984, approximately 7,500 families (17,000 children) received FIP benefits, which amounted to $17.5 million in expenditures for the 1983–84 fiscal year. Budget figures for 1984–85 indicate an increase in expenditures to $19.8 million in benefits payable to some 7,700 families.

Acknowledgements

The support of social service department officials from the four provinces covered in this paper is gratefully acknowledged. The programs were summarized from provincial legislation and policy, and they were subsequently verified for accuracy by Andre Bedard (Quebec), Bob Cooke (Ontario), Martin Billinkoff (Manitoba) and Dianne Anderson (Saskatchewan).

The introductory section of the text is based on my own experience in monitoring provincial social assistance programs.

4 Ideology and Income Supplementation
A Comparison of Quebec's Supplément au Revenu de Travail and Ontario's Work Incentive Program

ANDREW F. JOHNSON

Work-related income supplementation programs were unquestionably popular as devices to redistribute income in the provinces during 1979. In the spring of that year Quebec's minister of State for Social Development, Pierre Marois, introduced with a great deal of fanfare and publicity the Loi de supplément au revenu de travail (SUPRET) or the Work Income Supplementation Program.[1] And in the fall, Ontario's minister of Community and Social Services, Keith Norton, announced with no less pomp that a Work Incentive Program (WIN) would be implemented.

In addition to timing, the two programs shared other and more important similarities related to general program design. Both were lightly funded; incentives to work were emphasized within the context of each program; and both SUPRET and WIN were largely perceived as experimental. However, these broad characteristics were operationalized in ways that differed significantly. Thus, the purpose of this chapter is to explain the general similarities as well as the specific differences of SUPRET and WIN. In pursuing this purpose, the thesis presented is that the general characteristics shared by SUPRET and WIN—their inexpensiveness, their emphasis on incentives, and their experimental frameworks—may be explained by factors external to the welfare systems of Quebec and Ontario. However, the different ways in which these similarities have been operationalized are largely attributable to different ideological principles that have been diffused throughout the political systems of the two provinces. Moreover, these ideological principles, principles of Catholic social thought in Quebec and liberal principles in Ontario, are likely to promote a future expansion of SUPRET on the one hand but a retention of the status quo with respect to WIN on the other. A brief description of the programs' similarities and differences should further clarify the thesis.

SUPRET and WIN have been similar from the outset insofar as both have been modest ventures in the context of provincial public expenditure in Quebec and Ontario. But that is where this similarity ends. The $50 million originally allocated to SUPRET could hardly be viewed as a significant increment to the $650 million on transfer payments disbursed by Quebec at that time. However, it is something of an understatement to point out that that allocation was considerably more than the amount Ontario intended to spend on WIN. A mere $2 million was required to make WIN operational. Even that figure represented a windfall of $1 million for the Ontario government in light of the fact that the Low Income Supplement Experiment (LISE), which cost about $3 million, was cancelled just before WIN was introduced. Additionally, both governments expected to recoup much of the funds spent on SUPRET and WIN because of the savings that these programs would generate within their respective welfare systems. The raison d'être of both programs was and remains to provide low income earners with incentives to work so that they will not be compelled to draw social assistance.

Although the notion "work incentives" has been common to both programs, the conceptualization of that term in the context of each has differed in two respects. First, SUPRET benefits were initially targeted just to low income families. Families are still the main beneficiaries although coverage has since been extended to individuals.[2] WIN supplements have been primarily directed towards individuals. Second, SUPRET rebates were conceptualized as "residual" or preventative welfare, that is, the benefits were intended to prevent low income earners from becoming recipients of traditional types of social assistance; they were mainly intended to keep low income workers working. WIN rebates were viewed as palliatives or, quite bluntly, as cures for the disposition to remain on welfare; the program was intended to provide welfare recipients with financial incentives to find jobs.

Finally, both programs were experimental but once again the two governments differed in their interpretations of a similar term. In a recent interview the chairman of the task force that created SUPRET admitted that the program was experimental but emphasized that it was also intended with all sincerity to be a first step towards a guaranteed annual income. Indeed, the program was widely publicized as a "première étape" and Marois clearly indicated that this first step would be followed by others.[3] A first step was expected to allow the government to monitor and control costs as well as to redress possible administrative difficulties. Furthermore, the minister chose to speak in terms of a guaranteed income "policy" which left the impression that SUPRET would be one part of a greater whole, providing SUPRET was successful.[4] Thus, in terms of commitment WIN was more experimental than SUPRET. WIN was originally set up as a one year "test" project and as such did not even require its own legislative authority; the authority for WIN came under section 6(d) of the Ministry of Community and Social Services Act which authorizes the payment of grants for special projects.

In sum, there have been striking differences between Quebec's and Ontario's work income supplementation programs despite their broad similarities. The divergent values that Quebec and Ontario decision-makers have brought to bear on their respective policy-making processes account for the differences. The overall similarities, however, have been shaped by common socioeconomic and political circumstances that are external to the immediate jurisdictions of social welfare decision-makers in both provinces. A discussion of these external factors precedes an analysis of the relationship of ideological values to the development of SUPRET and WIN.

External Factors and the Development of SUPRET and WIN

Rick Van Loon had the Social Security Review in mind when he remarked that "social policy and particularly welfare reform are very much governed by factors external to the welfare system."[5] Hence, from Van Loon's perspective, towards the end of the 1970s a general mood of fiscal restraint was largely, but not entirely, responsible for the collapse of joint federal-provincial initiatives in the realm of welfare reform. However, Van Loon was also quick to point out that fiscal restraint did not stifle a federal initiative. On the contrary, fiscal restraint apparently inspired federal policymakers to create the Refundable Child Tax Credit (RCTC), an income supplementation scheme (albeit a financially limited one) which in effect was created with funds that were already within the social welfare system. However, while there is no available evidence to suggest that fiscal restraint spurred the creation of SUPRET and WIN, it is clear that spending cutbacks at both the federal and provincial levels of government greatly affected these programs.

Immediately prior to the introduction of SUPRET and WIN, the federal government reduced or threatened to reduce its expenditures on social policy in general and on social welfare specifically. First, Ottawa appeared to be determined to shave substantial sums from its transfer payments to the provinces for the established programs (medicare, hospital insurance, and post-secondary education). Second, the federal government imposed major cutbacks on unemployment insurance and on family allowances; federal savings on these programs were expected to result in increases in provincial spending on social welfare. Finally, in September 1978, the prime minister announced that the Canada Assistance Plan and related expenditures would be curtailed. Later, with a great hue and cry, Pierre Marois and Keith Norton made bids to gain federal financial support for their respective income supplementation programs. However, against this backdrop of federal cutbacks, their governments were fully aware that such support would not be forthcoming and that SUPRET and WIN would have to be modest ventures. More to the point, they were fully aware that their own hard-pressed treasuries would not yield sufficient funds for costly undertakings in the realm of social welfare.

SUPRET was developed under the shadow of a mounting deficit. Hence the task force, which drafted the program, was informed that the upper threshold of spending would be $50 million.[6] The task force did not run the slightest risk of exceeding that figure because the "take up" rate was expected to be considerably less than the original estimate. As it turned out, the actual cost during the first year was almost two-thirds less than projected. In addition, the financial extravagance of the then defunct "guaranteed family income program" stood at the cradle of SUPRET.[7] There was a feeling within the task force that this proposal of the former government had failed because estimates of costs had been excessive—about $253 million. Thus, the chairman of the task force alluded to the indirect relationship of the guaranteed family income proposal to the development of SUPRET when he recently remarked that "if you want something *not* to be done in government, you give something that is real expensive . . . [and] . . . I understood that."[8]

Expenditure on WIN in the context of Ontario's budget was not an issue. A $1 million disbursement in relation to a $550 million welfare budget was merely a "flash-in-the-pan." Furthermore and as noted above, WIN represented a saving by virtue of the demise of LISE for which it was a substitute. At any rate, Ontario's long tradition of fiscal conservatism, especially in relation to social security matters, is undoubtedly a factor that culminated in the meagre disbursement for WIN. Thus, a general mood of fiscal restraint was a powerful external factor which was stamped into the financial design of both. In addition, the experimental orientation of both SUPRET and WIN is also in part a result of fiscal restraint. The potential cost, however modest, of further developing either program became prohibitive as the economic recession deepened during the 1980s and as public revenues declined while public expenditures increased.

A general mood of fiscal restraint was paralleled by a general mood of social conservatism which also left a major imprint on both programs. In the aftermath of the controversy sparked by the federal government's reform of the unemployment insurance program, a strong current of public opinion held that social security disbursements generate disincentives to work. Therefore, a marketable feature of both programs was that they provided incentives to work. Work incentives were the raison d'être of WIN while they were a primary objective of SUPRET.[9]

Finally, there were other factors external to the welfare systems of Quebec and Ontario which not only shaped the general contours of these plans but which provided for their very existence in the first place. Both governments were midway through their terms of office. The time was ripe for initiatives in the realm of social security; if the initiatives were left to a later date they would have smacked of "politics" in the negative sense of the word. Accordingly, the Conservative Government of Ontario initiated WIN to knock its leftist opposition off balance. But the gesture was of a symbolic nature, that is, it was not a substantive reform. As a consequence, centre and right supporters of the governing party were not offended because Ontario Conservatives could claim to be concerned, but not overly concerned, about welfare issues by initiating the inexpensive WIN. The Parti Québécois could make the same claim with SUPRET and still satisfy its social democratic supporters by virtue of the relative generosity of the program and by virtue of implied promises for future expansion. The Parti Québécois not only had to face the electors in 1981; it was sponsoring a referendum in 1980. However, the Parti Québécois had yet to unfurl its social democratic colours in the sense of redistributing income. What better way to show these colours—colours that it could ill-afford to show—than by announcing SUPRET as a first step towards a guaranteed annual income?

To summarize the argument thus far, factors that were external to the welfare systems of Quebec and Ontario greatly affected SUPRET and WIN. Fiscal restraint coupled with social conservatism shaped general features common to both programs while electoral competition was a stimulus to their development. However, external factors only account for the similarities. Clearly, SUPRET and WIN contain specific differences despite the similarities. For example, although both are lightly funded initiatives, SUPRET was provided with twenty-five times the funding of WIN. How can that gap best be explained?

External factors do not account for the differing perspectives that public decision-makers of different provinces bring to bear on the welfare policy-making process. To put it another way, policies are not contrived exclusively in response to broad socioeconomic and political circumstances; decision-makers bring their own values and the values they represent into the policy-making process. In short, the cases of SUPRET and WIN demonstrate that ideological predispositions count in the development of social welfare policy.

Ideology and the Development of SUPRET and WIN

The social needs of Quebec were great when the Liberals came to power in 1960. Duplessis had refused to participate in federal social initiatives and to reap the concomitant financial advantages. In addition, the premier had lacked the financial wherewithal as well as the inclination to erect a social welfare apparatus. Thus, William Coleman explains that Lesage's Liberals were forced to choose between two options in order to satisfy Quebec's pressing social needs. They could have followed the recommendations of the Tremblay Commission and developed the economy in accordance with Catholic social principles.[10] Alternatively, they could have adopted the values of industrial capitalism and worked to ensure that the francophone community would benefit from that system. Coleman advances the widely accepted thesis that the Liberals chose the second alternative and, correspondingly, the values of the economy became the values of the social welfare system. From this perspective, Quebec's social welfare system is similar to the welfare systems of other provinces such as Ontario because it inheres in the values of industrial capitalism.

The general contours of Quebec's social welfare system do indeed appear to be similar to those of the other provinces. To be sure, that is precisely what is suggested in the brief discussion above that notes the general similarities of SUPRET and WIN. But, of course, differences—and differences which cannot be overlooked—are also noted. These differences, however, suggest that the economic cum social welfare alternatives facing Quebec during the 1960s were not entirely all-or-nothing propositions. It is far more likely that initially the Liberals and, subsequently, the governments of the succeeding decade and a half did opt for the alternative of advancing a system of industrial capitalism while attempting to retain as much as possible of the values of a Catholic social tradition, that is, a tradition which had come to be called Québécois.[11]

The proof resides in the repeated attempts of governments of

Quebec to wrest as much autonomy as possible from their perceived financial overlord, the federal government, in order to erect a social welfare system in harmony with Quebec values. Hence, it is to be expected that the Parti Québécois, as a vehicle for full independence, may well have been inclined to pay greater attention to advancing Québécois values than its Liberal predecessors. It is to be expected that these values would also be applied to its first and only major social welfare initiative. That is what is argued here: the values pursued by the Parti Québécois were basically the principles of Catholic social thought but packaged in secular jargon to appeal to a supposedly modern electorate. However, there is a major weakness in the argument which must be addressed immediately: a state-sponsored guaranteed annual income, a concept from whence SUPRET sprang, appears to have originated outside of the realm of Catholic social thought.

Participants in the development of SUPRET identify a complex web of factors as having been responsible for the promotion of the idea of a guaranteed annual income. The linkage that is frequently drawn starts with the Castonguay-Nepveu Report which originally sowed the idea in public circles; the report, in turn, inspired Claude Forget's guaranteed family income program which gave rise to the "blue book," the basis for SUPRET.[12] However, a variety of widely read American economists are said to have spread the idea among Quebec economists who participated in the preparation of these documents.[13] But then, the attempts of Northern European nations to secure full employment policies are also identified as sources of inspiration, as are the provinces of Manitoba and Saskatchewan with their income supplementation programs and the federal government with its failed attempt to establish the Family Income Supplementation Program (FISP). Whatever the specific sources, the general idea of a guaranteed annual income was very popular in Quebec in the sense that it was clearly accepted by all of the major political parties.[14] The Parti Québécois in particular endorsed the concept at every annual congress from 1970 onwards. Of course, a guaranteed annual income meant different things to different political parties and sometimes to different groups within particular parties. For the Parti Québécois, it meant a popular program that could be made consistent with Quebec's traditional Catholic values.

A guaranteed annual income appeared in the shape of SUPRET (and not in the numerous other variety of forms available) because of the principles of Catholic social thought that were clearly apparent in the thoughts and actions of the responsible minister—and the minister was undoubtedly responsible because he was a super-minister and as such decided on the main features of the program. In the Government of Quebec, unlike in the Government of Ontario or in the Government of Canada, ministers of state wielded considerable power largely because the four ministers of state were expected to be innovative and to draw up new programs. They constituted the "inner cabinet" and, thus, had the personal backing of René Lévesque in their policy-making activities. Moreover, Marois exerted full control over the policy-making process, according to the chief architect of SUPRET. Thus, the chairman of the task force took great pains to explain that in the final analysis Marois's preferences were etched into the program:

> ... Everything in that program was decided by the minister [Marois]. For every parameter that is in that program, for each and every one of them, the minister had choices that I presented to him personally.... There was a program-building process in which I collaborated and the minister decided everything.[15]

Pierre Marois confirms these remarks but adds that SUPRET was not only the outcome of his views on social welfare; it was also a product of the thoughts of other highly placed Péquistes, most notably Guy Joron and René Lévesque.[16] The three endorsed a "guaranteed minimum income" in principle while writing "Quand nous serons vraiment chez nous," one of the earliest statements of Parti Québécois objectives.[17] The manifesto was rather lean on details about this future program. However, it did contain the broad suggestion that such a program would contain principles that occupied the middle road between socialism and liberalism or metaphorically between utopia ("qui veut faire l'ange") and the jungle ("l'homme loup").[18] Although the authors did not say as much, the supplementary principle, a principle central to Catholic social thought, governed their intentions to create a social welfare program that would represent a middle course between liberalism and socialism. The supplementary principle was most certainly stamped into SUPRET as is apparent from the title of the program. However, the supplementary principle can best be explained in relation to two other principles of Catholic social thought from which it is derived.

The Tremblay Commission aptly identified and explained these principles of Catholic social thought as applied to social security.[19] They are as follows: first, initiative and responsibility for social security must, in the first instance, come from the individual. An individual has a duty to provide for himself and to provide financial protection for himself. Society, in turn, has a duty to provide an individual with access to work. Second, the principle of subsidiarity "regards society as a complete organism into which Man is placed through the medium of institutions, groups and communities which he creates himself through a natural need; these include families and various associations which contribute to the fulfillment of the common good. . . . "[20] The family is a basic component of society as an organic whole; the vitality of society is dependent on the vitality of the family. Thus, these two principles together suggest that social security should not be designed just for the individual good; it ought to be designed to promote the individual good for the sake of the collective good, the family in the first instance and society as a whole in the final instance. To put it another way, the individual good is entwined with the collective good. Furthermore "good" does not refer to material well-being but to freedom from want and to spiritual fulfillment. The concept is aptly summarized by the term "épanouissement," which is variously translated as blossoming, flourishing, or uninhibited development according to one's potential.[21] Epanouissement has long been a dominant theme in Quebec culture and, as might be expected, it is customarily applied to individuals as well as to Quebec society as a whole.

Finally, the supplementary principle holds that "the state is not the creator of the common good; it is its guardian."[22] The state is not a substitute for the initiative of individuals or of groups. Its responsibility is limited to stimulating, controlling, and coordinating private initiative. However, the state has a responsibility to act in the field of social welfare, if private initiatives are deficient.

Pierre Marois provides a view of SUPRET which most certainly expresses overtones of the supplementary principle. He points out that the Parti Québécois had long harboured intentions to launch a major fight against poverty. However, he and others wanted that fight "to be based not only on a social approach but also on an economic approach."[23] The "social" or socialist approach clearly involves the state as a creator of the common good. In other words, social welfare disbursements are expected to provide the necessary conditions for the attainment of the good of all individuals, that is, the common good. The "economic" or liberal approach on the other hand, promotes freedom for enterprising individuals to create the common good. In other words, liberalism holds that the private sector should be free to create jobs so that individuals can defend themselves against poverty by their own initiatives.

SUPRET is a compromise between these two approaches. Public funds are used to give employers "a break," as Marois puts it. According to Marois, work-related income supplementation encourages employers to establish "jobs at the margin of their operations, that is, jobs that are theoretically there but which would be too costly without income supplementation."[24] Thus, SUPRET is intended to bolster the economic approach. It is also designed to support the social approach because public funds are also used to give low income workers a break. SUPRET benefits provide the working poor with financial incentives to keep on working. In this sense SUPRET was touted as the missing link ("le maillon manquant") in Quebec's social welfare system.[25] Social assistance from Marois's perspective was not providing recipients with any incentive to improve their lot by work; in addition, low income workers were not being provided with sufficient incentives to continue working, given that they could benefit almost as much from social assistance. Thus, SUPRET as the missing link was intended to connect the social system to the economic system by helping recipients and potential recipients of social assistance to help themselves and by encouraging employers to create jobs so that low income workers could help themselves.

From this it is easily seen that individual initiative spurred by financial incentive was central to the design of SUPRET. Marois viewed work incentives as a means of upgrading the economic status of low income individuals; he also viewed work incentives as a means of enhancing an individual's self-worth. Indeed, Marois viewed the ability of SUPRET to generate individual dignity and growth in the broadest sense as the feature which distinguished that program from other types of social assistance. Remarks in which he compares the value of SUPRET expenditures to other types of social welfare expenditure are revealing in this regard:

> Si nous avons les moyens d'ajouter 500 millions au budget de l'Aide sociale, on doit toujours bien avoir les moyens, bon Dieu!, de développer une formule qui permette aux gens de s'épanouir convenablement et de retrouver simplement la dignité, la fierté de celui qui peut dire "Moi aussi, j'ai fait ma part."[26]

Of course, Marois's remarks echo a theme that has long been prevalent in the social security designs of the Parti Québécois: social security expenditures must be a force for productivity and thus a force for collective progress which includes individual development.[27] Marois puts the case in elemental terms: the individual has a duty to do his part, that is, to work and thereby to contribute to society. The collectivity or society, in turn, is expected to reciprocate by helping those who are unable to do their part, through no fault of their own, to work and thus to contribute to society.

However, the individual per se is not all important within the context of Marois's thinking on social welfare. The individual good is important insofar as it contributes to the collective good which begins with the basic collective unit, the family. The incentives may be directed towards the individual but it is the family which is strengthened by individual initiative within the context of SUPRET. After all, payments, which the Department of Revenue issues quarterly by cheque, originally required the signatures of both spouses. Clearly then the supplement was to benefit the family unit as a whole, not just one or the other spouse. Second, payments were originally made to families exclusively; coverage was only extended to individuals and to childless couples in 1981 and even then at a lower rate than for families. Finally, benefits have varied in relation to family size so that the greater the number of dependents the greater the supplement. However, families were never intended to be catapulted into a better economic status by virtue of SUPRET benefits. In 1982 the average annual benefit was about $731 which is hardly an amount that would be likely to cure poverty. It is an amount that would have just barely prevented low income workers from sinking into the quicksands of poverty. The intention has been to supplement, not to create, family income.

This leads us back to the supplementary principle to which Quebec closely adhered in the coverage and benefit levels of SUPRET. The intention was to proceed cautiously so that the government would remain in a position of merely supplementing incomes and not in a position of creating wealth for Quebec society. In Ontario, caution was also the norm with respect to WIN, although there was never any danger that costs would get out of control. In Ontario, the caution stems from a well-worn "liberal" reluctance to spend on social welfare. Indeed, as much as Ontario Conservatives would shudder at the suggestion, a strong liberal current has long pervaded the social welfare policy-making process in that province.

Liberalism embodies a wealth of principles but here it is sufficient to define liberalism in juxtaposition to the principles that are presented as integral to Catholic social thought. Classical liberalism, like the Catholic system of social inspiration, holds the individual responsible for taking care of his own needs. But that is where the similarity ends. Classical liberalism holds that state intervention in the market place will destroy individual initiative.[28] At best, the state should intervene to alleviate temporary financial difficulties experienced by individuals but it should intervene with the least disturbance to market forces. Basically liberalism holds that the state must exercise considerable restraint with regard to social welfare interventionism.

Although reform or contemporary liberalism recognizes that defects in market forces necessitate increased interventionism, there is a low threshold of interventionism beyond which the state must not venture lest it discourage individual initiative. Faith in the ability of the individual to provide for himself is also central to contemporary liberalism. Thus, the strengthening of groups or the collectivity via state interventionism is anathema to liberalism because of the sanctity of individualism. Similarly, the state as the creator of wealth is also a notion that is alien to liberalism because of the inviolability of individualism. The supplementary principle does not fare much better within the context of liberalism as is demonstrated by the case of WIN.

The income supplementation offered by WIN is designed to

relieve the state of its role as creator of wealth via the provision of social assistance. Indeed, the policy intent of WIN is crystal clear in this regard for its initially stated objective was "to encourage full-time employment and facilitate the transition from dependency on social assistance to complete financial independence by providing special cash incentives for two years."[29] The major benefit of WIN from this perspective is that it provides for the lesser of two evils; it provides for partial and temporary social assistance rather than for full and long-term social assistance. In other words, it is not necessarily a noble experiment in helping others to help themselves; it is largely a cost-saving device for a government which held and still holds an unfavourable disposition to social welfare of any type. Moreover, this disposition is largely accountable for the modesty of WIN as well as for its experimental orientation. Although WIN is intended to stimulate individual initiative, ironically, substantial social welfare investments of any type, and especially long-term investments, are ultimately viewed as threats to individual initiative.

WIN unquestionably upholds the principle of individual initiative. It provides transitional incentives to recipients, mainly single mothers with dependents, so that they can become independent of Family Benefits Act (FBA) disbursements.[30] It is primarily intended to facilitate the integration of employable welfare recipients into the labour market. In short, WIN is designed to make individuals responsible for their own welfare and, ultimately, independent of the state. Thus, WIN benefits, unlike SUPRET benefits, are not intended for the working poor or for the potential working poor. They are intended for FBA recipients and are, therefore, not intended to prevent poverty but to cure poverty. Furthermore, individualism as understood from the liberal perspective requires less support, if any, from income supplementation than does individual initiative as understood from a perspective dominated by Catholic social inspiration. After all, WIN benefits, unlike SUPRET benefits, have certainly not been discussed in terms of encouraging individual growth in the broadest sense of that concept. Finally and, perhaps obviously, the principle of subsidiarity is not related to the design of WIN benefits; single parent families, rather than traditional two parent families, are the main beneficiaries of WIN.

At least this is the way WIN has been perceived where it counts the most, in the Ontario public service.[31] The history of WIN, quite unlike the history of SUPRET, is not illustrious. WIN was largely the outcome of a decision which came from deep within the bowels of the Ontario Ministry of Community and Social Services following criticisms from social development groups that FBA regulations had created a "welfare trap."[32] There had been no talk of WIN as the first step towards a guaranteed annual income among leading politicians or among the major political parties. Furthermore, there has been no such talk despite the apparent success of WIN as "a positive first step in developing a new system to help people attain independence."[33] And there is unlikely to be any due to the strong current of liberalism which exists among Ontario's voters and decision-makers.

Conclusion: The Future of SUPRET and WIN

Too much and too little can be made of Quebec and Ontario's respective efforts to promote work-related income supplementation programs. In theory, income supplementation programs are potent measures to alleviate income inequalities. In practice, weaknesses in SUPRET and in WIN, especially with respect to funding, have limited their effectiveness in reducing poverty. More importantly, factors external to the welfare systems of Quebec and Ontario—particularly economic factors—are likely to preclude attempts to redress these weaknesses at least for the time being. Furthermore, prevalent ideological values in Ontario are likely to obviate any further development of WIN while dominant ideological norms in Quebec suggest that SUPRET-type programs are likely to face a bright future.

SUPRET and WIN have been weak in reducing poverty for the following reasons: first, each program represents a small step forward after many backward steps that have been taken in relation to the sheer level of social welfare disbursements in Quebec and Ontario. In the late 1970s, the federal government curtailed social welfare expenditures via cutbacks in unemployment insurance and in family allowances but partly redeemed itself by enacting the RCTC. However, the provinces appropriated a larger portion of the RCTC by lowering social assistance payments for those most likely to fully benefit from the tax credit.[34] Indeed, it was alleged that SUPRET was financed by these indirect appropriations. In short, lower income groups in Quebec and Ontario were as a whole no better off after the enactment of SUPRET and WIN than they were before.

Second, benefit levels have not been sufficiently generous to encourage recipients to sustain a long-term commitment to the labour force. Both Marois and Norton implicitly recognized that meagre benefits would not make an overwhelming difference in a recipient's decision to work. Hence, both requested federal financial support for their respective programs. Norton did not explicitly indicate whether federal funds would be used to expand the program and to increase benefit levels or simply to save more funds for the Government of Ontario. However, Marois made it abundantly clear that federal financial participation of any type would be used to increase SUPRET benefits. In the first instance, Marois engaged in a protracted battle with the federal government to ensure that benefits would not be taxed. He won the battle and low income workers have always received the full benefit of SUPRET payments. In the second instance, Marois attempted to induce the federal government to share the costs of SUPRET under the Canada Assistance Plan. Marois now claims that the federal government refused for the following reasons:

> ... they (federal officials) were afraid that if they had agreed to finance the program, I would have increased the benefits. Of course, I would have. They were also afraid that if the program worked well then several other provinces would have done the same thing and it would have cost them a lot. They would have had to reorganize their regime of public assistance. And we wanted them to do that.[35]

Thus, Marois suggests that the program cannot be developed further without federal assistance. However, his remarks by no means suggest a dim future for SUPRET. Marois points out that his main goal was to eventually secure fiscal autonomy for Quebec so that the social welfare system could be redesigned with a greater emphasis on income supplementation. In this sense, Marois was repeating a long-standing Parti Québécois position in government circles even after he left office.[36] More to the point, it is a position which has yet to be contradicted by the recently elected Parti Libéral. However, the government, like its Parti Québécois predecessor, also realizes that the growth of the Quebec economy is an absolute prerequisite to the improvement of SUPRET.

Work-related income supplementation programs have not been supported by economic growth. SUPRET has not been as successful as might have been expected in terms of participation rates because, in order to be eligible for benefits, one must be employed. In point of fact, SUPRET and WIN were announced just as unemployment in Canada began to climb dramatically.[37] Moreover, as critics of WIN are quick to point out, low income workers require educational infrastructure and job retraining in order to prepare them for the labour market.[38] In short, the success of work-related income supplementation programs has been short-circuited by the failure to develop a comprehensive social welfare system, which is, in turn, linked to the failure to revitalize the economy. The Parti Québécois, as the government of Quebec, recognized this shortcoming and, therefore, created an administrative structure which is expected to facilitate the formation of a comprehensive employment and social welfare system. Thus, the Ministry of Manpower and Income Security was created in the early 1980s with Pierre Marois as minister and the ministry has been retained by the Liberal government. However, this administrative unit alone cannot be expected to correct economic imbalances that cause unemployment. Nevertheless, an administrative unit which pools the resources of a variety of social programs may facilitate the implementation of measures designed to strengthen the economy and the social security system. In addition, the existence of the ministry is a symbolic recognition that employment and work-related income supplementation are connected and that the state must intervene to strengthen that connection.

In Ontario, liberal values clearly militate against a symbolic, not to mention a substantive, recognition of a need for greater economic and social intervention. The government is trapped by its own values in relation to WIN. A further development of WIN and complementary programs would produce the desired effect of integrating social assistance recipients with the labour force, that is, of stimulating individual initiative from the government's perspective. However, the further development of WIN and related programs as interventionist measures would also cripple individual initiative from its perspective. Liberal norms dictate that the Government of Ontario should expand WIN but the government is likely to leave well enough alone. Why should it stir a potential hornets' nest of anti-interventionism?

In Quebec, work-related income supplementation fits in with prevalent values that have been inspired by Catholic social thinking. The state is expected to promote individual and collective initiative by filling the cracks in the economy and in the social system. It is the duty of the state to supplement individual and collective initiatives when weaknesses occur. Thus, as we enter into the latter half of the decade of the 1980s the Government of Quebec is likely to give additional substance to its symbolic act of administrative reorganization. During its last months of office, the Parti Québécois promised to continue to encourage economic growth and to continue to promote a guaranteed annual income, promises which were not challenged by the Liberals.[39] It is clear that guaranteed annual income meant "greater financial incentive to low income workers to keep their jobs rather than becoming dependent on government assistance."[40] Indeed the maxim "plus ça change, plus c'est la même chose" aptly characterizes the expected direction of work-related income supplementation in Quebec and Ontario. In Quebec, there will likely be more income supplementation of the SUPRET variety. In Ontario there will likely be as little of WIN as there always has been. It could not be otherwise for social security is ultimately an expression of a society's ideological values, for better or for worse.

Notes

1. *Inventory of Income Security Programs in Canada* (Ottawa: Report for the Continuing Committee of Officials Reporting to Federal, Provincial and Territorial Deputy Ministers of Social Services, January 1984), 88, 93, provides a succinct description of the Supplément au revenu de travail and the Work Incentive Program. See chapter three of this text for a full description of each program.

2. Coverage was extended to individuals and childless couples during 1980. Currently, traditional two-parent families constitute slightly less than one-half of the households receiving SUPRET benefits. Pierre Frechete, "Un première regard sur les ménages bénéficiaires de Supplément au revenu de travail," texte presenté au 22e Congrès annuel de la Société canadienne de science économique, Université du Québec à Montréal, 12–13 mai 1982, presents a comprehensive description of recipients.

3. Quebec, *Débats de l'Assemblée nationale*, 29 mai 1979, 1442.

4. Une entrevue de Pierre Marois réalisée par Michel Pilon, "Vers une politique de revenu minimum garanti," *Carrefour des Affaires Sociales* 2 (September 1980): 26.

5. Rick Van Loon, "Reforming Welfare in Canada," *Public Policy* 27 (Fall 1979): 470.

6. Interviews. During October and November 1984, personal interviews were conducted with senior officials and politicians who had been involved in the development of the Loi de supplément au revenu de travail. During October 1983, interviews were conducted with officials in the Ontario Ministry of Community and Social Services.

7. The "guaranteed family income program" was introduced by Claude E. Forget, minister of Social Affairs, via the *Analyse d'un programme québécois de revenu familial garanti* (Québec: Rapport du Comité interministériel sur la revision de la sécurité du revenu, 1976). In a recent interview, Mr. Forget indicated that hearings on the report would have been held had he not been preoccupied with the hospitals' strike in the spring of 1976. The National Assembly recessed for the summer and an election was called for November 1976. Thus, Mr. Forget claims that the timing of the report, and not necessarily its cost estimates, was a main reason for its demise.

8. Interviews.

9. See Federal-Provincial Relations, *The Work Incentives Program (WIN)* (Toronto: Government of Ontario, November 16, 1981), 1; and Ministère d'Etat au Développement Social, *Le supplément au revenu de travail: orientations fondamentales* (Québec: Gouvernement du Québec, novembre 1978), 2.

10. William D. Coleman, *The Independence Movement in Quebec 1945–1980* (Toronto: University of Toronto Press, 1984), 136.

11. Frédéric Lesemann, *Services and Circuses: Community and the Welfare State* (Montreal: Black Rose Books, 1984), 43–78, effectively argues that major social reforms in Quebec resulted from compromises between the traditional and new technocratic elites. If his argument is accepted, then it stands to reason that the reforms manifested a compromise of the ideological values of both groups.

12. The "blue book" refers to the blue cover of *Les diverses hypothèses d'implantation d'une première étape de revenu minimum garanti* (Québec: Rapport du Groupe de travail sur la sécurité du revenu, 1978).

13. Interviews.
14. This includes the Union Nationale. See the remarks of M. Fernand Grenier in Quebec, *Débats de l'Assemblée nationale*, 29 mai 1979, 1442.
15. Interviews.
16. Interview, November 1984.
17. Le Conseil Exécutif du Parti Québécois, *Prochaine étape ... quand nous serons vraiment chez nous* (Montréal: Les Editions du Parti Québécois, 1972).
18. Ibid., 36.
19. David Kwavnick ed., *The Tremblay Report (Report of the Royal Commission of Inquiry on Constitutional Problems)* (Toronto: McClelland and Stewart, 1973), 68–69.
20. Ibid., 69.
21. Dale C. Thomson, "Introduction" in Dale C. Thomson ed., *Québec Society and Politics: Views From the Inside* (Toronto: McClelland and Stewart Ltd., 1973), 9.
22. Kwavnick, ed., *The Tremblay Report*, 69.
23. Interview, November 1984.
24. It has been argued that the supplement encourages capital to keep wages low and to extract greater profits. The argument has been advanced by Michel Pelletier, *De la sécurité sociale à la sécurité de revenu* (Montréal: à compte d'auteur, 1982), 96, and by Yvon Lebeau et Yvon Boucher, "Une prime au 'cheap labour'," *Le Devoir*, 17 juillet 1979. That may well be an effect of SUPRET. However, interviews with officials and politicians indicate that this has not been an intended effect.
25. *La Presse, Montréal*, 8 mars 1979.
26. "Vers une politique de revenu minimum garanti," 22.
27. René Lévesque, speaking on behalf of the Parti Québécois, articulated this theme as early as 1970: "Il faut également apprendre à regarder le coût des investissements sociaux bien faits non seulement comme un aspect de la justice la plus élémentaire, mais aussi comme un élément-moteur de la productivité, tout aussi important pour le progrès collectif que pour l'épanouissement individuel." See René Lévesque, *La Solution: Le programme du Parti Québécois présenté par René Lévesque* (Montréal: Editions du Jour, 1970), 51.
28. Classical liberalism holds that the least government is the best government while reform liberalism admits to the necessity for state interventionism to correct market failures that hinder individual initiative. However, a thread, which is common to both, posits that the state should intervene only when absolutely necessary—at best during emergencies—and even then it should act with restraint.
29. Ontario Ministry of Community and Social Services, Income Maintenance Branch, *Work Incentive Programme: Policy and Procedural Guidelines* (Toronto: Ontario Ministry of Community and Social Services, October 1981), 1.
30. WIN was aimed at sole-support mothers with dependent children and

the program was successful in reaching its target. In 1980, 84 percent of the WIN case load consisted of single mothers. See Hon. Keith C. Norton, *Statement by the Honourable Keith C. Norton, Minister of Community and Social Services, MPP Kingston and the Islands, to the Ontario Legislature Concerning the Work Incentive Program*, Thursday, 19 June 1980, 2.
31. Interviews.
32. For example, see Social Planning Council of Metropolitan Toronto and the Ontario Social Development Council, ... *And the Poor Get Poorer* (Revised Edition) (Toronto: Social Planning Council of Metropolitan Toronto, 1979), 78.
33. Hon. Keith C. Norton, *Statement*, 6.
34. Many of the provinces simply lowered or at least did not raise their social assistance payments to families with children thereby indirectly appropriating the RCTC. A complete explanation is provided in Andrew F. Johnson, "Restructuring Family Allowances: 'Good Politics at No Cost?'" in J. S. Ismael, ed., *Canadian Social Welfare: Federal-Provincial Dimensions* (Montreal: McGill-Queen's University Press, 1985), 109–11.
35. Interview, November 1984.
36. Ministère des Finances, *White Paper on the Personal Tax and Transfer Systems* (Québec: Gouvernement du Québec, 1984), 6, points out that the encouragement and maintenance of "the incentive to work and to entrepreneurship" is at the top of the government's fiscal agenda.
37. Jacques Rousseau, "Supplément au revenu de travail: les limites" in *Perception*, September/October 1979, 37, argues persuasively that high unemployment was a major factor that weakened SUPRET.
38. See Ontario Welfare Council, *"Settling for Less": A Response to the Work Incentive Program*, October 1979, and Ontario Status of Women Council, *Comments on the Work Incentive Program for Family Benefits Recipients Announced by the Ministry of Community and Social Services*, September 1979.
39. Ministère des Finances, *White Paper on the Personal Tax and Transfer Systems: Introductory Paper* (Québec: Gouvernement du Québec, 1984), 25.
40. Ibid., 25.

5 Welfare, Work Incentives, and the Single Mother
An Interprovincial Comparison

PATRICIA M. EVANS

EILENE L. McINTYRE

Since the mid-seventies, one of the most significant developments in social assistance policy has been the attempt by provincial governments to move single mothers from welfare to work. Provincial efforts to encourage entry into the labour force are evident in policies which include the imposition of work requirements, attempts to alter the benefit system to increase the rewards of low-paid work, and the provision of a variety of employment-related services. The result may be an erosion of the right to income maintenance for a portion of this group—those deemed able to enter the labour force.

In Canadian social welfare policy, the tension between the equity or welfare criterion and the efficiency criterion is perhaps nowhere more apparent than in the work incentive policies which underpin social assistance programs. These policies attempt to ensure that welfare is an unattractive alternative to low-paid work without imposing levels and conditions of benefits inconsistent with the conception of social justice in a liberal democratic society. Similarly, the strain between economic and social objectives has been apparent from the onset of major federal manpower programs in the mid-1960s.[1] Federal training dollars have been disproportionately allocated to areas of high unemployment as much to provide income to the unemployed as for realistic expectation of job entry.[2] When the economy is in recession and unemployment is high, the competition between social and economic goals emerges with particular clarity: the need to control social spending and enhance productivity increases while the demand for benefits mounts. Mildred Rein comments:

> In one form or another, society has always been willing to maintain those who cannot maintain themselves. But when a group that is being assisted becomes too large or its support too costly, attempts are made to distinguish those in the group who can maintain themselves from those who cannot—to separate out the non-deserving from the deserving. To single out employables is thus the essential strategy for containing the size of the assistance group under such circumstances.[3]

Definition as "employable" in Canadian welfare programs has consistently meant less eligibility: lower benefit levels, less security in the duration of the benefit, and more frequent and rigorous investigation of capacity and motivation to work, in comparison with categories of recipients believed to be unable to work. Historically, the distinction between employable and unemployable has shown considerable variation depending more on labour market and fiscal factors than on precisely articulated principles or criteria.[4]

The purpose of this chapter is to survey the trends in recent provincial work incentives for sole-support mothers, and to examine critically the issues that they raise. First, the economic, political, and sociodemographic factors which form the context of recent changes are identified. The second section discusses the findings of a survey conducted in March 1985 of the provincial and territorial governments' work incentive policies regarding single mothers on social assistance. Two major assumptions which appear to underlie the entire range of work incentives are examined in the third section. The paper concludes with a discussion of developments which seem essential both to the success of such programs and to the maintenance of a socially just balance between economic and social objectives.

The Rise of the Work Incentive

Mothers' Allowance legislation, enacted in a number of provinces between 1916–1935, established for the first time the right of eligible low-income single mothers to receive a monthly cash benefit on a regular basis. Advocated by the women's movement and social reformers, these early social assistance programs developed in part to provide an alternative to full-time employment, although part-time work was encouraged.[5] Following the exit of women from the work force at the close of World War II, even part-time employment was frequently discouraged.[6] From the mid-seventies onward, however, provincial interest in redefining the expectations of work for single mothers on social assistance has resulted in an increased emphasis on work incentive policies and programs.

Interest in work incentives for sole-support mothers on social assistance has developed within the context of economic, demographic, and political factors which include: 1) fiscal restraint; 2) the increased labour force participation of women; 3) the increase in single mothers in both the general and social assistance populations; 4) the changing structure of the labour market; and 5) the context of federal-provincial relations.

In a climate of economic restraint, social assistance programs have been an especially vulnerable target for social spending cuts. However, costs become increasingly difficult to contain as the efforts to control inflation produce further reliance on income support programs. The attempt to control expenditure is reflected in the decreasing purchasing power of welfare benefits,[7] and in efforts to ensure that all welfare recipients who can work do. Men, and women without dependents, traditionally have been subject to a range of work incentives. Despite some forays into "work for welfare," it may be politically and practically unrealistic to expect additional inducements to work amongst these groups to produce further savings.[8]

Additional factors have helped to identify single mothers as a particular focus for work incentive policies. The changing perceptions of women's role at home and in the economy have resulted in the dramatic rise in the labour force participation of mothers, which may well challenge the legitimacy of income support for single mothers, particularly at a time when they represent a growing share of the welfare caseload. In Ontario, for example, the number of sole-support mothers on social assistance grew by 400 percent between 1961 and 1982, and in 1984 represented almost one-third of the assistance caseload.[9] Other provinces may well share the concern expressed in a recent report produced for the Ontario Ministry of Community and Social Services which noted, " ... sole support mothers represent the largest potentially employable client group on the social assistance caseload."[10]

Changes in the structure of the labour market may further contribute to the redefinition of the employment expectations for the single mother on social assistance. Between 1975–1979, the largest gains in job creation were made in trade and service sectors, with its concentration of female employment. As Armstrong and Armstrong note, the majority of new jobs in this period were available in "female job ghettos."[11]

The influence of the relationship between the federal and provincial levels of government, important in the development of social security in Canada, has also been evident in the current interest in encouraging single mothers on social assistance to move into the labour market. The links between the social assistance work incentive programs, the programs of the Canada Employment and Immigration Commission, and provincial education and labour ministries were apparent in the data provided by the ministries in response to the survey questionnaire.[12] Eligibility for federal Manpower Training dollars, through formal and informal job training, offer clear financial advantages to the provinces, which may extend beyond the duration of training. Literature provided by the Deputy Minister of Social Services for Alberta, for example, notes:

> Even if participants cannot secure work after their E.S.P. [Employment Skills Program] placement, they become eligible for unemployment insurance benefits and are able to maintain, for a period, a continued uninvolvement with the social welfare system. This increases their self-esteem and may reduce their dependence upon other services of the department.

The degree to which this provides actual or potential relief to provincial expenditures awaits further research.

At the same time, some jurisdictions are assuming functions normally provided by Canada Employment Centres to the general population, and are operating directly or funding job readiness programs. It seems reasonable to suggest that, in the absence of demand for these arrangements from consumers or interest groups, a reason for their development may lie in political and administrative convenience, and in financial advantages to the provinces. These, then, are some of the economic, political, and social factors that have combined to identify single mothers as an attractive focus for work incentive policies.

Work Incentives Across the Provinces and Territories

Incentives can encompass both positive and negative forms of inducement. Rein identifies three major work incentive strategies, all of which are apparent in recent provincial initiatives.[13] At the negative end of the work incentive continuum lies the *restrictive* strategy which can encompass a variety of measures including low benefit levels, the use of stigma, and work requirements, to ensure that welfare is not preferred over work; this paper will only deal with work requirements. Secondly, a *financial* strategy is evident in efforts to alter the social assistance benefit structure to increase the monetary rewards of low-wage work. A third approach is the *service* strategy, which relies upon information, education, and training to improve the competitiveness of individuals in the work force, as well as the provision of employment supports such as day care.

Information regarding the scope and variation of current provincial work incentive policies affecting single mothers was collected primarily from responses to a questionnaire sent to all deputy ministers of social services in the ten provinces and two territories. All responded to this questionnaire and, wherever possible, additional sources supplemented these data.

WORK REQUIREMENTS: THE RESTRICTIVE STRATEGY
The restrictive strategy may incorporate a variety of measures (e.g., low benefits, stigmatizing practices); however, the single aspect examined in this paper is the explicit policy of work re-

Table 5.1   Presence of Work Requirements for Sole-Support Mothers by Province, 1985

	Children Under Six	Children Over Six
Newfoundland	No	No
P. E. I.	No	No
Nova Scotia	Yes	Yes
New Brunswick	No	No
Quebec	No	Yes
Ontario	No	No
Manitoba	No	No
Saskatchewan	Yes	Yes
Alberta	Yes	Yes
British Columbia	Yes	Yes
N. W. T.	No	No
Yukon	Yes	Yes

quirements. Work requirements for single mothers do not demand that recipients actually be employed to receive benefits; instead, they outline the activities that recipients must engage in to increase the likelihood of their employment, or to demonstrate their willingness to work. As Lurie points out, work requirements can vary along a number of dimensions which include: 1) the individuals to whom they apply; 2) the nature of the expectations that they impose; 3) the consequences of noncompliance; and 4) the rigour with which they are enforced.[14]

Half of the provinces and territories stipulate some form of work requirement for single mothers; this is illustrated in Table 5.1. At the present time, single mothers in Newfoundland, Prince Edward Island, New Brunswick, Ontario, Manitoba, and the Northwest Territories are not specifically included in work requirements, although, as will become apparent, this should not be equated with a lack of interest in their labour force participation. In Prince Edward Island, there is a work "expectation," rather than a requirement; work is encouraged but no formal sanctions are present. In the provinces which do impose work requirements, only Quebec exempts mothers with preschool children.

In 1978, Alberta introduced the most specific definition of single mothers who are considered employable and therefore subject to work requirements. This group includes single mothers with: 1) one dependent child over the age of four months; or 2) two dependent children, one or both of whom are of school age. British Columbia uses a very similar definition of employability.[15]

When work requirements are imposed, the formal expectations for compliance typically include provisions that the recipient shall: 1) look for work, which may entail registration with Canada Employment Centres; and 2) accept referrals to programs designed to improve his employability. In Nova Scotia, British Columbia, and Saskatchewan, there is an additional expectation that the single mother accept "suitable" employment. Alberta expects full-time employment which is defined as a minimum of 35 hours per week. In this province, providing child care for other families may be considered full-time employment if the single mother looks after more than one child and receives compensation deemed adequate.[16]

The consequence of failing to comply with work requirements can be the suspension or termination of eligibility for assistance. Although we have little information on the way in which work requirements are implemented, it seems unlikely that so drastic a penalty is invoked with any frequency. However, in 1981, British Columbia announced a policy which permitted reductions in benefits to unemployed but "employable" recipients; in addition, recipients can be required to reapply each month for assistance.[17]

In *The Collapse of Welfare Reform* Christopher Leman has described work requirements as "often ineffective, wasteful and basically unmanageable."[18] First, the assumption that the poor lack sufficient work motivation is not supported by research.[19] Second, an employment requirement for single mothers, in the absence of jobs and day care, simply cannot have much impact on the social assistance caseload. It serves only the political objective of ensuring the public that their tax dollars are properly safeguarded. In the process, however, the legitimacy of the single mother's entitlement to social assistance may be seriously undermined.

FINANCIAL STRATEGY

The second major strategy which may be used to improve the work effort of social assistance recipients is the manipulation of the fea-

Table 5.2   Retention from Net Monthly Earnings of $250 by a Single Mother, One Child, Employed Part-Time, by Province, 1983

	Earnings Exempted Before Reduction	% Deducted from Remaining Earnings	Earnings Retained
Newfoundland	$ 70*	Under $200:50%; then 100%	$160.00
P.E.I.	$ 90*	100%	$ 90.00
Nova Scotia	$200	75%	$212.50
New Brunswick	$200	75%	$212.50
Quebec	$ 60[a]	100%	$ 60.00
Ontario	$140	Under $240:50%; then 100%	$190.00
Manitoba	$125*	100%	$125.00
Saskatchewan	Varies[b]	100%	$250.00
Alberta	$155*	Under $200:50%; $200–$300:75%; then 90%	$202.50
British Columbia	$100	100%	$100.00
N.W.T.	$100	100%	$100.00
Yukon	$ 50	100%	$ 50.00

NOTES: * In jurisdictions where actual working expenses may also be deducted, this figure includes assumed expenses of $40.00 per month in addition to any regular exemption allowed.
[a] In Quebec, $40 per family and $5 for each child is exempted; in addition, work-related expenses amounting to either $25 or 6% of net monthly earnings, whichever is the lesser, is also permitted without benefit reduction (in this case $15). If the single mother is employed in a subsidized job placement, she is entitled to an additional $190.00 monthly earnings exemption.
[b] In Saskatchewan, a recipient may retain $100 plus 25% of the basic needs allowance (for purposes of the table, basic needs is assumed to be $750); in addition, working expenses are also exempt. In the case used in the table, these exemptions total $327.50.

tures of the income support system to increase the monetary rewards of low-wage work. These efforts identify the presence of disincentives within the welfare system, or conversely, the lack of incentives in the low-wage labour market as the obstacle to labour force participation. While some provinces have tackled this through programs available to the "working poor" population in general, this discussion is directed to incentives within the social assistance benefit system.[20] Financial incentives are evident in two

major mechanisms which govern the treatment of earnings by social assistance recipients: 1) the amount of earnings which are permitted without any reduction to the monthly benefit; and 2) the
rate by which benefits are reduced to reflect earnings beyond the
exempted amount. Table 5.2 illustrates the amount that a single
mother with one child and part-time take-home earnings of
$250.00 per month (after compulsory deductions) retains in each of
the twelve jurisdictions.

It is apparent from Table 5.2 that the treatment of earnings by
single mothers on social assistance varies widely amongst the
provinces. Treatment of earnings is most generous in Saskatchewan, where her entire take-home earnings of $250.00 are
retained. Nova Scotia, New Brunswick and Alberta are also comparatively generous: in those provinces, the single mother is
entitled to keep $212.50 and $202.50, respectively. In contrast, in
the Yukon, Quebec, Prince Edward Island, British Columbia and
the Northwest Territories, the combined effect of a low level of exemption and a dollar for dollar reduction rate produces little financial gain. The sole-support mother living in these regions
would have to be so thoroughly ingrained with the work ethic that
she was willing to work in spite of the fact that in terms of the
"costs" of employment, monetary and otherwise, she is likely to be
worse off.

Two recent provincial initiatives have extended the use of the financial strategy specifically to encompass single mothers who
leave social assistance to enter full-time employment but whose
earnings fall below a prescribed level. The provisions of Ontario's
Work Incentive (WIN) program, introduced in 1979, include an initial grant to cover "back to work" expenses, and a wage supplement, the value of which declines as earnings increase.[21] Nova
Scotia's 1983 Vocational Rehabilitation Program for Single Parents extends to the full-time worker the same earnings exemption
and reduction rate applied to part-time earnings of Family Benefit
recipients. In both provinces, provisions are made for easy re-entry
to Family Benefits to reduce the insecurity which may be caused
by the transfer from welfare to work.

Apart from the inequities to the nonwelfare poor which are inherent in financial strategies directed to recent social assistance
recipients, their effectiveness as a work incentive is severely con-

strained when pursued primarily as a cost-saving strategy. Allowing a larger amount of earnings to be exempted, and decreasing the rate of reduction, can rapidly expand the total costs of social assistance for several reasons. First, the incentives may need to be of considerable magnitude to produce the desired effect and to offset any loss or reduction in subsidies to other means-tested programs (e.g., housing, day care, drugs), which occurs as income increases. Secondly, as the income level permitted for eligibility is revised, the social assistance population may be expanded. These objectives are certainly worthy of pursuit from an anti-poverty perspective. However, as Martin Rein has noted: "To encourage work, to reduce poverty, and to contain costs are incompatible aims."[22] The current climate in Canada does not encourage optimism about which, amongst these competing objectives, will be given priority.

Unlike the work requirement, financial work incentives do not identify lack of individual motivation as a major employment obstacle. When applied to full-time workers in the form of wage supplements, the financial strategy attempts to redress the realities of the labour market; its remedy lies in the subsidy, rather than the reform, of low-wage employment. The financial strategy directed at part-time earnings may more accurately be viewed as an effort to reduce disincentives in social assistance programs rather than to provide positive incentives.

THE SERVICE STRATEGY

Employment Services   The third major work incentive strategy, the provision of services, has received the greatest emphasis in the recent provincial efforts to move single mothers from social assistance into employment. This section focuses on those services designed to increase the ability of the sole-support mother to compete effectively for employment in the labour market; day care is discussed in the following section. Since 1979, the provinces of Ontario, Newfoundland, Alberta, Saskatchewan, Nova Scotia, and the Yukon have ushered in programs exclusively or primarily targeted to the population of single mothers on social assistance; Prince Edward Island has programs in the very early stages of development. Only New Brunswick and the Northwest Territories reported no programs directed to single mothers on social assistance.

While programs vary considerably across the provinces, they can be divided, albeit somewhat crudely, into two major categories. The first category comprises pre-employment programs which typically foster the development of motivation, life skills, educational upgrading and job-finding techniques. The second category of employment related services includes those which attempt to increase directly an individual's labour market competitiveness through direct job placement, or referral to programs which provide formal training and informal on-the-job training.

The provision of employment services as a work incentive strategy is rooted in the assumption that increases to "human capital" will be rewarded in the labour market. This assumption is challenged by the evidence of the current levels of unemployment and the persistent segregation of women into low-paid and frequently unskilled work. Further, studies have suggested that while education may influence the entry into the labour market of a single mother on social assistance, it appears to have little effect on her earnings, the amount she works, or the type of work she does.[23] Education may offer to single mothers a range of other benefits; however, its ability to provide access to well-paid and secure jobs appears to be quite limited.

The track record of formal training programs does not necessarily suggest that they represent a better route to stable and relatively well-paid employment. A federal Task Force on Labour Market Development has suggested that expenditure for skill training appears to be used primarily to, " ... improve the general employability of the unemployed, to simply take people off the unemployment rolls or to provide extended income maintenance."[24] MacLellan has concluded from her examination of the manpower programs between 1979–1983 that women were over-represented in programs targeted to improve general "employability," that is basic skills, job "readiness" and occupational orientation.[25] There is little information regarding the extent to which employment services directed to the single mother on social assistance effectively improve her prospects for economic self-sufficiency.

A number of jurisdictions offer short-term work placements in an effort to increase employability: Ontario, Quebec, Saskatchewan, Newfoundland, Prince Edward Island, and New Brunswick all have programs which provide on-the-job training and work experience. Alberta's Employment Skills Program is representative in many respects. ESP was introduced in 1979, and places social assistance recipients in a variety of provincial agencies and departments; the work is largely clerical in nature, and is limited to six months. Information supplied indicates that for the fiscal year ending 1984, almost half (49 percent) were employed three months after completion or termination in the program. In order to assess the effectiveness of this program it would be important to examine employment duration over a longer period of time,[26] collect information on wages, and consider the exit from the social assistance caseload which occurs in the absence of program intervention.

The recent report of an evaluation of Ontario's Employment Support Initiative (ESI) Projects does not suggest that good jobs are an outcome.[27] These projects, piloted in nine areas across the province, provide some financial incentives, as well as pre-employment services, access to educational upgrading and training, and direct work placement. At the end of the first year of operation, one in five of the ESI participants had obtained part or full-time employment; the 25 percent projected full-time employment rate had been achieved by only 10 percent of ESI participants. In addition, the ESI program had no visible impact on the type of jobs participants obtained: although there was no information on wages, the percentages of those working in the service, sales, and clerical sectors before and after ESI enrollment were virtually identical.[28]

Day Care   The provision of acceptable, affordable and accessible day and after-school care is a prerequisite to employment for single mothers with young children. In New Brunswick, Nova Scotia, and British Columbia single mothers on social assistance receive day care subsidies on the same general terms and conditions as apply to other low-income earners; there is no special provision of space made available to them. The majority of other jurisdictions provide a measure of priority for subsidized day care space for children of mothers on assistance. All of these give "high" priority to single mothers leaving social assistance for full-time employment and, with the exception of Saskatchewan and Manitoba, to part-time workers. In addition, those searching for work are generally given high priority, except in the Yukon and the Northwest Territories.

Although licensed day care is the form of child care which seems to be preferred by parents, only a minority are able to exercise this option.[29] In Ontario, additional day care spaces were created for ESI participants. Despite this, less than one in every two (42.8 percent) of the children whose arrangements were known received licensed care, while less than one in three (30 percent) received licensed care provided in a day care centre.[30]

Since World War Two, subsidised day care in Canada has been regulated by provincially legislated standards, and access to subsidy has been conditional on care in a setting which met those standards. Ontario, Saskatchewan, and British Columbia now subsidise unregulated care as well as licensed day care and, as this information was not expressly elicited from the survey questionnaire, this policy may also apply elsewhere. Waiving the requirement to meet licensing standards is of particular concern when it occurs in relation to a population with few resources to object. In addition, the flow of public money to child care arrangements with no measure of public accountability may signal an erosion of the long-standing commitment of the provinces to safeguard the quality of care that children receive while their mothers work outside the home.

The Work and Welfare Link: The Marginal Labour Market

In addition to the implications of the specific work incentives, two major assumptions underpin current provincial strategies to improve work incentives to single mothers on welfare. First, implicit in strategies channelled through the social assistance system is the assumption that recipients represent the "nonworking" poor, a static population of individuals quite separate and distinct from the "working" poor. The second assumption is that jobs of the sort which permit long-term independence from social assistance are available; this section will assess the validity of these assumptions.

THE MIX OF WORK AND WELFARE

The view that single mothers on social assistance represent a static and stable group of recipients with little attachment to work stands in direct contrast to the findings from an expanding body of empirical research. Jean James's study of Toronto Family Benefit mothers, for example, has found that 39 percent of those sampled had received benefits for two years or less; when only those under thirty were considered, this figure jumped to 60 percent.[31] As these findings are based on a cross-sectional sample, they are likely to overestimate the use of welfare by the typical single mother who comes onto the social assistance caseload. The use of a cohort, a sample of those who come onto the social assistance caseload at the same time, avoids the accumulation of long-stayers.[32]

Work and welfare are not mutually exclusive sources of financial support. A study investigating the sources of income for a sample of low-income single mothers in Manitoba between 1972–1974 revealed that over half (54 percent) of those who had received income from social assistance during that period also reported earnings. James reported a lower, but still far from insubstantial figure: one-third had worked since receiving social assistance although less than one in five held jobs at the time of interview.[33]

Research which has established less reliance on welfare than conventionally assumed through the use of cohort samples has also noted a greater occurrence of the pattern of "cycling": going on and off social assistance. Rydell, et al. found that over one-third of their sample of single mothers with one child experienced more than one spell of welfare support. Similarly, Boskin and Nold report that more than one-quarter of those who left welfare returned within a five-year period.[34]

A study of the labour force participation patterns of all mothers with children under sixteen in Ontario shows that, in 1970, only 39 percent of all working mothers were employed full-time and full-year; differences were attributed to labour market factors and variable family needs.[35] Thus, it may well be that work patterns of sole-support mothers on social assistance are more similar to, than different from, those of all mothers of young children, particularly low-wage earning mothers.

In contradiction to the conventional separation of the role of work and welfare in the lives of single mothers, reflected in both stereotypes and work incentive programs, research has documented the interaction between social assistance and employment in the lives of single mothers. The evidence suggests, then, that sole-support mothers on social assistance not only *want* to work, but *do* work. Employment, however, does not necessarily equate with a temporary or permanent exit from social assistance: work and welfare are frequently "mixed" at the same time, and over time.[36] Nearly twenty years ago, Genevieve Carter described, in the following terms, the impact of the U.S. labour market on the patterns of work and welfare use:

> The game of musical chairs played by new cases, previous cases that return, and cases that close for a while or for good reflects the interaction of the welfare system with the unstable employment conditions of the irregular, dead-end job economy available to them.[37]

THE MARGINAL LABOUR MARKET

The single mother's use of welfare cannot be understood without reference to the marginal labour market. Low pay and occupational segregation are two striking characteristics which constrain the effective participation of women in the Canadian labour market.[38] There is abundant evidence which suggests that single mothers, before, during, and following periods of social assistance, work in jobs which are badly paid, unstable, and offer little chance for career advancement.[39]

Single mothers on social assistance are part of the broader and vulnerable population of mothers heading households on their own. As a general group, single mothers are more likely to work than their married counterparts. However, they are also more likely to be unemployed. Table 5.3 contrasts their labour force participation and unemployment rates with those of married women.

There are several points to note in an examination of Table 5.3. First, as previous research has indicated, the labour force participation rates of single mothers are higher than those of married women.[40] Table 5.3 also indicates that they not only have higher rates of unemployment but, in comparison to married women, single mothers are bearing an increasing share of female unem-

Table 5.3   Labour Force Participation and Unemployment Rates,
Single Mothers and Married Women, Selected Years,
Canada

| | Labour Force Participation | | Unemployment | |
	Single Mothers	*Married Women*	*Single Mothers*	*Married Women*
1975	47.4%	41.3%	7.3%	7.9%
1977	49.5%	43.8%	8.7%	8.9%
1979	53.3%	47.1%	9.8%	8.0%
1981	56.5%	50.2%	8.9%	7.6%
1983	57.0%	51.8%	13.3%	10.4%
1984	59.0%	53.1%	13.3%	10.5%

SOURCE: Statistics Canada, *Historical labour force statistics,* Cat. 71–201, February, 1985; annual averages cited from pp. 229, 195.

ployment. Between 1975–1983, the labour force participation rates of single mothers increased at a lower rate than married women's. This is partly a reflection of their initial comparatively high rates. However, over this period, the unemployment rate of female single parents nearly doubled (82 percent increase), while the unemployment rate for married women increased by only a third (32 percent). The labour force activity of single mothers is likely to reflect, in part, the high turnover rates in the service sector. Pat Armstrong and Hugh Armstrong comment: " . . . new employment and new unemployment are concentrated in the same industrial sector, in female job ghettoes."[41] It appears that whatever barriers women in general confront in the labour market may be of particular importance to the population of single mothers.

The structure of the labour market does not suggest that the position of women in the Canadian labour market is likely to improve. Neither predictions of the continued expansion of the service sector, or an increase in female unemployment suggest that the objective of long-term economic self-sufficiency for the single mother can be achieved without strategies directed to the demand for labour.[42]

Single mothers on social assistance, while as motivated to work as the nonwelfare population, have little confidence in their ability to find a decent job.[43] To the extent that this lack of confidence reflects an accurate, if depressing, estimate of job opportunities, programs which cannot also improve the likelihood that newly acquired confidence will pay off in the labour market would appear to be of marginal value.

Conclusions

This paper has reviewed recent trends in provincial efforts to move single mothers on social assistance into employment. Three major trends in work incentive strategies were identified: the increased use of the restrictive strategy of work requirements, the financial strategy which modifies features of the social assistance program to increase the monetary rewards from work, and the service strategy geared to employment preparation, job placement, and day care. There are three interrelated concerns regarding these programs which may: 1) encourage a short-term labour market entry approach; 2) possess important hidden costs; and 3) contribute to the erosion of the entitlement of the single mother to social assistance.

Although the solutions addressed by work incentive strategies span efforts to improve labour market competitiveness, supplement low wages, and reinforce the work ethic, they ignore the inadequacies of the labour market. In so doing, they encourage the identification of the problem as simply one of entry into employment, with little or no attention to its accompanying stability and rewards. In view of high levels of unemployment, single mothers on social assistance who do secure work may simply displace other workers in the revolving door of the marginal labour market. There is little evidence in current Canadian labour market research for optimism on the expansionary capacity of the labour market for women. Were "full" employment a short or even a mid-term economic goal, change to the occupational structure of the labour force would have to be addressed before it could be assumed that women, let alone underskilled women, would benefit.

Work incentive efforts directed to single mothers on social assistance may not merely be generally ineffective; they may be accompanied by a variety of costs borne by the single mother and her children. These hidden costs include the possibility of increased coerciveness in policies and programs, and the further deterioration in the quality of life for the sole-support mother and her children. The information available suggests that the majority of jurisdictions at the present time are attempting to enable rather than coerce the sole-support mother into the labour force. However, it may be that incentives to work which are not accompanied by action to ensure the availability of reasonably paid employment will inexorably become more coercive as their voluntary nature is perceived as inadequate to achieve the objective.

The attempt to marry the incompatible goals of cutting costs and upholding the single mother's best interests may increasingly push these policies across the thin line which divides motivation and manipulation, and the less restrictive from the more restrictive strategies. This has been true of the efforts directed to single mothers in the United States, and is also reflected in Canadian policies. In the last eight years, Alberta and British Columbia have implemented more stringent work requirements, and it has been suggested that Ontario has given recent consideration to their introduction.[44]

The collision between the efficiency and equity functions of our policies is likely to result in increased enforcement to work; however, programs may be cloaked in incentives. An area with considerable potential for coercion is the recent emphasis on individualized employment plans, an important component in Ontario's Employment Support Initiatives, and programs in P.E.I., Nova Scotia, Saskatchewan, and British Columbia. At the positive end of the spectrum, the development of individual plans can be helpful, affirming and enabling if undertaken by separate administrative authority from that providing assistance. In times of economic recession which herald increases in unemployment and pressures on both the federal and provincial purses, there is a very real danger that the vulnerability of the single mother, in contrast to the power of the social assistance worker and supervisor, may operate to singular disadvantage to the sole-support mother and her family. As Stein has observed: "When the explicit and implicit policies conflict, it is the latter that govern."[45]

A third danger inherent in ineffective work incentive programs is the increased jeopardy of the legitimacy of the single mother's entitlement to social assistance as viewed by the general public and welfare administrators. The focus on the pre-employment and employment strategies directed to "reform" women, in the face of high unemployment rates and the degree of concentration of women in low-paid, insecure, and unrewarding jobs, targets the wrong, if vulnerable, factor. It may serve to increase the rationale for cuts in social assistance benefits, in what is already a receptive bureaucratic/political climate.

Both manpower and social assistance programs are directed to the reform of labour supply. In their efforts to reform women and welfare, present trends in provincial policies ignore a critical factor in the work-welfare equation: the labour market. In a period of recession that coincides with major changes in the structure of the industrial and commercial base of the Canadian economy, the need is for reform efforts directed at the source of demand for labour rather than its supply. These might include job security policies similar to those in place in several European countries and measures to induce Canadian employers to engage in effective labour force planning and to promote joint employer-employee planning mechanisms.[46] The management of unemployment seems to have more to do with political variables than "objective" market forces, suggesting that Canadian provincial and federal bodies may need to turn their attention to policies which address the demand for labour.[47]

As long as policies attempt to reform women and welfare, and ignore reform of work, there can be no employment solution to the social assistance problems of provincial governments. At this critical stage in the evolution of work incentive programs for sole-support mothers, there are several directions which seem worthwhile to pursue. First and foremost is the improvement of the position of women in the Canadian labour market. Policies which emphasize the quality of work, legislation which promotes equitable pay, unionization which encompasses the particularly vulnerable worker, the strengthening of minimum wage policies, and the expansion of labour standards protection to part-time and temporary work, are all strategies which will help to place the incentive where it properly belongs: in work itself.

In addition to providing incentives through the labour market, the use of incentives directed only to that portion of the population which is the "visible tip" at one point in time is both economically and socially inefficient. The channelling of efforts through the social assistance system ignores the circularity between work and welfare, and the vulnerability of many single mothers who remain on the edge of welfare. It is not economically sensible to spend money simply to replace former workers with new in the revolving door of the marginal labour market. An emphasis on moving social assistance recipients into the work force, regardless of the marginal and short-term nature of their employment, cannot meet the goal of either the sole-support mother, or welfare administrator, for her long-term economic self-sufficiency.

Notes

1. Barbara Goldman, *New Directions for Manpower Policy* (Montreal: C. D. Howe Research Institute, 1976), 8–9.
2. Employment and Immigration Canada, *Labour Market Development in the 1980s* (Ottawa: Minister of Supply and Services, 1981), 33.
3. Mildred Rein, *Work or Welfare? Factors in the Choice for AFDC Mothers* (New York: Praeger, 1974), iv.
4. Jon Buttrum, "What is Employable?" *Canadian Welfare* 52, 3 (July–August 1976): 13–16.
5. The expectation of part-time work in the early Mothers' Allowances or Mothers' Pensions legislation was explicit in the policies of Ontario and New Brunswick and, as Strong-Boag suggests, implicit in the low level of benefits. The early provisions were limited in scope and frequently excluded deserted wives and unmarried mothers. See Veronica Strong-Boag, " 'Wages for Housework': The Beginnings of Social Security in Canada," *Journal of Canadian Studies* 14, 1 (Spring 1979): 24–34.
6. For Ontario see *One-Stop Service.* Report of the Joint Steering Committee on Integration, Monitoring and Evaluation, Ontario Ministry of Community and Social Services, December 1984.
7. For a report detailing the declining value of social assistance benefits in Ontario, see Social Planning Council of Metropolitan Toronto and the Ontario Social Development Council, *And the Poor Get Poorer,*

Toronto: September 1983, Revised Edition. Between 1982 and 1984, Alberta reduced its maximum benefit to a single mother with a child of four years old by 14.5 percent, while British Columbia's rate was unchanged. In addition, the following provinces kept their benefit increases below the rate of inflation: P.E.I., New Brunswick, Nova Scotia, and Saskatchewan. See the Social Planning Council of Metropolitan Toronto, "The Adequacy of Welfare Benefits: Responding to the Recession," *Social Infopac* 3, 4 (October 1984): Table 9, p. 8.

8. For examples of recent calls for "workfare" programs, see: Leslie Bella, "Work for Welfare: Alberta's Experiment in New Improved Work for Relief," *Perception* 7, 1 (September/October, 1983): 14–16; "Working-for-welfare plan step backward, critic says," *Globe and Mail*, October 6, 1982, p. 9; "Pick worms or lose your benefits official tells welfare recipients," *Toronto Star*, April 6, 1983, p. 1; "Proposals for welfare workers rejected," *Globe and Mail*, April 30, 1982, p. 4; "Welfare or workfare?" *Toronto Star*, March 19, 1984.

9. Leon Muszynski and David Thornley, "Women and Welfare," prepared for the Canadian Advisory Council on the Status of Women, for inclusion in the forthcoming publication, *Women in the Economy* (CACSW), 8.

10. Community Concern Associates Ltd., (On Behalf of the Ontario Ministry of Community and Social Services), *A Study of the Employment Support Initiatives Projects (Year 1)* October, 1984, 1.

11. Pat Armstrong and Hugh Armstrong, "Job Creation and Unemployment for Canadian Women," (paper presented at the Social Sciences and Humanities Research Council Workshop, "Women and the Canadian Labour Force," University of British Columbia, October 2–4, 1980), 11.

12. No specific question, however, was directed to program sponsorship or financing; information is therefore incomplete on the precise extent of joint endeavours. Information is based on responses to the open-ended question "Apart from those already mentioned (reduction rate, wage supplement, day care) does your Ministry provide specific services to single mothers on social assistance to help them enter the job market?" Respondents were asked to provide a description of services offered; many supplied brochures and additional statistical information.

13. Martin Rein, "Work Incentives and Welfare Reform in Britain and the United States" in Bruno Stein and S. M. Miller, eds., *Incentives and Planning in Social Policy* (Chicago: Aldine Publishing Company, 1973), 151–87.

14. Irene Lurie, "Work Requirements in Income-conditioned Programs," *Social Service Review* 52, 4 (December 1978): 551–66.

15. British Columbia's definition of employability is as follows: 1) those with one child over the age of six months; and 2) single mothers with

two children over the age of 12. Single mothers who have health problems themselves, or whose children do, are exempted from work requirements in both British Columbia and Alberta.

16. Gilles Séguin, "Social Assistance and the Single Mother: An Inter-
    Provincial Comparative Analysis," Health and Welfare Canada:
    Policy, Planning and Information Branch (January 1980), 11–12, 28.
17. Andrea Maitland, "Fighting new cuts in welfare," *Globe and Mail*,
    September 5, 1981, p. 8.
18. Christopher Leman, *The Collapse of Welfare Reform: Political Institu-
    tions, Policy and the Poor in Canada and the United States* (Cambridge,
    Mass.: MIT Press, 1980), 215.
19. Leonard Goodwin, *Do the Poor Want to Work?* (Washington, D.C.: The
    Brookings Institution, 1972).
20. Income supplementation to the working poor who lie outside of the
    social assistance system is provided in the following provinces: Brit-
    ish Columbia, Saskatchewan, Quebec, Alberta, and Manitoba. For in-
    formation on these programs, see National Council of Welfare, *The
    Working Poor: people and programs* (Ottawa: National Council of Wel-
    fare, March 1981), 108–17; and David P. Ross, *The Working Poor*
    (Toronto: James Lorimer & Company, 1981), 50–54.
21. The "back to work" grant is $250.00. The 1985 cut-off point for the
    WIN supplement occurs between $975–$1155 monthly income,
    depending upon family size. In all cases monthly earnings over $675
    are reduced by 50 percent. This program has had a low take-up rate: it
    has been pointed out that the program does the least for those with
    low levels of earnings (The Social Planning Council of Metropolitan
    Toronto and the Ontario Social Development Council, ...*And the
    Poor Get Poorer*, 78–80).
22. Rein, "Work Incentives and Welfare Reform in Britain and the United
    States," 158.
23. See, for example, findings of the following studies: Philip A. AuClaire,
    "The Mix of Work and Welfare Among Long-term AFDC Recipients,"
    Social Service Review 53, 4 (December 1979): 599; Jonathan Dickinson,
    "Labor Supply of Family Members" in James N. Morgan, Katherine
    Dickinson, Jonathan Dickinson, Jacob Benus and Greg Duncan, eds.,
    Five Thousand American Families: Patterns of Economic Progress, Vol.
    1, (Ann Arbor: Institute for Social Research, University of Michigan,
    1974), 236; Patricia M. Evans, "Work and Welfare: A Profile of Low-
    income Single Mothers," *Canadian Social Work Review 1984* (1985),
    85; Jean M. James, *Family Benefit Mothers in Metropolitan Toronto*
    (Ontario Ministry of Community and Social Services: Research and
    Planning Branch, March, 1973), 101.
24. Employment and Immigration Canada, *Labour Market Development
    in the 1980s*, 33; see similar comments in Goldman, *New Dimensions
    for Manpower Policy*, 8–9.
25. Dorothy MacLellan, "The Impact of Technological Change on Women

in the Labour Force" (unpublished paper, Faculty of Social Work, University of Toronto, November 1984); see also Rosalie Silberman Abella, *Equality in Employment: A Royal Commission Report* (Ottawa: Minister of Supply and Services, 1984), 165– 66.

26. M. Robertson and S. Bertrand, *Some Evidence of Labour Market Segmentation in Canada* (Ottawa: Department of Manpower and Immigration, October 1975) have found, for example, that important differences in the stability of "primary" and "secondary" employment emerged only when the length of job tenure exceeded three months.

27. Community Concern Associates Ltd., *A Study of the Employment Support Initiatives Project (Year 1)*.

28. Ibid., xix, 36, 202.

29. Margrit Eichler, *Families in Canada Today: Recent Changes and Their Policy Consequences* (Toronto: Gage, 1983), 250– 51.

30. Figures extracted from Community Concern Associates Ltd., *A Study of the Employment Support Initiatives Project (Year 1)*, 124.

31. James, *Family Benefit Mothers in Metropolitan Toronto*, 39.

32. The impact of the sampling method on the length of assistance receipt was graphically demonstrated in C. Rydell, T. Palmerio, G. Blais, and D. Brown, *Welfare Caseload Dynamics in New York City* (New York: The Rand Institute, 1974), Tables 2.9 and 2.10, pp. 20– 21. When a cross-sectional sample of the caseload was taken, only 36 percent of the single mothers with one child had used welfare for less than a three-year period; when an opening cohort was used, the figure climbed to 63 percent. These sampling methods address different questions, and both are of course quite appropriate. However, a cohort sample provides a more representative picture of the use of work and welfare by the population of single mothers who *ever* use welfare, rather than those most reliant on social assistance.

33. Evans, "Work and Welfare," 86; James, *Family Benefit Mothers in Metropolitan Toronto*, 98.

34. Rydell, et al., *Welfare Caseload Dynamics*, 21; Michael J. Boskin, and Frederick G. Nold, "A Markov Model of Turnover in Aid for Families with Dependent Children," *Journal of Human Resources* 10, 4 (Fall 1975); 473. See also Martin Rein, and Lee Rainwater, "Patterns of Welfare Use," *Social Service Review* 52, 4 (December 1978): 516.

35. Eilene L. McIntyre, "The Provision of Day Care in Ontario: Responsiveness of Policy to Children at Risk Because Their Mothers Work," University of Toronto Faculty of Social Work Publication Series: Working Papers on Social Work in Canada, Series 0317-8382-22, No. 6 (1981).

36. For studies linking entrances and exits from the social assistance caseload with employment, see Elizabeth Durbin, "Work and Welfare: The Case of Aid to Families with Dependent Children," *Journal of Human Resources* 8 (Supplement 1973): 119– 20; Judith Mayo, *Work and Welfare: Employment and Employability of Women in the AFDC*

Program (Chicago: Community and Family Study Center, University of Chicago, 1973), 29, 41.

37. Genevieve W. Carter, "The Employment Potential of AFCD Mothers in Six States," *Welfare in Review* 6, 4 (July–August 1968).
38. Carole Swan, "Women in the Canadian Labour Market," Technical Study No. 36, prepared for the Labour Market Development Task Force (Ottawa: Minister of Supply and Services, July 1981); Morley Gunderson and Harish Jain, "Low Pay and Female Employment in Canada with Selected References to the USA," in P. J. Sloane, ed., *Women and Low Pay* (London: Macmillan Press, 1980), 165–222.
39. James, *Family Benefit Mothers in Metropolitan Toronto*, 98; Mayo, *Work and Welfare*, 15; Joel Handler and Ellen Jane Hollingworth, *The "Deserving Poor"* (Chicago: Markham Publishing Company, 1971), 139; A. Abrahamse, D. de Ferranti, P. Fleischauer, and A. Lipson, *AFDC Caseload and the Job Market in California: Selected Issues* (Santa Monica, California: The Rand Corporation, 1977), vii; Edward Opton, *Factors Associated with Employment Among Welfare Mothers* (Berkeley, California: The Wright Institute, 1971), 140.
40. See also Monica Boyd, "The Forgotten Minority: The Socioeconomic Status of Divorced and Separated Women," in Patricia Marchak, ed., *The Working Sexes* (Vancouver: University of British Columbia, Institute of Industrial Relations, 1976), 56; Gunderson and Jain, "Low Pay and Female Employment in Canada with Selected References to the USA," 168.
41. Armstrong and Armstrong, "Job Creation and Unemployment for Canadian Women," 13.
42. Economic Council of Canada, *In Short Supply: Jobs and Skills in the 1980s* (Ottawa: Minister of Supply and Services, 1982), 18; Employment and Immigration Canada, *Labour Market Development in the 1980s*, 60.
43. Goodwin, *Do the Poor Want to Work?*, 112.
44. Michelle Landsberg (*Globe and Mail*, September 21, 1982: B1) cited an Ontario Cabinet document which explicitly suggested the possibility of imposing a future work requirement.
45. Bruno Stein, "Incentives and Planning as Social Policy Tools" in Bruno Stein and S. M. Miller, eds., *Incentives and Planning in Social Policy* (Chicago: Aldine Publishing Company, 1973), 81.
46. Roger Kaufman, "Why is the U.S. Unemployment Rate So High?" in M. J. Piore, ed., *Unemployment and Inflation: Institutionalist and Structuralist Views* (New York: M. E. Sharpe, 1979), 155–69; John Kenneth Galbraith, Presentation to the Annual Meeting of the Family Service Association of Metropolitan Toronto, November 9, 1984.
47. Walter Korpi, "Social Policy and Distributional Conflict in the Capitalist Democracies: A Preliminary Corporative Framework," *West European Politics* 3, 3 (October 1980): 296–315; Manfred Schmidt, "The Role of the Parties in Shaping Macro Economic Policy" in

Francis G. Castles, ed., *Impact of Parties: Politics and Policies in Democratic Capitalist States* (Beverly Hills: Sage Publications); Leon Muszynski, *Democracy, Equality and Canada's Economic Future*, A Brief to the Royal Commission on the Economic Union and Development Prospects for Canada (Toronto: Social Planning Council of Metropolitan Toronto, 1983), 62–65.

6 Feeding Canada's Poor
The Rise of the Food Banks and the Collapse of the Public Safety Net[1]

GRAHAM RICHES

Feeding Canada's poor has become a major preoccupation for the voluntary sector of churches and nongovernment organizations in the recent years. The most visible sign of this activity has been the establishment of food banks in all provinces with the exception of Prince Edward Island and Newfoundland, the heaviest concentration being in Western Canada and particularly British Columbia. While the current data on the rise of the food banks is subject to a number of qualifications it is possible to report that between 1981, when the first food bank was started in Edmonton, and the end of 1984 seventy-five organizations in Canada calling themselves food banks were set up.

This chapter will describe the development of food banks in Canada in terms of their operational definitions and typologies; their origins, auspices, and funding; and the people who are using them. It will then consider the collapse of the public safety net as one important explanation for the rise of the food banks. The term public safety net will be used to refer to unemployment insurance and social assistance programs. It will also examine the political and contradictory functions of food banks and the roles they could play in helping shape the current debate about Canada's public safety net.

Development of Food Banks in Canada

DEFINITIONS

In examining the topic of food banks as the most recent social welfare phenomenon to arise in Canada it is important to understand both how they differ from, and contribute to, a broad range of existing feeding programs. These services such as soup kitchens run by missions and churches, publicly and privately financed school meal programs, nutrition projects, meals on wheels services, and bed and breakfast facilities offered by bodies such as the Salvation Army have for decades formed part of the residual stopgap services of the Canadian welfare state. There is no known inventory of such services but they clearly provide services of last resort to many Canadians.

While some food banks are engaged in direct provision of food to hungry people, many people within the food bank movement would not see themselves as funding direct feeding programs. Their choice of definition would be along the following lines:

Food banks are centralized warehouses, or clearing-houses, registered as non-profit organizations for the purpose of collecting, storing, and distributing surplus food (i.e. donated and shared), free of charge, to front-line agencies which provide supplementary food and meals to the hungry.[2]

What is stressed in this definition is the aspect of surplus food in the food production and retailing system and the intent of the food banks to make that food, which would otherwise be wasted or dumped, available to organizations which can put it to good use. This is done either through bulk food deliveries to hostels and institutions serving a wide range of high risk groups or through emergency food hampers distributed through social agencies. The emphasis is upon conservation, sharing and the coordinating or clearinghouse function, not the direct feeding of the hungry which is handled by the churches and nongovernment organizations themselves.

However, if this is the intent it is important to note several exceptions. First, not all food is surplus given that some food banks

Table 6.1   Food Banks Reported by Province as of December 1984

	Numbers of Food Banks	Year First Food Bank Opened Doors*
Newfoundland		
Prince Edward Island		
Nova Scotia	2	1985
New Brunswick	2	1984
Quebec	2	1984
Ontario	4	1984
Manitoba	1	1985
Saskatchewan	5	1983
Alberta	12	1981
British Columbia	47	1982
Canada	75	

* Based on available information.

SOURCE: Food Bank reports

purchase food. In fact, food which is donated by individuals has in many cases already been purchased and is thereby not surplus to the food industry. In the same way surplus food donated by supermarket chains has already been paid for. It is essentially surplus to the requirements of profit. Second, not all food banks operate centralized warehouses. The Kitchener-Waterloo food bank makes use of a number of pantries and Montreal Harvest makes direct deliveries from hotels and restaurants to the social agencies. Third, the Greater Vancouver Food Bank distributes its food bags directly to people through line-ups while other food banks in British Columbia have emerged as, or developed into, food stores. In other words, in talking about food banks, it is important to beware of stereotyping them and assuming they conform to one particular model.

MODELS OF FOOD BANKS

Studies to date suggest it is possible to classify food banks in Canada into two broad models bearing in mind differences within each model. There are, as well, certain functions which particular food banks belonging to one model have in common with those in the second category.

The purpose of attempting such a distinction is two fold: as an aid to explaining the origins of food banks and as an indicator, and perhaps predictor, of the functions which they can and might play in the Canadian welfare system. Based on a consideration of the origins, auspices, activities, and functions of food banks operating in Canada in 1984 we can speak of the *voluntary/charitable model* and the *labour/union model*.

The Voluntary/Charitable Model   Food banks falling within the voluntary/charitable model are nonprofit registered charities having their roots in the church and nongovernment organization sector. As such they draw on a pool of traditional volunteers, though there are exceptions where people working through Community Fine Option programs are engaged. Neighbour helping neighbour is a key principle. They emphasize sharing, conservation and the salvaging of surplus food. All have become caught up in supporting directly or indirectly emergency feeding programs.

As indicated in Table 6.2, food banks of this type have developed in most provincial capital cities (9), as well as Ottawa and other major urban centres (6) of Canada. They are also to be found in a number of smaller cities (35) and help serve surrounding rural districts. Eighty percent of these food banks are located in Western Canada with the majority in B.C. and Alberta. The first food bank was established in Edmonton in 1981 followed by food banks in B.C. in 1982 and Regina in 1983. Food banks in central and eastern Canada became established more recently in 1984. The West certainly led the East in the establishment of food banks, though whether or not this is an accolade of which to be proud is debatable.

One fact, though, which should be noted is that almost without exception the larger food banks in Canada looked to the U.S. food bank movement for guidance in establishing their organizations. Food bank personnel either visited food banks in places such as Detroit or New York, received visits from staff working for the St. Mary's Food Bank in Phoenix, Arizona (the first food bank to be established in the U.S. in 1966),[3] or corresponded south of the border. The present director of the Greater Vancouver Food Bank

Table 6.2 Food Banks Reported by Province as of December 1984

	Voluntary/Charitable				Labour/Union			
	Capital Cities	Large Urban Centres	Small Cities	Sub-Total	UAC Food Banks	Stores	Sub-Total	Total
Newfoundland								
Prince Edward Island								
Nova Scotia	1		1	2				2
New Brunswick	1		1	2				2
Quebec	1	1		2				2
Ontario	2ᵃ	1	1	4				4
Manitoba	1			1				1
Saskatchewan	1	1	3	5				5
Alberta	1	1	8	10	2		2	12
British Columbia	1	1	21	23	18	6	24	47
Canada	9	5	35	49	20	6	26	75

ᵃ Includes Ottawa

SOURCE: Food Bank reports

worked as a food bank volunteer when she lived in the U.S. A key impetus at work in the early days of Canadian food banks, and one which remains so, has been the Catholic church and member organizations. Their staff have provided one of the most important links to the U.S. food bank movement.

It should not, however, be presumed that food banks included within the voluntary/charitable model are all replicas of each other. They display important differences in their distribution and rationing systems and, it would seem, in their approaches to public education and advocacy.

Food banks can be seen to differ principally in the ways by which they collect and distribute their food. The *centralized warehouse approach* (e.g. Edmonton, Calgary, Regina, Ottawa) results in the collection, storage, and sorting of surplus food and its distribution to member agencies (either in bulk or in food hampers) for dispersal to needy people. They thereby provide a coordinating function for frontline agencies and are only indirectly involved in the actual giving of food. Such food banks would regard themselves as the true example of what constitutes a food bank. However, other food banks including Moisson Montreal Harvest operate on a *direct food supplier to social agency* (e.g. from restaurant to hostel) basis; a *cooperative food buying arrangement* run by the Kitchener-Waterloo food bank; and a *direct feeding program* typified by the Greater Vancouver Food Bank and many of those in British Columbia and New Brunswick.

Food banks also differ in their approaches to government, public education, and advocacy. Many of the *voluntary/charitable* food banks receive direct or indirect financial support from the three levels of government. This may come in the form of federal Canada Works job creation funding; start-up and job creation grants from provincial authorities, and/or property or rent allowances from municipalities. One food bank in Prince Albert even received sixteen acres of land from the City Council. This source of funding is clearly important to the food banks though it does place them in a delicate position vis-a-vis government when it comes to criticizing those government social welfare policies which have resulted in so many people falling through the public safety net. Some food banks wish to avoid public debate, while others accept that they should be playing a stronger role with regard to public education and advocacy. This theme will be discussed in the final section of the paper.

The Labour/Union Model   This model of food bank organization refers to the twenty food banks (18 in B.C.; 2 in Alberta) and six food stores also operating in B.C. run through Unemployment Action Centres (UAC). While the data on these is subject to a number of qualifications it is possible to view the UAC food banks and food stores as based on somewhat different principles and practices to those of the voluntary/charitable model. These food banks were started largely through the unions as a response to the massive lay-offs the B.C. government created in the early 1980s. They are supported in B.C. through the B.C. Federation of Labour, and the staff are employed through the Federation mainly through federal grants. Not only is there more opportunity for the users of the food banks to act as volunteers but the UACs also work on advocacy questions. In other words, it is not just the request for food which is addressed but help is also provided with Unemployment Insurance Compensation (UIC) problems; social allowance appeals; rental questions and the whole range of welfare and legal rights issues.

Food stores—at least one of which, in Quesnel, B.C., has developed from a food bank—also stress the principle of participation and thereby work to maintain the self-esteem of those who are using such emergency food services. As well, the food stores also operate within the framework of the Unemployment Action Centres. They purchase certain food items at cost and have a very small mark-up. People using the food stores have to be unemployed and in receipt of some form of benefit (e.g., U.I. or social allowance) and be members of the food store.

Perhaps the most important thing to note is that food banks in Canada (as perhaps suggested by media coverage and public perceptions) represent not just the response of the churches and non-government organizations but also of the labour movement. It is these latter groups supported by the Labour Federations as well as the work of certain ecumenical groups, the United Church and organizations like Solidarity in B.C. which have seen the necessity of working at the same time on the political front. Given the numbers of people who have been turning to food banks since 1981 this should cause little surprise.

WHO IS USING THE FOOD BANKS?

It is difficult to present data on the users of all food banks which is reliable, can be aggregated, and lends itself to interprovincial comparisons. There are two primary sources for the information: the food banks themselves and the member agencies.

The categories and figures presented here are taken from the monthly compilations of a number of food banks which are published in newsletters and/or information kits. Where possible there has been verbal confirmation of the numbers. It should also be pointed out that the food banks mentioned here have been able to keep accurate data as they are able to record food received and distributed based on actual demand for bulk and emergency (i.e., individual/family) food.

During 1984 the Regina Food Bank distributed food to just under 50,000 people for periods of three to five days; for nine months in 1984 the Edmonton Food Bank gave out food to 67,000 people; the Calgary Inter-Faith Food Bank served 37,649 people with one to three weeks of food for eleven months in 1984; the Toronto Daily Bread Food Bank estimated it feeds 10,000 people a month; the Greater Vancouver Food Bank fed 308,000 people in 1984 based on approximate weekly hand-outs of 2,500 bags; the U.A.C. food banks in British Columbia fed 34,000 people in two weeks in February 1984.

Taken at face value these figures are little short of staggering, though it is important to remember that between 30 and 40 percent of those receiving food are returning more than once. In Vancouver it was estimated that 90 percent of those in the line-ups had been at least once before.

Such qualifications might lead one to think that the problem of hunger has been overdramatized. It should be remembered, however, that the figures quoted above refer to less than half of the reported food banks in existence. Also that some food banks only permit a limited number of visits per month, some turn people away and others, due to lack of food, simply hand out less per hamper. In short, it can be stated that at least hundreds of thousands of Canadians have been using the food banks since their inception in 1981.

The demographic characteristics of those receiving the food vary between food banks. While adults comprise the majority (between 40 and 87 percent) it should be noted that food banks in Vancouver, Langford, B.C., Edmonton, Calgary, and Regina report that between 35 percent to 60 percent of their recipients are children and young people. Families comprise the bulk of the recipients, underlining the fact that women along with children are heavily represented. Single parent families are a significant group. The "new poor" are also said to have swollen the ranks of food bank users.

Recipients of social assistance and unemployment insurance are major consumers of the emergency food hampers, and their numbers also include those with no income and others who have been cut off or are waiting for state benefits.[4] In fact, the Calgary Inter-Faith Food Bank only gives food to those *not* in receipt of benefit. Low income earners are also reported using the food banks as are numerous hostels and institutions for such as battered wives, the mentally ill, transients, and so on. This phenomenon seems more marked in Toronto and Montreal than elsewhere, pointing perhaps to the critical underfunding and short-term funding of these agencies.

The food donors comprise all members of the food chain from the producers and processors to the wholesalers and retail outlets such as supermarkets and the corner store. Cooked food is also donated by restaurants, hotels, and hospitals. Churches and service clubs provide food as do many thousands of individuals through private food and cash donations and food drives organized by football clubs and radio and television stations.

This somewhat brief description of the rise of food banks in Canada gives only a partial picture of the actions and activities of food bank supporters and staff since the inception of food banks north of the U.S. border in 1981. There are many more aspects which remain to be recorded and described. What we can perhaps begin to analyze at this point are the reasons for the emergence of food banks in Canada in the 1980s and the impact they are having and are likely to have on the concept of the public safety net in the years ahead. Given the existence of Unemployment Insurance in Canada as well as the Canada Assistance Plan and related provincial social assistance programs, what explains the rise of the food banks? Indeed we might want to ask whether the new Federal gov-

ernment's concept of "the social safety net" extends as far as unemployment insurance and social assistance?

The Collapse of the Safety Net

The thesis of this chapter is that the rise of food banks in Canada in
the 1980s can best be understood as both the symptoms and symbols of the crisis of confidence in the welfare state. This crisis has
been fuelled by governments' insistence that inflation and deficit
spending must be curbed through restraint; by a reliance on private sector led economic growth; by a lack of commitment to full
employment; by the alleged public perception that state social
spending is too high; and by the breakdown of political and public
support for a tax based system[5] of social security which provides
adequate safeguards (in cash and kind) against the risks and con-
tingencies of unemployment, sickness, accidents, pregnancy, and
so on. In other words food banks represent a retreat by government
from public services designed to compensate people against all
those interruptions to earnings, livelihood, and living that Marsh
in *Social Security for Canada* (1943) addressed over forty years
ago.[6] In this context the rise of voluntarism is not incidental.

As symptoms food banks are concrete evidence of the breakdown
of the public safety net. They also act, no doubt unintentionally, as
symbols of neoconservatism. They are tangible expressions of the
view that the social costs of change caused by demographic, technological, as well as deliberate government economic policies
should be passed back to the voluntary/charitable sector. The consequence of such policies is of course that the most vulnerable
members of the community—women, children, those on social assistance, the unemployed, people of native ancestry, and low income earners—end up carrying the fullest burdens of such change.
In the sense that food banks are acceptable to the public they can
be seen to act as ideological marker flags of the new right's thinking that welfare state spending has been profligate and a major
cause of economic and social decline.[7]

What, however, is the evidence for the collapse of the safety net?

First, some might argue that the growth of food banks can be explained without reference to ideological debates about the crisis of

the welfare state. If one accepts the assumption—as certain proponents of food banks appear to do—that food banks are primarily a direct and practical response to the surplus or wasted food in the food production system then it would seem that food banks are essentially supply driven. It is simply a question of moving food from point A to point B where it can be more appropriately utilized. Food is not wasted, or dumped, and costs, at least to the retailers, are kept down. Moreover, important values of sharing and conservation of resources are promoted and sustained. From an environmental perspective these arguments are significant.

However, what this view avoids mentioning are two things. One is that no questions are raised about the operation of the food industry itself including food pricing policies. The other is that it appears evident that the first food bank to be established in the U.S. in 1966, the St. Mary's Food Bank, right from the beginning linked surplus food to hunger. Its three purposes were: to reduce the food costs of charities by providing surplus food; to act as a food clearing-house and to help solve emergency food needs of local families.[8] The brochures of this charity speak of hunger, starvation, and waste. Clearly, it would seem, in the U.S. income assistance and food stamp programs were insufficient as public safety nets. Private, charitable effort was required and during the seventies food banks in the U.S., through the organization of Second Harvest, developed a national network. The view that food banks spring from the breakdown of the safety net and are evidence of the rise of voluntarism would seem to be borne out in the U.S. As noted earlier, U.S. food banks have been a major source of advice to Canadian food bank organizers.[9]

Second, the situation in Canada reveals that between 1981 and 1984, the period which was the inception and growth of food banks in this country, unemployment together with unemployment insurance and social assistance case loads grew dramatically and in some provinces in Western Canada exploded. For Canada as a whole the number of officially unemployed grew by 61 percent between March 1981 and 1984. While the percentage increases in central and eastern Canada, including Manitoba, were below the Canadian average, the growth for Saskatchewan (90 percent), Alberta (196 percent) and B.C. (144 percent) were well above (see Figure 6.1). In these three provinces for the same period the numbers of people receiving regular UIC benefits grew by 92 percent, 379 percent and 178 percent respectively, well above the Canadian average of 67 percent (see Table 6.3). Social assistance case loads likewise grew by 39 percent, 41 percent and 92 percent respectively in the same three Western provinces, again showing the highest increases (see Table 6.4). The above figures do not include unemployment insurance exhaustees nor registered Indians in receipt of social assistance.

These increases have resulted in the overburdening of the safety net which, of course, in terms of unemployment insurance was only designed to cope with short-term interruptions to earnings not long-term joblessness. Similarly provincial social assistance benefits have only performed a residual stopgap service for temporary unemployment. The increased strains on these programs have themselves led to policies of restraint and cutbacks. Ironically, in the thirties as Struthers points out, in order to cut costs the pressure by certain provincial and federal politicians was to increase state involvement, pressure which, along with other forces generating fears of social disorder, ultimately led to the establishment of unemployment insurance in 1940.[10] Today those arguments are either reversed or not advanced. Short-term job creation schemes are promoted while benefits are frozen or cut. Food banks have emerged in an attempt to cover the gaping holes in the public safety net and nowhere is this more evident than in the three western-most provinces, especially in B.C. It is little wonder that the West led the East in the start-up of food banks.

Third, it would be a mistake to conclude that food banks owe their existence simply to the rise of unemployment and consequent pressures created elsewhere in the social security system. Evidence presented by the Edmonton Food Bank[11] as well as that collected from a review of one agency's records in Regina points to the inadequacy of social assistance benefits as the major reason for people applying to the food banks. This is confirmed by food bank directors across the country. This of course should come as no surprise given the numerous poverty line and cutback studies pointing to such inadequacies in the seventies and eighties. These were conducted by such bodies as the Canadian Council on Social Development, the National Anti-Poverty Organization, the Social

Figure 6.1   Unemployment by Numbers and Rates (March 1984); and Total Percentage Growth by Province and Canada, (1981–1984)

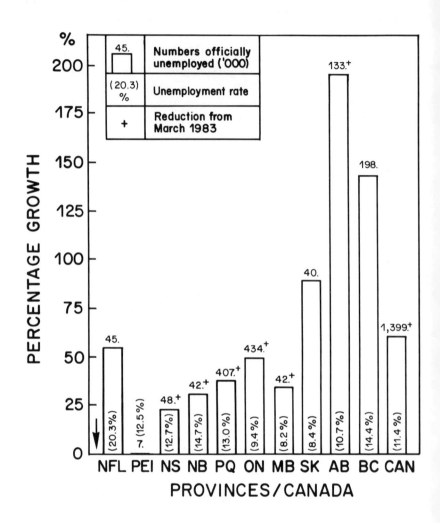

SOURCE: *Canadian Statistical Review,* June 1982 and November 1984.

Table 6.3   Unemployment Insurance Cases by Regular Benefits, Provinces, Territories, and Canada, March 1981–1984

	1981	1982	1983	1984	Total % Change 1981–84
Newfoundland	47,133	52,702	61,743	63,189	34%
Prince Edward Island	9,169	10,358	11,341	13,136	43%
Nova Scotia	40,530	50,423	56,490	55,764	38%
New Brunswick	50,666	57,962	63,863	68,676	36%
Quebec	281,806	381,549	423,683	389,053	38%
Ontario	193,491	262,091	383,162	316,131	63%
Manitoba	22,221	28,722	43,041	37,904	71%
Saskatchewan	16,463	22,023	31,590	31,563	92%
Alberta	20,223	40,524	103,809	96,870	379%
British Columbia	57,260	108,556	162,011	159,008	178%
Yukon	1,107	1,414	2,320	2,020	82%
Northwest Territories	623	872	1,595	1,328	113%
Outside Canada	124	179	258	193	56%
Canada	740,816	1,017,375	1,344,906	1,234,835	67%

SOURCE: 1978–1984 Statistics Canada, *Statistical Report on the Operation of the Unemployment Insurance Act*, Catalogue 73–001, April–June, Quarterly.

Planning Council of Metropolitan Toronto, the Edmonton Social Planning Council, the Social Administration Research Unit at the University of Regina, the *Report of the Manitoba Task Force on Social Assistance*, and so on.[12] The inadequacy of benefits is further attested to by the fact that all food banks included in the study stated that the heaviest demand periods were towards the end of each month when "welfare" cheques were exhausted. This fact is acknowledged by many government financial aid workers who refer their clients to the food banks. Overpayment reductions, cuts in rental allowances, harsher eligibility criteria for unemployed employables, and administrative delays are all cited as evidence of inadequate public welfare. This in turn has led to suggestions that the existence of food banks indicates that the public accepts low welfare benefits.

Table 6.4   Social Assistance Cases[1] by Province, Territories and Canada and Total Percentage Change as of March 1981–1984

	1981	1982	1983	1984	Total % Change
Newfoundland	20,275	20,009	20,747	21,800	8%
Prince Edward Island	4,563	4,958	5,010	4,400	–(3%)
Nova Scotia[2]	28,637e	29,441e	31,563e	32,200e	13%
New Brunswick	29,590	29,680	32,600	32,500	10%
Quebec	302,435	325,387	396,801	415,300	37%
Ontario[2]	203,255e	214,874e	253,097e	261,500e	29%
Manitoba[3]	23,612e	24,162e	29,010e	31,100e	32%
Saskatchewan	22,605	23,613	29,455	31,400	39%
Alberta	31,527	36,282	50,318	45,500	41%
British Columbia[4]	66,277	75,247	112,780	127,400	92%
Yukon	620	723	674	500	–(10%)
Northwest Territories	2,084	1,973	2,233	2,000	–
Canada	735,480	786,349	964,288	1,005,600	37%

e —estimate

NOTES: 1. A case represents any single person with no dependents, or a family in receipt of social assistance.
2. Family Benefits and General Assistance
3. Social Allowances and Municipal Assistance
4. GAIN: Basic Income Assistance only

N.B. Provincial program variation and program/statistical reporting changes may result in misleading comparisons and growth rates.

SOURCES: 1981 to 1983: *Inventory of Income Security Programs in Canada*, Health and Welfare Canada and Provincial Department of Social Services (or their counterparts), January 1984.

1984: Health and Welfare Canada—preliminary caseload data for all provinces/territories except British Columbia.

1984: British Columbia, Ministry of Human Resources, March 13, 1985.

Fourth, the fact of the inadequacy of social assistance benefits raises the whole question of the role of the Federal Government in interpreting and enforcing (or not enforcing) the conditions of the Canada Assistance Plan (CAP) (1966). CAP in its preamble and its provisions clearly indicates that people in need should receive adequate assistance.[13] While CAP itself provides no operational definition of what is meant by adequacy, it is clearly in the spirit of the conditions which govern the provision of the federal cost-shared dollars to the provinces. This topic is one which merits much deeper analysis than can be provided here. Suffice it to say that the Federal Government has permitted the erosion of the social rights and legally enforceable claims of Canadians in need to adequate assistance through choosing to ignore the general intent of CAP in relation to adequacy of benefits. It has also failed to relate the cost-sharing conditions to the ways by which provinces determine eligibility and operate appeal mechanisms (among other things). This is not simply a phenomenon of the eighties but has been a constant feature of federal-provincial social assistance arrangements in Canada in the seventies. Inevitably this policy of turning a federal blind eye has helped create the conditions in which food banks have emerged. Such policies have been aided and abetted by the introduction of more stringent eligibility criteria for unemployment insurance and the apparent unwillingness of the federal and provincial governments to move on long-term job creation through the public sector.

Fifth, while some might suggest that the inadequacy of benefits, dramatically increased caseloads and more stringent eligibility criteria are simply temporary or merely problems at the margin, we must ask ourselves what people experience on realizing that social assistance benefits are neither obtainable nor adequate. For them, at that point in time, there is no public safety net. It has indeed collapsed. They have no rights, no citizenship.

Lastly, it is clear that food banks are symbols of the shift away from institutional/citizenship rights models of social justice towards increasingly residual forms.[14] Such residualism espouses and promotes the development of voluntarism of which food banks are significant examples. In this sense, they reflect, perhaps unwittingly, the neoconservative presumption that private solutions to public problems are preferable in that they are less costly, promote self-reliance, and encourage community participation. Not unworthy goals if they were to work and if the reasons for such policy shifts had beneficial consequences for those most affected. Evidence from the food bank movement in the U.S. shows, however, that private charity cannot cope with the demand. Indeed, between 1983/84 when the U.S. economy grew, demand at the food banks increased by over 20 percent. Seventy-one percent of the emergency food programs surveyed reported that private charity could not cope.[15]

This commitment to neoconservative and privatized solutions in Canada stems from the era of restraint ushered in by the Federal government in 1975 when all Canadians were urged by Prime Minister Trudeau to dampen their demands. Even the NDP government of Saskatchewan in 1976 introduced a budget of "responsible restraint." Attacking the deficit and promoting economic growth through the private sector have now become the official policy of the new Federal government and most provincial governments. Questions of redistribution and the social rights of Canadians are unlikely to be given more than scant attention despite commitments to such concepts as universality and the social safety net emanating from Ottawa. Indeed, there has as yet been no official public recognition of the inadequacy of social assistance and unemployment insurance and the consequent rise of food banks. Has the shift from public welfare to private charity become accepted?

Political Functions of Food Banks[16]

Given this analysis, what functions are food banks likely to perform in relation to Canada's public safety net? It should at the start be noted that the development of the food banks in Canada serves a number of contradictory functions which depending on your ideological perspective can be seen as either progressive or regressive. From a progressive standpoint the media attention they have attracted has heightened awareness of the surplus and waste in the food production and distribution system. From an environmental standpoint these are important aspects of the debate and should not be lost sight of.

Food banks have also demonstrated in an immediate and visual way the enormous problem of hunger in Canadian society and the inadequacy of the public safety net. While politicians like to point to food banks as examples of public generosity and the voluntary spirit, they are sensitive to the charges that social assistance, unemployment insurance, and fixed income benefits are inadequate to put sufficient food on the table, let alone pay the rent. Thus the food banks are a constant reminder that unemployment remains the key social and economic problem in Canada. And that it is not simply a problem of single unemployed men but, significantly, of women, children, and families.

The response of the food banks has also shown that the voluntary sector (e.g. churches, nongovernment organizations, unions and corporations), albeit with some government support, is capable of organizing itself to respond to acute and pressing crises. It has helped give expression to people's sense of altruism and likewise fulfilled an important voluntary sector function of pointing to a need which demands public action. Most importantly they have fed thousands of Canadians who otherwise would have no food in their stomachs.

At the same time, food banks help to serve a number of social control functions, which could have serious and regressive implications for the development of social welfare in Canada. One of the most serious arguments made against food banks is that they serve to deflect public and political attention away from the need for long standing and urgent reforms in the social security system. Food banks can help us to believe the public safety net is working by leaving the public with the impression that the voluntary sector is simply providing a short term back-up service. They do this in two ways: first, food banks emphasize the point that their emergency food is only a supplement for people on social assistance. Mounting evidence, however, suggests the food is being substituted for public cash benefits. This is borne out by the heavy demand for food vouchers towards the end of each month when social assistance cheques run out and by the fact that government financial assistance workers are referring their clients to food banks. This action demonstrates official awareness, if not endorsement, of the inadequacy of benefits. Client organizations also fear that the value of food received through food banks will be deducted from social assistance cheques. This fear is not unfounded in Saskatchewan given the fact that social assistance recipients with children already have the amount of the federal family allowance deducted from their welfare benefits.

The second way food banks can allow governments to get off the hook is by fostering the public belief that food banks are capable of handling the crisis in the short- and long-term. The food banks are caught in an awkward dilemma. To raise food they need to convince the public and the suppliers that they are capable of meeting the need. Yet, as they do this they mask the problem of an inadequate system.

While it is true some food banks (Vancouver and Edmonton) have been calling for higher benefits and the need for governments to accept their public responsibilities,[17] the food banks are themselves not able adequately to meet people's emergency needs. U.S. food banks are not coping adequately with the problem of hunger, and those situated in Western Canada have been turning people away or reducing the amount of food received. Still, these may be facts the public does not wish to hear. To a large extent, the belief that food banks remain an appropriate response to a social problem of national proportions is sustained by the individuals, groups, and organizations who remain willing and able to contribute time, food, and money.

Food banks also help to undermine the concept of a publicly supported and financed safety net by treating assistance as a privilege and not a right; by returning to poor law principles of the deserving and nondeserving as they seek to ration a scarce resource in the face of growing demand; and by adopting the view that private agencies and relief committees can cope with the magnitude of the problem. In fact, as Struthers indicates, food banks help us to forget that the origins of public responsibility of income security in the thirties in Canada derived in part from a complete failure of the voluntary sector to cope with the massive problems of unemployment, hunger, and distress.[18]

The task of feeding people in the 1980s is also deflecting churches and nongovernment organizations from other priorities and activities. This is of concern to many in these organizations, particularly those who feel politicians are disregarding public responsibilities and legal mandates.

However, the most critical social control function of food banks is that, as they become extensions of the public relief system in Canada, they act to reinforce the work and productivity ethic through the part they play in ensuring the continued application of the doctrine of less eligibility. This doctrine which states no one on relief should receive more than the lowest paid wage earner is the basis on which relief policies are used to control the labour market. Poverty is held to be an individual problem and benefits are held at minimal subsistence levels. They are also widely accepted as adequate despite much evidence to the contrary. The true function of minimal relief is that it helps to keep the lid on wage demands and ensure that people on assistance will take jobs at any price. It assumes of course that the individual not the structure of the market is responsible for his or her joblessness. In that food banks act as extensions of public relief so they too come to play a similar function in helping to discipline labour. After all who wants the stigma of standing in a food bank line-up? How then should the food banks face the contradictions of their work?

A Way Through the Contradictions?

As voluntary agencies, food banks play their part in the network of welfare state provision like many others. They have to contend with the contradictions of their work which finds them ensuring surplus food is reaching hungry people while contributing to the maintenance of a welfare system based upon principles which increasingly deny people their rights.

Food banks and others associated with their work can find a way through these contradictions if it is accepted that gifts of food can be based on more than charity; if societal causes and not simply personal symptoms are acknowledged; if the long term can be considered and if public education and advocacy are seen as legitimate functions of food banks.

A number of questions which should be on the agenda include: what accounts for the increase in hunger in the 1980s? What changes need to be made in welfare state policies to recognize and adequately respond to people's basic needs? How adequate are current assumptions and concepts of poverty as guides to progressive economic and social policy? Where do government responsibilities end and voluntary agency support begin? Is food a negotiable item? Should food banks in Canada become a part of the welfare system as they appear to be in the United States? Is the current debate on Canada's "social safety net" sufficiently inclusive to take account of the collapse of the net itself? Should we be content to defend the current safety net? What short and long term considerations need to be taken into account in moving beyond it?

These questions and others are being asked in a number of food banks and organizations associated with them. The people concerned show an interest and a willingness to debate and work together not simply in terms of direct service but also through education and advocacy. Good examples of this are the Unemployment Action Centres in B.C.; the Food Action Coalition of Toronto; the research of the Montreal Diet Dispensary and Ryerson Polytechnical Institute into nutrition and poverty; the advocacy work of the Greater Vancouver Food Bank and of the Edmonton food bank agencies; and the questioning attitudes of the Regina Food Bank and its willingness to consider the issues it faces from various perspectives.

Food banks pose both a threat and an opportunity. The threat is they represent a return to the ineffective voluntarism and ad hoc residual relief of the thirties; their opportunity is to serve as catalysts for a re-examination of the public safety net and as promoters of social rights and entitlements. From this perspective the voluntarism of the food bank could have a critical and progressive role to play in shaping the debate about Canada's public safety net.

Notes

1. This chapter is a revised version of a paper given earlier at the conference on "Social Contexts and the Quality of Life, the Western Experience," organized by the Western Association of Sociology and Anthropology, University of Winnipeg, February 16, 1985. The research upon which this chapter is based is not yet completed. Data and findings should therefore be regarded as interim. Research undertaken on food banks included visits to major food banks and selected social

agencies and church organizations in B.C., Alberta, Saskatchewan, Ontario, and Quebec. Telephone interviews with food bank/food store operations in New Brunswick and B.C. were also conducted. A semi-structured open-ended questionnaire was used.

2. Compiled from the brochures of food bank organizations in Canada.

3. St. Mary's Food Bank, Phoenix, Arizona. Brochure, undated.

4. Sixty-two percent of those using the Edmonton Food Bank are receiving social allowance. Eighteen percent have no income. See *Hunger in Our City*, Edmonton Food Bank, February 1985, 5.

5. Unlike social assistance, unemployment insurance is only partially financed through general revenues. However, compulsory social insurance premiums are simply a different form of taxation.

6. See L. Marsh, *Report on Social Security for Canada 1943* (Toronto: University of Toronto Press, 1975).

7. See A. Moscovitch, "The Welfare State since 1975," paper presented to La Conférence de l'Association d'Economie Politique, 6–7 October 1983. See also P. Resnick, "The Ideology of Neo-Conservatism," in W. Magnussen, et al., eds., *The New Reality* (Vancouver: New Star Books, 1984).

> [Neo-conservatism] . . . invokes individualism against collectivism, and repudiates the principle of equality (both of opportunity and condition). It rejects the redistributive ethic of the welfare state and the interventionist role of government. It evokes populism and traditional morality in defending the social order of capitalism. It claims to be more democratic than its liberal or social democratic rivals (p. 138).

8. See St. Mary's Food Bank brochure.

9. It should be pointed out that not all Canadian food bank organizers accept all the advice of their U.S. counterparts.

10. J. Struthers, "The Rise of Public Welfare," *Briarpatch*, February 1985.

11. *Hunger in Our City*, 5–9.

12. See for example, *Canadian Fact Book on Poverty*, published in 1975, 1979, and 1983 by the Canadian Council on Social Development; *NAPO News*, quarterly publication of the National Anti-Poverty Organization; "The Adequacy of Welfare Benefits: Responding to the Recession," *Social Infopac*, published by Social Planning Council of Metropolitan Toronto to October 1984; *The Other Ontario*, a Report on Poverty in Ontario by the Ontario New Democratic Party Caucus, June 1984; *Income adequacy in relation to the poverty cut-off lines by family size, Montreal Census Metropolitan Area 1981: location and characteristics of the poor*, Surfacing the Poor Research Collective Montreal, July 1983; *The Unkindest Cuts: the impact of the recent Social Allowance Cutbacks*, Coalition of Human Service Agencies in Edmonton, September 1983; *Burdens and Benefits: Social Assistance in*

Saskatchewan in the 1980s, Social Administration Research Unit, University of Regina, May 1983; *Report of the Manitoba Task Force on Social Assistance,* September 1983.

13. The preamble to the *Canada Assistance Plan,* 1966–67, c. 45, s. 1, recognizes that "the provision of *adequate* assistance to and in respect of persons in need and the prevention and removal of the causes of poverty and dependence on public assistance are the concern of all Canadians. . . . " It further defines a person in need as someone "who by reason of inability to obtain employment, loss of the principal family provider, illness, disability, age or other cause acceptable to the provincial authority, is found to be unable (on the basis of a test established by the provincial authority that takes into account the person's budgetary requirements and the income and resources available to him to meet such requirements) to provide *adequately* for himself, or for himself and his dependents or any of them. . . . " Italics that of the author.
14. See R. M. Titmuss, *Social Policy: An Introduction* (London: Allen and Unwin, 1974).
15. See *Bitter Harvest,* a Status Report on the Need for Emergency Food Assistance in America, published by the Food Research and Action Center, Washington, November 1984.
16. The final sections of this paper, now revised, first appeared in "Feeding Canada's Poor," *Briarpatch,* February 1985.
17. See *Hunger in Our City,* 13.
18. See note 10.

Job Creation

7 Trends and Priorities in Job Creation Programs
A Comparative Study of Federal and Selected Provincial Policies

STEPHEN McBRIDE

Unemployment, Job Creation, and Economic Policy

Unemployment has the potentiality to become the most significant political issue of our times.[1] At present, it is far from realizing its potential. As an actual priority of governments unemployment has, in recent years, been regarded as less important than inflation. Job creation programs can be considered as one policy response to unemployment. But their role is limited by the basic political choice involved in making control of inflation the chief economic priority of government.

As the rate of unemployment has climbed governments have periodically proclaimed that job creation is a high priority and have introduced appropriate programs. Such programs do, of course, create jobs. But the analysis which follows suggests that, in general, it is not the intention of these programs, still less their effect, to significantly reduce the overall rate of unemployment.

In understanding the function of job creation policies, and the degree of priority they receive, it will be useful to analyze them in two contexts. First, job creation programs are part of broader labour market policy and should be considered as a subset of that area. Second, labour market policy, and within that area job creation, needs to be situated within the overall pattern of economic policy and the economic theory or paradigm which shapes it.

In most advanced capitalist countries, including Canada, the dominant economic paradigm of the post-1945 era, based on Keynesian economic theory, disintegrated at some point during the 1970s. A consequence, and indication, of the collapse of that paradigm was the much higher priority placed by governments on controlling inflation than upon maintaining full-employment.[2] No single economic school of thought has dominated the post-1975 period in the way that Keynesianism did the earlier period. Yet the various contending schools—monetarism, supply side, etc.—do add up, in the opinion of Thurow, to a re-emergence of the pre-Keynesian "equilibrium price-auction view of the economy."[3] In this sense one can speak of a new paradigm, though in its essentials it predates the one it replaced and is, perhaps, less unified.

The deep recession in the western world, and the present high rates of unemployment, are themselves partly the result of this change of priorities.[4] Similarly the anticipated persistence of high rates of unemployment can be attributed to the depth of the recession and to the deliberately slow speed of economic recovery, planned with control of inflation in mind.[5] If job creation policies are a response to unemployment they must be seen as a response to a situation which is itself partly the result of political choice.

In Canada, as in other western countries, the post-war Keynesian consensus brought with it a commitment to "high and stable levels of employment," generally interpreted as a commitment to full-employment.[6] It can be argued that in Canada this commitment was less absolute, and less honoured, than in some other countries,[7] but nevertheless until the mid-1970s the federal government did use the levers of demand management—fiscal and monetary policy—to assist in the achievement of levels of unemployment that were low by the standards of either the 1930s or the 1980s.

The Bank of Canada's conversion, in late 1975, to a policy of decreasing the rate of growth in the money supply marked the abandonment of this twenty-year policy commitment. In related moves the federal government announced, as part of its Anti-Inflation Program, that it would use fiscal and monetary policy to combat inflation and that the growth of government expenditures would be held to a rate less than the growth of GNP.[8] The progressive tightening of money supply targets, combined with the other measures, contributed to economic depression and rising unemployment from the late 1970s.[9] In Canada, therefore, a change in economic policy paradigms took place in 1975. In the second half of the decade full-employment was not an immediate priority of economic policy. Indeed the new paradigm was tolerant of, and to an extent predicated upon, rising unemployment.

In this context it seems reasonable to suppose that job creation programs would have less real priority than under the Keynesian paradigm. On the other hand public demands for governments to "do something" about unemployment could be expected to lead to some emphasis upon job creation as a response to the problem. While the new economic policies may recreate the conditions for profitable capital accumulation, which it has been argued were threatened in the mid-1970s, they do so at the expense of social legitimacy which is undermined by their harshness and deliberately induced unemployment.[10] Drawing upon these arguments it is suggested here that governmental emphasis on job creation, in the post-1975 period, is an attempt to legitimize overall economic policy, but that a dichotomy is likely to exist between the proclaimed and actual priority accorded job creation. This suggestion forms one of the hypotheses to be examined in this study.

A subsidiary question is whether the stated priority of job creation is primarily a function of economic variables, such as the rate of unemployment, or of political variables, such as the party in office, or the imminence of elections. Two further hypotheses flow from this question:

a) that the stated priority given to job creation varies with the rate of unemployment or changes in the rate of unemployment;

b) that the imminence of elections and the party in office makes little difference to the stated priority received by job creation.

Consideration of job creation as a subset of labour market policy will give rise to one additional hypothesis. Discussions of labour market policy typically classify its components into those activities which act on supply versus those which stimulate or create demand for labour.[11] Examples of supply programs would include placement services, career counselling, mobility assistance, training programs, immigration, and so forth. Programs acting on demand include job creation, wage subsidies, and other forms of assistance to industry aimed at creating employment, reduced hours legislation, regional development, and export marketing assistance. Clearly some of these, including job creation, act directly on the demand for labour while others operate indirectly and in the longer term.

During the 1960s Canadian labour market policy tended to concentrate on the supply side of the labour market.[12] The 1970s witnessed greater emphasis on demand side activities including a range of direct job creation initiatives. Comparative surveys indicate that such measures tended to incorporate goals additional to demand stimulation, for example, community benefit and improved employability of specified groups.[13]

Nevertheless, as the new paradigm replaced Keynesianism and became established, it would be reasonable to expect that demand side measures would be de-emphasized in favour of a more active supply side policy. This possibility provides our fourth hypothesis.

In evaluating the evidence on the four hypotheses experience at the federal level will receive the greatest attention, but two provincial jurisdictions—Ontario and Manitoba—are also referred to for comparative purposes. Before analyzing this material, however, it will be useful to provide descriptive background on the evolution of job creation policy in each of these jurisdictions.

Federal Job Creation

Our period (1968–84) begins with the cancellation of a traditional job creation program, Winter Works, designed to offset seasonal unemployment. In an era when the federal government relied heavily on fiscal and other general policies to combat unemployment, the program had been very much a "sidelight."[14]

In the early 1970s, however, there was considerable job creation activity through a variety of nontraditional programs: Opportunities for Youth (OFY) 1971–76, replaced in 1977–78 by the Young Canada Works Program; the Local Initiative Program (LIP), 1971–78; and the Local Employment Assistance Program (LEAP), 1971–83. Later in the decade, and in the early 1980s, other programs were added and finally consolidated in 1983 from twelve into four major programs.[15] These programs were Canada Works; Local Employment Assistance and Development (LEAD); the Job Corps; and the Career Access Program. The stated objectives of the programs were: (i) to meet employment problems caused by cyclical downturns in the economy or by unforeseen industrial developments (e.g., plant shutdowns or lay-offs); (ii) to encourage and contribute to local employment growth; and (iii) to support human resources development.

The programs begun in the early 1970s had emphasized smoothing out seasonal fluctuations in unemployment but had gradually evolved into a countercyclical effort.[16] In this sense the objectives of the consolidated programs of the 1980s reflected and built upon earlier experience. The severe increase in unemployment in 1981–82 did, however, stimulate a new generation of job creation measures including work-sharing arrangements, linked to unemployment insurance funds, and special programs for unemployment insurance "exhaustees."[17] Despite their innovative characteristics these new programs in many ways resemble more traditional "make work" projects rather than the early 1970s programs in which goals such as community benefit had received emphasis.[18]

Many, but not all (e.g., OFY) of the federal programs were devised with provincial participation in mind. The description of provincial job creation activity which follows deals mainly with actions *additional* to participation in joint ventures with the federal government.

Job Creation in Ontario

In the early 1970s Ontario Treasurers referred to job creation in the context of "full-employment budgeting" (for example, the Budget Speech, April 1971). Such job creation programs as were introduced tended to be traditional Winter Works type projects—for example, those announced in December 1971. By 1977, however, a plethora of programs was introduced—no less than five of which focused specifically on youth employment. One of these utilized

Table 7.1 Unemployment, Job Creation Priority, and Governing Party: 1968–1984

(1)	Federal			Ontario			Manitoba		
	(2)	(3)	(4)	(5)	(6)	(7)	(8)	(9)	(10)
Year	Unemploy-ment Rate	Job Creation Priority	Party	Unemploy-ment Rate	Job Creation Priority	Party	Unemploy-ment Rate	Job Creation Priority	Party
1968	4.5			3.6			3.9		CONS. MAJ.
1969	4.4		LIB.	3.2		CONS.	3.1		–
1970	5.7	mention	MAJ.	4.4	mention	MAJ.	5.4		NDP
1971	6.2	EMPHASIS mention		5.4	MAJOR THEME mention	–	5.7		MAJ.
1972	6.3		–	5.0		CONS.	5.4	mention	–
1973	5.6	mention	LIB. MIN.	4.3		MAJ.	4.5		–
1974	5.3		–	4.4			3.7	mention	NDP
1975	6.9	EMPHASIS	LIB.	6.3			4.5		MAJ.
1976	7.1	mention	–	6.2	mention	CONS. MIN.	4.7		–
1977	8.1	mention	MAJ.	7.0	MAJOR THEME	–	5.9	EMPHASIS	–
1978	8.4	mention	–	7.2	mention	CONS.	6.5	mention	CONS.

Year	Federal			Ontario			Manitoba		
1979	7.4	mention	CONS. MIN.	6.5	mention	MIN.	5.4		MAJ.
1980	7.5	mention	LIB.	6.9			5.5	mention	
1981	7.5			6.6		—	6.0		—
1982	11.0	EMPHASIS	MAJ.	9.8	EMPHASIS	CONS.	8.5	mention	NEP
1983	11.9	MAJOR THEME	—	10.4	mention	MAJ.	9.4	MAJOR THEME	MAJ.
1984	11.3	EMPHASIS	CONS. MAJ.	9.1	mention		8.3	EMPHASIS	

ELECTION YEARS:

Federal	Ontario	Manitoba
1968, 1972, 1974, 1979, 1980, 1984	1971, 1975, 1977, 1981	1969, 1973, 1977, 1981

NOTE: See note 22 for a fuller explanation of this table.

wage subsidies ($1 per hour) to those who would employ young workers. A major public construction program was also introduced. In the following year the creation of temporary summer jobs for young people received most attention. By 1980 the government was again relying on fiscal measures rather than direct activity to stimulate the demand for labour. These measures took the form of tax breaks for small business. Rising unemployment in the early 1980s led to new programs being introduced in the 1982 and 1983 budgets. A number of these were once again labelled youth employment programs but the bulk of the expenditures were for public works projects with most of the jobs to be created regarded as temporary.[19]

Job Creation in Manitoba

Most mentions of job creation in Manitoba Throne and Budget speeches in the 1970s referred to regional or seasonal make-work projects. The programs had only marginal impact on unemployment.[20] In 1978 a youth employment subsidy for summer jobs was introduced. It was not until 1983 that a major package of job creation programs was introduced under the rubric of a $200 million Jobs Fund. The Fund was to be used for a variety of job related initiatives including wage subsidies for new jobs, major and minor construction grants, matching grants to municipalities undertaking labour intensive projects, and a career-start program aimed at young people.[21]

Reviewing this descriptive material and the information presented in Table 7.1[22] it can be seen that job creation received greatest emphasis in three periods: 1970–71; 1975–77; and 1982–84. It is noteworthy that this policy instrument is mentioned more often in Federal Throne and Budget speeches (in 13 of the 17 years covered) than in either of the provincial jurisdictions. It should be pointed out though, that many of the federal programs were federal-provincial in nature. Provinces responding to such federal initiatives may not have viewed this as worth emphasizing.

The paper now turns to an examination of the four hypotheses developed earlier.

Table 7.2   Job Creation Priority and Increases in the
Unemployment Rate

Job Creation: High Priority Years*	Unemployment Rate	% Increase from Previous Year
Federal		
1971	6.2	8.7
1975	6.9	30.2
1982	11.0	46.2
1983	11.9	8.2
1984	11.3	− 5.0
Ontario		
1971	5.2	20.9
1977	7.0	12.9
1982	9.8	48.5
Manitoba		
1977	5.9	25.5
1983	9.4	10.5
1984	8.3	− 11.7

* i.e., years in which governments emphasized or made job creation a major theme (see Table 7.1).

NOTE: See note 22 for a fuller explanation of this table.

Stated Priority of Job Creation and the Unemployment Rate

Views about what is an "acceptable" rate of unemployment vary over time so it is, perhaps, more realistic to look at changes in the rate of unemployment rather than at the rate itself. For example, an unemployment rate of 6.2 percent in 1971 was enough for the federal government to emphasize job creation in that year but a decade later 7.5 percent unemployment was considered sufficiently satisfactory so as to require no special response.

Table 7.2 indicates that years in which governments stressed job creation tended to follow major increases over the previous year's unemployment rate.

The apparent anomaly represented by the 1984 decreases in the unemployment rate for Manitoba and the federal jurisdiction can probably be explained by regarding the continued emphasis on job creation as the result of the previous increase in the unemployment rate.

Generally it is unsurprising that government emphasis on job creation should follow significant increases in unemployment. In such circumstances political pressures on governments intensify and job creation programs are a logical and highly visible policy response for governments wishing to be seen to be "doing something" about the problem.

It is not true, however, that major increases in the unemployment rate always led governments to respond in this way. In Ontario, for example, between 1974 and 1975 the unemployment rate rose from 4.4 percent to 6.3 percent (+ 43.2 percent) without eliciting this type of policy response. In 1975 the Ontario government was becoming firmly wedded to expenditure restraint and to the control of inflation, if necessary, at the expense of rising unemployment. The Henderson Report considered that job creation programs were part of a "vicious circle of rising spending and inflation."[23] One of its key recommendations was that the expenditures of the Ontario government, as a percentage of Gross Provincial Product, should decline. In such a context job creation spending probably enjoyed a negative priority. Here ideological factors, or attachment to a new economic policy paradigm, seem to have overruled the political pressures emanating from rising unemployment.

The Dichotomy Between Stated and Actual Priority for Job Creation

Evidence drawn from the federal level will be examined to determine whether the actual, as opposed to the stated priority of job creation has declined with the adoption of a new economic policy paradigm. If a decline can be demonstrated there would indeed seem to be a dichotomy between pronouncement and performance.

Table 7.3[24] summarizes federal spending on job creation from 1971–85 in current and constant (1971) dollars. Figure 7.1 shows these trends in expenditure and in the unemployment rate. In general current dollar expenditures have tended to follow the fluctua-

Figure 7.1 Unemployment Rate and Federal Spending on Job Creation

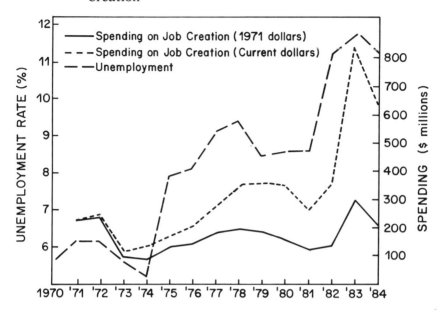

Table 7.3 Federal Expenditures on Job Creation

(1) Year*	(2) Expenditures	(3) Constant $**
1971–72	205.9	205.9
1972–73	223.5	210.3
1973–74	111.2	95.8
1974–75	120.3	93.5
1975–76	176.1	125.5
1976–77	200.1	132.3
1977–78	282.6	172.2
1978–79	356.8	199.6
1979–80	382.4	194.4
1980–81	356.4	163.1
1981–82	277.0	114.0
1982–83	378.5	143.3
1983–84	854.1	299.4
1984–85	634.9	211.9

NOTES: See note 22 for a fuller explanation of this table.
* Years in which job creation received emphasis or was a major theme (Table 7.1) are underlined.
** Based on the consumer price index with 1971–1972=100. Inflation for 1983–84 and 1984–85 assumed to be 5%.
SOURCE: Based on Douglas A. Smith, "The Development of Employment and Training Programs," in Allan M. Maslove, ed., *How Ottawa Spends 1984* (Toronto: Methuen, 1984), Table 5.4.

Figure 7.2 Number of Unemployed and Federal Spending on Job
Creation: Per Capita Unemployed Person

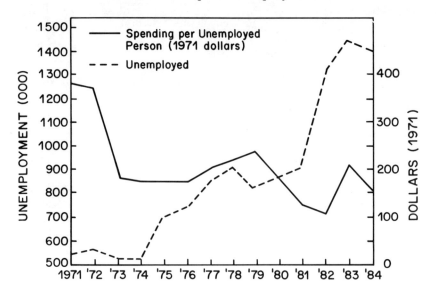

Table 7.4 Jobs Created by Federal Job Creation Programs as a
Percentage of the Number of Unemployed and as a
Percentage of the Labour Force

Fiscal Year*	Jobs Created**	As % of Unemployed***	As % of Labour Force***
1971–72	120	22.4	1.4
1972–73	116	21.0	1.3
1973–74	70	13.6	0.8
1974–75	60	11.7	0.6
1975–76	71	10.3	0.7
1976–77	47	6.5	0.5
1977–78	108	12.7	1.0
1978–79	106	11.7	1.0
1979–80	131	15.6	1.2
1980–81	133	15.4	1.1
1981–82	79	8.8	0.7
1982–83	86	6.5	0.7

* Years in which job creation received emphasis or was a major theme (Table 7.1) are
underlined.
** Based on Douglas A. Smith, "The Development of Employment and Training
Programs," in Allan M. Maslove, ed., *How Ottawa Spends 1984* (Toronto: Methuen,
1984), rounded to the nearest thousand.
*** Based on figures in Statistics Canada, *Historical Labour Force Statistics, 1984.*
These columns are based on the numbers (of unemployed, of the labour force) in the
year corresponding to the major part of the fiscal year (e.g., 1971 for fiscal year,
1971–72).

tions in unemployment. But while the shape of the constant dollar expenditure curve is similar, it is clear that these expenditures have scarcely increased over a period in which the unemployment rate has doubled.

Expressed in per capita terms, or in proportion to the size of the labour force or, as in Figure 7.2, to the absolute numbers of unemployed this represents a reduction in spending on job creation.

The impression of a decline in the actual priority given to job creation is confirmed by taking into account the number of jobs created under such programs. Table 7.4 expresses the number of jobs created as a percentage of the number of unemployed persons and as a percentage of the total labour force.

These statistics reveal a considerable fluctuation in the impact of job creation programs. The numbers involved are clearly significant and, as a result of these programs, many people have been removed, at least for a time, from the unemployment rolls, or conversely, have avoided becoming unemployed. The evidence does, nevertheless, support the interpretation that the actual priority of job creation has declined even though the unemployment rate has risen. The relative impact of these programs in 1971–73, the twilight of the Keynesian era, has not been equalled since.

Furthermore, since most of the jobs created are of a temporary nature the effect on the average annual unemployment rate is far less than the percentages in column 3 of Table 7.4. The effect of the programs is to "enable employment opportunities to be circulated among a larger number of people" by creating an additional number of employment opportunities.[25] But the number created is insufficient to significantly reduce the overall unemployment rate. Nor, in conditions of high unemployment, will job creation programs enable participants to re-enter the mainstream workforce at the conclusion of a project.[26] Participants may, of course, benefit psychologically and materially as a result of the projects. And, in terms of the legitimacy of the political and economic system, their potential disaffection may be assuaged.

Notwithstanding statements of federal government priorities, therefore, the real priority of job creation seems to have declined during a period in which unemployment has markedly increased. This finding is quite consistent with the anticipated effects of the change in economic paradigms in the mid-1970s. But where does it leave the emphasis and major priority which governments have claimed to assign to job creation? It can be said that in years in which the federal government emphasized job creation, with the exception of 1984, expenditures in both current and constant (1971) dollars did increase. As a year-to-year guide to real priorities, therefore, these government statements did have some validity. It is only when the longer term is considered that the statements cease to be a reliable guide to what was happening.

Viewed over the longer run, and taking into account the data presented in Figures 7.1 and 7.2 and Table 7.3, job creation, and the emphasis placed upon it in the early 1980s, takes on a quite different aspect from the situation in the early 1970s. In the earlier period job creation expenditures may have represented a real attempt by government to use this subsidiary policy instrument to restore full-employment. By the 1980s, in the context of the abandonment of the full-employment goal and the priority given to fighting inflation, the emphasis on job creation seems much more of an exercise in symbolic politics. Rather than playing a role in the achievement of full-employment, job creation policy had become a means of managing unemployment.

Political Factors, Job Creation, and the Supply Side Emphasis

It does not appear from Table 7.1 that there is a connection between elections and the priority given to job creation in government pronouncements. Table 7.5 summarizes the occasions on which the issue was emphasized or made into a major theme in Throne or Budget speeches in the year of and/or year preceding an election. The probable reasons for this lack of relationship are as follows:

i) from 1975 control of inflation tended to be designated as the major economic priority;
ii) even for those concerned about unemployment, job creation was only one of a range of policies that might be deployed;
iii) in the period under discussion the proportion of the labour force affected by job creation programs has ranged from 0.5

Table 7.5   Job Creation and the Electoral Cycle

Jurisdiction	Elections	Priority to Job Creation*
Federal	5	2
Ontario	4	2
Manitoba	4	1

* Number of elections in which job creation was a priority in preceding Throne and Budget speeches.

to 1.4 percent (Table 7.4). As conceived throughout this period, therefore, job creation *directly* affected only a tiny portion of the electorate.

How much impact does party have on job creation priority? No systematic attempt has been made here to measure the impact of party. But on the basis of an examination of the Throne and Budget speeches of the various governments, the following generalizations can be put forward:

i) all parties forming governments in the jurisdictions under consideration have been affected by the new economic paradigm. This influence is perhaps clearest in the cases of the Conservative government in Ontario and the Mulroney government in Ottawa;

ii) the Pawley NDP government in Manitoba is partially differentiated from the other governments by its identification of unemployment as Canada's number one problem and by its normative reassertion of full-employment as the chief priority of governments.[27] Even in this case, however, Premier Pawley foresaw the Jobs Fund moving from "the crisis-oriented job creation programs of [its] first year where government played the proactive role, to one in which more permanent economic development will occur, with government acting more as a catalyst to assist other sectors of our economy in seizing the opportunities upon which long-term growth is based."[28]

In Ontario a succession of Throne and Budget speeches, some of which contained direct job creation measures, place the issue in the context of the private sector being "the main engine of economic growth" (Ontario Throne Speech, 20 March 1980). Government's main role is defined as creating the climate or conditions in which the private sector will invest, grow, and, in the process, create jobs. A major theme in the creation of such a climate was expenditure restraint. The record reveals extensive use of direct aid and tax concessions to business in pursuit of this economic strategy. Direct job creation was very much subsidiary to the overall policy. Since studies[29] reveal that public sector job creation is considerably cheaper than stimulating private employment through the use of tax cuts or public expenditure, this emphasis can be attributed to the role of ideology or to the new economic paradigm.

A similar concern can be detected in Liberal government policy. In 1983 Employment Minister John Roberts summed up the government's approach to job creation ceding primacy to the private sector and placing government in a secondary role.[30] The Liberal government's overall strategy since 1975, as previously noted, stressed monetary and expenditure restraint.

This emphasis is even clearer in the case of the federal government of Brian Mulroney. The government's strategy towards unemployment in general, and job creation in particular, seems to incorporate the following features.

First, reduction of the deficit is the government's major stated priority.[31] The federal government expects deficit reduction to stimulate investor confidence and hence jobs will be created by the private sector. The greater emphasis on the deficit, as compared to the previous Liberal government, points to a fuller acceptance by the Conservatives of the post-1975 economic paradigm. Second, in a series of policy statements and press interviews, then Employment Minister Flora MacDonald stressed training rather than direct job creation as a major theme.[32] This suggests that demand side labour market policy is to receive reduced priority relative to supply oriented measures. This represents a trend towards the 1960s balance between the demand and supply aspects of labour market policy. How marked this trend will be remains to be seen, but its existence is a partial confirmation of the fourth hypothesis developed earlier in this paper. Third, there is a greater emphasis on the private sector role in job creation and on provincial involvement in federal labour market policy.

An overall conclusion of this rather impressionistic survey of the impact of party is that with the exception of Manitoba's NDP government which does present a contrast, the differences, which do exist, are at the level of degree rather than kind.

Conclusions

Five conclusions are suggested by the study. First, government statements emphasizing job creation tended to follow significant increases in the rate of unemployment. Such increases did not, however, always prompt governments to respond in this way.

Second, evidence from the federal level demonstrates that the actual, as opposed to stated priority given to job creation declined over the period as a whole despite rising unemployment. This was seen as the logical result of the adoption, in 1975, of an economic paradigm tolerant of rising unemployment.

Third, with the change in overall economic policy, job creation may be said to have changed its function. From being a policy aimed at full employment, it has become an instrument for legitimizing unemployment.

Fourth, party did make some difference in governments' approaches to job creation, though the differences between Liberal and Conservative governments were more nuanced than those between either of these parties and the NDP. The electoral cycle, though, seems to have had little impact on the priority of job creation policy.

Fifth, the Conservative federal government, seemingly more at ease with the implications of the post-1975 economic paradigm than its predecessor, seemed to signal a shift away from demand side aspects of labour market policy, such as direct job creation.

With the passing of the Keynesian economic policy paradigm the significance of job creation has declined. Further its function has changed from that of a useful adjunct in promoting or maintaining full employment to one of a largely symbolic response to unemployment: a means of creating legitimacy and hence, better managing the problem of the unemployed, a problem partially created by other aspects of government economic policy. If the election of a federal Conservative government signifies the consolidation of the new policy paradigm the need for legitimation

168   S. McBride

may be seen as less pressing and job creation's symbolic significance less necessary. As long as the term itself retains its mis-
leadingly "active" connotations, however, job creation programs
are unlikely to disappear completely.

Notes

1. Consider the public debate which followed the "Ethical Reflections
   on the Economic Crisis" issued by the Canadian Conference of Catholic Bishops in January 1983 and the continued salience of the issue in
   opinion poll results (e.g., *Maclean's*, 4 March 1985, 41). There is little
   agreement on the precise economic and social costs associated with
   unemployment. For two attempts to calculate these, however, see R.
   Deaton, "Unemployment: Canada's Malignant Social Pathology,"
   Perception 6 (1983): 14–19; and Social Planning Council of Metro
   Toronto, "The Social Cost of Unemployment Not Explored," *Globe
   and Mail*, 3 May 1983. For a comprehensive survey of the human impact see Sharon Kirst, *Unemployment: Its Impact on Body and Soul*
   (Ottawa: Canadian Mental Health Association, 1983).
2. Lawrence C. Hunter, "The End of Full Employment?" *British Journal
   of Industrial Relations* 18 (1980): 45.
3. Lester C. Thurow, *Dangerous Currents: The State of Economics* (New
   York: Vintage Books, 1984).
4. Bert Zoeteweij, "Anti-inflation Policies in the Industrialized Market
   Economy Countries," *International Labour Review* 122 (1983):
   563–78; 691–708.
5. S. F. Kaliski, "Why Must Unemployment Remain So High?" *Canadian Public Policy* 10 (1984): 127–41.
6. Department of Reconstruction, *White Paper on Employment and Income* (Ottawa, 1945).
7. Nixon Apple, "The Rise and Fall of Full Employment Capitalism,"
   Studies in Political Economy 4 (1980): 16, 18; Arnold J. Heidenheimer,
   Hugh Heclo, and Caroline Teich Adams, *Comparative Public Policy:
   The Politics of Social Choice in Europe and America* (New York: St.
   Martin's Press, 1983), 123.
8. David A. Wolfe, "The Rise and Demise of the Keynesian Era in Canada: Economic Policy 1930–1982," in Michael S. Cross and Gregory
   S. Kealey, eds., *Modern Canada 1930–1980s* (Toronto: McClelland and
   Stewart, 1984), 46–78.
9. Arthur W. Donner and Douglas Peters, *The Monetarist Counter Revo-
   lution: A Critique of Canadian Monetary Policy, 1975–79* (Toronto: Canadian Institute for Economic Policy, 1979): John McCallum,
   "Monetarism in Three Countries: Canada," in David Crane, ed.,

Beyond the Monetarists (Toronto: Canadian Institute for Economic Policy, 1981), 48–62.

10. Bob Chernomas, "Keynesian, Monetarist and Post-Keynesian Policy: A Marxist Analysis," *Studies in Political Economy* 10 (1983): 123–42. On legitimation and accumulation as functions of the capitalist state see James O'Connor, *The Fiscal Crisis of the State* (New York: St. Martin's Press, 1973).

11. G. Bruce Doern and Richard W. Phidd, *Canadian Public Policy* (Toronto: Methuen, 1983), 489; Klaus von Beyme and Ghita Ionescu, "The Politics of Employment Policy in Germany and Britain," *Government and Opposition* 12 (1977): 94; Barbara Goldman, *New Directions for Manpower Policy* (Montreal: C. D. Howe Research Institute, 1976).

12. Goldman, *New Directions for Manpower Policy*, 7.

13. Michael Jackson and Victor Hanby, "Job Creation in Western Europe and North America," *Industrial Relations Journal* 15 (1984): 37–45; Ray Marshall, "Selective Employment Programs and Economic Policy," *Journal of Economic Issues* 18 (1984): 117–42.

14. Doern and Phidd, *Canadian Public Policy*, 505.

15. Department of Employment and Immigration, *Government of Canada Job Creation Programs: An Overview* (Ottawa, 1983).

16. D. Dodge, *Labour Market Developments in the 1980s,* Report of the Task Force on Labour Market Development (Ottawa: Employment and Immigration Canada, 1981), 135.

17. Doern and Phidd, *Canadian Public Policy*, 522.

18. Jackson and Hanby, "Job Creation in Western Europe and North America," 38.

19. Ontario, Ministry of Treasury and Economics, *Ontario Budget 1982* (Toronto, 1982) and *1983 Ontario Budget* (Toronto, 1983).

20. James A. McAllister, *The Government of Edward Schreyer* (Kingston: McGill-Queen's University Press, 1984), 72.

21. Manitoba, *Manitoba Job Funds: Investing in Our Future* (Winnipeg, 1984).

22. In assessing the priority placed on job creation by the respective governments the following procedure was used:

> The judgement was based upon the governments' own statements of their priorities as outlined to their respective legislative bodies in Throne and Budget speeches (including mini-Budgets where appropriate). The data for all three jurisdictions were obtained from the summaries of throne and budget speeches (1968—84) contained in *Canadian News Facts*. A number of the summaries were checked against the original speeches and/or newspaper reports to ensure that this source adequately represented the content of the speeches. If job creation was mentioned in the summary of either throne or budget speech(es) for a given year, but without particular emphasis, "mention" was recorded in the appropriate column of

Tables 7.1–7.3. If job creation was emphasized "EMPHASIS" is
the entry. If job creation was identified as a major theme, "MAJOR
THEME" was entered. The intention is to give an indication of the
degree of priority accorded the issue in the governments' own pronouncements. This does not, therefore, necessarily imply that follow up actions reflected the same priority as the announcements.
Analysis of the tables is more detailed for the federal than for the
other two jurisdictions. In part, this is because better secondary
sources exist for that level of government.

Measures other than direct job creation were accepted as job
creation if they were tied *directly* to creating jobs (e.g., wage subsidies). Generally expansionary fiscal measures, which may have
been justified in terms of their job creating effect, were not counted
as job creation for these purposes.

23. Maxwell Henderson, *Report of the Special Program Review* (Toronto, 1975).
24. Based on Douglas A. Smith, "The Development of Employment and Training Programs," in Allan M. Maslove, ed., *How Ottawa Spends 1984* (Toronto: Methuen, 1984), Table 5.4.
25. Jackson and Hanby, "Job Creation in Western Europe and North America," 43.
26. In a somewhat different category are jobs "created" by the use of un-employment insurance funds to institute work sharing arrangements. The effect is to avert temporary lay-offs and unemployment which would otherwise have occurred due to the economic recession. Over 250,000 workers participated in work-sharing arrangements in 1982 and 1983. Approximately 120,000 lay-offs were estimated to have been averted. Excluding permanent layoffs which occurred (and which were not covered by the program objectives) a success rate of between 74 percent and 88 percent for 1983 was claimed. See Department of Employment and Immigration, *Pre-Evaluation Assessment: Developmental Use of Unemployment Insurance Funds for Job Creation* (Ottawa, 1983), and *Evaluation of the Work Sharing Program* (Ottawa, 1984).
27. Manitoba, Department of Finance, *The 1983 Manitoba Budget* (Winnipeg, 1983).
28. Manitoba, *Manitoba Job Funds.*
29. Cited in Dodge, *Labour Market Development in the 1980s*, 139.
30. Department of Employment and Immigration, *Government of Canada Job Creation Programs.*
31. Throne Speech (1984); Department of Finance, *A New Direction for Canada: An Agenda for Economic Renewal* (Ottawa, 1984); Honourable Michael H. Wilson, *Economic and Fiscal Statement* (Delivered in the House of Commons, 8 November 1984).
32. *Globe and Mail*, 18 January 1985, 15 February 1985; *Toronto Star*, 19 February 1985; Wilson, *Economic and Fiscal Statement*, 13.

8 Job Creation vs. Development in the Atlantic Provinces

MICHAEL BRADFIELD

This chapter reviews and evaluates recent development policies of the Atlantic Provinces and of the Federal Government. These policies are put into a theoretical perspective to show how they reflect or relate to the stages, export base, neoclassical and dependency theories. We indicate the inevitability of the major policy employed, the use of subsidies to attract firms to the region.

This development strategy is assessed in terms of its job creation impact and of its long-term development implications. The latter raises the question of changes in attitudes and institutions, and the need for alternative policies to provide a viable economy in the long run. These alternatives stress dispersed development and increased reliance on local resources, real and financial. Reference is made to the Mondragon region of Spain where such a strategy is succeeding.

Most of the job *creation* effort at the provincial level has gone into the manufacturing sector. Resource industries are seen more in the context of job *maintenance*. This reflects the conventional wisdom that the economic problems of the Atlantic region are the result of a weak and declining resource base. Economic strength is seen to lie in industrialization. This attitude is reflected in the very names of government departments, with departments of Industry or of Commerce being redesignated departments of Development. Thus to many, industrial development is a redundant term; industry is development.

While the resource sectors were not neglected, the attention they received was in the context of "industrializing" the resource sector. This includes the concentrated exploitation of resources, such as encouraging the use of the forest resource for a few pulp mills instead of small local saw mills. It has been suggested that such resources policies may not reflect intent, but rather the political difficulties involved in stopping the momentum generated by federal rural development programs.[1]

Twenty-five Years of Developing Policy

PROVINCIAL DEVELOPMENT CORPORATIONS

The Maritime provinces have been engaged in industrial promotion for more than twenty-five years. Nova Scotia's Industrial Estates Limited (IEL, formed in 1957) has been the high flyer. The New Brunswick Development Corporation (NBDC) was not active until 1963. Island Enterprises Ltd. (IEI), a carbon copy of IEL, was incorporated in 1965. There had been an earlier version, the Prince Edward Island Industrial Corporation, formed in 1949. The Industrial Corporation was active in the early 1960s and was not particularly successful.[2]

IEL and the NBDC adopted different approaches. IEL subsidized large multinational firms without regard to whether the firms had any economic links to Nova Scotia or to each other. IEL's approach was ad hoc, not subject to "the paralysis of analysis" as one of the corporation's executives was fond of saying. The NBDC, on the other hand, attempted to identify "keystone" industries which would fit the resources or needs of the province and would provide linkages with existing firms or attract new firms.[3]

Both IEL and the NBDC acted as "lenders of the last resort," but IEL viewed this as an entirely negative situation. Firms receiving support were thought to be marginal, unable to get financing through normal channels. IEL was secretive about who got support, fearing disclosure would indicate to a firm's creditors that it was in bad shape. The NBDC initially rejected a financing role, assuming that viable firms could get adequate funding from the traditional sources. When this proved not to be true, the NBDC undertook its funding role with much more openness than did IEL.

IEL's emphasis on large firms meant that it downplayed the possibility of assisting local firms. The NBDC recognized the potential in local firms and their need for management support services. They also made an effort to link local entrepreneurs with risk capital, both local and outside.

Both development corporations initially emphasized the provision of industrial parks to attract firms. However, whatever attraction such serviced sites might have had was overshadowed by the terms for the Regional Development Incentive grants introduced with the Department of Regional Economic Expansion (DREE) in 1969.

New plants or expansions of existing facilities were eligible for substantial assistance from the development corporations. IEL would provide up to 100 percent financing for land and buildings and up to 60 percent of the cost of machinery and equipment. The NBDC was also generous in its financing, initially funding an average of 67 percent of their clients' fixed asset investments. After DREE grants became available, the NBDC was providing an average of 47 percent of the financing of their clients' investments.

The late 1970s was a relatively quiet time for industrial expansion. Increasing unemployment and declining world demand, rising interest rates, and diminishing regional activity were the primary causes. The collapse of the Bricklin auto and of the Saint John Multiplex ventures led to the folding of the NBDC into the provincial Development Department, although the corporation should not be scapegoated for either failure.

In Nova Scotia, tough times in the international economy forced IEL to pay more attention to local opportunities and to the need for management support activities which had been growing since the early 1970s. There was also a revival of interest in industrial parks. Nonetheless, the dream of large "high tech" firms remained alive, evident in the fanfare generated for the announcement of $9 million in direct grants and as much as $41 million in training and infrastructure assistance to Pratt and Whitney, the aircraft manufacturer.

The Government of Nova Scotia's paper in 1984 on development, *Building Competitiveness*, emphasized small business, innovation, and technology to generate a more competitive environment in the province. However, much of the Government's attention was focussed on the hoped-for spin-offs from offshore energy development. Despite their public posture, however, they did not formulate policies or establish conditions which would generate long-term job creation activities from potential off-shore development.

Politicians seem to be attracted to mega-projects such as the offshore, Fundy tides, and nuclear power plants. A recent simulation study, however, indicates that even a very optimistic scenario for mega-projects in the Atlantic provinces would create only a series of short-term construction booms. These spurts of activity would add dramatically to provincial inflation pressures while doing little to bring the region toward full employment.[4]

FEDERAL INITIATIVES

After the Gordon *Royal Commission on Canada's Economic Prospects*, the Federal Government turned its attention to the deep and continuing regional disparities of Canada, particularly between the Atlantic region and the rest of Canada. The initial program, the Agricultural and Rural Development Act (ARDA), 1961, and Fund for Rural Economic Development (FRED), 1966, were focussed on rural areas, partly for rehabilitation and partly to aid the transition of older people away from declining agriculture. It was under FRED that the Federal Government and Prince Edward Island signed the 1969 Comprehensive Development Plan.

Industrial development policy for the Atlantic provinces was initially ad hoc, with special tax write-offs in the 1960 federal budget and again in 1963 when the Area Development Agency (ADA) was established. The tax concessions under ADA were available only in areas with the highest level of unemployment which tended to be the least attractive areas. Along with ADA, the Atlantic Development Board, later to become the Atlantic Development Council, was established to administer infrastructure funds and to provide long range planning, although it did little of the latter. By 1965, ADA's terms of reference were broadened to include the provision of development grants. APEC, the Atlantic Provinces Economic Council, was critical of these approaches, regarding the focus on "resource development and social infrastructure . . . as inappropriate considering the limited resource base and its implicit reliance on labour migration as a solution to unemployment."[5]

A major shift in federal policy occurred in 1969 with the formation of DREE. While it rationalized the existing rural development programs, DREE's primary emphasis was the stimulation of manufacturing employment. It was to assist twenty-three special areas with infrastructure and provide grants to processing and manufacturing industries. Regional Development Incentive grants have attracted the most publicity and analysis, but they amounted to less than one third of DREE's expenditures. In the Atlantic region RDIA grants were less than 25 percent of total costs from 1969 to 1974 and only 19 percent in 1982.[6]

DREE was reorganized in 1974, with emphasis on promoting opportunities by way of General Development Agreements and a series of subagreements negotiated with each province. In Nova Scotia's case, these subagreements reflected the focus on Halifax as a growth centre. In addition, parts of all provinces were made eligible for DREE funding, reducing the effectiveness of the subsidies available in the Atlantic provinces.

There is a feeling in the Atlantic Provinces that the federal government lost interest in their economic situation after the mid-1970s. DREE funding has been erratic and significant portions of their Atlantic expenditures have been on subagreements for particular projects such as the third Michelin plant in Nova Scotia and the Market Square development in New Brunswick. The Atlantic share of the Regional Economic Expansion budget has declined from an initial level of 54 percent to only 34 percent in 1980–81.[7]

Federal regional policy underwent another change in 1981 with DREE becoming part of the Department of Regional and Industrial Expansion (DRIE). The criteria for support were broadened in terms of firm size, sector, and location, so that even firms in Toronto now receive grants, albeit at a lower level of funding. Donald Savoie has noted that "by 1982 RDIA covered 93 percent of Canada's land mass and over 50 percent of the population."[8]

Evaluation

There are a number of criteria by which we might evaluate efforts to create jobs in Atlantic Canada. We will initially apply the measure of the agencies, jobs. Examining provincial and federal efforts separately, and restricting the cost analysis to financial costs, we conclude that these job creation activities are barely successful. When we remove the double counting of benefits and add in more of the economic costs, the balance tips against these efforts.

PROVINCIAL DEVELOPMENT CORPORATIONS

In examining provincial efforts, we rely heavily on APEC's 1973 study of the Atlantic development corporations, done at the end of their heyday. The most aggressive of the corporations, IEL claimed a total of 6,764 new jobs by the beginning of 1973. Of these, 5,537 were in firms which entered the province and about half of these were in one firm, Michelin. The NBDC took credit for creating 2,200 new jobs, of which 1,789 were in outside firms. They also claimed to have saved another 1,800 jobs which would have disappeared had firms not received Corporation assistance. IEI cited 1005 jobs created by their efforts to the end of 1972.[9]

What kind of jobs were these? The majority were in manufacturing and apparently were not significantly different from jobs in unassisted firms. APEC surveyed assisted firms and found that only one in six of the employees was given any on-the-job training of a formal nature, indicating that little skill upgrading was involved. This is confirmed by wage levels in the new firms. In Nova Scotia, average wages in the assisted firms were at the general manufacturing wage level—$5,331 in 1973. At $6,547, wages in NBDC-assisted firms appear to be significantly above the provincial average of $4,492. However, the sample was not sufficiently large that much reliance can be placed on these estimates.[10]

The corporations spent significantly different amounts on assistance, both absolutely and per job. APEC excluded the expensive blunders and counted only the firms still operating in 1973. Nonetheless, IEL provided assistance averaging $20,939 per job, with some cases running over $75,000. Assistance to outside firms averaged $22,937 per job, and 91 percent of IEL's funds went to outside firms. The NBDC had an average cost per job of only $7,697. This in part reflects greater efforts at supporting local firms which received 28 percent of their assistance. However, even assistance per job to outside firms was almost half as costly as IEL's, at $12,816. Island Enterprises fell between the other two agencies with a cost per job of $17,758. By 1973, one third of IEL's clients had gone out of business. The NBDC's failure rate was only 20 percent, but they were also a newer effort.[11]

Given the level of financial assistance, were the jobs a good deal? APEC's survey of their members, the majority of whom would be business people, showed that 63 percent felt that assistance per job should not exceed $10,000, or less than half IEL's average assistance.[12]

Roy George has pointed out that "on ordinary business criteria [IEL would] be classified a miserable failure."[13] Nonetheless, he concludes that there were enough social benefits in the form of wages and profits, direct and through linkages, to generate a net gain from the activities of IEL. However, the benefits are overestimated since the bulk of the profits did not accrue to Nova Scotians and we cannot assume that all of the incomes earned from the assisted firms are net gain. At least some of the workers would have been employed elsewhere, even if at a lower wage. Finally, two important costs are ignored: municipal and federal governments' expenditures and social costs.

As they are intangible, it is impossible to estimate precisely the social costs of development efforts. What effect has the industrialization of forestry had, as small sawmills closed? Have provincial governments been slow to introduce environmental or safety standards in order to save potential investors money? Forestry companies in both Nova Scotia and New Brunswick have been allowed to ignore forest management practices which are mandatory in other countries. Even the Ontario government has allowed environmental degradation and ill health in order to maintain jobs in metal reduction plants and paper mills.

We do have one clear case of the lengths governments are willing to go to protect the interests of the large companies. Michelin is considered a success by politicians as it has created over 3,000 jobs. It has been financed by Canadians as taxpayers and savers, through their governments and banks.[14] Michelin has manipulated politicians to prevent workers from forming unions to protect their interests. Major changes have been made in the labour legislation of Nova Scotia, at the request of Michelin. Despite workers' protests, these changes have been justified by successive governments as part of the price of jobs.

For a recent example of legislation to suit the corporations, we need only look to Newfoundland in 1984. The Provincial Government changed its legislation for a potential buyer of the Corner Brook pulp mill. The change relieves the company of $7 million in back wages. The workers are thereby made unwilling and unrecognized investors in their new employer.

If the workers who benefit from the jobs but pay the social costs argue that the costs are too high, should the rest of society assume the costs are reasonable? And if social costs outweigh social benefits and on strict financial criteria the development efforts are a "disaster,"[15] then clearly we must conclude that, from the provincial perspective alone, these job creation activities are hardly justifiable.

THE DEPARTMENT OF REGIONAL ECONOMIC EXPANSION

There has been considerable analysis of DREE questioning its net benefits, capital bias, and economic efficiency. The benefit generated by job creation depends on whether the jobs are actually new jobs or if the firm and the jobs would have been there without the subsidy. This is the "Catch 22" of business subsidies. If a firm would choose a location without the subsidy but receives a grant, then the firm has been given a windfall gain. There is a transfer from the rest of society to the firm but no change in firm behaviour. Given the regressive nature of our tax system and the concentration of wealth, this is a transfer from poor and middle income taxpayers to the wealthy. The unnecessary subsidy increases inequities in our economy.

On the other hand, if the subsidy is necessary to attract a firm to a region, it overcomes the disadvantages of the location. A subsidy which generates no windfall profit is then a measure of the degree of inefficiency inherent in the induced location choice. Thus, a subsidy generates inequities or inefficiencies, or some combination of the two.

The benefit to society of a subsidy is the gain in output which would not otherwise occur: the employment of labour which would otherwise have been idle. Thus, it is important to establish whether the jobs created in the subsidized firm are incremental, jobs that would not have existed otherwise. The Economic Council of Canada cites studies of incrementality for DREE grants ranging "from a low of 30 percent ... to a high of 80 percent ... "[16]

Even if the firms are incremental and need the subsidy to generate an Atlantic location, the jobs in a firm are not incremental if the workers moved from employment elsewhere and are not replaced. This is the "crowding out" phenomenon. The new firms may drive up wages or take vital labour or simply raise expectations so that existing firms are no longer able to operate on their previous scale. Of course, in a national program, there must also be concern that the firm has not led to the loss of jobs in other regions. There may be little national gain in employment in a case such as that of Pratt and Whitney if the company simply moves some of its Quebec operations to Nova Scotia.

There is also the question of capital bias because DREE's subsidies were tied to the firm's investment. Even that part of the subsidy related to the number of jobs created may be treated by the firm as a capital subsidy since it determines how much the firm will receive against its initial investment. A capital subsidy is less efficient than a direct wage subsidy in creating jobs.[17]

For 1970–72 grants, the Economic Council estimated net benefits of $290 million, $82 million, and -$94 million when incrementality was assumed at 40, 25, and 10 percent, respectively.[18] But the Council recognized that infrastructure expenditures are also part of the costs necessary to attract firms. Nonetheless they chose to ignore these expenditures and underestimated the costs of DREE's subsidies accordingly.

There are still other costs associated with firms receiving DREE subsidies. Many were granted corporate income tax and excise tax concessions, subsidies in the form of government tax expenditures. McLoughlin and Proudfoot have shown that the Federal government spent $4,439 million on Economic Development and Support in 1979–80, of which DREE represented 11 percent. However, tax expenditures for Economic Development amounted to $7,268 million.[19] Put in a different perspective, these tax concessions for one year were almost 50 percent more than DREE's entire 1969–81 budget of $5,059 million.[20] Thus tax concessions may exceed incentive grants as a cost of DREE's industrial promotion.

These hidden subsidies aside, if we were to assume that only half

DREE's infrastructure expenditures were necessary to attract the incremental firms, the costs of DREE's incentives would increase by $320 million, wiping out the positive net benefits estimated with a 40 percent incrementality. DREE would no longer be justified by the benefits generated.

DEVELOPMENT OVERVIEW

If DREE and the provincial development corporations are of marginal benefit when judged on their own, they collapse when judged together. And they should be judged together since they take credit for the same jobs. The direct assistance from provincial and federal governments often came to 80 percent of the total investment of a firm, as in the case of Michelin,[21] and is suggested by data provided privately by the NBDC and DREE. The benefits cannot be counted separately for the two sets of costs. As the benefits barely justify either set of costs, they are swamped when the costs are added together.

We can also measure the success of development efforts by examining Atlantic unemployment and market earnings relative to the rest of the country. The unemployment rate in the Atlantic provinces moved closer to the national average from 1963 to 1968. However, as unemployment climbed in the 1970s, it rose faster in the Atlantic provinces and exceeded the national rate by 4.2 percent in 1979, 11.6 compared to 7.4 percent, and has stuck at that level since.[22] The gap in wage and salary payments per employed person showed strong convergence from 1967 to 1975, but none since.

If regional development programs cannot stand up to scrutiny using their own criterion of success (job creation), are they saved by other benefits? Do they increase the stability of a region, its independence (from federal transfers or from reliance on outsiders for jobs)? APEC claims DREE grants increased employment instability in the Atlantic region.[23]

The concentration of jobs increases the sense of dependency on a few large employers. This has the effect of limiting political independence as the employer has considerable bargaining power both within the plant and in the community, as with Michelin's ability to affect labour legislation.

As would be expected, IEL's policies increased the proportion of provincial profits controlled by foreign firms in Nova Scotia. In the early 1970s, roughly 40 percent of corporate profits were foreign controlled. By 1980, this figure had risen to 47 percent. New Brunswick has a downward trend from a peak of 38 percent in 1971 to 18 percent in 1980. Newfoundland and PEI had very erratic patterns, with PEI showing a rise over the 1970s.[24] These data indicate both the extent to which profits and their investment potential are lost to local control and the increasing importance of decisions made outside the region.

Subsidizing large corporations in the resource sector has also been an expensive way to create jobs, and has served to stifle real development. Even where the Atlantic provinces have a competitive edge, the desperation for jobs has meant losing resource rents. According to the Economic Council of Canada, Newfoundland's resource giveaways have meant that "despite its substantial endowment of iron ore, base metals, forests, and hydro-electric potential, Newfoundland collects more money from taxing tobacco than minerals and more from registering deeds than from forest revenue." Thus "in 1975–76 Newfoundland received a scant 1.3 percent of the total value of mineral production; in contrast, the Saskatchewan government got 26 percent—the highest share of mineral revenue in Canada."[25]

THEORETICAL SUPPORT

If the subsidization of large, generally foreign-owned firms has been neither a financial nor a social success, why is it done? The answer lies in the theoretical perceptions of the relevant decision makers. The basic assumptions were that the Atlantic region had lost its economic base as technology and population shifted the center of economic activity to Ontario and Quebec. The resource base was either depleting (coal, forestry) or incapable of providing adequate incomes for substantial numbers (fish). The long-term solution, massive migration, was not politically popular, so work would have to be moved to the workers. Since plants did not move automatically to the Atlantic provinces, they would have to be subsidized to locate there.

A related factor is the dependency psychology which is so prominent in all aspects of Canadian life that it might be called the "Canadian disease." We assume we are second rate, that we can do nothing for ourselves. Our business community and politicians rely on foreign investment to bring technology, entrepreneurship, markets, even funds. We hope only to be workers in our own house; someone else must be master. Eventually we may build up our skills and our technology. In the short run we look to foreign investment to start the process. The problem, of course, is that the long run is made up of a series of short runs. Our dependence today is a function of our unwillingness to break our dependence in the past.

There are several theoretical props to the basic approach followed in the last twenty-five years. The staples theory argues that an underdeveloped economy must get its economic stimulus from the export of basic raw materials. In the optimistic scenario of the staples theory, the initial reliance on raw materials diminishes as the economy diversifies into manufacturing. Thus the resource sector is seen partly as a stimulator, partly as providing a job maintenance function while manufacturing provides the real growth. This is also consistent with various stages theories, with development moving an economy from concentration in the primary sector to a strong manufacturing base which leads to a growing service sector.

Of course, economies have and do move through these stages. Unfortunately, many identify development as the process of moving through the stages, not as the increase in output which allows the economy to become more service oriented. Converting corn fields to steel mills will not develop Kansas nor has converting small scale agriculture to tourism helped the bulk of the population in the Caribbean.

Both the stages and the staples theories emphasize exports in the development process. The market is the main mechanism and the government secondary in the development process, although a more pessimistic scenario can be developed in the staples theory, a scenario not very different from the metropolis-hinterland theory's hypothesis that power leads to the development of some at the expense of other regions.[26]

Another strong theoretical strand in Canadian policy has been the growth poles strategy based on the idea of urban scale economies, of public and private savings by locating activities in large urban areas. This has led to the concentration of infrastructure spending in a few urban centers to push them to a hypothetical threshold size after which they generate sufficient agglomeration economies to perpetuate growth. Despite limited empirical evidence of urban scale benefits and radically different interpretations of what generated them, the concept continues to underlay development strategies.

An alternative interpretation of the growth of cities is provided by centre-periphery theories which see the wealth of large cities as reflecting their economic power and control rather than their inherent efficiency.[27] However, Canadian policy makers generally ignore economic power, being content to pretend that our economy is a perfectly competitive system which needs only the occasional prodding by government to make it work faster to achieve an efficient outcome. Conventional analysis promotes this view: the Economic Council of Canada's *Living Together*, for example, contains no reference to centre-periphery theories or to monopoly.[28]

In short, the policies of the last twenty-five years are neither effective nor surprising. The poverty of the analysis limits the alternatives considered and the approaches taken. Because of a narrow definition of development, development policy has been a jobs creation policy. Since Canadian business shares the dependency psychology, the approach was predetermined. The lack of significant net benefits was also predictable.

Certainly jobs have been created, but the economic and social costs have been high and the benefits low. If we see ourselves dependent on outsiders for jobs, location in our country or region must be made attractive. We must give to them, we must not demand from them. Because they are profit maximizers, we give them large subsidies. Because they maintain their traditional sources of supply, spinoffs are minimal. Because they control the profits generated, future funds are constrained. Because they continue to do their research and development activities at head office, our technical capacity is not enhanced.

Changes in development policies reflect changes in international conditions rather than in analysis. Illustrative of this is the 1985 *Intergovernmental Position Paper on the Principles and Framework for Regional Economic Development*, which contains traditional attitudes toward development with only one reference to alternative organizations such as cooperatives.[29] How serious are federal and provincial decision makers about promoting a climate for the development of small local enterprises? Moreover, the specious job creation argument for Canadian participation in the U.S. "Star Wars" venture indicates that nothing has changed.

Tangible evidence of this can be found in the 1982–1983 Annual Reports (joint) of the Departments of Industry, Trade and Commerce, and of Regional Economic Expansion. These departments provided almost as much in Defence Industry Productivity grants ($131,965 million) as they did in regional industrial incentives ($142,756 million). Apparently our politicians do not agree with the picket sign "we may be dying for a living, but we don't want to kill for one." An industrial strategy based on subsidized Canadian dependence on military contracts would be the ultimate perversion of economic development.

Alternatives

If we are to break the "jobs at any price" approach to development, we must redefine what we mean by development. Economic targets are not the goals of society, they are part of the means to society's goals. Even the Economic Council of Canada recognized society's goals as "well-being for individuals and equity among them."[30] And well-being is not strictly material but "the extent to which the material, socio-cultural, psychological, and other needs of society are met." Unfortunately, the Council quickly confused means and ends, stating "the ultimate goal is surely to improve income and employment opportunities."[31]

But if we restrict development to economic goals, we will ignore or dismiss noneconomic costs, be they political, cultural, environmental, or social. This is not good economics, since society must use its scarce resources to meet all of its needs, not just its material needs.

Economic development can only be defined within the context of what kind of society we are working towards. Are we to be more self-reliant, as individuals and a society, more in command of our lives? Will greater output allow us more leisure to enjoy cultural and political activities, or will the cost of growth be the further deterioration of our culture, of our independence, and of our environment? While jobs and incomes cannot be ignored, particularly in regions where so many are without secure jobs or adequate incomes, a broader definition of development forces us to seek strategies consistent with all our goals.

Our development policies should recognize that unemployment represents a potential as well as a crisis. The potential is the additional output which society can achieve from job creation. But that implies not any jobs, but jobs which meet society's needs. Thus, the unemployed should not be seen as a burden but as a possibility, as squandered savings which could be invested to build a better society.

It should also be obvious that the sense of dependency on foreign investment cannot be explained by an inability to save and invest. Atlantic Canada generates a substantial share of the investment funds financing the real investment in the region. Unfortunately, those funds are either taken out of the region or turned over to foreign "investors" who receive control and profits while Canadians take the risk.

There is one other bit of mythology that needs to be laid to rest: that development and productivity are a function of a "favourable" (large) resources to population ratio. It is true that many areas got their initial market stimulus from the development of resources, but many regions and countries have experienced rapid economic growth and prosperity without resources. For instance, Japan's phenomenal success has been despite its lack of resources and its large population. A major factor in Japan's success is its people, their willingness to save, their imagination, their drive. As Levine pointed out, "Effective entrepreneurship— private or state—is the most important single progenitor of economic development."[32] While an abundance of resources clearly makes economic growth easier, it is neither a sufficient nor even a necessary condition for success.

But to do more ourselves we have to be prepared for a process which is certainly less dramatic and perhaps slower, at least in the initial stages. The process also involves challenges to and changes in economic structures.

We need a long-term strategy to build our regions through and for people. This starts with identifying the needs and aspirations of those people: What are we building for? It requires an assessment of human skills and natural resources: What are we building with? It involves an understanding of the region's weaknesses: What must be built up? Among these weaknesses must be included the institutions and forces which have retarded development: What are we up against? And finally, the strategy must relate the internal possibilities to external conditions, markets, and trends.

This is not an isolated process, pretending the outside world does not exist. Rather it means being more selective in how we relate to the rest of the world, finding alternative ways to deal with it. It is a refusal to be co-opted and exploited. It involves developing alternatives to very powerful institutions: strengthening credit unions, stimulating workers' co-ops, promoting industrial democracy.

MONDRAGON

One example of local development is in Spain where a strong cooperative movement has developed successfully in the Mondragon region. It is a coordinated and integrated strategy which blends democratic worker control and social consciousness with economic growth. While not a model to be adopted totally, it provides useful insights.

The Mondragon cooperative movement began with a clear conception of what it was working for—the personal development and dignity of workers with local control over their economy. The founders also knew what they were working with—a tradition of industrialization and of cooperation even among farmers, a tradition of hard work and saving, and a pool of industrial skills. But they also recognized their weaknesses and the importance of dealing with them before they became binding constraints on development.

The first project in Mondragon began with the need for greater training; a technical school was started in 1943. To provide a creative work environment, a small manufacturing company was formed in 1956. The need for financing independent of traditional institutions was soon recognized and a credit union was established in 1959. As their manufacturing and finance base broadened, the need to strengthen their entrepreneurial, managerial and technical capabilities became obvious and in 1969 the central credit union set up a management services division. By 1978, it employed more than 100 economists, accountants, and other experts.

Thomas and Logan have documented the success and growth of the Mondragon cooperative movement. Two decades after the first small firm was opened, the Mondragon accounted for one of every eight industrial jobs, its credit union had 13 percent of the region's deposits, and its educational co-ops went from nursery school to technical school.[33] Moreover, this rapid growth was accompanied by only one failure!

The success of the Mondragon co-ops can also be seen in their wage levels. The workers annually have voted to keep their wages down to the level of the capitalist firms, to plough back the surplus for greater expansion of activities and jobs. The absenteeism rate in the 135 co-ops, with their 15,000 cooperators, is one half to one third of the absenteeism of the capitalist firms.[34]

Judged by their criteria of economic success, Thomas and Logan felt that the Mondragon is efficient, despite their cooperative basis and social goals. In analyzing the reasons for this success, Bradly and Gelb conclude it is *a function* of their cooperative organization and goals.[35] This performance far outstrips that of IEL which was set up in Nova Scotia at the same time the Mondragon was establishing its first manufacturing plant. IEL had additional federal funds and tax concessions; the Mondragon faced the antipathy and harassment of Franco's government. Yet IEL has created fewer than half as many jobs and has lost about one third of its funds. In Atlantic Canada, job creation policies, federal and provincial, have alienated workers in their jobs, in their communities, and from control over their lives and their economy. Mondragon has increased self-reliance and local control over production, finance, distribution, marketing, and technology. In other words, the Mondragon has been able to achieve significant economic development accompanied by impressive social achievements which many Atlantic Canadians no longer even dream of.

The Mondragon co-ops have gradually built their own institutions for the different phases of production and finance. While not totally independent of traditional institutions, they created viable parallel structures. They have maintained the principle of worker control and showed that it can be at least as efficient as private capitalism.

The Mondragon experiment shows what can be done when people are determined, even if they are not particularly prosperous. While the Atlantic provinces lack the history and cohesiveness of the Mondragon region, we also do not suffer from as many weaknesses or constraints.

There are Canadian examples as well. In Quebec, both the unions and the Government are attempting to consolidate local savings for local investments.[36] Quebec also provides the example of Tembec, a pulp mill rescued from the scrap heap and made viable by its workers.[37] In Nova Scotia, there are businesses which have penetrated international markets, sometimes using traditional skills for new products and sometimes using traditional resources with new marketing insights. Other firms are developing a market niche in high technology. There are also local examples of community development corporations.[38]

Conclusions

Can the success of a few firms or even of a region justify a complete reversal of policy? Are there enough jobs in a local development strategy or would it condemn people to unemployment and poverty? IEL's own experience financing small business has shown that it is less costly than the large firm approach. The $13 million lent to small firms—roughly equal to just the interest subsidy to Michelin—created 2,500 jobs, a cost of only $5,200 per job.[39] In the U.S., of the 9.6 million jobs created from 1969 to 1976, "the *Fortune* 1000 companies accounted for only one percent.... The small business community accounted for ... more than 75 percent."[40]

Traditional approaches to development, even to job creation, have not been successful. There is a need for alternative strategies. An important component, and one which is paid lip service in existing policies, although not in expenditures, is the development of a viable small firm economy, with emphasis on community development corporations and workers' co-ops.

No single approach will provide all of the solutions to Canada's regional disparities. Past policies have been too expensive and too narrow. Relying on military exports is also a no-win proposition. We must put our funds and our energies into approaches which come to grips with the underlying causes of disparities and meet society's many needs. This means radical changes in policies and in institutions. Examples like the Mondragon are therefore crucial if people and governments are to recognize that these changes are possible.

Acknowledgement

Thanks, but not blame, are owed to Patrick Kerans for his many suggestions on various drafts of this paper, and to an anonymous reviewer.

Notes

1. Mike Cleland, "The General Development Agreement and Provincial Economic Development," in Barbara Jamieson, ed., *Governing Nova Scotia* (Halifax: School of Public Administration, 1984), 163–79.
2. Philip Mathias, *Forced Growth* (Toronto: James Lewis & Samuel, 1971).
3. New Brunswick Development Corporation, *Annual Report* (1964), (Fredericton: NBDC, 1964), 4.
4. Melvin Cross and Michael Bradfield, *Major Investments in the Atlantic Provinces, 1983 to 1995* (Calgary: Canada West Foundation, 1983).
5. Atlantic Provinces Economic Council, *An Analysis of the Re-organization for Economic Development* (Halifax: APEC, 1982), 6.
6. Economic Council of Canada, *Living Together: A Study of Regional Disparities* (Ottawa: Minister of Supply and Services, 1977), 151; Department of Industry, Trade and Commerce and Department of Regional Economic Expansion, *Annual Reports 1982–83* (Ottawa: Minister of Supply and Services, 1984), 55.
7. APEC, *Analysis of the Re-organization*, 20.
8. Donald J. Savoie, "Cash Incentives Versus Tax Incentives for Regional Development: Issues and Considerations," *The Canadian Journal of Regional Science* 8, 1 (1985): 4.
9. APEC, *Seventh Annual Review: The Atlantic Economy* (Halifax: APEC, 1973), 63, 66, 104–5.
10. Ibid., 69.
11. Ibid., 66–69.
12. Ibid., 68.

190   M. Bradfield

13. Roy E. George, *The Life and Times of Industrial Estates Ltd.* (Halifax: Dalhousie Institute of Public Affairs, 1974), 107.
14. Michael Bradfield, "Michelin in Nova Scotia," *Canadian Forum* 66, 714 (1981): 9–11.
15. George, *Industrial Estates Ltd.*, 106.
16. Economic Council of Canada, *Living Together*, 161.
17. George H. Borts, "Criteria for the Evaluation of Regional Development Programs," in W. Z. Hirsch, ed., *Regional Accounting for Policy Decision* (Baltimore: The John Hopkins Press, 1966), 206.
18. Economic Council of Canada, *Living Together*, 165.
19. Kevin McLoughlin and Stuart B. Proudfoot, "Giving by Not Taking: A Primer on Tax Expenditures," *Canadian Public Policy* 7, 2 (1981): 334.
20. APEC, *Analysis of the Re-organization*, 20.
21. Bradfield, "Michelin in Nova Scotia," 9–11.
22. Economic Council of Canada, *Living Together;* Bank of Canada, *Bank of Canada Review* (1984), (Ottawa: Bank of Canada, 1984), S 118, S 120.
23. APEC, *Industrial Incentives Programs in the Atlantic Economy* (Halifax: APEC, 1982), 164.
24. Statistics Canada, *Corporations and Labour Unions Return Act*, Part 1: Corporations (Ottawa: Department of Industry, Trade and Commerce), 61–210.
25. Economic Council of Canada, *Newfoundland: From Dependency to Self-reliance* (Ottawa: Minister of Supply and Services, 1980), 36, 109.
26. Stuart Holland, *Capital Versus the Regions* (London: Macmillan Press, 1976).
27. John Friedmann, "A General Theory of Polarized Growth," in Niles Hansen, ed., *Growth Centers in Regional Economic Development* (New York: Free Press, 1972), 82–107. David Harvey, *Social Justice and the City* (London: Edward Arnold, 1973).
28. Economic Council of Canada, *Living Together*.
29. *Intergovernmental Position Paper on the Principles and Framework for Regional Economic Development*, 12.
30. Economic Council of Canada, *Living Together*, 11.
31. Ibid., 18.
32. APEC, *Retardation and Entrepreneurship* (Halifax: APEC, 1965), 2.
33. Henk Thomas and Chris Logan, *Mondragon: An Economic Analysis* (London: George Allen and Unwin, 1982).
34. Ibid., 33.
35. Keith Bradley and Alan Gelb, "The Mondragon Cooperatives: Guidelines for a Cooperative Economy?" in Derek Jones and Jan Svejnar, *Participatory and Self-Managed Firms* 1 (Lexington: Lexington Books, 1982), 155.
36. Ted Jackson, *Worker Ownership and Economic Democracy*, Research Report 14 (Ottawa: Canadian Centre for Policy Alternatives, n.d.), 8, 18.

37. A. Booth, "Tembec: The Little Mill that Wouldn't Die," *Financial Post*, 1 October 1983.

38. DPA Consulting Ltd., *Towards a Provincial Policy on Community Development* (Halifax: DPA Consulting Ltd., 1982). See also Greg MacLeod, *New Age Business* (Ottawa: Canadian Council on Social Development, 1985).

39. IEL, *Annual Report* (1982), 5.

40. James Keith MacDonald, *The Economic Performance of Small Businesses in Nova Scotia: A Comparative Study* (unpublished M.A. thesis, Dalhousie University, 1982), 7.

9 "Half a Loaf Is Better Than None"
The Newfoundland Rural Development Movement's Adaptation to the Crisis of Seasonal Unemployment

RICHARD P. FUCHS

The European settlement of Newfoundland occurred because of fish. The English and the French were attracted to the large island in the North Atlantic because of the bountiful cod stocks on the Grand Banks. Unlike other colonies, where settlement was encouraged to secure access to land-based natural resources and other sources of revenue, in Newfoundland mercantile trading practices were directed at maximizing the return on prosecuting the lucrative salt fish trade while minimizing the costs associated with the governance and administration of an otherwise barren and foul-weathered rock.

The type of salt fish trade which was prosecuted from small trap boats, with the fish being dried on shoreline flakes, promoted the dispersion of the fishing activity to the numerous bays and inlets surrounding the island. It was from these widely dispersed bays and inlets, rather than from the neatly parcelled land grants and lots of colonial administrators in other parts of British North America, that Newfoundland settlement would proceed. It was from this unique settlement history that the word "rural" would come to have different meanings in the major development conflicts which would occur three centuries later.

While rural life is the heartland of Newfoundland culture, it is perceived as the bane of the province's contemporary "modern" economy. The rural factor has been the main impediment in the province's almost single-minded efforts to reproduce the industrial culture of North America within Newfoundland society. During the early years of Confederation with Canada, the provincial government began the first of the now infamous series of household resettlement programs (1955–1975) in which 28,000 people were relocated to what were called "growth centres."[1] The émigrés from these isolated rural fishing communities, having been lured, on the one hand, by the promise of better services and superior income opportunities, and pushed with the other, by the withdrawal of essential services from their original settlements, all too often became a new underclass which was artificially grafted on to the traditional social structures of the receiving communities.

Beyond the efforts taken to physically relocate entire communities, massive investments of public funds were made into the "Great Modernization" of education. In many areas of the province the one-room school came to be replaced by the consolidated regional school with children from outlying areas being bussed long distances to attend. In Newfoundland the federal Department of Regional Economic Expansion became involved in financing the construction of these regional schools. Like the resettlement programs, education was seen to be an essentially economic development program. Modernization and industrialization required a centralized and formally educated labour force.

Attendant with these initiatives were centralizing patterns of medical and transportation service which continue at an even more rapid rate today. The completion of the Trans-Canada Highway across the island and the paving of roads to the province's major peninsulas removed the transportation dependence on the sea which was the reason for the original settlement of most of the province's rural communities.

Contemporary Rural-Urban Disparity

Despite the massive pressures to centralize people, employment, and services the population of the province remains largely rural. Since 1971 the proportionate share of the province's population has remained essentially stable at about sixty percent of total population, having experienced net population loss in the two pre-

194   *R.P. Fuchs*

vious decades.² This relative stability is maintained by a considerably higher birth rate and is a thinly veiled disguise for the large scale out-migration of young, occupationally mobile rural residents.³

Rural communities today are comprised of a population which is both very young and very old with proportionately smaller components of people of labour force age.⁴ The unemployment rate is considerably higher in rural areas than it is in the towns and cities even in the best of times and becomes dramatically higher during the winter months when fishing activity is at a lull. Income levels in rural areas are much lower even when accounting is made for the subsistence component of household income.⁵ Despite the massive public investments in education almost 50 percent of rural adults have completed less than Grade Nine education in contrast with a 25 percent completion rate for this level of schooling in the urban areas. Local access to medical services has, in fact, declined relatively over the last decade with, for example, 84 percent of the 4,077 new medical and hospital jobs created over the last ten years having been located in urban areas.

Without reciting a litany of rural/urban disparity,⁶ the almost unarguable verdict which must be reached is that rural communities in Newfoundland have experienced a process of underdevelopment. Those who become educated in rural areas see their certification as a ticket out of the more limited opportunities afforded by employment in primary production there. Small businesses perceive the newly paved highway as a subsidy to the market penetration of externally manufactured products into the local economy. Fishermen and fish plant workers find that the new highway serves as a mechanism through which their small inshore fish plant becomes consigned to the current euphemistic status of the "social fishery."⁷ The construction of the large regional hospital in the regional centre becomes the death sentence for the local cottage hospital.

The Rural Development Movement

The Rural Development Movement was born in Newfoundland in the 1960s, largely in response to the deterioration of economic and social opportunities in rural areas. While historians and local activists still argue as to where it really first began, it is commonly thought to have emerged first in the Port au Port region in 1964 and later on in the Great Northern Peninsula with the formation of NARDA, the Northern Area Regional Development Association, in 1967. Other development associations came to be formed in Eastport, Green Bay, Fogo, and Bell Island in the late 1960s. With no forms of local or regional government there to express their interests, people in rural areas felt that planners and bureaucratic decision-makers in St. John's and Ottawa were uninformed and insensitive to the local potential which was, in fact, available for regional, rather than centralized, forms of economic development. The simple and straightforward solution was to band together to identify opportunities, seek financing for local development projects and lobby for improved services. Johnstone described the growth of these associations, as follows:

> The community development groups which came to be known as Development Associations first emerged in Newfoundland in the 1960s in such areas as Fogo, Eastport, Green Bay, Bell Island, Placentia and Burin, for the most part as a reaction to economic and social problems and especially as a response to government plans for resettlement. . . . Given the lack of municipal government, and given the political and developmental rather than municipal nature of the issues, as well as the geographic dispersion of communities, this resistance crystallized into regional community development groups which came to be known as Development Associations.[8]

By 1974 this citizen-led approach to economic and social development had become part of public policy with the signing of the first of three federal-provincial agreements for rural development.[9] A provincial Department of Rural Development was created to administer the funds provided within the Agreements and rural areas had access to a special fund which was designed around the philosophy of promoting development through voluntary planning and opportunity identification. What is, perhaps, most interesting about the public embrace of this approach was the fact that rural Development Associations were supposed to provide an opportunity for participation in decision-making among groups who were largely ignored by public policy. The notion was that a local idea is more likely to work than an imported strategy for economic development, and that the identification with a common regional interest could overcome the cleavages of community rivalry, religious differences, ethnicity, and social class. In a word, Regional Development Associations were to be a pluralist approach to voluntary planning and the promotion of economic development.

Rural Development Associations are voluntary organizations incorporated under the provincial Companies Act and consist of a board of directors representing at least 75 percent of the communities in a specified geographic region. In each community a "local committee" is elected which, in turn, selects a representative to serve on the regional Board of Directors. In 1983 there were approximately 1200 volunteer regional directors and fifty salaried "development coordinators" who work as the animators for each Association. A provincial umbrella organization, the Newfoundland and Labrador Rural Development Council (NLRDC) consists of volunteer directors (8) elected by regional constituents and an executive which is elected annually by the entire membership and serves a lobbying and coordinating function for the whole movement. The NLRDC has four permanent staff and is located in Gander in the centre of the island.

The pluralist composition of Development Associations is reflected by the fact that the volunteer directors come from a wide range of occupational groups as is reflected in Table 9.1.

Inshore fishermen predominate in the organizations but are joined by a broad-based representation of other rural occupational types. Given the importance of the fishing industry in rural areas, many rural Development Association members equate economic development with the fishery so it comes as little surprise that such a large proportion of the volunteer directors are, in fact, fishermen. Indeed, the overwhelming focus of development project activity by rural Development Associations has been in providing fisheries infrastructure with job creation funds in the local areas. The concentration of rural development membership and activities in the fishing sector is so considerable that most of the Associations suspend their operations during the summer fishing season.

A further indication of the pluralist composition of Development

Table 9.1   Occupational Representation of Development

Association Board of Directors	
Occupational Group	*Percent of Directors*
Fishing	26
Managerial, Administration, Clerical	12
Business Person	9
Homemaker	9
Construction Trades	7
Labourer (NEC)	7
Retired	5
Sales and Service	5
Fish Processing	4
Mechanic, Repair, Transport, Equipment Operator	4
Teacher	4
Farming, Forestry, Logging	3
Other	5
Total	100

Based on 705 members of 1982 Boards of Directors for thirty-four development associations.

SOURCE: Department of Regional, Agricultural and Northern Development and Department of Regional Industrial Expansion, "Regional Development Association Evaluation" (unpublished manuscript, St. John's, 1982).

Associations is the degree to which women have become active in these organizations. Traditional rural organizations are characterized by sex cleavage where men and women join their own separate groups (e.g., Women's Institutes). Women comprise 19 percent of the directors' positions in rural Development Associations and hold 22 percent of the executive positions. While considerably less than their proportionate share of the population, many women have been able to secure leadership and decision-making positions in this rural development system.

What is also significant about the Rural Development Movement is that it is a locally developed secular form of organization. Unlike organizations tied to religious institutions, national service club structures, or trade union affiliations, the Rural Development system is accessible to all segments of the community. These up-start organizations, which attract relatively large amounts of pub-lic spending, can run afoul of traditional hierarchical elites. Taylor refers to this in two regions where she states:

> The differences between Trinity South and the Southern Shore are related to the more prominent role of the Church in the lat-ter. There have been general changes in this pattern, particu-larly over the past fifteen or twenty years in both regions, which appear to be associated with the establishment of local govern-ment and local development associations. Nevertheless, in these regions, both the "traditional" and the "contemporary" styles exist in a mixture which is considerably complex and some-times conflictual. In Trinity South, the Rural Development As-sociation is an expression of the "contemporary" style in that it involves "mostly fishermen, plant workers, then also tradesmen and laborers." In both areas there is a distinction between people whose businesses involve more than one generation of their family and those who have started their own business re-cently. The latter are involved in the Rural Development Associ-ation, the former are not. This pattern tends to be the case on the Southern Shore as well. "Businessmen are connected to Churches and lodges (in Trinity South). They've got their own class of people. A few mix with ordinary people."[10]

Despite the occasional competition for leadership with tradi-tional regional elites, rural Development Associations have been able to secure their own niche within the pattern of rural life. In a recent (1981) attitude survey conducted with a random sample of adults on the Avalon and Burin peninsulas, respondents were asked which organization they would join if they wanted to take a greater part in community affairs. The responses to this question, as reflected in Table 9.2, are illustrative of the wide base of support for rural Development Associations.

It should be noted that the Avalon and Burin peninsulas are among the most highly urbanized regions of the province and one would expect the prominence of rural Development Associations

Table 9.2   Organizations that the Respondents Would Join if They Wanted to Take a Greater Part in Community Affairs

Organization	Percent of Respondents
Local Development Association	35.5
Religious Association	21.1
Residents Association	19.0
Union	12.2
Women's Institute	12.2
Political Party	7.2
Board of Trade	6.3
Other	2.0
	100.0
	(N=1003)

SOURCE: MacLaren Plansearch/Lavalin, "Social Attitudinal Survey" (unpublished manuscript, Mobil Oil Canada Ltd., St. John's, 1981), 36.

to be even greater in the other more rural sections of the island and Labrador.

A key element in the growth of rural Development Associations has been the role played by the Rural Development Branch of the provincial Department of Rural, Agricultural and Northern Development (RAND). This department provides a field staff which works with these associations in every region of the province. It also offers a social development training process for the volunteer directors which concentrates on providing assistance in the development of group process, leadership and conflict resolution skills. In the period 1978/79 to 1982/83 ninety-nine training seminars were held involving 1,999 volunteers and development coordinators with forty-one associations. In a recent (1983) evaluation the Development Association presidents and coordinators identified that these seminars were either very successful (62 percent) or partially successful (24 percent) with only respondent (N=85) indicating that the training exercise was a failure (NR=13 percent).[11]

At the hub, however, of the Department's role is the fact that it provides an annual administration grant of $26,500 to each of the fifty-two Development Associations in the province which meets the minimum eligibility criteria of having representatives from seventy-five percent of the communities in a region and conducting an annual general meeting. Commenting on the Department's role with the associations Johnstone states:

> As observed earlier, the power structure involved in the Program of the Department and the Development Associations is about as undirective as it could be without leaving the Program open to the opposite charge of lack of proper guidance and accountability procedures. As far as the larger issue of co-option is concerned, while such possibilities always exist, if the fact of government seed funding and other support is in some way necessarily co-optive then a large number of people and groups, ranging from ballet companies to middle class academics paid out of public funds, are necessarily co-opted. Presumably a systematic process of co-option would manifest itself empirically in some way, in the activities and view of the government field workers and the Development Associations, and such evidence is not apparent.[12]

By 1985 Regional Development Associations had grown in number to fifty-two representing more than 80 percent of the province's rural communities and had successfully navigated through the troubled waters of federal-provincial relations to have a new cost-shared program amounting to $22,000,000 signed by the two orders of government in June 1984. While the staying power of these groups is a testament to their development as organizations and the successes which they have achieved in generating local employment, their growth occurred at a time when rural unemployment was increasing due to the recession and restructuring in the fishing industry. The result has been that rural Development Associations, rather than becoming the leading edge of rural economic change, have come to play the role of mollifying the impacts of national and provincial policies which continue to centralize public investment in the towns and cities.[13] The planning of new economic development opportunities has had to take a back seat to the management of the recurring crisis of unemployment in rural areas.

Table 9.3   Funding to Development Associations by Source of Funding

Source of Funds	1977/78–1981/82	
	Value of Funding ($)	Percent of Distribution
Canada Community Development Program	19,839,876	59.7
Rural Dev. Sub-Agmnt.	5,098,822	15.3
Small Craft Hr. (DFO)	2,365,356	7.1
LEAP (CEIC)	1,519,349	4.6
Other (CEIC)	1,751,792	5.2
Provincial Fisheries	626,969	1.8
Public Works (Fed.)	465,800	1.3
All Other Sources	1,566,632	4.7
Total	$33,234,598	100.0

SOURCE: RAND, Research and Analysis Division, *Annual Survey of Regional Development Associations.*

"Half a Loaf Is Better Than None . . . "

The major focus of activity of rural Development Associations has come to be in the area of facilitating the implementation of job creation programs sponsored by both the federal and provincial governments. In the period from 1977 to 1982 Development Associations were responsible for the expenditure of $33,234,598 in public development funds as is reflected in Table 9.3.

Caught between the myriad job creation programs which governments sponsored to manage the unemployment crisis and the community expectations that these organizations would do something to blunt the sharp edge of winter unemployment, Development Associations became the intermediary between local employment aspirations and the bureaucracy. A recent evaluation of the previous Canada-Newfoundland Rural Development Agreement described it this way:

To the novice the bureaucratic maze can be awesome. Development associations, however, are not novices to the process and their familiarity with what needs to be submitted to whom, by when and in what form has, by dint of experience, become almost intuitive.... Indeed, development association coordinators (salaried staff) and Presidents have come to be the "professionals" in many areas for knowing the rules associated with funding from all government programs. Community Councils, recreation committees, fishermen's committees, action groups and service clubs will commonly seek the advice of development association coordinators on program funding selection.[14]

In 1982/83 Development Associations sponsored 251 projects which employed 2,398 people and maintained or enhanced the employment of a further 4,226 people as is reflected in Table 9.4. In one year alone more than 6,500 people in rural Newfoundland and Labrador had their employment status directly affected by the activities of rural Development Associations. In many regions of the province the rural Development Association is the largest single employer during the winter months as the organization manages the various rules and regulations of publicly sponsored job creation programs. Managing the rural unemployment crisis in this way is no easy chore. In order to ensure that community rivalry does not become a divisive factor, project priorities will often be developed on a community rotational basis in order to ensure that one community is not perceived to have too much clout in the organization. The selection of project workers is an even more sensitive process. Each representative on a Development Association wants to be able to deliver some benefits to his/her community. As such, Development Associations will go to great lengths to ensure that no one community is receiving undue preference. One Association on the Northern Peninsula hires its project workers at a meeting of its twenty-three volunteer directors where each community representative votes by secret ballot for the applicant whom they think should be employed.

This intermediary role which Development Associations play helps to remove the bureaucracy from the actual process of selecting who will receive the seasonal job. For special employment programs, like the Section 38 provision of the Unemployment Insurance Act, Development Associations receive lists of eligible un-

Table 9.4   Sectoral Distribution and Employment Impact of
Projects Funded by Regional Development
Associations for All Sources of Funds, 1982–83

Type of Project	No. of Projects	Total Value ($)	Average Project Value ($)
Fisheries	158	8,787,228	55,615
Tourism	13	231,544	17,811
Agriculture	12	420,374	35,031
Handcrafts	2	25,836	12,918
Data Collection/Studies	5	48,670	9,734
Food Processing	3	45,545	15,182
All Community Servicing	58	2,026,760	34,944
—Recreational Facilities	17	191,322	11,254
—Health Care	2	15,909	7,955
—Fire Protection	5	212,690	43,538
—Utilities	3	157,630	52,543
—Community Centres	7	290,459	41,494
—Other	24	1,158,750	48,281
Total	251	11,585,957	46,159

Jobs Created

Permanent		Short Term		Enhanced/ Maintained
F.T.	Seasonal	4 Mths	4 Mths+	
12	78	1,366	941	4,228

SOURCE: RAND, Research and Analysis Division

employed persons from the local CEIC office and assume the sensitive job of selecting project workers. The provincial Department of Social Services will similarly send prospective social welfare recipients to the development association for consideration in project hiring.

Development Association projects are comprised mostly of support to infrastructure improvements such as wharves, slipways, and related fishery improvements, developing social facilities like regional meeting halls which are then rented out as office space to local interests and actual commercial enterprises such as fish plants, aqua-culture projects, and mink ranches. While most of the project activity is of the infrastructure type, the place where Development Associations would prefer to invest their time and energy is in these latter long-term employment creation projects. Development Associations have become tired of their role as brokers of job creation programs. They are dissatisfied with their dependence upon government funds, although they are somewhat fatalistic about their chances of doing much about it as the following statements by Association representatives suggest:

> I don't see how they could (become financially independent) in this area. Everything in this area depends on government. There's not much industry in this area. Even forestry is dependent on government for the FESP (Forestry Economic Stimulation Program) and the fisheries is dependent on government. I don't say any association would be any different.
>
> It would be better (to be financially independent) but I can't see how we can raise money in the times that we have. People haven't got money.
>
> There's only a certain amount of time that volunteers can give. It could only work if you had someone like a millionaire sponsoring you. It would be a flop without government support in rural Newfoundland.

Many Development Associations have tried to remove themselves from the double-bind in which they find themselves by engaging in various economic planning exercises. While this process can be as rudimentary as identifying which community needs a wharf the most, it can also become rather sophisticated where strategic and sectoral forecasting in a new resource area like aqua-culture development requires considerable self-education in appropriate technology, marketing, and fish habitat science. The idea behind these planning processes is a good one. If the Association can look five or ten years into the future to identify what it actually wants to achieve it is in a stronger position to direct job creation funds and possible sources of private capital to achieve their economic and social objectives in an incremental way.

Confounding this process, however, is the fact that planning is something other than a value-free exercise. When a plan is made it reflects the planner's values and preoccupation with achieving certain objectives. In the case of development associations, that objective is clearly and unmistakeably job creation in the local area. Development Associations begin their planning with the issue of creating jobs while governments in the resource sector start with planning decisions that will protect and manage the resource and business persons with a focus on what will provide the best return on investment. These planning interests are not necessarily exclusive of one another but they can often be overlapping or in conflict. The government department that wants to control the growth of fish plants because they add to the surplus processing capacity which already exists can find itself at odds with the Development Association that has already received funds from another government agency to provide the infrastructure for a new plant that will create local employment.

Despite this, Development Associations have been ingenious in their attempts to create longer-term employment. In one area the local fish plant building is owned by the provincial government but all of the cutting lines, freezing capacity and solar drying equipment belong to the Association, having been financed by job creation funds with the occasional bank loan to smooth out disruptions in cash flow. In another area, an aqua-culture project has been developed from the ground up with a patch-work of government job-creation funds. The Southern Avalon Regional Development Association has mixed and matched energy conservation, job creation, and other public development funds to commence a fledgling peat fuel substitution enterprise from the local peat bog resource. In a fourth area a woolen mill has been started and eventually leased to a private operator. In southern Labrador a drying facility for salt fish has been installed through the collaboration of a newly formed fishermen's cooperative and the local Development Association, again with the discriminating use of job creation funds and modest amounts of private savings. Even these attempts, however, have been troubled by the structural limitations of a voluntary organization trying to operate a commercial enterprise along with the lack of experience with and control over markets for their products.

The primary role, however, which development associations

have begrudgingly assumed is that of matching community development priorities with the various layers of government bureaucracy involved in job creation programs. Their pluralist composition leads them to seek development projects which both provide enduring general community benefit and create local seasonal employment. They are remarkably successful in doing this. Their aspirations to become involved in activities which will provide stable and secure employment remain generally unfulfilled. Other than the development funds of various job creation programs, they have access to no forms of capital with which to pursue long-term economic development. The lower incomes and higher tax rates in Newfoundland generally make it such that the savings rate is much lower than in other parts of Canada, reducing the prospect of locally generated savings as a form of investment financing.[15]

Future Prospects

The Rural Development Movement has recently come to actively consider a closer alliance with the small cooperative/credit union system in the province. The experience of cooperatives in Newfoundland is a mixed one with many of the older rural co-ops having declined after Confederation and the most successful recent cooperative growth having occurred in the larger towns and cities.

On paper, at least, the alliance between the two would have much to recommend it. The cooperative and credit union systems have assets in excess of $108,000,000 which could conceivably go some distance to securing locally generated forms of investment capital. The Development Associations, on the other hand, offer the promise of assisting the cooperatives to move into the rural commercial and financial markets where they now have little presence. This marriage made in heaven will, however, require an extended courtship. The rural marketplace is widely dispersed and the incomes are generally low.

In May 1984, the Federation of Newfoundland and Labrador Cooperatives and the Newfoundland and Labrador Rural Development Council began the courtship when they co-sponsored a conference on workers' cooperatives in which more than 250 rural development volunteers participated. At the proceedings the question of worker cooperatives as a vehicle for regional economic organization was presented and discussed. The recent growth of fledgling fisheries cooperatives in Labrador and on the Avalon peninsula was a subject of considerable interest as was the formation of employment cooperatives in the St. John's area.

Perhaps the most promising development has been the formation of the Eagle River Credit Union in Southern Labrador. Faced with the prospect of the closure of their regional sub-branch of a chartered bank, this area of 2,500 people, through the cooperation of the Southern Labrador Regional Development Association and the Newfoundland Fishermen Food and Allied Workers Union lobbied, cajoled, and organized to form their own credit union which, one year later, has cash assets of more than one million dollars. The formation of this credit union is worthy of a separate historical accounting but it provides a glimmer of promise with clear implications for other rural regions of the province.

It was in southern Labrador that the notion of a pluralistic regional interest held sway over other narrower sets of interests. In the vacuum created by the bank closure there was initial competition between the concept of an open regional credit union and a bond-of-association, fishermen-only credit union organized by the Fishermen's Union. After considerable soul-searching it was agreed that one regional credit union would be formed with initial operating capital provided by the Union, the building provided by the development association, and an agreement to expand the service to include fishermen further north along the Labrador Coast. The local Caisse Populaire in Blanc Sablon agreed to provide cheque clearing at cost and the people of southern Labrador, through their own devices, with their own money, and using their own organizations were able to establish a viable financial service. This combination of a large anchor founding organization and broad-based regional interest group holds promise for other regions of the province as well.

Conclusion

Notwithstanding this notable exception, rural development associations may have to continue to play a truncated role in regional development over the coming years. They will become even more proficient in maximizing the community utility of job creation programs and will maintain their important social development role for individuals who would otherwise have little access to participation in meaningful decision-making roles within their community and region. The prospects, however, for a dramatic alteration in rural economic opportunity still lie beyond their immediate grasp. To the extent that public policy decisions in the resource and employment sectors are made without direct reference to their interests as "rural" people, their role will remain a largely ameliorative one.

Rural Development Associations have been an important source of social and employment development for rural communities in the province. They provide an easily accessible secular institution through which the interests of one community can become part of a regional approach to social and economic development. It should come as little surprise that they have, as yet, been unable to reverse the centre-periphery polarization of economic opportunities that has plagued Newfoundland throughout its history. The major testament to their success is that, after a period of almost twenty years, when other community and regional development initiatives have come and gone, they not only still exist but remain strong and active.

Notes

1. The Newfoundland household resettlement program(s) were initiated by the province in 1954 with the Federal government contributing financial assistance from 1965 to 1975. During this period of time 255 communities were completely evacuated and a further 312 communities partially resettled.
2. This definition of "rural" is that employed by the provincial Department of Rural, Agricultural and Northern Development (RAND) and identifies a community as rural if it has a population of 5,000 people or less and is not part of the St. John's Census Metropolitan Area or any other Census Agglomeration Area in the province. A comparison of the RAND and Census definitional population changes is as follows:

Year	% of Popula-tion Rand	Rural Census	% of Popula-tion Rand	Urban Census
1961	67.0	—	33.0	—
1966	64.3	—	35.7	—
1971	61.7	41.0	38.3	59.0
1976	60.1	41.0	39.9	59.0
1981	60.4	41.0	39.6	59.0

3. Rural/Urban Net Migration Change from 1971–1981 was as follows:

Year	Rural	Urban
1971–1976	-13,346	5,136
1976–1981	-18,061	-9,146

4. Rural/Urban Dependency Ratios from 1971–1981 were as follows:

Year	Rural	Urban
1971	1/.847	1/.678
1976	1/.751	1/.593
1981	1/.652	1/.530

5. The value of subsistence income sources as a significant proportion of household income in rural areas is, now, more a matter of folklore than fact. A recent study of unemployment in five communities put it this way:

> Moreover, even if market values of subsistence products were underestimated by one hundred percent, which seems unlikely, the economic gains to the households of the unemployed through subsistence production when compared to the employed is quite small. The most realistic assessment is that subsistence production compensates very little for the loss of earnings by the unemployed. Thus, there is little evidence in these data to support the idea that unemployment is a less serious problem in this province because the unemployed can compensate for lost earnings through the production of income in kind.

> Robert Hill, *The Meaning of Work and the Reality of Unemployment in the Newfoundland Context* (St. John's: Community Services Council, 1983), 238.

6. For a comprehensive overview of rural/urban disparity in Newfoundland see R. Thompson, *Persistence and Change: The Social and Economic Development of Rural Newfoundland and Labrador* (St. John's: Department of Rural, Agricultural and Northern Development, 1983).
7. The "social fishery" is a phrase which has crept into bureaucratic language in recent years and is referred to in the Kirby Report on the Atlantic Fishery. Its essential meaning is that those communities where the local fish plant is uneconomic as a separate unit of production and where there is no alternate employment for large numbers of people are referred to as being engaged in the "social fishery."
8. Frederick Johnstone, "Rural Development in Newfoundland: The Newfoundland Rural Development Program in the 1970s" (unpublished manuscript, Department of Sociology, Memorial University of Newfoundland, 1980), 25.
9. The major change took place in the signing of the Canada/Newfoundland General Development Agreement in 1974 under which two of the three Subsidiary Agreements for Rural Development were signed. The General Development Agreement provided for a move away from resettlement approaches to rural development where it stated:

   The broad objectives of this Agreement are to increase the number and quality of viable long-term employment opportunities and improve access to those opportunities by the people of Newfoundland to *increase opportunities for people to live in the area of their choice* with improved real standards of living (p. 15) (emphasis added).

10. M. Taylor and J. Gavin, "An Examination of Individual and Community Adaptation to Atlantic Fishing Industry Reductions Using the Taylor Model" (unpublished manuscript, Fisheries and Oceans Canada, 1984), 266.
11. Department of Rural, Agricultural and Northern Development, and Department of Regional Industrial Expansion, "Rural Development Associations (Evaluation Survey)" (unpublished manuscript, St. John's, 1983).
12. These funds are now cost-split (rather than cost-shared) by the federal Department of Regional Industrial Expansion and the provincial Department of RAND on a 50/50 basis (approx.). Johnstone, *Rural Development in Newfoundland*, 106–7.
13. The Economic Council of Canada, in its report entitled *Newfoundland: From Dependence to Self-Reliance* (Ottawa: Minister of Supply and Services, 1980) stated it this way:

    Within each major peninsula, the services, infrastructure, and related employment opportunities should generally be located in one or two urban centres on or very accessible to the Trans Canada Highway. The highway should be upgraded to link these urban centres with two major entrance points (p.162).

14. RAND/DRIE, "Rural Development Associations," 47.
15. A recent (1983) feasibility study for credit union development in Labrador identified the Newfoundland average savings rate as a percentage of income as *1.23* and that of Canadians as *9.37* for the years 1976 to 1981. (Derived from Statistics Canada Catalogue 13–001 Annual.) R. Fuchs, R. Thompson et al., *A Preliminary Assessment of the Feasibility of Extending Credit Union Services to the Lake Melville/Coastal Labrador Region* (St. John's Credit Union Council of Newfoundland, 1983).

10 The Bloom Is Off the Lotus
Job Creation Policy and Restraint in B.C.

PATRICK J. SMITH

LAURENT DOBUZINSKIS

Two themes stand out in the examination of public policy responses on unemployment and job creation in British Columbia in the 1980s: (i) the appropriation and use of language in agenda setting and (ii) the effectiveness of the strategies adopted by government in seeking to respond to the realities of its provincial economy during a period of recession. Orwell's "Politics and the English Language"[1] stands out as a classic on the first. Thomas Walkom's "Tory-Talk" has added a contemporary (and Canadian) version on the manipulation of language, where words prevent people from examining meanings.[2]

Such appropriation of the language of debate by government represents one of the inherent biases existing in any political system, according to Cobb and Elder.[3] In seeking to have "need perceptions" placed on the public policy agenda, proponents of action need also to confront the fact that the range of issues and alternative decisions that will be considered by the polity is restricted. This is partly a factor of capacity, but perhaps more the fact that "all forms of political organization have bias in favor of the exploitation of some kinds of conflict and the suppression of others."[4] In this policy struggle, where government determines the language of debate, this represents a substantial advantage to incumbency. It is a contention of this chapter that such a process describes the politics of agenda building on job creation policy in British Columbia. In determining public policy responses to the 1980s recession in British Columbia, this initial advantage favoured the incumbent Social Credit government.

This chapter is divided into four parts. The first is concerned with briefly establishing economic and political characteristics of British Columbia prior to the 1980s, and the situation confronting government in the province between 1980 and 1986. This overview includes reflections on the general budgetary strategies adopted under the "restraint program" introduced by Social Credit in 1983 (and continued through to 1985). In Part II, significant dimensions of the public policy responses to job creation are examined, and the value assumptions underlying them assessed. Here, three dimensions stand out: (i) the political; (ii) the economic, and (iii) the social. Part III concentrates on an analysis of the social policy initiatives undertaken by the Bennett government on job creation and unemployment. The question addressed here is this: How effective were government strategies in responding to the employment "imperatives" of a provincial economy in recession? In Part IV, concluding comments address the impact of governmental style, and the significance of manipulating language to limit agenda setting. In dealing with unemployment, the agenda-limiting strategy of the B.C. government seriously (and negatively) affected its choices of response.

I

The external image of British Columbia throughout the 1950s, 1960s, and 1970s can be substantially characterized by the unofficial appellations attached to it: from "God's Country" and "Across the Great Divide" to "the Spoiled Child of Confederation" and "Lotus Land." It was not an image without substance: whether in resource diversity and richness, personal wealth, or a political climate which reflected "high optimism, satisfaction, interest, and a relatively high sense of efficacy," B.C. ranked above the national average.[5]

The very resource-based richness which produced the wealth of the post-war period affected the nature and extent of the economic downturn in B.C. during the 1980s: with its "dependence on uncertain export markets with the resulting instability and fluctuating unemployment, high capital intensity (and participation rates below those regions with more diversified economies) and, ultimately, limitations on growth reached with the maximization of sustainable yields in renewable resources or exhaustion of nonrenewable ones,"[6] the economic downturn in British Columbia was not surprising. It is here contended, however, that governmental policies significantly exacerbated the economic problems confronting the province.

Following the introduction of restraint policies in 1983, B.C.'s unemployment rate and ranking has increased substantially: while the national unemployment average has declined (from 11.9 percent in 1983 to 11.6 percent in 1984 and 11.0 percent in February 1985), B.C.'s rate has gone up—13.8 percent and 4th ranking in 1983, 15.0 percent and 3rd ranking in 1984, and 15.0 percent (and 3rd position) as of February, 1985; currently it is over three full percentage points above the Canadian jobless rate, with B.C. fluctuating monthly between second and third position in unemployment.[7]

And after three years of such restrained government, recovery in British Columbia resembles the quest for an economic holy grail—long sought and fundamentally elusive. More importantly, though the B.C. government (re-elected on May 5, 1983) faced a number of serious problems including "an appalling budgetary outlook," their July 7, 1983 appropriation of language, the Restraint Program[8] "jeopardize(d) not only the real resource base on which (B.C.) depend(ed) in the longer run, but more importantly, the social tolerance and community institutions which ... enable[d] [the province] to work together to utilize those resources most effectively."[9]

The bottom line on "restraint" is that after three years, rather than (as intended by the B.C. government) having "led the way" for other jurisdictional responses to the recession, the B.C. case remains a public policy anomaly. As one observer concluded, "the fact is that B.C. is now a much poorer place, spiritually and financially than it was when Bennett launched his restraint program.... The deficit's up. Unemployment is up. Welfare is up. Bankruptcies are up."[10] For Dobell, "the longer-term consequences of the B.C. program, in terms of damage done to processes for consultation, negotiation and conflict resolution in the community seem likely to be large and lasting."[11] The basis of this policy evolution is examined in Part II.

II

THE POLITICAL ASPECTS OF JOB CREATION

Political discourse deals in symbols; it creates order in the chaos of ordinary experience and gives apparent meaning to the intractable problems of the day. For example, the idea that reducing the deficit will create a more favourable climate for investment gains credence if only the economic aspect of unemployment and job-creation policies are taken into account by opinion leaders and governmental officials. This is precisely the kind of theme, derived more or less directly from the new economic orthodoxy—supply side economics—which is encountered in any B.C. official pronouncement or ministerial statement.

Faced with a serious financial problem such as the value of B.C. exports declining sharply, the government had to convince public opinion that a) it had assessed the situation carefully, and b) a solution was in sight. The B.C. government's response was typical: confronted with a "new reality," (B.C. government's vernacular for its 1983 restraint program) government must practice "restraint" and encourage initiatives in the private sector in order to bring about a recovery, while maintaining essential social services. This language introduced in 1983 carefully avoided administrative or scientific jargon at a time when confidence in the bureaucracy was at a rather low point; it was intended to create the impression that common sense was on the side of government.

With the caveat that democratic governments in pluralistic societies are rarely, if ever, in a position to pursue entirely coherent strategies for very long, it seems that the B.C. government's strategy behind the rhetoric was twofold: first, the emphasis upon the need to restore the competitiveness of the B.C. economy in the context of increased international competition (i.e., the "new reality") implied a concomitant reduction in the size of the public sector which was targeted as unproductive. In fact, the provincial government downsized the provincial public service by at least 25 percent between 1983 and 1985.

This was an argument that the government exploited systematically, for it exonerated the government from the responsibility of developing public make-work projects. As Premier Bennett said in October 1983:

> Most would agree that governments do not, and cannot, create the jobs our people want. It is the private sector that can best create the jobs our people need. Governments can, however, assist the private sector, by creating a prior climate for investment, by expanding markets, and by attracting new industry to diversify our economy.[12]

(Eighteen months later, however, Premier Bennett acknowledged that recovery might require more than simply creating a climate for investment, and his government introduced its new "partnership in enterprise" program.)

Secondly, the "new reality" rhetoric provided a rationale for restructuring power relations in society, in particular as far as labour relations were concerned. The emphasis has clearly been on deregulation of the work place.

To put these observations in perspective, it is necessary to look back at the events of the last two to three years. The Social Credit government of Premier Bill Bennett entered the 1983 campaign running behind the New Democratic Party in the opinion polls. However, Premier Bennett successfully closed the gap by hammering the point that only the private sector could create permanent jobs: economic recovery and a policy of restraint were repeatedly said to be mutually dependent goals. Restraint became the major issue during the second half of the campaign, after Dave Barrett had made the tactical mistake of declaring that, if he were returned to power, he would dismantle the Compensation Stabilization Program (an early component of restraint of government) that had been introduced early in 1982. Premier Bennett's majority increased from 31 to 35 — though popular vote totals changed little.

What Premier Bennett had in mind when he campaigned for restraint in government was not really clear until July 1983 when twenty-six bills were introduced in legislature. These ranged from an act allowing the provincial government, as well as other public sector employers, to terminate the employment of public sector employees without cause (Bill 3),[13] to the abolition of the Rent-alsman and of the Human Rights Commission.[14] Thus the scope and import of the restraint program involved far more than simply controlling wages in the public sector, as had been the purpose of the Compensation Stabilization Program, yet this was the only meaning that voters could reasonably have attached to the term "restraint" during the campaign. Not unexpectedly, this controversial legislative package was met with fierce resistance from the Opposition in the legislature, but to no avail. After a slow start during the summer months, the cabinet managed to reach most of its legislative objectives in the Fall. Operation Solidarity/Solidarity Coalition—an umbrella organization established by labour and human rights activists on July 15, 1983—proved to be the most visible and arguably the most effective counterforce. Large rallies were staged in Victoria (July 27) and in Vancouver (August 10 and October 15), and a petition was circulated. Against this background, Art Kube, the leader of Operation Solidarity, threatened to organize a general strike if the lay-offs of 1,600 civil servants planned by government were carried out on October 31. The B.C.G.E.U. membership, followed by the teachers, went on strike at the beginning of November. This dispute was resolved by the personal intervention of the Premier who negotiated with Jack Munro, a vice-president of the B.C. Federation of Labour, a compromise according to which seniority was to be taken into account when considering any lay-offs in the future. But the restraint program, in the end, has been implemented virtually in full.

In spite of the fact that many programs were either abolished or affected by severe cuts, the overall level of expenditures in the 1983/84 budget had risen by about 12 percent. Finance Minister Hugh Curtis attributed this increase to debt servicing charges and to the need to pay for job creation programs.[15] In the 1984/85 budget the estimated expenditures were actually reduced by 0.2 percent. (However, not all ministries have been able to stay on target; there has been overspending on highway construction, health and welfare assistance.)

When the 1985/86 budget was introduced (on March 14, 1985) an important element included measures "that will secure employment for years to come." For the first time, Mr. Curtis mentioned unemployment explicitly in his 1985–86 budget speech and by offering substantial tax cuts to business he had moved more decidedly in the direction of "supply side" economic management in an attempt to encourage investors more directly than by simply providing a favourable sociopolitical climate. However, it may be argued that since 1983 the overall tax burden has been increased by 5 percent, despite the announced tax cuts in the "renewal budget" for 1985–86.

In discussing political communications it is important to consider not only the source of the messages (i.e., generally government authorities) but also those who receive the message—voters. While symbols are powerful instruments for mobilizing support, their effectiveness decreases over time if they cannot be reconciled with experience. The Social Credit victory in May 1983 showed support for the idea of restrained government (though few anticipated its real meaning until confronted with the July 1983 Restraint Program.) But public opinion polls taken since then indicate that, while restraint in the abstract continued to be a popular idea, there has been considerable dissatisfaction with the specific priorities and policies of the provincial government. In fact, these policies were very much an issue in the two by-elections that took place in November 1984. The government lost one seat in a constituency that since 1952 always had returned a Social Credit MLA, and in the other riding—the N.D.P. stronghold of Vancouver-East— the Social Credit candidate placed third, behind a Liberal.

Faced with polls showing a 25 percent decrease in governmental popularity, Premier Bennett promised to adopt a more active job creation strategy in his February 1985 televised address and in the throne speech in March. But here again, it is the language rather than the content that strikes the observer as being the important element—most observers noted indeed that these pronouncements were short on specifics. The new symbols have become "consultation," "consensus building," and "economic renewal." Interestingly, the official opposition has adopted a similar strategy, insofar as it also tried to project an image and to articulate symbols, rather than to propose counter-plans and specific targets. In this case, it is precisely the language of consultation and conciliation that Bob Skelly had spoken ever since he was selected as provincial leader of the N.D.P.

In brief, the ability to create images, for example, new jobs in a revitalized private sector, is an essential condition of political success—this is something that both Government and Opposition understood clearly. However, the capacity of the political system to deliver actual benefits depends also on concrete structures that are part of the institutional/constitutional dimension.

From a constitutional point of view, job-creation is neither an exclusively federal nor provincial responsibility, although unemployment insurance has been exclusively a federal responsibility since 1940. The requirements of the constitutional/institutional dimensions of job creation are that consultation and cooperation between the two levels of government should be the *sine qua non* for the development of a coherent and rational job-creation policy.

At present, the climate in federal-provincial relations has improved considerably but negotiations between Ottawa and Victoria on items such as reforestation, construction of a natural gas pipeline to Vancouver Island, Special Economic Zones, and provincial uses of EPF funds (re: post-secondary education), etc. will put this new cooperative federalism to the test. Here both economic and social factors will impinge on the outcome.

ECONOMIC DIMENSIONS OF JOB-CREATION POLICY

Economists traditionally divide unemployment into four components: frictional, structural, cyclical, and seasonal. *Frictional unemployment* is due to the fact that the labour market is in a constant state of change as some workers leave and others re-enter the work force for a variety of reasons. Under such terms, economists argue that full employment is compatible with a residual level of unemployment (i.e., there is a natural rate of unemployment). *Structural unemployment,* on the other hand, is caused by more fundamental inadaptations such as (i) structural rigidities (e.g., restrictive labour practices, discrimination against certain groups, obstacles to the mobility of the work force, etc.) and/or (ii) technological changes that result in a mismatch between the demand for and the availability of certain skills. *Cyclical unemployment* occurs when the economy is operating at less than full capacity as has been the case in B.C. for the last three years because of the slackening of demand for natural resources. Today this may be looked at more as a continuing structural problem than as a short term cyclical variation in demand. Finally, *seasonal unemployment* results from the seasonal nature of certain industries such as construction, fishing, or forestry. All of these have important impacts in British Columbia.

Depending on the relative weight given each of these components, different job-creation policies are required. For example, if unemployment is thought to be of a cyclical nature and if a recovery is expected, then short-term programs are appropriate (e.g., small scale municipal public works projects). If, on the contrary, unemployment is caused by structural factors, then a carefully planned policy designed to match the qualification of the labour force with the technological requirements of new industries would be required. However, there will be a time lag between needs in the economy and retraining programs.

Admittedly, the difference between cyclical and structural unemployment is often difficult to maintain in practice. The forestry industry is a case in point. Seasonal factors and cyclical trends (e.g., high interest rates) have had a negative impact on the demand for wood products in the recent past; but the forestry industry also faces serious structural problems (e.g., exhaustion of resources, inefficient mills, etc.). Under these conditions, one might expect policy-makers to develop a mix of policies devised to deal with both the cyclical and structural weaknesses in the provincial economy (such as the overgrown size of an unproductive public sector), as well as with the changes occurring in the global economy (e.g., increased competition from Pacific Rim countries). This found reflection in the rhetoric of the "new reality," though the economic renewal strategy signals a move toward a more balanced approach. However, as Dobell argued at the beginning of the restraint exercise, it may have significantly damaged the capacity to ensure the success of this "partnership" approach.

The comparative merits of stimulative budgetary policies and of a return to something like a laissez-faire approach are the object of ongoing debates among economists.[16] The Keynesian models from which the economic management ideas of the 1950s and the 1960s were derived have come under sharp attacks. Monetarism and supply side economics have replaced these as the foundation of the new economic orthodoxy.[17]

Just as Keynes' demand theory of inflation and unemployment was not new—it could be traced back to Cantillon's writing in the early 18th century—the ideas of the modern monetarists (e.g., M. Friedman) and supply siders (e.g., A. Laffer, R. Mundell) are in many ways similar to those of J. S. Mill or Irving Fisher. For the latter, inflation was not induced by excessive demand but by restrictions on credit. The cost of money is pushed up by government and public sector enterprise borrowing to finance their debts, thereby crowding out private sector investors (under this economic assumption, the solution is to eliminate budgetary deficits). Moreover, government interference with market mechanisms also increases the cost of labour and of many other factors of production. In order to create jobs, the supply siders have advocated massive tax cuts, especially in favour of high income earners, who are "more likely to invest," and for business, even if the outcome of these measures is a deficit in the short time (in this respect, monetarists and supply siders are not in complete agreement). In "Tory-Talk," this means "unlocking the genius of the market" vs. turning resources over to wasteful public bureaucracies.

Clearly, the B.C. government rejected the Keynesian orthodoxy arguing that government could not create "real" jobs and that "we cannot spend our way out of a recession." The downsizing of government is entirely consistent with supply-side theory. However, under the restraint program, the B.C. Government was very reluctant to commit itself to a tax reduction strategy, even as the mining industry found itself at a disadvantage in comparison with several other jurisdictions. In fact, the government collected an extra $1.5 billion in new taxes between 1982 and 1985.[18] At the same time the B.C. government was prepared to reduce or eliminate certain still unspecified taxes for the benefit of *new* firms willing to move into the proposed "special economic zones."[19] In March 1985 it also announced creation of a commissioner of Critical Industries, whose function is to help financially troubled firms by means of tax relief, loans, and other incentives, on the condition that both labour and management in these firms cooperate to improve productivity. This kind of belated intervention is certainly not compatible with supply-side economics.[20]

While professional economists may be puzzled by the apparent lack of consistency of the provincial government's economic strategy, it still remains the case that, especially in B.C., job-creation has always been perceived as an essentially economic problem by the Social Credit governments. A market economy is regulated by natural laws, or so we are told. Therefore, British Columbians were also told that hard choices had to be made, and that we had to adapt to changing circumstances, or risk the slide into economic and technological decline.[21] At the same time, and for related reasons, compassion for the victims of hard times and other nonmarket/social values did not figure prominently in official discourse in B.C. This is not necessarily a matter of callousness; but it is a logical consequence of the policy-makers' preferences for economic justifications of their policies. (Of course, all economists are not equally unconcerned with the ethical implications of their theories—in fact, Adam Smith, Alfred Marshall, and J. M. Keynes were keenly aware of the broader philosophical questions associated with the study of economic affairs; however, contemporary "marketism" being exclusively preoccupied with the defence and promotion of the idea of freedom from coercion is unable to articulate a coherent social philosophy.)[22] We contend that these noneconomic implications of unemployment and job-creation policies ought also to be taken into account. In B.C. government thinking, they were essentially by-products rather than agenda items.

SOCIAL DIMENSIONS AND ETHICAL IMPLICATIONS

Unemployment in the aggregate is very different than unemployment in the particular. With that truism, it is also arguable that the plight of the unemployed is not as dramatic today as it was in the 1930s. The safety net of social services in the 1980s seeks to ensure minimal levels of support. Even where these services are limited and staff resources strained—as in B.C. under restraint—there are a variety of interpretations of the implications of such social support: for example, on the political right, there is a considerable body of economic literature that suggests that generous unemployment benefits are one of the causes of the high reported rate of unemployment.[23] Alternatively, it is suggested on parts of the left that U.I. benefits and welfare support ensure system maintenance by limiting/blunting more fundamental challenges to the economic and political order.

Whatever the interpretation, unemployment and underemployment are obviously conditions that are associated with all the particular and personal tragedies and social ills related to poverty in a society. In British Columbia, bread/soup lines, food banks, and voluntary relief operations of various kinds are becoming a more familiar part of the provincial urban environment.[24] For more than a year now, it has been the case that one out of five B.C. residents lives on unemployment insurance or on welfare payments (the latter frozen for three years).[25]

When these facts are viewed not as the regrettable consequence of external forces, but as an integral part of the image of social relations that informs our understanding of reality, job-creation programs raise obvious ethical questions: Is full employment the desirable outcome of economic growth, or is it an end in itself? Is economic efficiency compatible with the common good? Is laissez-faire a morally defensible position? and so forth.

The nature of the political debates is changing as redistributive (e.g., tax reform) and moral issues (e.g., disarmament, abortion, human rights, etc.) become more pressing. This is also evident in the way in which job-creation policies are discussed in the political arena. Two years ago, for example, politicians had to respond to the challenge presented by the report of the conference of Catholic Bishops entitled *Ethical Reflections on the Economic Crisis.* This report suggested that i) there should be "a preferential option for the poor, the afflicted, and the oppressed," among whom the unemployed obviously were to be included; and that ii) the dignity inherent in human work requires that labour intensive forms of investment must have priority over capital intensive ones. (While in Newfoundland, the Pope proclaimed a similar message in 1984.)

In B.C., the morality of the "new reality" has been questioned most forcefully by the extra-parliamentary opposition. This is not to say that the N.D.P. opposition has been completely silent in this respect, but Bob Skelly, the N.D.P. leader, seems to be more interested in practical issues and in improving the democratic process than in questions of principle. On the other hand, the provincial government has tried successfully not to get involved in this kind of debate with its opponents; however, Patricia Marchak has argued that Social Credit rhetoric implicitly alludes to moral values. The term restraint, in particular, connoted not only fiscal responsibility but also "discipline and the curbing of excess" in all areas of our public and private lives (e.g., the involvement of women in society, education, industrial relations, and so forth). These connotations appeal to those who long for a return to "more puritanical" times, at no cost to their own position in society.[26] Indeed, the groups most adversely affected are those least part of what Apostle and Pross have referred to as "the central work world."[27]

The extra-parliamentary opposition began to organize in July 1983. In August 1983, the Solidarity Coalition was formed by the merger of community groups and of Operation Solidarity, which had been organized by both the B.C. Federation of Labour and B.C. Federation Unions. (The phrase "solidarity coalition" is in itself interesting: on the one hand, it refers to the Polish Solidarity labour movement fighting for altered union relations/status and, on the other hand, it explicitly rejects the individualism of the new right.) Those who have lost jobs or fear losing them are more likely to need to turn to a third party when dealing with their landlord or their employer, the government. However, the restraint program abolished the Rentalsman office, the Human Rights Commission and the Human Rights Branch, cut legal aid and consumer group funding. (The rationalization for these measures is to be found in the neoconservative repudiation of the notion of positive liberty: the only legitimate role for the state is to guarantee "negative freedoms," i.e., the freedom to act as one pleases so long as no one else's freedom is threatened—but, as L. Allison observed, there exists no convincing argument for the dichotomization of concepts such as freedom since complex concepts of this kind are admitting of any number of interpretations.)[28] The Solidarity Coalition mobilized a large number of community activists and ordinary people against these restraint measures. This unexpected opposition explains, in part, why the government let Bill 27 (the Human Rights Legislation) die on the order paper. But it was reintroduced almost unchanged in April 1984 as Bill 11 and passed then. Indeed, though the Solidarity Coalition continues its work, its impact on the administration seems limited. The nature of majority parliamentary government has led to some change in tactics.

In brief, the social and ethical dimensions of unemployment have been recognized and public opinion has been alerted to some of the most glaring violations of the social contract that had prevailed in B.C. until recently. However, it has been difficult to maintain the high degree of mobilization which had been established in the summer and fall of 1983. The events of this troubled period have accentuated the political and social divisions which are so characteristic of B.C.'s political culture. This will make the transition to a more consultative and cooperative approach all the more difficult. Where proofs are in puddings, the "new reality" of restraint in B.C. seems likely to remain an ongoing factor in subsequent relations between Government and its provincial public. This is nowhere more apparent than in the actual job-creation approaches of the B.C. government during 1982/3—1985.

III

On March 12, 1984, (virtually in the middle of the Restraint Program) the premier of B.C. designated a new class of provincial citizenship—"Bad British Columbians." It was Bill Bennett's response to those who booed his announcement of an extension of the Greater Vancouver Rapid Transit megaproject across the Fraser river to Surrey (thus keeping a pre-election promise to the community if they returned only Socreds to the Legislature). Human Resources Minister Grace McCarthy added that "there is no other province in Canada, where the premier could be booed for announcing $200 million of public expenditure for job creation."

In the same month, the provincial Ministries of Labour and of Industry and Small Business Development announced another job creation initiative entitled the Student Venture Capital Program. With overall provincial unemployment then the second highest in the country (at 15.5 percent for February 1984), with the student grant program eliminated in the February 1984 provincial budget, and with youth/student unemployment at 25 percent, this program offered "interest free loans of up to $1,000 to students who wish to operate their own small business." (The loans, through a Canadian bank, were to be interest free from April 1 until October 1, the same year.) This public policy response represented "a new

initiative of the government of British Columbia to create employment and to provide business experience for students." ("It's a
great way to ... BE YOUR OWN BOSS this summer!").

Both initiatives were entirely illustrative of the public policy approach to social policy on job creation in British Columbia between 1983 and 1986. At least since the July 7, 1983 budget (which
sparked the Solidarity response) the stated policy of the government has been "to downsize" its own operation, "to privatize"
much of the current public and human resource sector (whether
the private sector had any intention to respond to these initiatives
or not), and "to re-establish the risk taker"—the only positive image extant in governmental thinking (viz., the Student Venture
Capital Program, etc.—following on from the 1979 initiative to encourage "little capitalists" through the BCRIC Share turnover).

Yet both initiatives represented significantly different strategies
to cope with unemployment and job creation needs. One has been
described as "Smoke and Mirrors,"[29] the other as "the Edifice
Complex."[30] Moreover, it is here argued that neither has represented an adequate strategy to provide anything but the shortest
term employment. Indeed, coupled with the restraint program's
cuts of expenditure on social programs and education,[31] these
policy responses have actually contributed to unemployment in
B.C.

In order to sustain this contention it is necessary to offer a
sample of both types of employment strategies: the megaprojects
and the make-work projects.

MAKE-WORK POLICY—B.C. RESTRAINT INITIATIVES

"Make-work" in B.C. during the 1980s (as in many jurisdictions)
has been more creative than the apocryphal refilling of the hole
just dug. Yet for its creativity, it has not necessarily been more successful in responding to employment needs. In B.C. much of this
lack of success has been a direct result of the policies—and implementation—of the provincial government. Some examples will
illustrate the point, and support the contention that "Smoke and
Mirrors" is a not inadequate description of the mini-project
strategy.

i) In the Spring of 1982, a Federal-Provincial Cost Shared program "to bridge the gap to economic recovery during the economic

recession"[32] was joined by B.C. Other provinces were involved in their own versions of the *Employment Bridging Assistance Program*. In British Columbia the program was to cost $10 million in provincial government support—and a total of $34 million—to employ U.I. recipients to clean up B.C.'s forests, thus promoting more productive utilization of the resource. It was expected to provide employment with up to 10,000 jobs.[33]

Within six months of the April 1982 initiation of the program, the province decided to divert the second half of its remaining funds into jobs outside of the forestry sector. By March 1983 the Government (in an unusual display of candor for make-work scenarios) announced it was thinking of eliminating the Employment Bridging Assistance Program. By June 1983, it did, despite an offer of an additional $11 million in federal support to keep the program until September.[34] EBAP in B.C. had created 5,000 jobs, for a $6 million provincial government investment. Yet by June 1983, the remainder of the funds initially allocated for the program were diverted to another "new initiative" by the province,[35] and 5,000 jobs were lost. The rationale, according to Human Resources Minister Grace McCarthy, was that "the period of greatest need is over and we now look to encouraging the private sector and slowly recovering economy to take over the job creation role."[36]

ii) In some instances, ministers literally fell over one another in announcing these "new initiatives" or where these were lacking simply created fictitious job creation announcements to promote the image of governmental commitment to the job creation task.

As one example of the latter, the same Grace McCarthy who (following the May 1983 election) had stated that job creation was to be a private sector role, only three months previously announced the spending of $510 million in provincial funds to create 32,000 jobs through highway construction. For Mrs. McCarthy "it is better to pay out for job creation than welfare."[37] A small amount of investigative journalism discovered that these figures merely represented an acceleration of existing Ministry of Highways estimates. Mrs. McCarthy got front page. The rebuttal was less prominent.[38]

In September 1982, the B.C. government announced the *Winter Employment Stimulation Program*—$10 million in provincial funds to create 8,000 workplaces for new entrants. It was subsequently announced by the Minister of Human Resources, then the Ministers of Science, of Tourism, of Agriculture, of Industry, and finally, the Provincial Secretary—all in the space of one month. When eliminated in six months it had temporarily created less than 2,000 jobs (under 25 percent of those announced) and only spent $3 million. The leftover funds could then be redirected for other "new initiatives" and multiple announcements.[39]

Generally, the pattern remained the same—substantial publicity for announcements on job creation initiatives, underspending of funds announced, substantially fewer jobs created, even temporarily, and then the quiet dismantling of the program so that temporary jobs were lost, only to rise again phoenix-like from their own ashes. Where federal funds were involved, Canada Employment officials would laugh and remark that "here it comes again."[40]

iii) The $5 million unspent by the province in EBAP were reconstituted as the *Community Recovery Program*—a joint Federal-Provincial program initiated in 1982 to assist the unemployed by supplementary U.I. benefits. It was axed by the province within months, having temporarily created approximately 3,000 jobs. Only $2,399,856 were spent (47.99 percent of the funding announced) when this program was eliminated.[41]

iv) The only year-round job creation project in B.C. under restraint was the *Apprenticeship and Employment Training Program* (AETP). This program was intended to provide job training for those on welfare, employment and training for women in non-traditional workplaces, summer jobs for students, and wage subsidies. During 1982 and 1983, the Labour Ministry underspent this program by $4 million.

When confronted in a newspaper article, Labour Minister McClelland failed to respond to the $4 million figure, but claimed distortion of the government's initiatives on job creation.[42] While $2.6 million was allocated for AETP in 1984–85, with $575,000 for the retraining of welfare recipients component—only $155,000 had been spent by the tenth month of the annual program; and only $175,000 of $520,000 (less than one-third) had been spent on its programs of training women for the "nontraditional work world."[43] McClelland wrote a three-page letter of complaint/response to the initial newspaper article.[44] In it he stated that "unspent" AETP dollars were "not returned" to his Ministry. Rather they were "redirected" to other initiatives such as the EBAP. (EBAP itself spent only one-half of its funds before being cut one week prior to the July 7, 1983 Restraint budget.)[45]

v) In February 1984, a "new initiative" in student employment was suggested as forthcoming. When it did, for the summer of 1984, it was announced as the *Student Venture Capital Program*. As noted earlier, this program sought to encourage young entrepreneurs and promote risk-taking. Students were offered up to $2,000, interest free, for six months, — "to provide students with the opportunity to create their own employment and at the same time obtain practical business experience."[46] There was, of course, little enough employment opportunity elsewhere. With the major reason for small business failure as undercapitalization, and with bankruptcies extremely high in B.C., it was hardly surprising that only 600 jobs were created for the summer at a cost of $250,000.[47]

vi) A range of other programs, with acronyms such as NEED (New Employment Expansion Program) and LIFT (Low Interest Funding Today), were included in the provincial job-creation galaxy.

According to Labour Minister McClelland, $25 million was "earmarked" for "successful employment job creation initiatives" in 1982, and a further $40 million during 1983.[48] Press investigations of the Public Accounts concluded that less than $15 million is spent in B.C. on direct job creation, despite its 15 percent plus official unemployment. Of this, 1982–84 figures showed that at least $14 million in job funds promised since 1982 were not spent on the intended programs.[49] Indeed $10 million had "disappeared . . . in a maze of cancelled programs and fund transfers. Often the government announced a new job creation program, spent half the promised amount, used the rest to fund another job creation program, spent half that amount, and so on."[50]

For Sandra Nichol of the Organization of Unemployed Workers, the fact that job funds in B.C. did not end up providing the intended jobs was not surprising: "I don't think this government has ever had any intention of providing jobs. They don't now and they didn't two years ago."[51] Perhaps refilling holes just dug would have been more productive. Certainly the Federation of Canadian Municipalities had an interesting variant in this make-work category, when they sought $10 billion over the next decade to rebuild Canada's urban infrastructure. And recognizing the need to "Tory-Talk," the F.C.M. posed this as more than job creation—their Spring 1985 proposals were to provide a solid basis for economic growth and renewal.

MEGAPROJECTS AS JOB CREATION

In some ways, the megaproject strategy of the Bennett government was nothing more than the logical extension of the "hole-digging" approach. Without extending the symbolism too far, North-East Coal might fit such a categorization. Together with B.C. Place/Expo 86, Greater Vancouver's Advanced/Automated Light Rapid Transit (ALRT), the Coquihalla Highway Project (and, looming on an uncertain horizon, the Vancouver Island Natural Gas Pipeline and the Site C Hydro Electric project to supply power to California), these megaprojects gave substantial credence to the "Concrete Mentality," indeed to the "Edifice Complex" of the Social Credit government of B.C. in the early 1980s (though these roots are over thirty years old);[52] yet it is as an approach to job creation that their effectiveness should be judged.

B.C. Place/Expo 86   B.C. Place is the proposed twenty-five year development of approximately 300 acres of downtown Vancouver property (on the north shore of False Creek/old C.P.R. terminus site) by a provincial Crown corporation. Early work has included the construction of the 60,000 seat B.C. Place covered stadium. Expo 86 is the World's Fair, organized by another provincial Crown corporation which will use most of this site until the exposition is concluded.[53]

Total provincial investment in the B.C. Place megaproject is estimated at $2.4 billion (1981 dollars), with initial estimated employment of approximately 40,000 job years.[54] The project has represented an ongoing provincial-municipal irritant with debates over the orientation (public versus market), saving the 1887 C.P.R. Roundhouse, public participation, waterfront access and community amenities/parks, transportation links, parking, housing densities and mix and commercial/office concentrations, and social and planning impacts on the region.[55]

On the job creation aspects, recent information from B.C. Place officials (in February, 1985) suggests that the general economic decline has put much of this market development on hold. Some of the temporary Expo buildings might even remain on the site.[56] Little of the proposed activity is planned. For example, after contentious debate—and the threat of a total provincial pullout by B.C. Place—over the height/density of a major hotel in the first development parcel, the anticipated hotel group has been unable to construct the building.[57]

Expo 86 was undertaken by the provincial government to (according to Dobell) "demonstrate that British Columbia is a good place to invest."[58] Government Reports (for example in February 1984) anticipated that Expo would add $1 billion to the local economy, with an additional $2.5 billion in spinoffs during the actual fair itself.[59] Yet according to other B.C. (nongovernmental) economists "many of the real costs of Expo will never appear on its financial books."[60] For Blackorby, Donaldson, and Slade, the history of modern world fairs has been one of promise unfulfilled: "of the last eighteen world fairs, fifteen have lost money."[61] Their projections for Expo 86 are that it will lose more than $500 million, with additional millions siphoned off from other B.C. tourist destinations.[62]

The job-creation role claimed for the fair is equally tenuous. In a February, 1985 meeting with an official of Expo 86, she proclaimed that "there will be jobs for everyone in B.C. in 1986." When queried about the substance of her projections she admitted that the jobs would be temporary and at minimum wage.[63] The reality of Expo has been that other aspects of the economy particularly in tourism were negatively affected; the actual Expo deficit when finally calculated is anticipated to be between $200 million and $300 million dollars.

With Expo altering attendance spending estimates, and chairman Jim Pattison arguing that the fair was never expected to make money, the emphasis has shifted to how to pay for its estimated $800–900 million costs. The government has stated that financial losses will be made up out of lottery funds versus taxes, thus "not costing anything" to the B.C. taxpayer.[64] Yet, when these funds are traditionally used to provide a broad range of community funded projects throughout B.C., their use for Expo represents a major subsidization of the fair by taxpayers outside of the lower mainland; and with tax dollars being needed to replace these lost funds, Expo will doubly impinge upon the well-being of the B.C. taxpayer.[65] Even if it was predicted that "everyone in B.C. will work in 1986," Expo was little more than a "mega-make-work project" in terms of job creation.

Of the several other megaprojects, perhaps two others will complete the illustration of the genre.

Automated/Advanced Light Rapid Transit (ALRT)   In the Spring of 1983, the province of B.C. removed responsibility for transit planning from the regional districts and placed it in the hands of a provincial Crown corporation.[66] With the ALRT as a showpiece for Expo 86, the apparent rationale for this intrusion into local control was the perceived need by the province to ensure timely completion of the megaproject.

One example will demonstrate this perceived need: while most of the initial twenty-one km transit route is being built on existing B.C. Rail right-of-way, in one neighbourhood (Commercial Drive in Vancouver East) the elevated guideway represented a significant disruption and ongoing feature of community life. With assistance from city council members, the area pressured for a covered, i.e., less disruptive, routing in the area. When City Hall indicated it might use its powers (under the Vancouver Charter—its own provincial legislation outside of the Municipal Act) to hold up this section's construction, the province responded with the view that Vancouver did not need to have such powers. For Vancouver Mayor Mike Harcourt, this represented "the nuclear option" vs. the "conventional warfare" that is usual in politics between a left-oriented city council and a Socred provincial administration.[67] And with a year to its opening, there are major provincial-municipal disputes over who will bear the costs of operating the system, and finance the debt. At a March 1985 international seminar on transit in Vancouver, experts from other nations expressed appreciation at the engineering sophistication of the ALRT, but considerable concerns about its costs and operability.

On job creation, the cost of ALRT will be approximately $1 billion (1983 dollars), with $200 million for a phase two Fraser River Crossing—Surrey Extension. The construction phase of this megaproject will have created 7,500 job years. Yet with the highly automated (driverless) state of the technology, only 550 work positions are expected to exist when the system opens in 1986.[68]

With the parallel 1986 closing of Expo, it is easy to see why other megaprojects are being created on the next (post 1986) construction horizon. Prominent amongst these are the Coquihalla Highway, a 180 km toll highway which is to involve $375 million in phase one/two construction (there are three phases) and to create 10,000 direct and 16,000 indirect jobs during its construction;[69] and recent pressures by the provincial government on Ottawa for funds for a Mainland-Vancouver Island natural gas pipeline.[70]

The North East Coal Megaproject   In 1983, the B.C. Ministry of Finance proudly proclaimed "the North East coal project (as) the largest mining development in B.C.'s history, and the largest mining development in Canadian history."[71] Started by the provincial government in 1980, it has involved the provision of approximately $3 billion provincial subsidization of infrastructure, including the building of a complete townsite (Tumbler Ridge), serviced by a new 127 km long B.C. Hydro transmission line, a 129 km branch line of the B.C. Railway, a 92 km new highway link, and major upgrading of the Ridley Island port facility at Prince Rupert. About $1 billion of this public support is written off as creating the right economic climate.

In job creation terms, about 5,000 temporary construction jobs resulted. The expected mining/other permanent workplaces were to be approximately 2,000,[72] but these figures have proven to be overly-optimistic: indeed, one report, by Hal Halverson, a B.C. mining consultant, concluded that this particular megaproject (though intended to demonstrate all of the positive economic potential of the megaproject strategy) might actually result in job losses. In supporting his critique of North East coal, Halverson has cited (a) job losses in the traditional coal fields of southeastern B.C. (e.g., in February 1984, up to 500 miners lost jobs in the South East coal fields—a half year before the opening of the North East project[73]); (b) a substantial overestimation of the future growth of the Japanese Steel industry (the original catalyst for the NE Coal megaproject was long-term contracts at perceived to be fixed prices with the Japanese Steel industry[74]); and (c) an underestimation of world coal markets (to be economic, NE Coal needs to sell for approximately $90 a tonne; yet in 1982, South East B.C. Coal was selling on world markets for $82 per tonne; and by 1983 some of this was being marketed at $69 a tonne—only three-quarters of the break-even point for NE Coal.[75])

Importantly, as well, Denison Mines and Quintette Coal, two of the three private companies involved, also have received provincial subsidization. Yet, after officially opening the facility recently, B.C. Premier Bennett renounced any responsibility for subsequent economic developments regarding the project when Japanese Steel executives announced the need to cut the coal price (within hours of the opening ceremonies). In early 1986, Quintette Coal wrote off over $400 million of its investment in North East B.C. Coal as a bad debt.

Halverson's report concluded that coal could have been supplied more economically, with less infrastructure costs, and less economic dislocation, with South East Coal development. The B.C. government did not show "good judgement in its investment in North East Coal.... Subsidy to one segment of an industry at the expense of another, and job creation in one part of the province that contributes to unemployment in another is hardly wise use of the tax dollar."[76]

IV

The appropriation of language by the Social Credit government of B.C. between 1982–83 and the present was an important tactic in its ability to limit the subsequent debate over its restraint program. By ensuring that the language of political discourse was "Socred-Speak" (the provincial equivalent of "Tory-Talk"), the ability of other views (including "Bad British Columbians") to impact on the political agenda was circumscribed. Yet this restriction did not serve the needs of public interest well. By developing a defensive style, the provincial government failed to manage its new economic reality, and in implementing the strategy of restraint failed to deal with unemployment and job creation by limiting its choices of response.

In examining the July 7 restraint budget, Dobell contended that "two notions [were] central ... and frequently repeated. The first

[was] the concept of the employer's 'ability to pay'—the suggestion that there is no more money. The second [was] the concept of 'productivity'. *Neither can bear the weight placed upon it.*"[77]

By centralizing tasks, by limiting input and by distrusting criticism, the style of the B.C. government robbed it of the opportunities for dialogue. While substantial political heat (and even some fire) resulted from this style of political management, little light resulted.

The lack of light produced two results. First, the process by which we tend to do political business was altered. Dobell predicted (in 1983) that "the longer-term consequences of the B.C. program, in terms of damage done to processes for consultation, negotiation and conflict resolution in the community seem likely to be large and lasting."[78] In turn, the "Fortress B.C. government" approach that emerged from that altered process affected the second result. Stumbling in a darkened polity, the choices of public policy responses to the economic recession were too limited. Having closed itself off from its critics (though the latter remain), the B.C. government made inappropriate policy choices. A legislature which has returned to part-time status (with only fifty-seven days sitting last year), a government preoccupied with polls, and packaging (the P.R. budget for the government was increased in 1983–85), and an administration which "has to put out its own newspaper because Vancouver newspapers don't present the 'true facts' "[79] all support the "fortress" contention.

On the issue of job creation, the bottom line on such policy initiatives is effectiveness. Peter Drucker has contended that "efficiency is doing things right, effectiveness is doing the right things."[80] Job creation programs in B.C. during the 1982–83—1985 period were neither, particularly the latter. Importantly, this is not because they might not have been but rather as a by-product of having limited the process and as a result of deliberate governmental policy. For example, on make-work, the Smoke and Mirrors/Double Bang Shuffle, and on megaprojects, public funds were used to provide infrastructure for private development. The latter would be defensible if it worked. In B.C. it did not.

Certainly, substantial numbers of jobs were created; these were short-term and of limited effect. Hence, the need for new megaprojects. Unemployment has not decreased; rather the opposite. In the language of "Socred-Speak," the government has simply lacked the "political will." It has systematically sought to organize unemployment off the political agenda in B.C. With a straight face, the Minister of Finance could address the B.C. legislature and argue that "record unemployment aside, British Columbia is showing Canada the way to prosperity."[81]

Those who would search out hidden agendas might conclude that a grand design was being served. When B.C.'s high unemployment is coupled with Special Economic Zones and legislation to (in the words of "Socred-Speak") "ensure workplace democracy," the result is a less unionized, lower paid workforce. That such would interest many investors seems certain. The premier has declared B.C. "an open province"—and government has promised to restrain its interference. This was to ensure the proper economic climate for what is now termed "Partnership and Renewal." Yet as a job creation strategy the policy has simply been a failure. Rather than stimulating the economy and creating jobs, the restraint approach has pulverized it. And even where restraint was ignored—in the megaprojects—these have not significantly altered employment.

Throughout all of this, the province also virtually ignored its major industry, forestry. One minister perceived it as "one with a limited future." In the Spring of 1985, it had become (in Iacocca's terms) "a critical industry." To flip-flop so fundamentally on such an important cog in the provincial economic wheel illustrates the rampant ad hoc practices of governmental policy.

One irony of the B.C. forestry policy as a component of job creation in the province stands out in this confusion: between 1980 and 1986, a group of small-town mayors on Vancouver Island have demonstrated the capacity of municipally-initiated forestry renewal to create jobs—in a province that anticipates a loss of 18,000 jobs and 30 percent of its forest harvest by the year 2030. In one example, North Cowichan Municipality has employed several hundred previously unemployed workers since 1980 to weed, prune, fertilize, thin, and replant a 500 hectare site. This and other projects have been so successful that the House of Commons Standing Committee on Forests and Fisheries has endorsed an extension of the plan across Canada; the creation of as many as

300,000 jobs is possible with a renewed forest generating continuing revenues for government forty-five years down the road. While
the provincial government has shown some interest, its policy
thrust has been primarily directed toward the job creation and job
maintenance of continuing a first cut policy (vs. reforestation) as
demonstrated in the battles over South Moresby, Meares Island,
and the Stein Valley.[82]

In winning the battle of words, the Bennett government so constrained political discourse as to limit policy input and its own
policy options. While it is recognized that all policy-makers are
constrained in their choices,[83] the B.C. government's policy
predicament was substantially of its own making.

Notes

1. George Orwell, "Politics and the English Language" in Sonia Orwell
   and Ian Angus, eds., *The Collected Essays, Journalism and Letters of
   George Orwell*, Vol. 4 (London: Secker and Warburg, 1968).
2. Thomas Walkom, "Tory Talk: How the Conservatives Captured the
   English Language," *This Magazine*, 6 February 1985, 5–8. For a B.C.
   Social Credit version of "Tory-Talk" see also P. Marchak "The New
   Economic Reality: Substance and Rhetoric" in Warren Magnusson,
   W. K. Carroll, C. Doyle, M. Langer, and Rob Walker, eds., *The New
   Reality: The Politics of Restraint in B.C.* (Vancouver: New Star, 1984),
   22–40.
3. Roger W. Cobb and Charles D. Elder, *Participation in American
   Politics: The Politics of Agenda Building* (Boston: Allyn and Bacon,
   1972). See also R. Cobb and C. Elder, "The Politics of Agenda Building," *Journal of Politics* 73, 4, (November, 1972): 892–915.
4. Cobb and Elder, "The Politics of Agenda Building," 900–902.
5. M. A. and W. M. Chandler, *Public Policy and Provincial Politics*
   (Toronto: McGraw-Hill Ryerson, 1979), 79. See also Paul Phillips,
   Regional Disparities (Toronto: Lorimer, 1982), 156–57, 66 regarding a
   variety of economic wealth indices.
6. Phillips, *Regional Disparities*, 156.
7. Source: Statistics Canada, Monthly/annual unemployment reports,
   and Keith Fraser, "B.C. Falling as Country Looking Up," *The Province*,
   13 January 1985, 18; "B.C. Jobless Total Up, National Figures Fall,"
   The Sun, 8 March 1985, C6. At the end of February, 1985, 215,000 Brit-

ish Columbians were *officially* unemployed (and an additional 100,000 were counted as "discouraged"—no longer looking for work)—one-third of these among "under 25's". See Glen Bohn, "The Great Job Hunt: Despair Reigns Among Young," *The Sun*, 3 November 1984, H16, and "Cities' Jobless Tally Still Grim," *The Sun*, 8 February 1984, C5.

While 1986 unemployment figures for Canada have dropped below 10 percent, for the first time in four years, in B.C., unemployment remains at about 13 percent. In February 1986, for example, official unemployment in the province was set at 12.9 percent. See Statistics Canada, *Monthly Employment Report*, 7 February 1986, and passim.

8. For a list of the 26 Bills that comprised the July 1983 "Restraint Programme" (and for commentary on it) see Magnusson, et al., *The New Reality*. The B.C. "restraint" period included three budgets which compounded the impact of these conditions and offered little by way of redress for the provincial unemployed: The *1983 budget* took away union rights, eliminated rent controls, limited community power over local school boards and colleges, cut funds for child abuse programs, eliminated family support workers, shut down the B.C. Human Rights Commission (apparently because its three directors had sought to enforce existing legislation, particularly that concerning disadvantaged groups in need of such support—working women, farm workers, etc.) cut legal aid, eliminated funding for organizations such as the Vancouver Status of Women and the Consumers Association of Canada and eliminated tribunals such as the Rentalsman, ensuring more costly judicial remedies for landlord-tenant disputes. Equally importantly, the July 7, 1983 budget *increased* government expenditures by more than 12 percent—more than double the inflation rate and representing "real growth in excess of the average of *all* other provincial governments and in excess of its own record for most of the past thirty years." Rod Dobell concluded that the budgetary exercise "can only in jest be called a budget of expenditure restraint."

The *1984 budget*, in keeping with the "restraint of government" theme, privatized a variety of governmental (particularly social) services, fired 4,000 public servants, reduced welfare rates, increased pharmacare costs, introduced a health maintenance surcharge tax, cut funds to municipalities, and deregulated a variety of governmental functions, such as the elimination of motor vehicle safety inspections. It also paid $470 million to pay out the debt of the B.C. Railway.

The March *1985 budget* continued education cuts, eroded postsecondary spending for the third year (by 5 percent), cut $1.7 million from medical and dental services to the poor, left welfare rates unchanged for the third year but increased expenditure on highways by 38 percent, and offered $1 billion in tax concessions to the corporate sector over three years.

None of this created jobs, and indeed the 1983, 1984, and 1985 bud-

get statements made only the most oblique references to unemployment (for example: "Partly as a result of ... previous strength, B.C.
suffered a much larger decline in economic activity and employment
during the major downturn of 1982," B.C. Budget Statement 1984)
and offered positively cryptic messages on job creation.

9. Rod Dobell's paper became the most-quoted unpublished source in
B.C. in 1983 and 1984. While subsequent versions of it have been published and presented as public lectures, this quote is from the 'third,
revised draft' of September 1983. See A. R. Dobell, "What's the B.C.
Spirit: Recent Experience in the Management of Restraint," (University of Victoria, Centre for Public Sector Studies, September 1983),
26–27.

10. M. Nichols, "A Farrago of Contradiction," *The Sun*, 19 February 1985,
A5.

11. Dobell, "What's the B.C. Spirit?" 24.

12. *The Sun*, 21 October 1983.

13. In the final and amended version of Bill 3, termination of employees
is justifiable when there is insufficient work, or when "there are insufficient current operating funds budgeted to maintain current levels of
employment" (provisions are also made for a "change in the organizational structure" or the discontinuation of a programme).

14. The Human Rights Commission has been replaced by a less independent Council of Human Rights.

15. Direct job creation expenditures were as follows: $170 million for
capital improvement to medical facilities, $190 million for highway
construction, $11.7 million for dyking programmes, $3.7 million for
agricultural plans and $40 million for miscellaneous job creation pro-
grammes.

16. For a good review of these debates, see J. Jacobs, *Cities and the Wealth
of Nations* (New York: Random House, 1985).

17. For a sympathetic exposition of the themes of the new orthodoxy, see
the various publications of the Vancouver-based Fraser Institute, as
well as Bruce Barlett and Timothy P. Roth (eds.), *The Supply-Side
Solution* (Chatham, N.J.: Chatham House Publishers, 1983), and
Supply-Side Economics in the 1980s—Conference Proceedings (West-
port, Conn.: Quorum Books, 1982); for a more critical perspective, see
L. Dobuzinskis, "A Critical Analysis of the Fraser Institute's Approach
to Political Economy," (paper presented to the Annual Meeting of the
Canadian Political Science Association, Montreal, Quebec, June
1985), and Nick Bosanquet, *Economics: After the New Right* (Boston:
Klawer-Nijhoff Publishing, 1983).

18. Marjorie Nichols's column, *The Sun*, 9 March 1985.

19. 1) Firms moving into the "special Enterprise Zones" would take advantage of further tax cuts. 2) So far only one zone has been planned,
in Delta. 3) The economic rationale for these special zones is outlined
in Herbert Grubel, *Free Market Zones: Deregulating Canadian Enter-*

prise (Vancouver: The Fraser Institute, 1983). 4) For a contrary view, see D. Donaldson, "Does B.C. Need Special Economic Zones?" (B.C. Economic Policy Institute, paper No. 0-85-01, January 1985).

20. Premier Bennett explicitly referred to Lee Iacocca's autobiography *(Iacocca)* in his televised speech as being the source of some of his ideas. In fact, Iacocca advocated the establishment of a "critical industries commission" that would facilitate cooperation between government, labour, and management: but similar ideas can also be found in Felix Rohatyn, *The Twenty Year Century* (Mr. Rohatyn is an investment banker who was instrumental in bailing out New York City in the late 1970s). See also M. Nichols's and V. Palmer's columns, *The Sun*, 7 March 1985.

21. For an insightful criticism of the argument of necessity (i.e., we have to adapt to technological change, or else . . .) see Geoffrey Vickers, *Freedom in a Rocking Boat* (Harmondsworth: Penguin Books, 1970).

22. On economics and morality, see David McQueen, "Of Repeated Folly," *Policy Options* (September 1984): 15–19. The term "marketism" was coined by Lincoln Allison in his *Right Principles* (Oxford: Basil Blackwell, 1984). At its "edge," the political/economic right does take on not only moral and philosophical ascriptions, but also religious ones. The attitudes of W. Block (of the Fraser Institute) in establishing the Centre for the Study of Economics and Religion suggest that political and economic fundamentalism claims religious roots.

23. A typical example is H. G. Grubel and M. A. Walker, eds., *Unemployment Insurance: Global Evidence of its Effects on Unemployment* (Vancouver: The Fraser Institute, 1978). In a paper published last year by the Canadian Federation of Independent Business, it was claimed that about 170,000 jobs throughout Canada are not filled because they are unattractive to the recipients of unemployment insurance benefits (*Globe and Mail*, 15 November 1984).

24. For example, the "Food Bank" in Vancouver distributes between 2,600 and 3,000 bags of food every week; on average, these bags are used by 2.3 persons. About 85 percent of the recipients are on welfare. The Food Bank was established in December 1982 and since then the amount of food that it distributes has never decreased (the overall rate of increase has been in the order of 25 percent during this period). For an examination of the growth and implications of Food Banks see Chapter 6 — Graham Riches, "Feeding Canada's Poor: The Rise of the Food Banks and the Collapse of the Public Safety Net," pp. 127–48.

25. Out of a population of 2.8 million, approximately 240,000 people are collecting unemployment insurance and more than 245,000 others are receiving welfare benefits.

26. See Patricia Marchak, "The New Economic Reality: Substance and Rhetoric," in Magnusson et al., *The New Reality*, 32.

27. See Richard Apostle and Paul Pross, "Marginality and Political Culture: A New Approach to Political Culture in Atlantic Canada," (paper for the Canadian Political Science Association, Halifax, Nova Scotia, May 1981). Apostle's and Pross's paper is part of the much broader "Marginal Work World" study, centred at Dalhousie University.

ture: A New Approach to Political Culture in Atlantic Canada," (paper for the Canadian Political Science Association, Halifax, Nova Scotia, May 1981). Apostle's and Pross's paper is part of the much broader "Marginal Work World" study, centred at Dalhousie University.

28. Therefore "there can be no such thing as a purely or even primarily negative or positive approach to freedom." Lincoln Allison, *Right Principles*, 115. For other thoughts on the tendency to dichotomized ideas, see P. Smith, "Dichotomies, Hyperlexis and Eclecticism: Misleading Clarities of the Policy-Administration Debate," *London Review of Public Administration* (January, 1986).

29. "Smoke and Mirrors" is hardly unique to B.C. What it represents is the clash which occurs when "symbolic language" meets "reality" and of attempts of government to "postpone" this collision. On B.C. specifics see, for example, R. Dobell, "Doing a Bennett," *Policy Options* 5, 3, (May/June 1984): 6–10; and in Magnusson, et al., "The Illusion of the Provincial Debt," 56–74; John Malcolmson, "The Hidden Agenda of 'Restraint'," 75–87; and Stan Persky and Lanny Beckman, "Downsizing the Unemployment Problem," 192–208; see also Terry Glavin, "Review Shows Job Cash Diverted," *The Sun*, 30 October 1984, A16. See also Thomas Walkom, "Tory Talk," 5–8 on "The New Language."

30. Again while not uniquely British Columbian, the tradition of creating "monuments" forms a special component of the Pacific periphery's political culture. See, for example, Martin Robin, "The Social Basis of Party Politics in B.C.," *Queen's Quarterly* 72 (1966); or M. Nichols, "Edifice Complex," *The Sun*, 30 January 1980, A4.

31. See, for example, William Schworm, "The Economic Impact of the B.C. 'Restraint' Budget" (B.C. Economic Policy Institute, paper No. P-84-9, May 1984).

32. British Columbia, Ministry of Finance, *Financial and Economic Review* (Victoria: Queen's Printer, October, 1983), 73.

33. Ibid.

34. See D. Togan, "Bennett Flayed for Killing Job Project," *The Sun*, 30 June 1983; E. Sopow, "B.C. Puts 5,000 Out of Work," *The Province*, 30 June 1983.

35. In the vernacular of bottom lines, political mileage, obfuscation, and job creation policies in B.C., this might be termed "two bangs for the buck."

36. Sopow, "B.C. Puts 5,000 Out of Work."

37. E. Sopow, "Socred 'Job Plan' is Trickery Says NDP," *The Province*, 11 March 1983. Such creativity is not unique to B.C. A March 1985 study by the Economic Council of Canada has concluded that "Statistics Canada is deluding us on the magnitude of unemployment . . . and playing politics with the figures." See: "Jobless Figures a Sham, Says Study," *The Province*, 29 March 1985.

38. Ibid.

39. B. Kieran, "Socreds Fall Short of Goals in Job Pledges," *The Sun*, 12 March 1984.
40. Interview, official of Canada Employment, February 1985; the laughter—like the humour, was black.
41. Government of B.C., Public Accounts figures.
42. T. Glavin, "Millions Unspent in Jobless Plan," *The Sun*, 22 October 1984.
43. T. Glavin, "Review Shows Job Cash Diverted," *The Sun*, 30 October 1984, A16. In October 1985, the B.C. Government simply cut apprenticeship classes in the province's vocational schools by 16 percent for 1985–86. A letter to B.C. college principals from the Education Ministry said the classes were being cut because "employers have been unable or unwilling to hire and retain new apprentices in sufficient numbers to sustain the province's apprenticeship training program." The cuts represented a halving of apprenticeship classes in two years. See B. Power, "Apprenticeship Classes Slashed," *The Sun*, Vancouver, 12 October 1985, p. A12.
44. Glavin, "Millions Unspent in Jobless Plan."
45. Glavin, "Review Shows Job Cash Diverted."
46. Bruce Pepper, "Plan for Student Jobs," *Vancouver Courier*, 1 April 1984.
47. Michael Sasges, "Making Jobs vs. Taking Jobs," *The Sun*, 16 June 1984. The 1985 version "is shaping up as a flop" according to recent reports. See, for example, "Student Work Plan 'IN TROUBLE'," *The Province*, 29 March 1985, 112. This program continues as the Student Venture Loan Program in 1986.
48. B. McClelland, Letter to Vancouver *Sun*, October 1984.
49. Glavin, "Review Shows Job Cash Diverted."
50. Ibid.
51. Cited in ibid.
52. Martin Robin has pointed out this "engineering component" of the Socred vision: "B.C. Social Credit advertises neither the populist idyllic past, nor the socialist golden future. Its vision extends no further than the next highway or bridge." Robin, "The Social Basis of Party Politics in B.C.," 690. And indeed the vision (if limited) was very infectious. B.C. Hydro (a Crown Corporation) only recently discovered that it had built too many dams. Current supply (and potential) significantly outstrips demand.
53. For an extensive discussion of the B.C. Place component, and other provincial initiatives in Greater Vancouver, see P. J. Smith, "Planning at Cross-Purposes: Provincial Municipal Relations in Greater Vancouver" (Paper for the Canadian Political Science Association, Vancouver, June 1983), particularly pp. 6–9; and P. J. Smith, "Planning and Open Government: Recent Policy Options and Applications in Canada," *Planning and Administration* 11, 2 (Autumn 1984): 54–62.
54. See, for example, B.C. Ministry of Finance, *Financial and Economic*

Review, 37. Alvin Narod, then B.C. Place Chairman, put the figure at $2.5 billion (1981 dollars), *The Sun*, 16 January 1981.

55. See Smith, "Planning at Cross-Purposes," 6–9.
56. Author interview, B.C. Place official, 20 February 1985.
57. Ibid.
58. Dobell, "Doing a Bennett," 7.
59. "Expo to Provide Billion Dollar B.C. Boost," *B.C. Economic Bulletin* 2 (January/February 1984): 4.
60. See Charles Blackorby, Glen Donaldson and Margaret Slade, "Expo 86: An Economic Impact Analysis" (B.C. Economic Policy Institute, paper No. P-84-11, August 1984), 1.
61. Ibid., 4.
62. Ibid., 27. The basis of this projection was the counting of only "new expenditures within the province."
63. Author interview, Expo 86 staff official, 20 February 1985, the official also admitted that she would be "looking for work" by the end of 1986, as well.
64. See V. Palmer, "Minister Dismisses Economists' Expo 86 Pessimism," *The Sun*, 12 October 1984, 4. In February 1986, Provincial Secretary Grace McCarthy announced a $500,000 expenditure from the Lotteries Fund to help B.C. students *to travel* to EXPO. With four years of decreased educational funding in the province, B.C. educators reacted negatively to the priority such funding represented. See "Lottery Cash Aid Students to Visit Fair," *The Sun*, February 15, 1986, p. A15.
65. See, for example, Gordon Hamilton, "Charities Cry Foul on Lotteries," *The Sun*, 7 February 1985, 1: "the government is putting $250 million from its (lottery) revenues into Expo. I know Expo is a problem (said a Charities spokesman), but we don't want to see it paid for on our books. Now it looks like Expo is a charity too."
66. See Smith, "Planning at Cross-Purposes," 9–13.
67. See P. J. Smith and A. M. Goddard, "Provincial-City Relations in British Columbia: 'Vancouver' Cases, Seattle Comparisons," (Paper for the Pacific Northwest Political Science Association, Olympia, Washington, November 1984).
68. British Columbia, Ministry of Industry and Small Business Development, *Major Projects Inventory*, Vol. 7–1,000 (Office of Procurement and Industry Benefits, September 1984).
69. See, for example, V. Palmer, "Toll Highway in the Works," *The Sun*, 26 September 1984, B2.
70. See Don Whiteley, "B.C. Balks at Ottawa's Plan for Bucks," *The Sun*, 22 March 1985, A1.
71. B.C. Ministry of Finance, *Financial and Economic Review*, 63. See also Minister Don Phillips's thoughts on the N.E. "Hole" in V. Palmer, "Globetrotter Takes Time Out to Smite a Few Enemies," *The Sun*, 20 March 1984, A4.
72. See "N.E. Coal, A Complex Deal Costing Billions," *The Sun*, 10 May

1982, B1; *Planning for B.C.'s North East Coal Development*, and *A Report Covering N.E. Coal Development: Background and Agreements* (Victoria: Ministry of Industry and Small Business Development, 1981).

73. See Suzanne Fournier, "Firing Up a Fight Over Coal," *Maclean's* 97 (27 February 1984).

74. Hal Halverson, "The Dubious Economics of Developing North East Coal," *The Sun*, 21 April 1983, A5.

75. Ibid., B1.

76. Ibid.

77. R. Dobell, "What's the B.C. Spirit?" 10. Emphasis added.

78. Ibid., 24.

79. Hon. Jim Chabot, Provincial Secretary, in defending the $100,000 cost of producing 1.2 million copies of *The B.C. Government News* for every household in B.C., following the March 1985 budget. See Lisa Fitterman, "Government Newspaper Give 'True Facts': Chabot," *The Sun*, 22 March 1985, A12, and *B.C. Government News*, 30 (March 1985). On Friday, 29 March 1985, Provincial Secretary Chabot announced a further $300,000—$400,000 expenditure on promoting the new budget—three two-minute T.V. commercials the minister called "mini-documentaries" on job creation. The rationale: "to stimulate people, to stimulate them so there's employment created." See Peter Comparelli, "B.C. Spending up to $400,000 to Promote Enterprise Budget," *The Sun*, 30 March 1985, A16.

80. See Peter Drucker, *The Practice of Management* (New York: Harper and Row, 1954).

81. See Ron Barrett, "B.C. Showing the Way to Riches, Curtis Says," *The Sun*, 14 March 1984.

82. See, for example, M. Munro, "Forest Plan Would Grow Trees, Jobs," *The Sun*, 17 February 1986, p. A3.

83. See George Edwards and Ira Sharkansky, *The Policy Predicament: Making and Implementing Public Policy* (San Francisco: Freeman, 1978). The early prognosis of the Vander Zalm government in British Columbia is that it is not so constrained. See P. J. Smith and L. Dobuzinskis, "From Lotusland to Fantasyland: The New Politics and Policy of Employment in British Columbia," paper for the 3rd Conference on Provincial Social Welfare Policy, Banff, Alberta, April, 1987.

11 How Ottawa Decides Social Policy
Recent Changes in Philosophy, Structure, and Process

MICHAEL J. PRINCE

As leaders and governments are elected and defeated, as issues move up and down the attention cycle, and as experience judges previous reforms, the ideas, structures, and procedures of governments are modified or replaced. This chapter seeks to understand how the federal government decides social policy by examining the principal decision-making structures and processes in and around the Cabinet, where several important changes have recently taken place.[1] The chapter comprises four main sections. The first analyzes the social policy philosophy of the Mulroney Progressive Conservatives by considering their general perspective on social welfare. The second section briefly describes the main government organizations involved in Ottawa's social policy decision-making system, comments on the abolition of the Ministry of State for Social Development, and notes the importance of the interface between social and economic policy agencies in the federal government. In the third section, the policy and expenditure management system and Social Development budget, and program evaluation and restraint, are examined. The final section considers the implications of recent developments for how Ottawa may decide social policy. Reforms of policy structures and processes always involve choices and tradeoffs between values and between interests. Recent changes in the federal social policy system promote financial restraint, political rationality, and debureaucratization.

The Social Policy Philosophy of the Mulroney Conservatives

Ideologies and values form an important part of the context for Canadian social policy and are, therefore, useful analytical tools in understanding the role of the federal government.[2] Ideology expresses and reflects particular interests, justifying certain actions and nonactions by the state. Ideas and values are the currency of political discourse. They serve as weapons in partisan debate, as general guides for behaviour and as signals to outside groups and officials inside the bureaucracy about a government's intentions. The Conservative view of social policy embraces a number of ideas related to their general political ideology, basic conception of social welfare, preferred values and assumptions in this policy field, and specific social development goals and priorities.

IDEOLOGY: RELUCTANT BUT PATERNALISTIC COLLECTIVISTS
Though the Conservatives are anti-collectivist on many economic development and energy policy issues, they are reluctant but paternalistic collectivists on most social policy matters. Mr. Mulroney, for example, has characterized social programs as "the dimension of tenderness" in Canadian society which relates to "the vital responsibility of government to demonstrate compassion for the needy and assistance for the disadvantaged. Of all the challenges of government, none is more noble, no obligation more sacred."[3] These notions of *noblesse oblige* and social policy as tenderness entail a belief in the benevolent potentialities of government action and a rejection of social Darwinism. With respect to employment, justice, health care, pensions, and other aspects of social development, the Tories accept and support government action to ensure the security of Canadians.

The Mulroney Conservative view of social policy is not fundamentally different from the current Liberal view. Indeed, there always has been considerable overlap between the basic values and positions of the Liberals and Tories on social policy issues.[4] Since September 4, 1984, when a majority Progressive Conservative government was elected, the Tories have repeatedly stressed that they have a mandate for change. In their Throne Speech, budgets, and in debates in the Commons, the Tories have asserted that there is much more to be done in social policy and that the opposition parties do not have the exclusive claim to compassion.[5]

SOCIAL POLICY PARADIGM: SAFETY NET WELFARE

In a statement forecasting their party's social policies as the new government, the Tories say they are proud of their role in the development of the social "safety net" in Canada. They make two commitments: "first, we will maintain the strongest support of the safety net, particularly at a time of real need because of the economic crisis facing so many Canadians; second, we have specific goals for improvements in social programs."[6] In large part, the Tories articulate a "residual" conception of social policy which holds that most government social benefits and services should come into play only when the family, local community, and the market economy break down. Social policy is identified with protecting the less fortunate—the poor and the sick—and the elderly. There is an emphasis on helping the truly needy and the deserving poor, with an appeal to voluntary action and corporate social responsibility.

The Mulroney Tories' social policy paradigm is closely linked to their belief in the need to revive the private sector and restrain the public sector. The Tories suggest that social programs must be reexamined and have to be more selective in *impact* if not in *delivery*. In the current period of fiscal restraint, they assert, it is vitally important that job creation and other social programs be streamlined so that taxpayers' dollars are spent more efficiently.

The Conservatives are concerned that federal spending, much of which is social spending, is ineffective in many areas. They are concerned, too, that social programs are discouraging individual independence, the work ethic, and economic renewal. In his November 1984 economic statement, Finance Minister Michael Wilson stressed that the state of Ottawa's finances cannot support the costs of many new initiatives. The need, therefore, is to reorder priorities, strengthen the economy, and do less in some program areas if the federal government is to do more in others. Over the course of their mandate, the Conservatives intend to implement many new social policies within this framework of "fiscal responsibility." According to the finance minister, "the goals of deficit control and increasing job opportunities cannot be separated."[7]

Controlling and reducing the deficit will rebuild private sector
confidence which is the key to economic growth and job creation.
A review of social programs is seen as contributing to this strategy.
Mr. Wilson has said:

> We must ensure that growth will be for the benefit of all Cana-
> dians and that the costs of change will not fall on those least
> able to bear them. To provide this assistance, we must make cer-
> tain that those who really require social assistance receive it.
> We must also ensure that our social support systems encourage
> self-reliance rather than create a dependency on government.
> We will examine our child benefit, old age security and unem-
> ployment insurance systems to see how they may be improved
> within this framework.[8]

The Tories express a particular view of the relationship between
social policy and economic policy. Social development is seen as a
function of economic growth. Despite the federal deficit and tenta-
tive/economic recovery, the Tories pledge to not weaken the basic
income support programs. "Indeed," says Finance Minister Wilson, "we will seek to find room within our capacity and through
stronger economic performance, to provide even greater assistance
to those Canadians who truly need it."[9] In addition, the Finance
Minister has said: "Let us remember that a strong economy leads
to strong democracy to greater protection of our basic values."[10]
The Tories contend that reviving the private sector will offer
security to senior citizens, unemployed youth, and others in need
of help by generating the new income and wealth on which our social welfare system depends. National Health and Welfare Minister Epp has noted "the fact that good social policy is best protected when there is economic growth."[11]

Conservatives believe that Canada is a world leader in social
welfare. This view leads them to conclude that while there is a
need to help the victims of the economy and the truly needy, many
important social reforms cannot be undertaken until the economy
fully recovers and the government's own fiscal status improves. An
implication of viewing social reform as mainly a function of economic growth is that social welfare expenditures are regarded as
unproductive expenditures and a burden on the economy. Never-

theless, the Tories believe that maintaining existing social programs supports not only social harmony but also economic stability. Hence, a major reduction in the "safety net" is rejected since it would jeopardize public order as well as private enterprise. Also, the Tories claim they "will ensure an integration of economic and social policies, which is the key to both paying for social programs and ensuring that economic policy will not have negative social effects."[12]

THE DOMINANT IDEAL OF TORY SOCIAL POLICY: EQUALITY OF
EMPLOYMENT OPPORTUNITY

Against the background of a reluctant collectivist ideology and safety net perspective, the central values of Conservative social policy are social welfare and social justice. The value of social welfare refers to the responsibility of the state to provide for those who cannot provide for themselves. The social justice concept as used by the Tories refers generally to equitable treatment and, more specifically, to equality of opportunity to participate in society, especially in the paid labour force. The dominant ideal of Conservative social policy is the equality of employment opportunity.

In their discussion paper, *A New Direction for Canada*, the Mulroney Conservatives proposed a sweeping and fundamental review of federal social policy.

The government agrees that a frank and open discussion is timely, and that there is considerable scope for improving and redesigning social programs based on the twin tests of social and fiscal responsibility. *Social responsibility* dictates that wherever possible, and to a greater extent than is the case today, scarce resources should be diverted first to those in greatest need. *Fiscal responsibility* suggests that the best income security is a job, and that government expenditures must be allocated to provide immediate employment opportunities and better ensure sustained income growth.[13]

A number of key assumptions and ideas are evident in this statement. Social responsibility is linked to the notions of welfare, redistribution, selectivity, and the social safety net policy paradigm. Fiscal responsibility asserts that the best income security is a job. While most Canadians would accept this claim, its validity must be examined in the current context of the Canadian economy. There can be no doubt that this principle, however laudable, rests on shaky assumptions. Clearly, jobs are not available for all those Canadians wanting to work and will not be for some time. Present wage levels in many cases are inadequate to keep workers out of poverty, and many jobs are unstable and offer few opportunities for advancement. Moreover, because of individual and systemic biases, the labour market discriminates among groups as potential and actual employees. The Tories' principle of fiscal responsibility that employment is the best income security fails to acknowledge that:

> Even with full employment there is still a need for income maintenance for those unable to work; for those with low incomes or special income needs often related to family size; for those who find themselves intermittently unemployed; and for those who have retired from the labour force.[14]

As well, there is a need for income maintenance for the working poor and compensation to injured workers, veterans, and victims of crimes, among others, for lost income.

Although the federal Health and Welfare Minister contends there is no incompatibility between the principles of social and fiscal responsibility, their juxtaposition raises the following issue: what should be the balance between financial support for employment policies on job creation and retraining, and income security policies for reducing disparities and compensating diswelfares? That many Mulroney Tories are committed to promote stability and fairness in social programs need not be doubted.[15] Overall, the major social policy thrust of the new government is on employment with a focus, first, on increasing work opportunities in the private sector and, second, on equalizing work options. They believe that social needs are better addressed through economic renewal policies than income redistribution policies. It is this emphasis on work in the market economy as the best income security policy that reveals the residual nature of the Tories' social welfare policy thinking.

Yet, in contrast to the neoconservative movement and the

Reagan Republicans in the United States,[16] the federal Tories support the extension of opportunity for work options, the compensation of past deprivations and stress the importance of consultation in making policy.

When Mr. Mulroney entered the federal Conservative leadership race in March 1983, he expressed concern that some Tories were infatuated with the economic policies of U.S. President Ronald Reagan:

> This is not the United States. We have evolved over the years our own society which has always been hallmarked by a degree of compassion which should under no circumstances ever be vitiated.
>
> Most of all, we Conservatives must show the Canadian people that we have about us a dimension of tenderness. We shall be judged both as individuals and as a political party by the manner in which we care for those unable to care for themselves.[17]

Furthermore, the Mulroney Tories are not nostalgic for a past social order. The first Throne Speech of the Mulroney government spoke of a new era of social justice, saying the government would ensure that justice in Canada keeps pace with evolving social needs and circumstances. With respect to social policy generally, the government's message was that "Canadians value and support the comprehensive social security system that has been put in place over many years by the federal and provincial governments. Many areas of this system must be strengthened to respond to the changing nature and needs of our society."[18] In *A New Direction for Canada*, the Tories said:

> Special effort is required to ensure that certain groups who have been disadvantaged in the past are given the occasion to become equal partners in a fair society. Barriers restricting full participation by natives, women, visible minorities and the disabled must be pulled down, and obstacles that prohibit individuals from participating fully in Canadian society must be removed. These are the reasons why, for example, the government is committed to affirmative action.[19]

For the Tories, the proper social mission of Ottawa in the 1980s is as an "employment opportunity—welfare state." Conservative social policy ideas at the federal level are concerned with helping those in greatest need by removing barriers and eliminating discriminatory practices in the economy to ensure the chance for full participation.

SOCIAL POLICY OBJECTIVES, PRIORITIES AND TARGET GROUPS

Five social policy objectives were articulated in the Tories' 1984 Throne Speech: improve job opportunities for Canadians; promote the economic equality of women; support and strengthen the Canadian family; comprehensively overhaul the national pension system and promote individual retirement savings; and modernize the criminal law and correctional system. To pursue these broad objectives, over twenty social policy measures were promised. These measures are itemized in Table 11.1.

Typical of a Throne Speech, the measures are wrapped in rhetoric, totally lacking in many vital details, and covering a wide territory of issues, client groups, and agencies. At least half the promises involve negotiations and agreements with the provinces and the private sector, pointing out the reality of divided jurisdiction in the Canadian welfare state. Many specific measures are from the unfinished business of the last Parliament and can be found in the Liberal Throne speeches of April 1980 and December 1983. Virtually the entire law and order package in the Tory Throne Speech contains such recycled promises. The Throne Speech is also significant in what it did not say or promise. It was silent on medicare, extra-billing and opting-out, as well as on a minimum tax for high-income earners. Some of these issues were subsequently addressed in the Wilson budget of May 1985 and in other ministerial statements.

The Throne Speech identified sixteen target groups for attention in the development of new social policies. These target groups are summarized in Table 11.2. Four groups appear to be high priority groups—women, unemployed young people, the elderly, and families needing child care and income assistance.

During the 1984 federal election campaign, the Tories placed considerable emphasis on issues of particular interest to Canadian women. The Throne Speech described the greater participation of

Table 11.1   Social Policy Measures Promised in the 1984 Throne
Speech

—Implement equal pay for work of equal value in the private and public
sectors

—Increase employment opportunities for women in the federal
government

—Removal of the discriminatory clauses in the Indian Act

—Amendments to the Divorce Act

—Measures to control pornography and sexually abusive broadcasting

—Establish a national system for the enforcement of maintenance orders

—Provide additional assistance to the victims of family violence

—Bring those who suffer from physical and mental disabilities into the
productive mainstream of Canadian life

—Enter discussions with provinces on reform of the pension system

—Consider measures to encourage Canadians to save for their retirement

—Increase federal support for community-based health care

—Extend the Spouse's Allowance to widows and widowers aged 60 to 64
regardless of the age of their spouse at death

—Improve the financial situation of Canada's war veterans

—Address in a variety of areas the challenge of encouraging cultural,
artistic, and athletic endeavours

—Strengthen the comprehensive social security system

—Eliminate certain problems and abuses in the corrections system, and
address other anomalies in criminal and correctional law

—Undertake measures to protect better the public and peace officers

—Amendments to the Criminal Code to deal more effectively with impaired
driving, soliciting, computer crime, and sentencing

—Work closely with the provinces in the areas of family law, crime
prevention, and assistance to victims of crime

—Support official language minorities

—Foster the rich multicultural character of Canada

—Improve job opportunities through expanded market-oriented skill
training and retraining programs

Table 11.2   Social Policy Target Groups Identified in the 1984
Throne Speech

Priority Groups	• Women
	• Unemployed youth
	• Elderly
	• Families
Other Groups	• Workers who need skill upgrading
	• Victims of family violence
	• Official language minorities
	• Other cultural groups
	• Disabled
	• Veterans
	• Victims of crime
	• Artists, performers, and athletes
	• Police and correctional officers
	• Prostitutes
	• Drunk drivers
	• Computer criminals

women as the most significant development of recent years in Canada; acknowledged their rightful claim to equality with men everywhere in our society; and admitted there is some distance between the principle of equality, widely accepted, and its reality, still far short of achievement. Expressing the Tories' reluctant collectivist inclinations in this area, the Throne Speech stated: "It is the duty of Parliament and government to help ensure that Canadian society travels that distance as quickly as possible. This will sometimes require the exercise of your power, and it will always need the power of your example." Table 11.2 shows that about half the social measures promised in the Throne Speech are directly concerned with advancing the equality and well-being of women.

The Mulroney government calls unemployment "Canada's most debilitating problem and most critical national challenge."[20] Renewing economic growth is seen as essential to address the tragedy of youth unemployment. According to the Tories' statement on social policy, a youth employment strategy will be implemented focusing on the following:

• a Refundable Employer Tax Credit, enabling cash-poor companies to hire and train young school leavers;
• an information strategy, including a computerized National Registry, putting unemployed young people in touch with potential employers;
• an economic development strategy based on initiatives by local communities; and
• a training program, making Unemployment Insurance benefits payable for the purposes of training, and a range of other training initiatives for all socioeconomic categories.[21]

For the elderly, the Tories' main focus is on pension reform and retirement income security. With respect to pension reform, their long-term goal is to maintain a mix of public and private sector pension schemes. "Opportunity for individual planning for income security must be able to coexist with the Canada/Quebec Pension Plan, if the long-term viability of the CPP is to be maintained."[22] In their Throne Speech the Tories promised several initiatives dealing with the income needs of the elderly. In addition, the Tories have promised to pursue negotiations with the provinces to include a Homemaker's Pension in the CPP; to introduce a Registered Pension Account to improve pension portability; and to convert the existing income tax deduction for contributions to retirement savings plans to a 40 percent tax credit.[23]

The Throne Speech stated that the Mulroney government "has as a high priority measures to support and strengthen the Canadian family, which is the cornerstone of our society. The need for accessible and affordable child care has in recent years come to the forefront of the social agenda." The Tories believe that "expanded access to quality child care is an important objective both for single parent families and for families with both parents in the workforce."[24] A parliamentary task force will examine the levels and nature of public support as well as the roles of the private and voluntary sectors, in an effort to reach a national consensus on policy options for child care.

The Mulroney philosophy of policy making has important implications for the relationship between the federal and provincial
governments in the development of social welfare policies. A fundamental priority of the Tories is to inaugurate a new era of national reconciliation and consensus. They intend to maintain a
constant process of consultation with provincial governments at
the ministerial level so as "to eliminate irritants and to improve
services to people where the federal and provincial governments
have joint responsibilities." The Mulroney government's approach
to federal-provincial relations has several objectives: to harmonize
policies of the two orders of government, to ensure respect for their
jurisdictions, to end unnecessary and costly duplication, to foster
the multicultural character of Canada, and to cooperate in supporting official language minorities and ensure the equality of the
two official languages.[25]

In health care, *the* major provincial social welfare policy field,
the Mulroney Tories pledge continued support for universal
medicare. They also believe that advances can be made in both the
quality and efficiency of health care in a number of areas. Specifically, they want funding to place greater emphasis on preventive
medicine, community and home-based care, and efficiencies in institutional care. Further, they hope to see the amount of medical
research increased in such areas as the needs of an aging population.[26]

The dark cloud of restraint, however, looms over this bright new
day of cooperative federalism. The Tories' objectives of restraint
and intergovernmental cooperation seem to be uneasy partners in
social policy. In his November economic statement, Finance Minister Wilson said:

> The federal deficit must be reduced to limit the steadily rising
> federal debt burden.... Bringing the deficit down will require
> restraining the growth of federal outlays. A reduction of $10–15
> billion from projected expenditure levels, phased in by the end
> of the decade, would be a prudent and realistic target.... To
> achieve the target will necessitate a careful examination of all
> federal expenditure—economic and regional development, so-
> cial programs, federal-provincial transfers, official development
> assistance, defence—to develop an orderly plan to slow their
> growth, while re-shaping their composition.... [27]

The federal Tories' agenda paper, *A New Direction for Canada*, as well as their budgets, leave little doubt that transfers to provinces—which include equalization payments to the lower-income provinces, block funding for health and post-secondary education, and cost sharing for the Canada Assistance Plan—will be subjected to Ottawa's restraint policy. Health and post-secondary education are highlighted as areas where both levels of government can contain financing and use existing resources more effectively and efficiently. "Mr. Mulroney," observes Jeffrey Simpson, "determined to spread his charm across the landscape of federal-provincial relations, is trapped. Harmony, which he desires, will require giving the provinces money. Saving money, which he needs, will require saying no."[28]

Federal Social Policy Structures

Within the federal government, more than fifty agencies, boards, committees, and departments have responsibility for some aspect of social policy. It is understandable then that Van Loon says that "the politics of the policy and planning process in Ottawa are really a kind of democracy among institutions."[29] Our focus is on the cabinet system and central agencies.

The Mulroney cabinet is the largest ever with forty members, eleven more than the short-lived Turner cabinet and three more than the last Trudeau cabinet. The Mulroney cabinet has eleven committees, excluding ad hoc committees, one more than was in the Turner cabinet and two less than in the final Trudeau cabinet system. Located at the centre of the policy process, the cabinet structures constitute an active and dominant decision-making system. The Cabinet Committee on Priorities and Planning (P&P) is the inner cabinet or executive committee of cabinet. P&P is chaired by the prime minister and usually meets weekly. Its membership of sixteen in 1985 included four social policy ministers—John Crosbie, Jake Epp, Flora MacDonald, and Marcel Masse. P&P determines the annual fiscal framework and overall priorities of the government; allocates budgets to each cabinet policy committee and resource envelope, including the social development budget; reviews and ratifies the decisions of all other cabinet committees; deals with major issues such as federal-provincial relations, the government's Throne Speech and legislative program; and has program responsibility for fiscal arrangements and the public debt.

The Cabinet Committee on Social Development (CCSD) contains fourteen ministers representing the major social departments. In addition, the deputy prime minister, president of the Treasury Board and minister of Finance are *ex officio* members of CCSD. CCSD is chaired by Mr. Epp, the minister of National Health and Welfare. In several respects, CCSD is the organizational focal point for how Ottawa decides social policy. The large number of organizations overseen by CCSD include Communications, Employment and Immigration, Environment, Indian Affairs and Northern Development, Justice, Labour, Health and Welfare, Secretary of State, Solicitor General, Treasury Board and Veterans Affairs. CCSD is responsible for resource allocation questions and strategic policy planning within the social policy field. It had been one of the most active cabinet committees in terms of the number of proposals considered, but recently CCSD has been meeting far less regularly because of general expenditure restraint.

The Treasury Board Cabinet Committee is a key structure in the social policy process since, along with the Finance Minister and Department, it oversees the budgetary system and guards the public purse. Treasury Board is the cabinet committee responsible for managing the operations and preparing the *Estimates* of the federal government. It approves detailed expenditure and person-year plans of departments, monitors the continuing allocations of existing program expenditures (the "A" budget) and assesses the financial aspects of new initiatives (the "B" budget). It is also designated as the employer for federal collective bargaining purposes and responsible for departmental administrative procedures. A further point about the Treasury Board vis-à-vis federal social policy has been noted by Hartle:

> On the biggest policy issues, such as the introduction of Medicare or a proposed major increase in family allowances, the Board as such has little input. But the President and Secretary can have an impact on these decisions depending upon peer group assessments of their power, influence and ability, their intensity of feeling about the issue and the cogency of their comments.[30]

Two other Cabinet committees are relevant to social policy matters. One is the Cabinet Committee on Economic and Regional Development which deals with social welfare-related issues such as farm credit, consumer protection, resource development in the north, labour policy, regional expansion, and transportation safety. These examples illustrate that many public issues overlap policy committee boundaries and program budget categories. In fact, some of these issues have involved disputes over which committee should fund certain initiatives. The Cabinet Committee on Economic and Regional Development is further involved in the social policy field in terms of competing with CCSD and individual social ministers and departments for limited expenditures, personnel and tax assistance provisions.

The other Cabinet committee which potentially has major consequences for federal and provincial social policy is the special committee of ministers headed by Deputy Prime Minister Erik Nielsen. The Nielsen task force included Justice Minister John Crosbie, Finance Minister Michael Wilson and Treasury Board President Robert de Cotret. This group, aided by a private sector committee, was in operation from September 1984 to late 1985, reviewing nearly all federal government programs. The purpose of this special Cabinet committee was to consolidate and simplify programs, end duplication, improve service to the public, and eliminate programs that no longer serve a vital public purpose. The conclusions of the Nielsen committee will undoubtedly remain "on the shelf" as an inventory of possible program cutbacks and changes over the course of the government's mandate.

To support the collective work of ministers and facilitate Cabinet decision-making are several central agencies. These include the Finance Department, the Prime Minister's Office (PMO), the Privy Council Office (PCO), and the Federal-Provincial Relations Office (FPRO).

The Department of Finance is involved in virtually all matters of economic significance with a mandate extending far beyond narrow fiscal issues. Finance is primarily responsible for stabilization policy (including monetary, exchange rate, fiscal and debt management policies), taxation policy, fiscal aspects of federal-provincial relations, that is, transfer payments, and the evaluation of departmental proposals with respect to major changes in economic and social welfare programs. Thus, Finance is the primary advisor to the government on economic policy and an important advisor on social security and welfare legislation. On federal-provincial cost sharing programs, its influence is frequently decisive. Because of its private market ideological framework, "Finance takes an anti-interventionist stance more frequently and more firmly than any other department or agency."[31]

The PMO advises the prime minister on policy in the context of parliamentary, electoral, and intergovernmental politics. Unlike other central agencies, the PMO is comprised of political staff, not permanent public servants. Traditionally, the PMO has generated few policy innovations, being "more a partisan machine devoted to the survival of the government."[32] Mr. Mulroney, however, is substantially expanding his staff resources in policy advice. The group of aides in the Mulroney PMO include Geoff Norquay as director of policy development. Mr. Norquay is the lead advisor on social policy matters as well as in briefing the prime minister for the daily business of the House of Commons. Mr. Norquay was formerly director of research for the Tory caucus and, before that, for the Canadian Council on Social Development. Another major source of advice and briefings for the prime minister is the FPRO. It deals with federal-provincial matters and the intergovernmental implications of other issues facing Ottawa.

The PCO has both an administrative and policy advisory role. Its function is to facilitate the process of Cabinet decision-making and advise on policy matters. Primarily a secretariat to Cabinet and most Cabinet committees, the PCO manages the paper flow of submissions, agendas, background papers, and decisions. The PCO also provides briefings to the prime minister on various policy issues.

Legislatively, the Department of National Health and Welfare (NHW) is the main federal social welfare policy agency. The department has general responsibility for matters relating in any way to the health, social security, and welfare of the people of Canada not assigned to other federal ministers and departments. NHW has the largest department budget in the Canadian government, representing around 25 percent of federal expenditures.[33] In the Mulroney Cabinet system, the NHW Minister, Jake Epp, chairs the CCSD as well as sits on the powerful P&P Committee.

The most significant recent changes in federal social policy organization are the abolition of the Ministry of State for Social Development (MSSD) and the committee of social policy deputy ministers. Those two structures along with others were abolished by Prime Minister Turner in July 1984. The Trudeau Liberals established MSSD in June 1980 to assist the government in integrating current social programs and developing more equitable policies. During its short life, MSSD was a relatively small, professional staff agency headed by its own cabinet minister. Its role was to help CCSD ministers set priorities, allocate resources, establish trade-offs, and help integrate social programs within an overall social development strategy. MSSD also briefed the chairperson of the CCSD, initiated policy ideas and evaluated the efficiency and effectiveness of departmental program proposals before they went to the social Cabinet committee. Thought by some observers to represent the wave of the future, MSSD is now a relic of the past.

Several "mirror committees" of deputy ministers, roughly reflecting the composition of the policy sector Cabinet committees, have also been wound up, including the committee of social deputies. Some Liberal ministers resented these "mirror committees" as second-guessers. The Social Development Deputies was a committee composed of the secretary of MSSD and the deputy ministers of the main departments represented on the CCSD. This deputy ministerial committee enabled interdepartmental consultation by senior officials before final ministerial decisions were taken at the social policy Cabinet committee. The Social Deputies committee was concerned with questions of program effectiveness, policy coordination, and delivery systems.

This inventory of federal social policy structures points out the organizational plurality and complexity of the decision-making system, the social-economic policy interface, and the crucial role played by ostensibly nonsocial policy agencies such as Finance in income security and social services. Doern argues that "key social spending decisions are *not* being made by social ministers. They are being made increasingly by others on cabinet committees that manage energy and economic development."[34]

In a similar vein, Banting contends that "the guns of social reformers need to be trained even more steadily on ministers of finance and their officials. Taxation and other economic policy decisions can—overnight—overwhelm the progress achieved through years of social policy effort."[35] Aucoin has described the balance of influence in the social-economic nexus as follows: "social policy ideals have not been the major determinants of most economic policy and especially not fiscal policy. For the greater part, social policy follows rather than leads economic policy."[36] Thus, to appreciate how and why Ottawa decides social policy a certain way, it is essential to view social welfare in a much broader and more dynamic way than is usually the case.

Federal Social Policy Processes

Two key processes in federal social policy-making are the expenditure management system and program review and restraint. Of course, there are several other processes, but these two are at the heart of the Conservative approach to policy-making.

THE EXPENDITURE SYSTEM AND SOCIAL DEVELOPMENT ENVELOPE

Most social spending by Ottawa is contained within the social development envelope which is one of eight expenditure parcels into which the federal government's expenditures are allocated. This larger "envelope system," known as the Policy and Expenditure Management System (PEMS), is linked to the Cabinet committee system. PEMS was introduced by the Clark government in 1979, was maintained by the Trudeau and Turner governments, and has been retained and modified by the Mulroney government. Throughout, the basic purpose of PEMS—integrate policy-making with expenditure control—has remained constant.

A new set of guidelines outlining the principles and procedures of PEMS was issued by the PCO in September 1984, replacing earlier statements. The main principles and responsibilities of the system are:

(a) the integration of policy and expenditure decision-making to ensure that policy decisions are taken in the context of expenditure limits with full consideration of the cost implications and that, in turn, expenditure decisions are taken in the context of the government's priorities;

(b) the establishment of expenditure limits (i.e., "envelopes") for broad policy areas consistent with the fiscal framework and the government's priorities;

(c)   the responsibility of the minister of Finance for macro-
       economic and tax policy, to recommend the fiscal frame-
       work and the annual envelope levels and to advise on the eco-
       nomic effectiveness of new proposals;
(d)   the responsibility of chairmen of policy committees to ensure
       that committees review existing expenditure priorities and,
       where appropriate, reallocate resources within the envelope;
(e)   the responsibility of the Treasury Board for the overall integ-
       rity of the financial and other resource systems, the
       maintenance of the envelope accounts and provision of re-
       ports on the status of reserves, the accuracy of costing of pres-
       ent and proposed policies put before ministers and Parlia-
       ment, as well as for timely advice to ministers of the efficient
       and effective management of public resources generally; and
(f)   the discretion of individual ministers to make expenditure
       decisions below certain thresholds without Cabinet approval
       where they judge that the policy or political implications of
       the decision are not sufficient to warrant collective Cabinet
       examination.[37]

Key changes to PEMS include the consolidation of certain envelopes, the promise of greater individual ministerial discretion,
and the more restricted access to "policy reserves" to finance new
proposals.

From 1979 to 1984, federal social spending was located in two
resource envelopes—the Social Affairs and the Justice and Legal
envelopes. They have now been consolidated to form the Social Development envelope. This is not a significant change since the two
original envelopes were managed by the CCSD and were already
treated as one policy sector for purposes of establishing priorities
and trading off new policy initiatives within the financial con-
straint of the sector. A potentially more substantial change to
PEMS concerns the greater discretion that individual ministers
now have to make expenditure decisions and reallocations within
their approved departmental resources without having to obtain
Cabinet approval. "This is intended to simplify decision-making
and increase the ability of individual ministers to exercise their
discretionary authority within broad corporate management standards."[38]

Another important change to PEMS is that below a certain dollar level (unspecified in the guidelines) new initiatives will be

financed out of departmental resources rather than the policy reserve. Under PEMS, a policy reserve may be allocated to an envelope to finance new or enriched programs. Whether a Cabinet policy committee receives a policy reserve and what amount is determined by P&P during the annual priority setting exercise and review of the government's fiscal framework. For the fiscal year 1985–86, the Social Development envelope had no such policy reserve for the financing of new initiatives. A social policy reserve could conceivably be created by CCSD itself or by an individual minister by reducing or eliminating existing social programs. Any revenue-generating proposals for new initiatives by reducing tax expenditures or increasing user fees requires the approval of the Finance minister, the president of the Treasury Board and possibly the P&P Committee.

The Social Development envelope is by far the largest envelope in the expenditure system, accounting for about half of federal outlays. Besides its massive size, another outstanding feature of the federal social budget is its nondiscretionary nature. Social development is arguably the most rigid sector of the federal budget because of the number and magnitude of statutory and quasi-statutory programs in the social sector and the indexation of several of these programs. Statutory and quasi-statutory programs are nondiscretionary expenditures, at least in the short to medium term. Such expenditures have been given continuing authority by acts of parliament and therefore require no new parliamentary approval. Moreover, changes to certain statutory payments not only require federal legislative amendments but also require consultation and agreement with the provinces. The shared-cost social programs require notice to the provinces of one to five years in advance of intent to change the programs. How Ottawa decides social policy, therefore, is mostly determined by statutory or quasi-statutory provisions and by agreements with the provinces. The CCSD has real discretion over about only 10 to 15 percent of the Social Development envelope.

PROGRAM REVIEW AND RESTRAINT

Over the 1980–84 Liberal years the CCSD initiated reviews covering most of the social development field. Programs reviewed included Unemployment Insurance, human resource development, fiscal transfers, broadcasting, culture, the child benefits system, pensions and retirement policy, the RCMP contracts with several provinces, and social housing. As a result of these reviews, some program cuts and cost reductions were made, some of a one-time nature, others on-going.

The Mulroney Tories have taken action on several fronts in formulating and implementing a restraint policy. In September 1984, Treasury Board President Robert de Cotret announced a temporary freeze on staffing and discretionary spending. The freeze was not a cost-saving effort but was meant to give ministers a chance to gain control of their departments before new staffing and funding was approved. Also in September, a ministerial task force headed by Deputy Prime Minister Erik Nielsen was established to review departmental programs and formulate an action plan for each federal department to deliver programs more efficiently and simply. This massive review of hundreds of federal programs was expected to produce considerable expenditure savings in programs.

Then, in October 1984, de Cotret advised his Cabinet colleagues to identify a combination of reduced spending and cost recovery measures that would trim 10 percent from the operating expenses of government programs. Since such spending accounts for about 30 percent of total federal expenditures, it meant an overall cut of 3 percent from federal outlays for the 1985–86 fiscal year. Economic and social policy ministers and their officials had to identify programs that could be trimmed, eliminated or made to generate new revenue in the form of user fees. The results of this exercise were then considered by the P&P Cabinet Committee and a first round of restraint measures to reduce the federal deficit was announced by Finance Minister Michael Wilson in his November economic statement.

The expenditure review exercise was guided by the following objectives: to promote growth and employment, to treat all regions equitably, to ensure that those in need are not unduly affected, to honour existing agreements with provincial governments, and to fulfill election pledges.[39] The package of expenditure and revenue increases and cuts announced by Messrs. Wilson and de Cotret yielded a net saving in the 1985–86 fiscal year of $4.2 billion—$3.5 billion in expenditure cuts and $732 million in increased revenues. Table 11.3 presents the main social spending cuts and additions.

Table 11.3 Main Social Expenditure Changes in the Economic
Statement, November 1984

Social Spending Cuts		Social Spending Additions	
($ million, 1985–86)			
CBC	$ 75.0	Spouse's Allowance	$ 200.0
Other Cultural Agencies	7.5	Veteran's Pensions	22.0
Employment Assistance	200.0	Canada Works	200.0
Summer Canada Employment	85.0	Employment and Skill Training	1,000.0
Foreign Aid	180.0		
Canada Student Loans Programs	5.0		
Unemployment Insurance	295.8		
Environmental Programs	46.0		
CMHC	39.0		

The Mulroney government claimed these expenditure reductions were "even-handed" and that new expenditure measures demonstrated the Tories' commitment to social justice, the safety net and to providing opportunity to Canadians to participate in economic renewal. In contrast, social workers and reformers across Canada saw these measures as an attack on the unemployed; as blaming the victims of the economy and regulating the poor; as creating more unemployment not less; and as the first step in a series of moves to weaken the social welfare safety net.[40]

The Mulroney government has frequently argued there is no hidden agenda for expenditure cuts. This is true in the sense that the government has identified the areas of change under review and possible options for reform. Yet, though the agenda may be visible it is an unclear agenda surrounded with considerable uncertainty as to the direction, extent, and timing of reforms, and the policy mechanism to be used. Some uncertainty is inevitable given a new government that is promoting consultation in the policy system. At times, however, the Tories have appeared to have little coherence or sense of direction in their statements and actions on social policy. Moreover, the focus of their social agenda has been unduly narrow, concentrating on universality and direct expenditures, giving little attention to taxation and tax expenditures.

Implications of Recent Changes

Reforms by the Turner and Mulroney governments have particular significance for the federal social policy system. There are now fewer Cabinet committees, fewer expenditure envelopes and fewer central agencies, the sectoral Deputy Minister committees are gone, and the PEMS procedures have been revised.

An important implication of these structural and procedural changes is their impact on the distribution of power within the federal government. With the abolition of MSSD, the Finance Department gains increased responsibility for evaluating the effectiveness of new program initiatives. Finance advises Social Development ministers, and through PCO, the chairperson of the CCSD, on the economic impacts of proposals. PCO regains the role of briefing the chairperson of the CCSD and thus enjoys increased influence. Treasury Board Secretariat also regains some influence over government spending decisions. Along with PCO and Finance, the Treasury Board Secretariat will serve as a major source of advice to the CCSD and other policy committees of Cabinet. Social policy formulation remains within departments, as before, but with MSSD gone, the onus is now on departments to ensure that appropriate interdepartmental consultation occurs in program development. As well, the onus is on Mr. Epp, the chair of the CCSD, to see that an integrated and equitable approach to federal social policy is promoted. In reality, the ongoing annual provision of "sectoral" strategy and overview in social development is not being performed as it was over the 1980–84 period. This function could shift to the PMO where Mr. Mulroney's policy unit has been expanded in order to develop policy and political strategy, liaise with ministers and follow-up with Cabinet and its committees. The abolition of the committee of Social Deputies means "there is no regular review of Cabinet committee items by officials collectively in advance of ministerial discussion. This will require more reliance to be placed on *ad hoc* meetings between representatives of the concerned departments."[41] Such meetings are to be called by the lead department on a given issue or proposal.

Changes to the public policy system always involve choices between certain interests and ideas. Recent innovations in the structure and processes of cabinet government in Ottawa reveal several choices and some shifts in interests and ideas.

The latest reforms continue to emphasize the need to link the budgetary process and the policy-making process, that is, expenditure management and political priority setting. Second, and closely related, the current approach to budgeting is premised upon very limited growth in public spending, and is, therefore, designed to review programs and terminate or reduce some expenditures. The Mulroney Tories intend to substantially slow the growth rate of federal spending and pursue financial self-discipline.

Recent changes suggest that increasing bureaucratization is not an inevitable process in complex organizations, including the federal government. In fact, several changes indicate a move toward a more informal, less complex executive in Ottawa. By streamlining PEMS and the Cabinet committee system, and abolishing some central agencies and deputy committees, the process for Cabinet decision-making has, to some extent, been debureaucratized. This may well mean that the power of senior bureaucrats in Ottawa will decline relative to executive politicians. The tendency toward debureaucratization involves a reduction in the professional autonomy, rules and values of the appointed officials for purposes of political flexibility, sensitivity, and control by the elected leaders.[42] Comprehensive rational reforms introduced in the late 1960s and through the 1970s in Ottawa were not costless. Such reforms delayed decision-making, placed heavy time demands on Cabinet, weakened the representational role of ministers, and submerged their political visibility and individuality. It is to be expected, then, that new adjustments have endeavoured to promote political rationality and individual ministerial authority.

Politics has its own logic, dealing with unforeseen events, incomplete knowledge, competing values and interests, and the electoral cycle. Under the Mulroney government there seems to be a greater emphasis on partisan and political considerations in policy making. Given their huge majority and desire to "correct the damage" done by twenty years of Liberal rule this is understandable. It is most evident in the expansion and upgrading of the PMO and individual ministerial offices, and the elimination of the economic and social policy central agencies and deputies' committees. These changes will likely reduce the input and impact of "objective analysis" in the policy and expenditure system. In short, there will be a decrease in bureaucratic rationality and greater emphasis on political rationality.[43] This suggests a further shift towards ministerial authority relative to bureaucratic responsibility in how Ottawa decides policy.

Notes

1. A more comprehensive and far lengthier analysis would, of course, include Parliament, pressure groups, intergovernmental relations, advisory bodies, the mass media, the voluntary social welfare sector and others. See, for example, Harry Chapin and Denis Deneau, *Access and the Policy-Making Process* (Ottawa: Canadian Council on Social Development, 1978).
2. See John McCready, *The Context for Canadian Social Policy: Values and Ideologies* (Toronto: University of Toronto, Faculty of Social Work, 1981); and Peter Aucoin, *The Role of the Federal Government in Canadian Social Policy* (Ottawa: Canada Mortgage and Housing Corporation, 1981).
3. See *Maclean's*, 28 March 1983, 27, and 11 April 1983, 20–21. The reluctant but paternalistic approach to social policy combines a belief in self-sufficiency for the majority of citizens with a social conscience of concern for the elderly, the sick, and the disadvantaged. On the notion of noblesse oblige, see Kathleen D. McCarthy, *Noblesse Oblige* (Chicago: University of Chicago, 1982).
4. See John Porter, *The Vertical Mosaic* (Toronto: University of Toronto Press, 1965), Chapter 13; Kenneth Bryden, *Old Age Pensions and Policy-Making in Canada* (Montreal: McGill-Queen's University Press, 1974), Chapter 9; and A. W. Djao, *Inequality and Social Policy* (Toronto: John Wiley and Sons, 1983), Chapters 1–3.
5. The Hon. Michael H. Wilson, "Economic Statement," *Commons Debates* (8 November 1984): 99. A similar theme was echoed by the Minister of Health and Welfare, the Hon. Jake Epp, in *Commons Debates* (15 November 1984): 278.
6. "Statement on Social Policy of Progressive Conservative Government," published in *Perception*, 8, 1, (September/October, 1984): 8.
7. Wilson, "Economic Statement," 98.
8. Ibid., 100.
9. Ibid., 97.
10. Ibid., 103.
11. Epp, *Commons Debates*, 278.
12. "Statement on Social Policy," 8.
13. The Hon. Michael H. Wilson, Minister of Finance, *A New Direction for*

Canada: An Agenda for Economic Renewal (Ottawa: Department of Finance, 8 November 1984), 71.

14. Canadian Council on Social Development, Social Policies for the Eighties (Ottawa: CCSD, 1981), 40.
15. See for instance, the remarks by Epp, Commons Debates, 277–80.
16. See Sar A. Levitan and Clifford M. Johnson, Beyond the Safety Net: Reviving the Promise of Opportunity in America (Cambridge, Mass: Ballinger, 1984).
17. Reported in The Globe and Mail, 22 March 1983, 5. See also Michael J. Prince, "Here are policies Tory government might follow," The Citizen (Ottawa), 7 June 1983, 9.
18. Speech from the Throne to open the First Session, Thirty-third Parliament of Canada, 5 November 1984.
19. Wilson, A New Direction for Canada, 69–71.
20. Speech from the Throne.
21. "Statement on Social Policy."
22. Ibid.
23. See Michael J. Prince, "Startling Facts, Sobering Truths and Sacred Trust: Pension Policy and the Tories," in Allan M. Maslove, ed., How Ottawa Spends 1985: Sharing the Pie (Toronto: Methuen, 1985), Chapter 5.
24. "Statement on Social Policy."
25. Speech from the Throne.
26. "Statement on Social Policy."
27. Wilson, A New Direction for Canada, 84.
28. Jeffrey Simpson, "Tale of two provinces," Globe and Mail, 20 February 1985, 6.
29. Richard J. Van Loon, "Kaleidoscope in Grey: The Policy Process in Ottawa," in Michael S. Whittington and Glen Williams, eds., Canadian Politics in the 1980s, Second Edition (Toronto: Methuen, 1984), 432.
30. Douglas G. Hartle, The Expenditure Budget Process in the Government of Canada (Toronto: Canadian Tax Foundation, 1978), 18.
31. Ibid., 9.
32. Van Loon, "Kaleidoscope in Grey," 420.
33. Michael J. Prince and James J. Rice, "The Department of National Health and Welfare: The Attack on Social Policy," in G. Bruce Doern, ed., How Ottawa Spends Your Tax Dollar (Toronto: Lorimer, 1981), Chapter 3.
34. G. Bruce Doern, "Statement on Federal Spending," in Canadian Council on Social Development, Issues in Canadian Social Policy Reader, Volume 2 (Ottawa: CCSD, 1984), 32.
35. Keith G. Banting, "The Social Policy Reformer in the 1980s," ibid., Volume 2, 51.
36. Aucoin, The Role of the Federal Government in Canadian Social Policy, 9.
37. Privy Council Office, Policy and Expenditure Management System:

Principles and Procedures, (Ottawa: 18 September 1984), 1–2.

38. Ian D. Clark, *Recent Changes in the Cabinet Decision-Making System* (Ottawa: Privy Council Office, 3 December 1984), 15–16.

39. Wilson, "Economic Statement," 99. Also see, the Hon. Robert R. de Cotret, President of the Treasury Board, *Expenditure and Programs Review* (Ottawa: Treasury Board Secretariat, 1984).

40. See Wilson, *A New Direction for Canada,* 69; and Victor Malarek, "Social Welfare Advocates Decry Cuts in UIC, Job Training Subsidies," *Globe and Mail,* 10 November 1984, 14.

41. Clark, *Recent Changes,* 24.

42. See S. N. Eisenstadt, "Bureaucracy, Bureaucratization, and Debureaucratization," *Administrative Science Quarterly* 4 (1959): 302–320.

43. Van Loon, "Kaleidoscope in Grey," 413, distinguishes between bureaucratic rationality and political rationality as follows:

    Bureaucratic rationality emphasizes efficiency and systematic approaches, depends on maximum amounts of quantifiable information and demands concrete objectives and clear directions. Political rationality emphasizes the provision of maximum satisfactions for voters in the relatively short run and thereby utilizes information which makes many bureaucrats uneasy and thrives on flexible objectives.

12 Critical Compromises in Ontario's Child Welfare Policy

GAIL AITKEN

This chapter reflects the fact that erosion of the welfare state in Canada has far-reaching implications for the entire field of social policy and profound impacts on human well-being. It raises the additional concern, quite apart from issues of fiscal restraint, that processes of policy formation indicate increasing centralization of decision-making within government.

The chapter is based on analysis of policy processes in Ontario, using major changes in child welfare legislation as case examples. Adoption policies are the primary focus because it seemed instructive to examine how, in two different periods, the government came to implement highly controversial policies which were strongly opposed by significant interest groups.

This study was conducted with the assumption that, since conflict and consensus are both variables characteristic of the policy process, consensus, like conflict, should be treated as an interesting variable, not as a presupposition.[1] A further assumption was made that the policy processes would essentially be what Hall et al. have characterized as "bounded pluralism." According to this view, diverse contending factors are influential and the policy process is not neutral or wholly closed to groups not considered to be among the elites.[2] This conception holds that, while decisions are made through compromises among competing interests, there are severe limits placed on the extent of influence of diverse interests on the pluralist dynamic. This is partly due to controls placed by government both upon issues which enter the decision-making arenas and upon those which are excluded.[3]

The analysis reflected a trend in Ontario under the Progressive Conservative government towards increasing limitations on the pluralistic dynamic of the policy process. This examination of policy revealed serious economic and political compromises which have negatively affected the lives of children in the care of the state.

The first part of the chapter focuses on methods and outcomes of revisions effected through the 1965 Child Welfare Act.[4] Specific attention is directed to changes in adoption policy which were intended to ensure that all Crown wards would be considered adoptable until proven otherwise. The study reveals how weak government policies and provincial parsimony compromised the well-being of many of the "hard-to-place," mostly nonwhite or handicapped children beyond infancy. It demonstrates consequences for the rights of children as well as the rights of their natural, foster, and adoptive parents when government is ambivalent about its commitment to social welfare.

The second part of the chapter compares earlier processes with those around the recent development of omnibus legislation, the 1984 *Child and Family Services Act,* much of which came into effect on July 1, 1985.[5] It assesses shifts in the dynamics and indicates actors, issues and events influencing both process and outcomes. Clearly evident are the increased "withinputs," that is policies generated within government, and the decreased responsiveness of government to the input of diverse social welfare interest groups.[6] Such trends indicate increasing limitations on the pluralistic nature of the policy-making process. The chapter also raises concerns about conflicts of interest involving key social policy-makers. It highlights the confusion of rights and responsibilities implicit in the new legislation.

The Development of the 1965 Child Welfare Act

RISING DEMANDS FOR REVISED CRITERIA OF ADOPTABILITY

The major changes in criteria of adoptability advanced during the 1960s in Ontario and codified in the 1965 Act were the consequences of a drawn out process which began in the late 1950s. From the time of Ontario's first adoption legislation, the Adoption Act of 1921, until the 1954 Child Welfare Act which incorporated adoption legislation, the state's role was viewed largely as ensuring the legality of the child's status.[7] Regarding adoption placements, The Children's Aid Societies, which had (and still have) the responsibility for implementing the legislation, often apparently focused on meeting the needs of prospective adoptive parents.[8]

Gradually in the post-World War II period, the government of Ontario responded to social, political, and economic trends, as well as to changing conceptions of childrens' rights and child development, by assuming greater responsibility for the lives of children. The 1954 Act was intended to serve their "best interests." However, by the late 1950s, despite the improved and consolidated legislation, officials of Ontario's Lepartment of Public Welfare became alarmed about escalating costs of caring for a growing number of permanent wards under the care of the largest agencies.[9] By this time many of the fifty-five Children's Aid Societies, partially government funded and governed by voluntary boards of directors, were in dire financial straits, especially those agencies in the rapidly expanding major cities. Their situations were paradoxical: on the one hand, they required much more substantial and more stable provincial funding; on the other hand, they were increasingly concerned about threats to their autonomy.[10] Records of the Ontario Association of Children's Aid Societies also indicate mounting frustration among that organization's executive and within member agencies due to the increasing inaccessibility of provincial department officials who were apparently less responsive to policy inputs from the Association than formerly.[11] To make matters worse, many child welfare workers were opposed to provincial policies. For example, in April 1959, the deputy minister of Public Welfare had certain Children's Aid Societies notified by telephone, and without prior consultation, that an adoption promotion campaign was being started immediately which would advertise children available for adoption in the classified columns of daily newspapers.[12] However, the success of the campaign convinced some skeptical social workers of the efficacy of the approach, if only because it did result in homes being found for "hard-to-place" children. It also lent further support to the department's increasingly dominant position in determining policy.

By the early 1960s demands for revised criteria of adoptability mounted. Resources of both the voluntary and public social welfare sectors were severely strained by burgeoning demands. Just as in the early 1980s, an economic downturn forced the societies to struggle with larger numbers of children in long-term care. Caseloads grew enormously, but there were insufficient financial resources available to increase staff complement.[13] The particular plight of the Toronto societies heightened their executives' efforts to gain more financial stability through greater provincial and municipal commitments.[14]

Interestingly, at the time there was growing acceptance by both the public and policy-makers that economic circumstances rather than parental inadequacies were often the basis of the children's dependence on the social welfare system. As awareness grew of stress within the Children's Aid Societies, there was heightened public debate about the nature, funding, and auspices of child welfare services.[15] Particular attention was given to the cost as well as the plight of unadopted children who remained in institutions or experienced a succession of foster placements.

Although criteria of adoptability had been liberalized by 1960 as adoption became more generally accepted, it was still the case that the children most easily placed were healthy, white, Anglo-Saxon infants under two years of age with "good histories." Interracial adoption was sanctioned, but many professional social workers retained serious reservations about the practice.[16] Along with children of mixed or nonwhite racial origin were those with poor health or family medical histories; any abnormalities presented an impediment to adoption, to the extent that grossly abnormal children tended to be categorized automatically as unadoptable. Older wards—those over three years—were also generally considered by the agencies as "unmarketable."

Religious criteria of adoptability caused the most controversy. Efforts were made as they always had been to match the religious affiliation of the adoptee's natural and adoptive parents. Agnostics and atheists were not considered suitable candidates for adoptive parenthood. In Toronto, territorial prerogatives established earlier gave the Catholic Children's Aid Society responsibility for all Catholic children needing care, yet the agency was unable to find sufficient adoption homes within the expanding Catholic community.[17] Although key child welfare figures, including the executive director of the Children's Aid Society of Metropolitan Toronto, were convinced that religious differences should not preclude adoption placement, there was little softening of the Catholic agency's position.[18] The church establishment not only dominated the Catholic agency but was also a potent force in the determination of provincial policy.[19]

By the early 1960s, the consequences of using existing criteria of adoptability and criteria for adoptive parents resulted in ever increasing stress in what were poorly resourced provincial residential institutions. In May 1960, the Social Planning Council of Metropolitan Toronto released results of a Child Welfare League of America study of Toronto's children's institutions, which revealed hazardous dilapidated facilities and an appalling lack of qualified staff.[20] The ensuing controversy in the press led to a clearer articulation of demands by child welfare agencies and municipal governments for more resources and better regulations.[21] Controversy over the religious issue and the inadequacies of institutional care created sufficient "disturbance" within the political system that the Department of Public Welfare was forced to begin a formal process to revise policies.[22] In this, conflicting aims appeared: provincial authorities wanted to economize and maintain political support by quieting controversy but various child welfare interest groups wanted to attain better quality care for dependent children.

THE FIRST PHASE OF THE PROCESS: THE ADVISORY COMMITTEE ON CHILD WELFARE

The first phase of the formal process began in May of 1961 when the Government created the Minister's Advisory Committee on Child Welfare.[23] It was a mechanism intended not only to obtain information and policy proposals, but also to create an illusion of government action and control and to quell criticism, much of it directed at the minister by the child welfare field.

Among the twelve members of the Advisory Committee were representatives of the Ontario Association of Children's Aid Societies, municipal government, child welfare officials, educators, a retired judge, and a newspaperman.[24] However, "withinputs," perspectives of those within the provincial service, had extensive influence on the Committee. The deputy minister selected the mem-

bers and appointed the director of Child Welfare as an ex-officio
member and a social worker with the Department became its executive secretary.[25] Over three years the Committee conducted or
sponsored fact-finding in consultation with children's aid societies.[26] The Committee also heard twenty-one delegations from
both private and public organizations, many of which were already represented on the Committee.[27]

In June 1964, after three years of internal wrangling, the Committee produced an impressive report which documented wide inconsistencies in the quality of Children's Aid Societies' services
and an appalling lack of both resources and qualified staff. It
decried the extensive use of long-term institutional care for permanent wards and the lack of resources and competence of many
societies in homefinding.[28]

Among the fourteen major recommendations three pertained
directly to adoption:

- That more specialized resources to serve children in care be
  developed and utilized, such as group foster homes; and that
  constructive planning for each child towards a permanent type
  of care (e.g., an adoption home), be undertaken at the earliest
  possible stage and be carried progressively forward.
- That there be no denial of a "good home" to a child on the
  basis of the religion or lack of religion of the adopting parents.
- That continued emphasis be placed on expanding and improving the quality of adoption services.[29]

The Report pointed out that all findings of the Minister's Advisory Committee on Child Care and Adoption Services of 1953 remained valid, as were those of the 1954 Advisory Committee on
Field Services, most of which had not been implemented.[30] Major
thrusts of the Advisory Committee Report concerned the government's apparent inconsistencies and confusion in relation to its
role and responsibilities and the question of the autonomy of the
Children's Aid Societies.[31]

Despite dissenting opinions about the desirable relationship of
the Children's Aid Societies to provincial and municipal governments, there was a degree of consensus among nongovernment
child welfare interests about major demands, including the need

for greatly strengthened provincial financial support of the societies. By the end of this first phase of the formal policy process, the three years of the Advisory Committee's activities, the government was in a much more advantageous position to enact important changes in child welfare policy, particularly respecting adoption, than it had been three years earlier.

As it happened, the three years of the Advisory Committee's activities was a time of marked change in adoption practice in Ontario. With growing frequency adoptions were being made across racial, religious, and international barriers.[32] More people were willing to accept the risks of adopting children with known or anticipated problems. In part as a result of an intensified advertising campaign run by the provincial government, and in part because voluntary organizations in Toronto sponsored a major project to promote the adoption of black children, public acceptance of adoption increased, especially of adoption without the emphasis on matching of race and religion.[33]

THE SECOND FORMAL STAGE: THE "HENDRY" COMMITTEE AND THE LEGISLATIVE PROCESS

The stage was set for major changes which could result in permanent placements for all but the most grossly handicapped or disturbed youngsters in care. But the government became aware that such policy thrusts would require significant increases in resources and greatly strengthened provincial government leadership.[34] Officials of the Department of Public Welfare expected that extensive revisions would create political turmoil, especially if they concerned either the accountability and financing of the societies or religious criteria in adoption. Any evidence of marked shifts in provincial priorities or interference with the Roman Catholic church's stand on religious matching within their agencies would have required the government to grapple with sensitive, value-based policy issues. Marked shifts were clearly not to be forthcoming from a government which was ambiguous about its commitment to the welfare state.

In seeking compromises among competing demands, the government delayed drafting new legislation based on the Advisory Committee's work, and interposed an intermediary group, the "Hendry" Committee, ostensibly to deal with the Advisory Committee's recommendations and draft the new Child Welfare Act.[35] In this way provincial authorities continued to maintain the appearance of involving nongovernment interests in determining policy. In fact, the Hendry Committee was created months before the Advisory Committee Report was made public, and it was very much a creature of the provincial department, orchestrated by the deputy minister, a member of the group.[36]

Hendry fully recognized that both the process and the provincial government's objectives were first and foremost political, and would involve delicate compromises. The evidence suggests that both he and the executive secretary of the Ontario Association of Children's Aid Societies, a committee member, were co-opted by the deputy minister. Such consultation as the "Hendry" Committee did engage in was limited, selective, and complied with Departmental direction. Only a few powerful nongovernment actors gained access to this stage of the formal policy process other than by carefully considered invitation. Decisions made complied with the policy directions of the province which were to control social welfare expenditures without creating political waves.

The Hendry Committee's efforts led to the introduction of Bill 119 in the legislature in April of 1965. The proposed legislation reflected the fact that the most contentious issues raised by the Advisory Committee had been reduced, or set aside, in internal processes. Conflict was avoided by backing away from the crucial issue of restructuring or reorganizing the societies. Nor were the societies assured of sufficient resources to implement the legislation, in part because the Bill was in many respects unspecific and contained permissive provisions, such as in regard to preventive programs.[37]

In relation to criteria of adoptability the government ignored inputs from various interest groups, even demands expressed convincingly within the legislature.[38] During both second and third readings of Bill 119 both Liberal and New Democratic members articulately urged clarification of legislation with regard to religious criteria in adoption. Stephen Lewis, N.D.P. Social Critic, stated:

> The legislation is clever—almost inscrutable—it is so ambivalent. The religious factor in adoption may have been taken

out, but, if so, the Act needs some clarity. It should not be left in its present hazy and confused way for the courts to interpret. If the Honourable Minister's intentions are to allow inter-faith adoption let him say so unequivocally.[39]

These demands were echoed in the press and diverse social welfare groups.[40] An amendment was proposed by a Conservative member to the effect that no child should be denied a good home (either adoptive or foster) because of the religion or nonreligion of the parents.[41] But, in what Lewis described as "inexplicable maneuvering behind the scenes" the amendment was not brought forth by the government.[42] Direct reference to race and religion was avoided and specific action to assist adoption programs was not taken.[43] The legislation afforded amazingly little direction to the judiciary hearing adoption cases and fell short even in dealing with unofficial adoption policies already being implemented by the more progressive agencies. However, despite the vagueness of the Bill and widespread discontent, Bill 119 received Royal Assent on June 22, 1965, long before the Hendry Committee had completed drafting the Regulations and long before the implications of the legislation for the societies and the children in their care were carefully studied.[44]

Clearly the desire of the government to avoid conflict with Roman Catholic interest groups was significant in this process. The societies were left with much discretion in their adoption practices, and they, in turn, had to rely on the courts to make controversial decisions which could vary greatly from one jurisdiction to another.

This second phase of the formal process reflected the ways in which significant demands were resisted, and portrayed techniques used by the Department of Public Welfare and government leaders to control both the decisions and the "nondecisions" of the Hendry Committee and the legislature.[45] In fact, the "authorities" responsible for the outputs of this policy process froze out significant inputs from major nongovernment interest groups and from members of all parties of the legislature. This phase clearly reflected the government's overriding concern about political priorities and its reticence to assume increased commitments to social welfare.

Despite its limitations, the 1965 Child Welfare Act was, in many re-spects, undeniably progressive in its attempts to enshrine "the best interests of the child." However, even as this second phase of the formal policy process ended with the proclamation of the 1965 Child Welfare Act it was abundantly evident to some of the interest groups involved that political compromises had been made which would have serious implications for many dependent children re-quiring permanent homes, the very children the Act was intended to assist and protect. Although the legislation was a marked im-provement over its predecessor, it was immeasurably weakened by the government's failure to risk dealing effectively with politically sensitive issues and its refusal to reorder its priorities or allocate greater resources for the defence of the rights of Ontario's children.

The government could not expect that problems within child welfare institutions would be resolved, or that consistently high standards of service would be provided as long as responsibilities and accountability remained vague and ambiguous. Yet they were clearly apprehensive about the political consequences of assuming markedly greater authority for child welfare services through restructuring the service delivery system. They were especially aware of the risks involved in assuming direct control of the func-tions of children's aid societies.[46] It was convenient to have these quasi-voluntary agencies serve as buffers to bear the brunt of the intense public criticism whenever poor standards were exposed. So it was that policy initiatives, especially those related to the societies' structure or to religious criteria of adoptability, re-mained flaccid and innocuous.

During the implementation phase the consequences of the law's ambiguity and its compromises quickly became evident to govern-ment and child welfare agencies. However, as a result of the Act, greater emphasis was placed on adoption promotion and there was some increase in the department's resources and initiatives. The number of adoptions continued to climb, but so too did the number of children for whom adoption homes were unavailable or who were classified as "unsuitable for adoption."[47] In many cases children were not candidates for adoption because early preven-tive intervention had not occurred or because treatment facilities continued to be inadequate or inaccessible. Another factor which meant missed opportunities for adoption was that adoption promotion by both the Department and the societies was hampered by resource limitations. Potentially progressive adoption promotion policies and initiatives were only partially and inconsistently implemented, apparently due in large measure to the government's ambiguity in relation to social goals.

Meanwhile, the emergence of alternative life styles and changing social pressures, particularly on women, added to the demands placed upon agencies to provide long-term foster or group home care for a growing number of older children. With greater acceptance of interracial adoption and rather less stringent emphasis on religious criteria than there was in the early 1960s, adoption homes were being more readily found for children in sibling groups and for some children with disabilities. Government penury was, however, at least partially responsible for the fact that some Crown wards were not provided with permanent placements, and that other adoptions of "hard-to-place" children with special needs broke down because the agencies were unable to provide adequate on-going services to the family.

Despite assurances to interest groups during the formalized policy process, specifically to the children's aid societies during the Hendry Committee's limited consultation process, there were insufficient resources to implement the Act. Change came with the advent of the Canada Assistance Plan in 1966 under which federal cost-sharing led to a decrease in the net costs of the societies to the province.[48] Despite apparent public readiness for and the anticipation of extensive policy shifts, in fact the provincial authorities demonstrated a long-standing adherence to a liberal ideology which supported limited government provision of social welfare services. Although under the 1965 Act responsibility was assumed "in loco parentis" for Crown wards, in practice the authorities remained equivocal as to the extent to which the province would be considered accountable for child welfare. Since ambivalence about the state's role in social welfare provision imbued the legislation it is not surprising that it failed to respond to the needs and rights of many "hard-to-place" children. To a large extent the outputs of the process were determined by internally established political priorities.

Certainly, policy processes are cyclical.[49] Demands for extensive legislative revisions were bound to increase as early as the late 1960s as the Act's deficiencies were demonstrated.

Policy Developments Two Decades Later

The process around the development of the 1984 Child and Family Services Act involved nongovernment interests in largely a reactive way. By contrast, although the earlier process reflected tight government control and the dominant role of "withinputs," the provincial authorities recognized the political significance of involving nongovernment interests in a major way, particularly during the first phase, and even appeared to recognize the need for utilizing their expertise. By the 1980s, the order of the day was to rely on strong internal staff resources (many of them not social workers or experienced in child welfare services) to draft plans and policies. This was a trend which developed in relation to the government's efforts during the early 1970s to gain increased accountability and controls over the burgeoning social welfare system.[50] Although the trend developed during a period of rapid expansion of services, it has been reinforced during the period of retrenchment since the mid-1970s.

Unlike the earlier process, policy development of the 1982 to 1985 period reduced to insignificance the role of nongovernment interests, despite the fact that the bill was intended to be a comprehensive piece of legislation incorporating several laws currently in force.[51] Responses were invited to several consultation documents in the years prior to 1982, before the formal policy process began.[52] Then, in October of 1982, a very general paper of 180 pages, entitled *The Children's Act: A Consultation Paper*, was drafted by an internal Ministry working group and circulated.[53] Although this document listed twelve organizations and forty-nine individuals who contributed ... "valuable comments in the early stages of the development of this paper" (termed by Ministry staff "the mini-consultation process"), some of these were other Ministry or government employees, and only four were employees of a children's aid society.[54] Some of those listed have said they were only asked to comment on a particular issue or practice. There is a striking contrast between the research and documentation acquired directly from the field in the preparation of the 1964 Report of the Advisory Committee and that for the preparation of the 1982 Consultation Paper and the ensuing consultation period which followed. After the release of the Consultation Paper, a six-month period was allowed for reaction. Active lobbying on the part of several major child welfare organizations and related interest groups took place.

Staff were directed to draft the recent legislation while keeping in mind the need for financial restraints and the need to avoid politically damaging conflict or controversy with major interest groups.[55] Under two consecutive ministers and throughout the entire policy process from 1983 onward, staff were also under instructions that no proposals resulting in the liberalization of adoption information disclosure would be tolerated.[56] Certainly this seems characteristic of what Nordlinger has described as a "state-centred" as opposed to a "society-centred" model of social policy.[57]

In December 1983 the then minister of Community and Social Services presented to the legislature and circulated to child welfare agencies the proposed Child and Family Services Act; he allowed a six-week interval (including Christmas vacation period) in which responses would be accepted.[58] In February of 1984 a number of delegations submitted briefs and made oral presentations to the Standing Committee on Social Development, a committee of the legislature comprised of representatives of all three political parties. The Ontario Association of Children's Aid Societies, the Children's Aid Society of Metropolitan Toronto, the Ontario Association of Children's Mental Health Centres, the Ontario Association of Professional Social Workers, and the Ontario Medical Association were among groups which made presentations in which they highlighted weaknesses in Bill 77.

Some of the concerns raised by these bodies led to modifications. In fact it can be argued that ministry initiatives to lessen existing program difficulties and to increase the degree of protection of children's rights were altered as a consequence of these interest groups' inputs and the threat of political damage in the event that particular demands were not heeded. Some groups regarded the government's proposals as largely positive and thought that some of their concerns were considered.[59] However, many sources of discontent remained, particularly about the excessively legalistic nature of the controls applicable to children's aid societies, the increased powers to be retained by the Ministry, and the nondisclosure of even nonidentifying information from adoption records. These issues were unresolved when Bill 77 went to the legislature for its first reading on May 18, 1984.

THE SECOND PHASE: THE LEGISLATIVE PROCESS

Second reading, incorporating some changes made by the Social Development Committee, came a month later.[60] Further hearings in July 1984 drew protests about the persistence of major flaws in the draft legislation.[61] Significant amendments were also moved and defeated in late November during an intense two-and-one-half hour debate of the Committee of the Whole in the legislature and during third reading on December 11.[62] Despite the continuing and widespread criticism, Bill 77 received Royal Assent on December 14, 1984.

Throughout the legislative debates there was protracted controversy about the adoption sections relating to disclosure. Despite well-reasoned arguments by Liberal and New Democratic Party members, all significant amendments were rejected by the minister with the backing of the cabinet. Great concern was expressed both within and outside the legislature that Bill 77 would prohibit the currently widespread practice of disclosing to adult adoptees, upon request, nonidentifying information from birth records. The new legislation was intended to prevent this occurring except in special circumstances necessary to protect the individual's health.[63] A Liberal member moved an amendment, far short of permitting full and free disclosure (Subsection 152.2) to permit:

The disclosure by a director to a person who is adopted and has attained the age of eighteen years of information that relates to the adoption and does not identify an individual by name or make him or her readily identifiable by other means.[64]

In supporting this amendment, the N.D.P. critic charged the minister with imposing his own narrow, personal views on the entire province.[65] In rejecting the amendment the minister disagreed that he was imposing his own will, stating that "the legislation reflects the policy and the position of cabinet and the government caucus."[66]

As was explained in the daily press, a coterie of influential cabinet members, some of whom were adoptive parents, had fashioned the adoption policies of this Bill on the basis of their own personal values and vested interests. In respect of disclosure, the outcome of the policy process varied widely from the inputs of both the public at large and child welfare interests directly involved in service delivery. Neither did the outcome reflect the policy recommendations of the Ministry's own policy unit and staff dealing directly with child welfare.[67]

While sections of the Act relevant to adoption clearly reflected personal self-interest, in other contentious sections government initiatives were directed towards economizing or avoiding political controversy. Publicly known information about the particular politicians and senior government bureaucrats who influenced the adoption policies of this legislation gives rise to serious questions of conflict of interest.

It should be noted that these particular sections relevant to the disclosure of adoption information and the adoption register were inconsistent with the government's claim that the legislation was intended to protect the rights of Ontario's children as well as those of other parties involved.[68] Several other sections of the Act did, in fact, incorporate ministry initiatives in defence of the child's rights, such as those concerning children in institutional care.[69]

However, with regard to the sections pertaining to adoption, the rights of the adoptive parents seem to have been the focus of attention. If implemented this regressive adoption legislation would have withdrawn from adult adoptees access to information regarding their personal histories which for some years had been made available to them by most of Ontario's children's aid societies.[70] Adult adoptees would have been prevented from possessing basic personal information about themselves, information which well-intentioned and supportive adoptive parents would be willing to give (if they could).

As passed, Bill 77 would have removed from the professional social worker the freedom to disclose appropriate information to adult adoptees from their birth records, even nonidentifying information.[71] It would also have done nothing to activate and improve the Adoption Register which, since 1978, had facilitated a relatively small number of reunions of adult adoptees with their birth mothers when such a meeting was mutually agreeable.[72] If the Act had been enforced as passed, power to disclose information from birth records would have rested with the director of Child Welfare or his/her appointee. Such information would have been released only in exceptional circumstances and only for health reasons, ill-defined in the legislation.[73]

It should be noted that several interest groups, including the opposition during the legislative debate, conceded that there was some credibility in the official ministry position that it was necessary to safeguard the rights of adoptive parents who had not anticipated future disclosure of birth-record information to their adopted child. Of particular concern was information which might identify the birth parents, who had not anticipated an adoption registry.[74] However, in the legislature Liberal and N.D.P. spokespersons argued that for future adoptions, adoptive parents should anticipate the possibility of disclosure of information and even the reunion of the adult adoptees with their natural parents.[75] However, even with this concession to the contractual law concept, the minister refused amendments which would have aided adult adoptees of the future to gain access to information which might have helped them come to terms with their own identities.

In fact, the minister contended that the Child Welfare Act as amended in 1978 did not permit the release of information from birth records to the extent that some agencies had been doing.[76] He was supported in this contention by the ruling of County Court Judge J. Kileen of 18 January 1983 with regard to the Ferguson case.[77] He had ruled that Elizabeth Ferguson, a fifty-five year old woman who expressed no urgent reasons for information from her birth record but a need to dispel a sense of incompleteness, must be denied her request.[78] He condemned the legislation for failing to differentiate between identifying and nonidentifying information and pointed out the lack of powers afforded the judiciary.[79] He pointed out that it failed to give an active role to the registry itself by mandating the communication of full information about the registry to prospective members of the adoption triangle and the public.[80] Judge Kileen also pointed out that the 1978 Act did not incorporate the recommendations of the 1976 Report of the Ministry's Committee on Record Disclosure to Adoptees which he called a "comprehensive and scholarly document," and noted that the Committee had made recommendations which reflected fairness to the sometimes conflicting interests of members of the adoption triangle and satisfied public interest considerations.[81] He also noted that amongst the Committee's major recommendations were that "with minor limitations, nonidentifying information should be made available to adoptive parents, adult adoptees and the biological parents upon request."[82] The Committee had also urged the creation of an active Adoption Registry through which identifying information could be exchanged amongst the parties to the adoption.[83]

Notwithstanding the critically constructive comments in the Kileen judgement concerning the inadequacy and passivity of the adoption sections of the previous legislation, the government orchestrated the passage of Bill 77 with its equally restrictive provisions.

THE RESULTS AND PROSPECTS

The 1984 Act, as passed, contained even greater inconsistencies than the 1965 Act with regard to two of its stated objectives, defending the best interests of the child and protecting children's rights. For example, for the past twenty years child welfare agencies had been promoting the adoption of children in care who were beyond infancy, and recently the thrust in practice had been towards the concept of open adoption. An increasing number of older wards had been encouraged to maintain contact after their adoption with selected members of their birth families on the basis that this was beneficial to the healthy emotional development of the child. However, as passed, the 1985 legislation required the utmost confidentiality after the adoption has taken place (and some interpreted Bill 77 to indicate that such confidentiality also would have applied during the adoption process).[84] It was easy to predict the dilemma of the worker who had been involved for many months with a particular six or seven year old child: suddenly, the day after the adoption process began, the worker would have had to tell the child that they could no longer talk about a much-loved grandparent or sibling.

Further inconsistencies arose due to the government's eagerness to respect the distinct needs and the autonomy of the native population. For instance, the native community's controls over their child welfare services have been increased, which is highly commendable, providing the necessary resources are available.[85] However, the law stipulated the band council must be notified about the adoption of all band children.[86] This provoked questions as to how it was possible to maintain confidentiality on the reserve, or for that matter in any instance, when the concept of open adoption within the community is encouraged. It was also asserted that the law violated principles inherent in the Canadian Charter of Rights and Freedoms as it treated native children differently from others.

Under the legislation as passed, social workers would be torn between their responsibility to abide by the law and their responsibilities to work in the best interests of clients. Breaches of the confidentiality required by this Act would be frequent. Good legislation must be based on clear goals and it must be seen to be appropriate and possible to implement.[87] The Child and Family Services Act as passed failed to balance the rights and responsibilities of the children, their families and child welfare agencies, and could not be implemented effectively due to inconsistencies, ambiguities and inadequate resources. As James Anderson has pointed out, without adequate resources "actions ostensibly directed towards meeting material wants or needs may turn out to be more symbolic than material in their impact."[88]

Trends in the past two decades have tended to centralize the powers of the Ministry of Community and Social Services over child welfare agencies. Increasingly the policy inputs of experienced service deliverers are ignored.[89] Children's aid societies have expressed anxiety about the "excessively legalistic" processes which have been instituted and are in prospect.[90] They have stated that these processes have threatened to increase costs greatly, delay necessary treatment, prolong adoption processes, and extend the sanctioning and reporting procedures required by the ministry. Certainly the legislation as passed defied a basic tenet of good management that authority should always be commensurate with responsibility; those designated with the responsibility for service provision require the freedom of professional discretion and the resources to meet their responsibilities.

The Child and Family Services Act of 1984, like the 1965 Child

Welfare Act, reflected the particular political, economic, and social pressures of the time. It was complicated by the government's increasing reticence to assume responsibility for social welfare services and it espoused strategies of minimal professional interference with family autonomy. It illustrated the dilemmas of the quasi-voluntary agency, mandated and funded to implement legislation that in many respects did not reflect the agency's own policy recommendations. It also raised long-standing controversial questions about the role of the quasi-voluntary agency.

Like the 1965 Child Welfare Act, the new legislation had some strong points. However, like its predecessors it reflected government parsimony and compromises based on political expediency, compromises of critical significance to many Ontarians. Even more clearly than the earlier law, the new legislation presented a confusion of rights and responsibilities.

Since Bill 77, the Child and Family Services Act of Ontario, was passed in December 1984, many events have occurred which further illustrate the extent to which its limitations were realized. Following Premier William Davis's resignation in February 1985 a new minister of Community and Social Services was appointed. By April, Dr. Ralph Garber, dean of the Faculty of Social Work at the University of Toronto, was named as a one-man commission to study adoption disclosure and report back in September 1985. The implementation of several portions was delayed, including Section 157 dealing with adoption disclosure as well as parts dealing with policies regarding native children, records and confidentiality, and residential placements. At the time of writing it remained to be seen what improvements would be made under the new Liberal minority government which took office in June 1985. However, the question remains as to how, despite the knowledge and resources which were available, legislation so replete with faults came to be passed.

UNRESOLVED ISSUES
Like earlier instances of provincial policy development the process around the 1984 Act and the legislation itself lacked clearly articulated goals, values, or ideological bases.[91] Like earlier child welfare policies it portrayed the paradoxes and ambiguities inherent in liberalism. However, while earlier policies and processes indicated

the Progressive Conservative government's ambivalence about the state's responsibilities in relation to social services, the recent process reflected erosion of government's commitment to social welfare and reinforcement of limitations on the pluralist dynamic.

As has been stated in relation to a recent analysis of human services policy in British Columbia, "it needs to be acknowledged that the choice of approaches at any stage of the policy-making process will be determined more by the personality of the minister and his senior staff than by careful analysis of the most promising approach in a given situation."[92] The development of the 1984 Act indicated centralized control, which, the evidence suggests, rested with a small coterie within cabinet. The process was largely unilateral with reduced potential for significant inputs from diverse nongovernment interests. As Manzer has acknowledged, "pluralist regulation has stabilized the domestic social order by accommodating the interest conflicts of whatever social groups prove too powerful to be coerced with a consequent clouding of social justice."[93] This provoked serious questions, beyond the scope of this chapter, about ways of reducing the relative impotence of social welfare interest groups and opposition political parties.

In addition, the development of the 1984 Act illustrated very clearly the need to examine closely the definitions of conflict of interest in current Canadian law, and the need to determine how decision-makers with serious conflicts of interest can be prevented from having almost untouchable control over major social policy processes. It raised questions as to how methods used by powerful officials, elected or employed, to influence policy decisions can be monitored and, if necessary, controlled through democratic processes. Such issues are of critical concern to those eager to protect a pluralist dynamic in a democratic framework and to those wanting to engender intensified commitment to social welfare priorities.

Notes

1. Phoebe Hall, Hilary Land, Roy Parker, and Adrian Webb, *Change, Choice and Conflict in Social Policy* (London: Heinemann, 1975), 13.
2. Ibid., 130–51.
3. Valuable analyses in this regard are presented in Peter Bachrach and Morton S. Baratz, *Power and Poverty: Theory and Practice* (London: Oxford University Press, 1970), Chapter One, "Two Faces of Power," 3–16, and Chapter Three, "Key Concepts: Decisions and Non-Decisions," 39–51.
4. Ontario Statutes, 1965, 13–14 Elizabeth II, Chapter 14, *The Child Welfare Act*.
5. Ontario Statutes, 1984, 32–33 Elizabeth II, Chapter 55, *An Act Respecting the Protection and Well-Being of Children and Their Families*.
6. The term "withinputs" as distinct from "inputs" (significant interest group demands) is derived from David Easton, *A Systems Analysis of Political Life* (New York: John Wiley and Sons, 1965). See pp. 38–50.
7. See the Ontario Statutes, 1921, 11 George V, Chapter 55, *The Adoption Act;* and Ontario Statutes, 1954, 3 Elizabeth II, Chapter 8, *The Child Welfare Act*.
8. See the report to the Ontario Association of Children's Aid Societies (OACAS), "Review by the Standing Committee on Adoption of the Report to the Minister of Public Welfare of His Committee on Child Care and Adoption Services" (March 26, 1954).
9. These included a great many "hard-to-place" wards for whom adoption homes were not found or even sought.
10. As the former Executive Director of the Children's Aid Society of Metropolitan Toronto, Lloyd Richardson, stated, by the late 1950s the societies were thoroughly frustrated in their attempts to cope with larger numbers of children in long-term care on a hand-to-mouth basis. Personal interview, May, 1980.
11. See OACAS, Minutes of Board of Directors meeting, December 1, 1960.
12. Personal interview with the former executive director of the Children's Aid Society of Metropolitan Toronto, May, 1980.
13. At the Children's Aid Society of Metropolitan Toronto, for example, there was an increase of 32 percent on protection cases and of 50 percent in children under three years brought into care. Yet during that time period the social work staff increased by only 2 percent, from 199 in 1958 to 203 in 1963.
14. This, however, provoked renewed questioning about their proportionately high costs by contrast to the smaller societies.
15. Many press editorials supported the government's restrictive position in relation to social welfare spending, such as those entitled "Enough Welfare Already," *Globe and Mail*, 2 December 1960, and "The New Poor," *Globe and Mail*, 22 February 1961.

16. The Ontario Association of Children's Aid Societies, "A Statement of Practice and Procedure in Adoption" of 28 March 1960 stated "In general, efforts should be made to place a child in a family of the same racial origin as himself, or at least in one which he most nearly resembles in appearance."

17. An estimate derived from available records of the Roman Catholic agencies and published by Peter Ward in the *Toronto Telegram*, 17 August 1960.

18. Based on personal interviews with Lloyd Richardson, former executive director of the Children's Aid Society of Metropolitan Toronto on 9 May 1980, and with Mrs. Collette Lecour Cardinal, former adoption supervisor of the Catholic Children's Aid Society of Toronto, 18 June 1980.

19. Senior Roman Catholic clergy, such as Bishop Marrocco, directly affected the Catholic agency's policies and participated actively on the Board.

20. Social Planning Council of Metropolitan Toronto, *Report on Children's Institutions in Metropolitan Toronto* (Toronto: May 1960).

21. Examples of press controversy are to be found in: the *Toronto Telegram*, 28 March 1960, the *Toronto Star*, 28 and 29 March 1960, and the *Globe and Mail*, 29 March 1960.

22. This is following a concept described by Easton. See *A Framework for Political Analysis* (Englewood Cliffs, New Jersey: Prentice-Hall, Inc., 1965), 90–91.

23. Ontario, Department of Public Welfare, *Report to the Minister of the Advisory Committee on Child Welfare* (Toronto: Queen's Printer, 1964), 1.

24. Ibid., i.

25. Ibid., 67–68.

26. Ibid., ii–iii.

27. Ibid., 26.

28. Ibid., 12.

29. Ibid., 2.

30. Ontario, Department of Public Welfare, *Report of the Minister's Committee on Child Care and Adoption Services* (Toronto: Queen's Printer, 1953), and *Report on Field Services* (Toronto: Queen's Printer, 1954).

31. Ibid., 41.

32. When interviewed, key adoption workers of both Toronto societies of that time also spoke of lessening resistance on the part of fellow social workers.

33. Social Planning Council of Metropolitan Toronto, *The Adoption of Negro Children* (Toronto: July 1966).

34. The government of Ontario had consistently, through the early sixties, tried to restrain the expanding costs of social welfare services, although their rationale for doing so was not consistently or clearly stated.

35. Gail Aitken, "Criteria of Adoptability in Ontario, 1945 to 1965: The Circumstances, Processes and Effects of Policy Change" (Ph.D. dissertation, University of Toronto, 1983). This committee was also known as the "Legislation" Committee but was formally named the Committee on the New Child Welfare Act as indicated in minutes of the committee retained in the files of Dr. Charles Hendry, at the archives of the University of Toronto.

36. This is evident in the minutes of meeting of the Committee on the New Child Welfare Act, for example, those of 9 March 1965 and 14 April 1965.

37. See *The Child Welfare Act*, 1965, Part I, Section 6:2 c.

38. Ontario, Legislature of Ontario, *Debates*, 1965, 2773–2778.

39. Ibid., 2773–2774.

40. For example, *Globe and Mail* article and editorial, 12 November 1965.

41. Ontario, *Debates*, 1965, 2776.

42. Ibid., 3754.

43. *The Child Welfare Act*, 1965, Part IV.

44. Yet, as one senior government official of that time later stated:

    Under Band [the deputy minister] all the legislative changes were probably less significant than the changes in the regulations which accompanied them.

45. For a discussion of the concepts of nondecisions see Peter Bachrach and Morton S. Baratz, *Power and Poverty: Theory and Practice* (London: Oxford University Press, 1970), 39–51.

46. Experience had taught that public attention could be directed very readily to child welfare issues, perhaps more readily than to issues in other human service areas.

47. Records of the Catholic Children's Aid Society indicate that the number of Crown wards in care rose from 718 in 1965 to 869 in 1968, an increase of about 21 percent. At the CAS of Metropolitan Toronto the costs of maintaining children in institutions climbed from $250,000 in 1957 to $3,000,000 in 1967, an enormous increase, even considering the change in dollar value.

48. Canada, *Statutes of Canada*, 1966, 14–15 Elizabeth II, Chapter 45, *The Canada Assistance Plan*, proclaimed July 15, 1966. By this Act the federal government agreed to cost-share with the province 50 percent of a broad range of social services for people "in need or likely to be in need." These included most of the costs, other than capital costs, to the provincial and municipal governments of children's aid societies programs.

49. See, for example, William W. Boyer, *Bureaucracy on Trial: Policy-Making by Government Agencies* (New York: Bobbs Merril, 1965), 166–77.

50. See, for example, Urwick, Currie and Partners, Ltd., *A Study of the Managerial Effectiveness of Children's Aid Societies in Ontario* (com-

missioned by the Government of Ontario), (Toronto: 1968), and Ontario, Committee on Government Productivity, *Report to the Executive Council of the Government of Ontario*, 10 volumes (Toronto: Queen's Printer, 1970–1973).

51. The Act was intended to consolidate the Child Welfare Act; The Training Schools Act; The Children's Mental Health Services Act; The Children's Residential Services Act; The Day Nurseries Act and others. See Ontario, Ministry of Community and Social Services, *The Children's Act: A Consultation Paper* (Toronto, October 1982), 9.

52. For example, *Children's Services: Past, Present and Future* (December 1980); *Funding of Children's Services in the 1980s* (December 1979); *Child Advocacy: Implementing the Child's Right to Be Heard* (October 1980).

53. Ontario, Ministry of Community and Social Services, *The Children's Act: A Consultation Paper* (1982).

54. These four, Douglas Barr, Robin Vogl, Dorothy Harrison and Sandra Scarth, were all with Metro Toronto Children's Aid Society at the time.

55. This was corroborated by several persons directly involved in the process.

56. Ibid.

57. As Nordlinger has proposed, one of the characteristics of a "state-centred" model of social policy, as opposed to a "society-centred" model, is that "When state and societal preferences diverge, public officials periodically capitalize upon their autonomy-enhancing capacities and opportunities to free themselves of societal constraints, and then they translate their preferences into authoritative actions." See Eric A. Nordlinger, *On the Autonomy of the Democratic State* (Cambridge, Massachusetts: Harvard University Press, 1981), 7.

58. The shortness of the interval was a frustration to agency representatives who stated that they required much more time to respond adequately.

59. See The Ontario Association of Professional Social Workers submission to the Legislature's Standing Committee on Social Development (February 1984), 5.

60. Ontario, *Debates*, 20 June 1984.

61. For example, Children's Aid Society of Metropolitan Toronto, *Notes for an Appearance Before the Ontario Legislature's Standing Committee on Social Development Regarding Bill 77: "An Act Respecting the Protection and Well-Being of Children and Their Families"* (18 July 1984).

62. See, for example, Ontario, *Debates*, 22 November 1984: 437.

63. *An Act Respecting the Protection and Well-Being of Children and Their Families*, 1984, Section 157, Subsection 2,d.

64. Ontario, *Debates*, 22 November 1984: 4374.

65. Ibid., 4382.

66. Ibid.

67. Since 1976 internally prepared policy documents had recommended that:
    i) Nonidentifying information should be made available to adoptive parents upon request, and
    ii) Nonidentifying information should be available to adult adoptees without adoptive parental consent.
    It had also been recommended that the Ministry administer a "basically passive" adoption Registry whereby adult adoptees, adoptive parents, and biological parents might register for personal contact or information giving. Child Welfare Branch, Ministry of Community and Social Services, *Report of the Committee on Record Disclosure to Adoptees* (Toronto: 22 July 1976), 18–25.
68. However, see the comments of the Minister which stress the concerns for the rights of the adoptive parents. Ontario, *Debates*, 22 November 1984: 4383.
69. See: *An Act Respecting the Protection and Well-Being of Children and Their Families*, 1984, Part IV, Section 90.
70. Children's Aid Society of Metropolitan Toronto, *Notes for an Appearance Before the Ontario Legislature's Standing Committee on Social Development*, 13–20.
71. *An Act Respecting the Protection and Well-Being of Children and Their Families*, 1984, Section 157.
72. Ibid., Section 158.
73. Ibid., Section 157 (2).
74. Ontario, *Debates*, 22 November 1984: 4382–4383.
75. Ibid., 4384–4385.
76. Ibid., 4377.
77. County Court of the County of Middlesex, *Elizabeth Ferguson vs. Director of Child Welfare, Ministry of Community and Social Services*, London, Ontario, 18 January 1983.
78. Ibid., 3.
79. Ibid., 10, 42.
80. Ibid., 25.
81. Ibid., 20.
82. Ministry of Community and Social Services, *Report of the Committee on Record Disclosure to Adoptees*, 18–20.
83. Ibid., 20–24.
84. This ambiguity has been a source of concern to lawyers connected to child welfare agencies and to the provincial government.
85. The consultation paper had recommended that there should be native representation on children's aid societies board of directors where indicated and that the minister should be empowered to establish a native child welfare agency. Apparently these recommendations were generally supported, according to Ontario Ministry of Community and Social Services, *The Child and Family Services Act: Draft Legislation and Background Paper* (Toronto: November 1983), 7.

86. *An Act Respecting the Well-Being of Children and Their Families,* 1984, Section 156.

87. Also, as James Anderson has pointed out, "when the goals of a policy are unclear, diffuse, or diverse, as they often are, determining the extent to which they have been attained becomes a difficult and frustrating task." See James E. Anderson, *Public Policy Making,* 2nd ed. (New York: Holt Rinehart and Winston, 1979), 157.

88. Ibid., 155–56.

89. Although the Ministry structure is decentralized, with regional and area offices extensively involved in program development and monitoring, policy-making, and resource allocations are centralized.

90. See note 74; also Children's Aid Society of the Region of Peel, *Bill 77, "An Act Respecting the Protection and Well-Being of Children and Their Families,"* (n.d.), and the brief presented to the Standing Committee on Social Development by the Ontario Association of Children's Aid Societies, February 1984.

91. This concern is well expressed in Kenneth R. Hammond and Jeryl Mumpower, "Formation of Social Policy" in *Knowledge: Creation, Diffusion, Utilization* 1, 2, (December 1979): 245–58. They state:

    —Because citizens have no good mechanism for explicitly considering tradeoffs among values, and because their expression of values is episodic, it provides a poor guide for social policy makers. (p. 248)

    and:

    The present chaotic, unsystematic method of policy formation relies on the adversary system. . . . Adversaries simply organize the facts into two classes, those that can be used to support their position and those that cannot. Those facts that *can* be used *are* used, those that *cannot* be used are *ignored* or their importance is diminished. (p. 251)

92. Michael Clague, Robert Dill, Roop Seebaran, and Brian Wharf, *Reforming Social Services* (Vancouver: University of British Columbia Press, 1984), 248.

93. Ronald Manzer, *Public Policies and Political Development in Canada* (Toronto: University of Toronto Press, 1985), 189.

13 Social Policy and Some Aspects of the Neoconservative Ideology in British Columbia

CHRIS R. McNIVEN

Between 1945 and 1973, the system of practices and state institutions which became known as the Keynesian Welfare State was developed in most western countries. In Canada, the national version of the welfare state was able to grow fairly rapidly. It was linked to the promises of guaranteed improvement in the economic security and quality of life of all Canadians and it benefited from a lengthy cycle of economic growth and a climate of political stability which fostered the emergence of enlightened social innovations.

In the early 1970s, however, and shortly after the Liberal party which was in power at the time had announced the arrival of the "Canadian Just Society," almost every version of the welfare state began to encounter increasing difficulties in fulfilling its economic and social goals. The problem was caused by factors that had not been present, or clearly anticipated, when the initial model of a state which could be a viable solution to the socioeconomic problems generated by capitalism had been invented. Three of these factors—a sharp increase in the price of fuel oil, a growing competition amongst world nations for control of consumer markets, and widespread changes in communication and work technologies—affected the normal utilization of the labour force in almost every western country. As economic growth slowed down, unemployment and inflation rose, and it did not take long before concerns were expressed about the feasibility and wisdom of expanding further national social security systems and social welfare programs. By the middle of the decade, the ideological and theoretical basis of the welfare state was being questioned openly and the search for an appropriate post-welfare state ideology was gaining popularity.

The formulation of this new ideology could have come primarily from the left end of the political spectrum and consisted of a renewed attack upon capitalism and capitalist notions of social welfare. The left, however, had lost some of the influence it had enjoyed before 1968. The ideology that was to guide eventually the policies and priorities of several western governments came instead from the neoconservative right and took the form of reaffirmation of faith in the value of capitalism and free enterprise, coupled with a strong determination to get rid of the allegedly debilitating burden of state welfare. Right-wing governments were elected or re-elected in the United Kingdom, the United States, Germany, and Canada between 1978 and 1984 and they all proceeded rapidly to develop their own models of the post-welfare state era. A parallel development has occurred in British Columbia, where two political parties, the Social Credit Party (SOCRED) and the New Democratic Party (N.D.P.) have formulated and reformulated socioeconomic welfare policies several times since 1952.

Following a brief overview of the nature of this welfare system in British Columbia, before 1976, this chapter explores some of the changes that have been made to this system after a Social Credit government was returned to power in December, 1975.

Social Welfare Trends in British Columbia from 1952 to 1975

The domination of the British Columbia political scene by liberal conservative coalitions ended in 1952 with the election of the province's first Social Credit government. While it may not have been impressed with the progressive and optimistic views of state welfare popular in the fifties and sixties, the new government allowed nevertheless a group of dedicated social welfare professionals to develop a fairly substantial welfare system in the public and voluntary sectors.

The system suffered from a number of structural weaknesses and social allowance rates were inadequate but, compared to the systems operating in other provinces at the time, it was considered to be well above average.

During the sixties, if there was any dissatisfaction, it was directed at the provincial welfare department that had been renamed the Department of Rehabilitation and Social Improvement in 1963 following the appointment of its first full-time minister. The department was criticized, not only for failing to provide adequate services but also for its harsh and insensitive ways of dealing with clients.

Between 1969 and 1972, a trend away from welfare and in the direction of control and restraint began to grow but it was halted in 1972 when the N.D.P. obtained a long awaited opportunity to form a majority government and to implement new social welfare policies. Armed with a mandate for changing the system of social service delivery in British Columbia, which had come primarily from the social welfare establishment, the government launched a community resources board experiment characterized by a massive service decentralization, coordination and integration and by a strong emphasis on citizen participation.[1]

A realistic assessment of this approach to social welfare in British Columbia between 1972 and 1975 is difficult because the experiment was of short duration and conducted in a rather ad hoc fashion. In retrospect one may wonder whether the party of reform did have a clear and comprehensive set of policy guidelines but its intentions were good and the disadvantaged and needy had hopes of being treated more humanely and fairly than at any previous time in the history of the province.

The 1976 to 1983 Phase

The 1975 election did not turn out to be a routine event for B.C. It ended abruptly the brief reign of the only party capable of opposing the Social Credit party, halted moderate left wing social policy initiatives and launched the career of a new political leader.

The new premier was the son of the Social Credit party founder, who had retired in 1972 when an N.D.P. victory had interrupted his twenty year incumbency as premier. He had lived in the shadow of this popular father, did not have much political experience and, although he was re-elected again in 1979, he had to move with caution initially. Lacking the charisma and air of self-confidence projected by some of the other Canadian politicians of the 70s and 80s, the new premier did not lack energy and ambition, and it is not too far fetched to speculate that the need to establish his own political identity and to show that he was not an inferior copy of his father has had some influence on the political process that unfolded after 1976. His strong determination to turn British Columbia into a high profile province capable of trading with international partners, even more successfully than the senior eastern provinces could hope to do, may have been rooted to some extent in a need to be recognized and respected.

Until 1980, the achievement of this goal of economic prosperity seemed to be realistic. While specific economic policies often elicited mixed reviews on the ground that they were short-sighted, and leading to the depletion of British Columbia natural resources for the benefit of foreign investors,[2] they nevertheless appeared to be successful and the economy of the province grew on the average at an annual rate of a little over 5.5 percent between 1975 and 1980.

During this period of time social welfare policies were influenced, of course, by a Social Credit ideology which included an approach to economic development that emphasized the value of investing resources in the private sector while making relatively more parsimonious allocations of resources to the public sector. The Community Resource Boards established by the N.D.P. government were dismantled, new approaches were tried that restricted the scope of child welfare services and new procedures were introduced which reflected a determination to slow down the increase in the cost of social welfare programs, but the level of public assistance benefits remained higher still than the Canadian average and the overall quality of social services fairly adequate when compared to the quality of similar services in other Canadian provinces.

The welfare policy orientation followed in British Columbia between 1976 and 1981 could be characterized as one of containment rather than retrenchment and social welfare administrators and workers continued to be able to use professional discretion in the implementation of policies and procedures.

Between 1980 and 1981, the economic picture changed rather abruptly as British Columbia joined the rest of Canada in experiencing the impact of a worldwide recession. The economic events which occurred have been analyzed by William Schworn, a British Columbia economist, who wrote that:

> B.C. is suffering from the worst recession since the 1930s. The Recession is world-wide and was initially caused by factors outside the control of B.C. The central bank in the U.S., followed by the Bank of Canada, practiced a tight monetary policy which pushed interest rates up to unprecedented levels. The high interest rates induced large reductions in investment, housing construction, and the purchase of consumer durables. The resulting loss of business revenues plus the high cost of borrowing resulted in widespread bankruptcies and layoffs.
>
> B.C. necessarily participated in this economic recession. First, consumers and businesses in B.C. faced the same high interest rates that caused the recession throughout the world. This has caused businesses to postpone construction projects and households to reduce housing construction. The consequence has been a precipitous decline in the construction sector of the economy. Second, the reduction in housing construction in the U.S. reduced the demand for B.C.'s timber and lumber exports. Third, a fall in metal prices, especially copper, caused a major decline in the mining sector of the economy. Fourth, the recession in the U.S. and in the rest of Canada has sharply reduced the revenues from tourism. Finally, the reduced personal incomes caused by unemployment, lower real wages, and lower business profits together with higher interest rates on loans have forced consumers to purchase fewer consumer goods with depressing effects on the trade and service sector of the economy. These events have combined to create the extremely depressed economic conditions in B.C.[3]

Not only did the recession cause the level of unemployment to rise in B.C. from 6.5 percent in 1980 to 13.5 percent in 1983 and to

14.9 percent in 1984, but it also cut sharply into provincial revenues. According to economist John Malcolmson:

> During the 1982/83 fiscal year, the resource sensitive sectors of
> provincial revenue nearly collapsed. Corporate income tax,
> which in the previous year had provided $580 million, fell to
> just over $180 million. Energy revenues dropped from $357 mil-
> lion to $229 million, mineral revenues from $62 million to $33
> million and forest revenues from $107 million to $86 million.
> This situation, when combined with the increases in social ex-
> penditures triggered by the recession, produced B.C.'s first
> deficit on operating expenditures since the mid-1970s.[4]

Faced with this dismal situation and with the evaporation of the
dream of economic prosperity, the B.C. government took a series of
steps between 1982 and the spring of 1983 to cope with the difficulties. These steps consisted for the most part of reductions in the
allocation of funds to the public sector and were similar to the
steps already taken by the Federal government. The Compensation
Stabilization Program, introduced early in 1982, was to keep public sector wage increases down to a maximum of 14 percent, and
approximately 6 percent if the public sector work force was to be
reduced, mostly through attrition. Other key measures included
the termination of the Denticare program, reductions in the grants
to provincial school districts, post-secondary institutions and hospitals, and a freeze of the welfare rates.

In February 1982, the premier announced the beginning of a
restraint program. In October 1982, the government was forced to
relinquish its pay-as-you-go philosophy and to borrow money to finance the maintenance of government services. By the beginning
of 1983, the recession had become even more acute. The deficit was
increasing and because more people had to apply for public assistance there was an estimated $100 million overrun in the
1982–83 budget of the Ministry of Human Resources. In the spring
of 1983, the government called an election and asked for a
mandate to implement a policy of fiscal restraint.

The nature of the request became subsequently a controversial
issue. The Social Credit party has maintained that its political
platform had been made perfectly clear to the electorate and was
endorsed fully by a majority of voters. The opposition has claimed

that the agenda was vague and that the voters did not have a genuine opportunity to understand the real meaning and far-reaching aims of the concept of fiscal restraint which the government had in mind.

Whether or not the voters understood the implications of the policy, the Social Credit party was re-elected in May with a substantial majority of seats in the legislature and a popular mandate of very close to 50 percent of the B.C. electorate. On July 7, 1983, the budget speech and the legislation introduced by the government revealed to the public the first segment of the B.C. post-welfare state blueprint called by the premier "the new economic reality," a term which was abbreviated soon to "The New Reality."

The 1983 Blueprint and the Transformation of Socioeconomic Welfare in B.C.

The New Economic Reality concept and the program designed to implement it are not new. Although they both contain specific objectives and have characteristics that are derived from the local situation, they fall within the confines of the neoconservative trend which has swept North America and western Europe during the past decade. The character and coherence of neoconservatism is, like all ideologies, somewhat difficult to identify and pinpoint. It includes a broad array of political, social, and economic beliefs as well as specific opinions about the nature of society, of human behaviour, and of human relations. Moreover, the content of the ideology varies from country to country and its interpretation is distorted fairly often, by both its supporters and detractors, for political reasons. As Nevitte and Gibbins have suggested:

> Public debate does little to clarify the dimensions of neoconservatism; its opponents link it to a variety of noxious social attitudes while its proponents defend it in the language of cherished though often ambiguous, democratic values such as "freedom."
>
> The internationally acclaimed standard bearers of neoconservatism like Hayek, Kristol, Friedman and others may disagree about the exact boundaries of the ideology, but there is a con-

sensus that, at a minimum, neoconservatism involves a core set of beliefs which include a preference for down-sizing government, a belief in the efficacy of private enterprise and hence a preference for deregulating the economy. The widespread support for the Thatcher and Reagan governments is ample testimony to the response of these neoconservative principles with the British and American policies. The different national policies of these governments also indicates how similar general ideological principles become translated into different specific policy outputs. By comparison, the nature of Canadian neoconservatism is far more difficult to determine. There is no single, widely acknowledged Canadian neoconservative manifesto, no sustained record of neoconservative legislation and no systematic evidence which lays out the attitudinal structure of Canadian neoconservatism.[5]

The core set of beliefs mentioned by Nevitte and Gibbons applies partly to the B.C. experience, where the solution to the economic crisis is seen by the government as lying in the vigorous support of a renewed and modernized version of the traditional tenets of capitalism, combined, however, with an attempt to move rapidly from an industrial to a post-industrial society. No manifesto has been published, but the blueprint for change can be inferred from comments made by Milton Friedman about the British Columbia experiment in his book, *Bright Promises*, from the writings produced by the Fraser Institute, a neoconservative institute located in British Columbia, and mostly from a series of fiscal and legislative measures introduced by the B.C. government since July 1983. Initially, the new measures could have been interpreted as being simply a more extensive version of standard efforts to reduce government spending and prevent the growth of a deficit. But, when the various components of the 1983 blueprint, and the additions introduced subsequently, are brought together it becomes apparent that the basic premises underlining the version of state welfare which had been taken for granted in Canada for several decades, were to be denied in B.C.

In retrospect, it is fairly evident that the transformation was planned, and small parts of it were installed, before the 1983 election. Three years later, in 1986, it is even more obvious that the process of transformation is continuing and will continue as long as the Social Credit party remains in power under the same type of leadership.

To understand the nature of the transformation of the welfare state taking place in B.C., one must look beyond the benevolent image of a system created out of a collective and unselfish commitment to the well-being of all members of society who are in need. The original model, the Keynesian Welfare State, can be (and has been) conceptualized instead as an invention to reconcile the interests of broad sectors of the population, through redistributive programs and appropriate employment policies, with the requirements and operations of industrial societies.[6]

The cluster of state institutions, practices, and legal entitlements providing citizens with claims to transfer payments and services, and covering a variety of well-defined needs and risks, performed reasonably well as long as the economy was growing and the requests for benefits limited. But as we have seen, the 1981 recession cut into public revenues and increased the demands for assistance, not only from unemployed workers but from the business sector which had learned to depend on tax breaks and the infusion of public funds to stimulate the economy during periods of stagnation. Moreover, the B.C. economic recession is not caused by temporary factors but is of a structural nature. Jobs are disappearing permanently and the deficit, as well as the volume of claims on public resources and services guaranteed by the welfare state, will continue to grow until the economy has been restructured and the province has learned to cope with the transition to some version of post-industrialism.

The B.C. government had essentially four choices available. It could pretend that the problem would disappear if left alone. It could tinker modestly with the Keynesian Welfare State formula. It could attempt to transfer an adaptation of the economic growth paradigm which has prevailed in advanced capitalist societies for nearly two centuries to the realities of a post-industrial world. Or it could be very radical and develop a new paradigm. The B.C. government selected a version of the third option.

The model of welfare state which is unfolding in B.C. is concerned primarily with the development and requirements of a post-industrial society but only slightly with the safeguard of the economic, social, and even political interests of people who are unable or unwilling to find a niche in this society. The process of change from a semi-industrial to a post-industrial province is taking place very rapidly but is also quite complex and it reaches into all sectors and levels of B.C. society.

The economic sector is being reorganized and strengthened through the use of legislation and selective allocations of provincial revenues. The welfare sector is also being reorganized, some parts have been dismantled, some are kept under tight controls, and others maintained or allowed to grow a little, if growth cannot be avoided.

The Keynesian Welfare State culture is under attack and the power needed to move forward the process of change has been centralized within the inner cabinet where it seems to rest increasingly in the hands of the premier and a few trusted advisors. Public participation is minimal and limited to commentaries and suggestions from selected segments of the population about the implementation of basic policy decisions made by cabinet. Every one of these policy decisions and every step taken for over three years has been subordinated to the achievement of one central and consistent aim: to pull or push into the twenty-first century a prosperous and fully post-industrialized British Columbia.

The Process of Implementation

The process required to implement what is essentially a major policy shift from one pattern of socioeconomic development, inherited from an epoch of old-fashioned moderate conservatism, to a pattern rooted in a post-industrial version of neoconservatism has involved a detailed program as well as a sophisticated strategy to prevent or squash resistance. The key element in the blueprint for change is the transformation of the B.C. economic sector. It is based on the following and increasingly familiar assumptions: The immediate economic crisis can be overcome if government expenditures are reduced in the allegedly nonproductive public sector and the money thus saved allocated to cover the costs of major projects able to benefit the current and future economy of the province and to create employment.

The future economic growth of the province depends on a straightforward strategy which consists of attracting foreign investments, securing economic markets and trade relationships around the Pacific Rim and broadening the occupational and revenue bases in the province. This last step requires, in turn, a progressive shift from a strong dependency upon the primary sector (forestry and fishing) and the secondary sector (mining) to a greater dependency upon the tertiary sector (high technology and special services).

Policy changes instituted since 1983, or projected for the near future, have included tax reforms, special financial incentives in the form of low interest loans, forgivable loans and grants to firms for capital investment in B.C., the creation of industrial or commercial projects such as the North East Coal project, highway construction, a rapid transit system in the lower mainland, the establishment of industrial parks, the B.C. Place project, plans to install free trade zones in partnership with the federal government, and Expo 86.

The job creation policies merit close observation since they must be subordinated to the long-term economic aim of growth and prosperity through transformation into a state of post-industrialization. Initially the policies call for the relocation of segments of the workforce into quasi-public work projects because the private sector does not appear to be able to create enough new jobs. However, the nature of future job creation arrangements could be different if the economy could prosper with the help of a much smaller, highly skilled labour force and, as in the case with Japan, with a growing supply of computers and robots. Moreover, if the dismantling of the welfare state ideology were sufficiently advanced, surplus labour could be prodded, through the use of very restrictive social assistance policies, to leave the province or to accept relocation into isolated and cheaply run camps. This scenario may sound extreme but labour camps have been used in B.C. in the past, public assistance benefits can be reduced to a bare minimum and replaced with hand-outs from food banks and the policy justified on the basis that the economic prosperity of the province depends on a "realistic" handling of those who have become obsolescent economically.

A persistent failure of the current job creation policies is important in financial and political terms only, and as long as a substantial portion of the labour force, 75 percent to 80 percent for instance, is working or can hope to work again, the electorate may not be sufficiently concerned to object to the callousness of a survival of the fittest policy and to brutal slashes in public welfare rates. Whether a post-industrial society operates with a very small labour force or whether it encourages job sharing and a return to greater dependency on local community economic development (the strategy favoured by the neosocialist left), the customs, habits, attitudes, and expectations of industrialized society workers must change. The type of worker considered desirable in a neoconservative version of post-industrial society, or even during the transition phase, is certainly not an individual interested primarily in self-actualization and cooperative enterprises, nor is it a trade union member determined to ensure the protection of his or her seniority and collective bargaining rights.

The economic recovery and development envisaged in the economic component of the B.C. plan could not be implemented in the absence of major changes in the patterns of labour-management relations, in the labour code and in the structure of the work force itself. It is not surprising, therefore, that since 1983 the government has enacted measures indicating to Canadian and foreign investors its determination to increase the power of employers and to decrease the power of organized labour.

Between 1983 and 1985 numerous pieces of legislation and several labour code amendments have been introduced to weaken the power of the unions and lower real wages below the level to which they would have risen normally. Labour has lost some of the bargaining advantages and rights it used to have and the public sector work force has been made aware that its members could be hired, fired, demoted, or relocated at the pleasure of their employer, the government. In the March 1985 budget—as in the two previous ones—there were no provisions for salary increases for direct government employees or for employees in organizations funded by the government, including schools, colleges, and universities.

The 1982 compensation stabilization program has become a permanent feature of the labour code of B.C. and the size of wage settlements will continue henceforth to be determined by the employer's "ability to pay" principle, as well as related to increased productivity. These criteria are vague and when they are set by management they can be used effectively to justify lay-offs or to keep an insecure labour force in a state of docility. In February 1986, changes to this particular program have been promised which should make it less restrictive but then premier Bill Bennett called once again for a continued wage freeze in the public sector because "top priority must be jobs for the unemployed, not more money for those already working."

The right to job security regarded as universal and basic in all respectable welfare states is rapidly vanishing and being replaced by a growing acceptance of the merit principle. Workers, including professionals, must continuously show proof that they deserve to keep their jobs because they are able to maintain a high level of productivity as well as an above average performance. Raises and promotions can be obtained only on the basis of outstanding performance. Equality of opportunity may be promoted, in theory at least, but those who do not make effective use of their initial opportunity may not be granted a second chance to do so.

The policy of job creation pursued by the government does not include a deep concern for the quality of the work experience. Finding and keeping a job is the responsibility of the individual while sound working conditions, long-term job security, adequate wages, and work related benefits cannot be guaranteed and should not be expected any longer by members of the labour force.

The reorganization of the provincial economy has affected the educational sector. This was inevitable because, from the point of view of the government, the sector suffered from two major problems: increasing costs, and a highly autonomous work force not particularly willing to accept externally imposed changes to educational programs that were not adapting fast enough perhaps to the demands of a neoconservative version of the post-industrial society.

Between 1983 and 1986 the government used its control over the allocation of funds to address both problems. Funds were reduced several years in a row to save money, force several school boards to lay off teachers and compel these boards, as well as institutions of post-secondary education, to become more docile.

The process reached a high level in 1985 when the overall school budget was increased by 4 percent but a $20 million portion had to be reallocated to increase support to private schools. School boards across the province were ordered to stay within specific limits when preparing their budgets and two disobedient boards, including the left wing dominated Vancouver board, were dismissed and replaced by government appointed trustees. There were no salary increases for teachers, many layoffs and some programs had to be terminated or curtailed.

In Vancouver the trustees ended up with a deficit larger by several millions than the deficit projected by the disbanded board. The government at that point called a board election, leaving the returned board with a difficult decision to make. It could recommend an inadequate budget or use the authority, given recently to school boards to hold referenda asking residential property owners for an increase in their property taxes. Hardly a popular request when the nonresidential property share of taxes has been decreased by $90 millions as part of the business stimulation policy.

Also in 1985/86 the B.C. post-secondary institutions already on very tight budgets for several years in a row, saw their funding cut from $536.6 millions to $511.6 millions and 5 percent of the money had to be used to improve core programs. A dozen tenured professors had their contracts terminated and a new principle was established: the government could earmark funds for those programs considered important enough to be priorized.

In February 1986 the premier announced the establishment of a $110 million excellence fund for B.C. schools, colleges, and universities which was to be above and beyond ordinary operating funds. But, almost immediately, there were indications that strings were to be attached to the use of these funds. They were to be allocated to programs which could prepare students for work in areas to be highly developed in a post-industrial society. These programs deal with new scientific knowledge and advanced technology in physics, chemistry, biology, medicine, and in such mega-sciences as computer science and artificial intelligence. Pacific Rim studies and the teaching of Asian languages were to be given a high priority also.

This growing control over the setting of educational priorities and over wages and work conditions has led to a series of harsh confrontations with teachers and the universities and, each time, the government has emerged as the victor.

A secondary element of the 1983 blueprint for change has been dealing with a reorganization of the social welfare system to complement the reorganization of the economic and educational sectors. To suggest that the New Reality ideology has all but ended government spending on social programs in B.C. would be misleading. The March 1985 budget indicated that the government expected to spend $9.05 billion in the coming year against anticipated revenues of $8.16 billion for an $890 million deficit, 3 percent higher than in the previous year. But it indicated also that the social spending slice of the budget, health, education, and welfare would receive $5.9 billion, an increase of $1.4 billion since 1981.

Between 1985 and 1986 the Health Care sector fared best. It is always the most popular and acceptable sector in the eyes of the government and of the general public. The 1985–86 budget projected an increase of 5 percent over the 1984–85 budget to $2.68 billion and in February 1986, the premier announced that health was going to be an area of high priority in the coming months.

Within the Health Care sector, problems seem to be related to shifts in priorities over the choice of goods and services to be purchased with the money that is made available. Since the purchases are expected to help the private sector and maintain the popularity of the government with influential interest groups—a custom which is hardly unique to Social Credit governments—the funds are allocated selectively every year and reductions in the number of public health care personnel or salary freezes are seen as more desirable than reductions in hospital construction or in the purchase of special equipment.

There are indications that health care users will be expected to pay an increasingly larger share of hospitalization and of services which used to be free or extensively subsidized, but the government is moving slowly in this direction since the public would object probably to strong measures of retrenchment in their health care system. A battle was launched in 1984 to control the deployment of physicians across the province by denying Medicare billing numbers needed to claim reimbursement for services rendered to physicians who insist on practicing in urban areas already saturated with qualified professionals. Eventually, the government had to retreat but the battle could be resumed, following the next election if the government is returned to power again.

The cost of the social welfare sector has remained higher than the government would like. The inability of the government to reduce substantially the high level of unemployment means of course that more people have to apply for welfare when their Unemployment Insurance benefits are exhausted, and that more people remain on welfare for longer periods of time. Had the B.C. economy remained prosperous, the task of reorganizing the B.C. social security system would have been simpler and public assistance could have been provided to the unemployable only on the grounds that jobs were available. The social welfare policy thrust which has been emerging in the past few years is a blend of selective spending, selective forms of privatization, an increasing use of administrative and legislative controls, and a distinct lack of sympathy for most of the disadvantaged and their advocates.

The policy of privatization, while not new in B.C., is being implemented on a growing scale. Privatization is directed at two categories of services: statutory services contracted out to the nongovernmental sector and nonstatutory services which this sector is expected to provide without subsidies or grants from the provincial government. All the pieces of the new model of service delivery are not yet in place, but the underlying concept of welfare is clearly residual: the bulk of the social services should be provided by families, friends, and volunteer networks and profit-making organizations are encouraged to play a role since they can meet the demand coming from high income groups for counselling, child care, or institutional care for physically and mentally handicapped adults.

The B.C. policy has some features which are not found in policies concerned with radical models of privatization. The actual delivery of many services is provided by nongovernmental agencies under contractual arrangements, with the government retaining responsibility for service funding and control over many important areas of client access to the social service system. There have been no indications that the government wanted to terminate its mandate in relation to child protection services and federal cost-sharing programs, in the case of the nonnative Indian population at least. While full privatization is financially attractive, the retention of control over the social welfare system is also important since it is a major component of the economic blueprint and should not be left to operate without some government supervision.

A valid assessment of the B.C. policy of partial privatization is not possible because extensive research findings are not yet available. There are, however, several areas of concern to social workers, including the fact that the standards of service delivery, the nature of the monitoring system and of the procedures to safeguard the right of clients have not been made public. In addition, one may wonder whether families and communities are able and willing (or should be expected) to shoulder again the social service duties and the compulsory altruism imposed on them in the prewelfare state era.

A number of policy initiatives and principles have been identified by social workers. They have not been enunciated officially but can be inferred from steps taken by the government since it began to revise systematically its social policy priorities. The old distinction between worthy and less worthy clients has reappeared. Those who can be absorbed fairly rapidly in the new work force are more valuable than those who cannot. Nonaged poor and female-headed families whose number will probably increase should receive a modest level of help because they could become an expensive burden to the public sector if they were encouraged to expect yearly raises in their benefits.

A second principle seems to be that the money needed to finance increases in the cost of public assistance or health care should come from savings in other programs. To use a description which is fast becoming a cliche, high priority programs can cannibalize other programs. Prevention types of services in the child welfare field and some social services for the aged have low priority and have been victims of this increasing tendency to shuffle the same funds around rather than allocate new money.

A third policy trend, which is a special aspect of the B.C. privatization policy, consists in the replacement of benefits and services by legislated forms of control. Welfare recipients who cannot survive on an allocation that has not kept pace with inflation do not receive an increase in cash benefits or support services. They receive instead a more extensive program of antifraud control. There also is more interest in the development of legislation and measures to punish child abusers, particularly sexual abusers, than there is in provision of better services to prevent abuse and to attempt to rehabilitate abusers.

A fourth policy trend is hardly surprising but a profound cause for concern. The search for greater equality, greater protection of human rights, and for the enhancement of social solidarity which has been at the core of all liberal versions of the welfare state is being replaced by an emphasis on the survival and well-being of the superior individual who has the competence and skills useful in a new post-industrial society and who does not need to claim enforceable rights.

One of the first victims of the 1983 blueprint of change was the B.C. Human Rights Commission: it was dismantled and replaced by a system guaranteed to discourage those who wanted to complain of discrimination from applying for help in obtaining redress. The office of the provincial ombudsman was progressively retrenched and has been pushed into a state of obscurity since 1985 when the term of the first ombudsman the province ever had ended. The next incumbent, who was not appointed right away, has not been able or willing to be very visible.

The government has not made any pronouncements which could be construed as racist, and politically unsound. Members of ethnic communities that have ties with current or future economic trade partners appear to be reasonably safe from overt discrimination. The problem of sexism tends to be ignored, however, while the government stance toward native Indians is characterized by a refusal to negotiate land claims coupled with a willingness to privatize the troublesome area of native Indian family welfare through a transfer of responsibilities to Indian Bands.

A Strategy to Implement the Program of Transformation

The successful implementation of the initial and crucial phase of such a massive program of transformation over the brief span of time available between two elections required skills and a carefully planned strategy.

The government has had many advantages working in its favour.

A key one, of course, has been the possession of a substantial majority in the House, since the new policies and programs could be established easily through the help of appropriate legislation and funding allocations. Moreover, the government could point out that a little over one-half of the active electorate and probably well over one-half of the nonactive electorate appeared to have either more faith in the neoconservative approach to the restoration of economic prosperity than to a neosocialist approach or more confidence in the Social Credit style of administration than in the N.D.P. style.

There were some problem areas. The potential victims of the transformation of the economic sector included many segments of the labour force: civil servants, teachers, health personnel, university professors, private sector unionized workers, nonunionized workers who wished nevertheless to obtain some job security, and small independent business entrepreneurs whose fate can be as precarious as the fate of hired workers in a society in transition between industrialism and post-industrialism. In other words, large segments of the population had to be convinced that they could not successfully obstruct the new order or that it was in their interest to support it.

The strategy of implementation has used two approaches: direct and indirect. The direct approach has included the formidable package of legislation which accompanied the July 1983 budget, the series of budgets and additional legislation promulgated in 1984, 1985, and 1986 and the myriad of administrative procedures enacted within all ministries. The indirect approach has included several tactics: the creation of a special language, and the projection of selected images, partial control over information, the centralization of full fiscal and policy-making power in the cabinet and the partial suppression of alternate arenas of decision-making.

All these tactics have been carried out relentlessly and with a ruthless determination that does not allow for compromises. The creation of a special language has been a very effective tool which deserves praise, or opprobrium, depending upon one's point of view. Some words have been substituted for others. Unemployment, for instance, has been replaced by the more positive concept of job creation. Democratic participation has become government decisions made following review of the input from relevant constituencies, while complaints from boards and institutions unable to cope with massive and prolonged cuts to their budgets are redefined as attempts to make political statements about situations created by incompetent administrators.

The government has succeeded so far in projecting an image of prudent fiscal management leading to economic recovery and to salvation from the dangers of unbridled socialism and social decay. The image has blurred the edges of reality well enough to protect the politicians from awkward questions and it has kept a heterogeneous group of supporters under a common umbrella. Several controversial or reactionary policies and measures, introduced and enacted in the name of restraint, have been accepted or even praised, not only by staunch Social Credit supporters but by other segments of the population, because to question the policy of restraint is seen as tantamount to endorsing the squandering of the basic economic resources of B.C. and condemning most British Columbians to a future of economic misery.[7]

The tactic of partial control over information does not bear any resemblance to the media control and suppression of information which occurs in countries ruled by authoritarian governments. The press, members of the academic community, and members of various groups opposing government policies have been left fairly free to voice their protests and to write numerous papers, articles, and documents showing, statistically or otherwise, that the policies are inappropriate, increase rather than deflate the economic recession and are creating a substantial amount of human suffering and social disorganization. But, it is difficult to obtain dependable and comprehensive data about the internal operations of various ministries and public departments, civil servants cannot release information or be quoted and recently cabinet ministers have begun to sue political commentators and critics.

The government has a budget to provide official news releases on T.V. and radio or in the form of booklets and government publications but these releases invariably give an optimistic view of government initiatives and the exact costs of major job projects, notably Expo 86, have not been revealed to the public.

The government has made use also of specific tactics too numerous to list in this chapter. The most interesting or original have included: the reduction in the number of sittings of the legislature to

the minimum required to ensure passage of the legislation introduced by the government, the extensive use of polls (the results of
which are not released to the general public), considerable delays
in the introduction of yearly budgets, and a vast array of measures
and activities to defeat, befuddle, exhaust, or inflict acute stress
and chronic anxiety upon actual or potential opponents. If one approach does not work, the government appears to retreat only as a
prelude to a renewed attack on firmer grounds.

Since 1983 the government has pursued also a broad and per-
vasive strategy to weaken labour through the use of indirect tactics, pitting private and public sector unions against each other,
fostering confrontations between unionized and nonunionized
labour or between different categories of workers, and presenting
to the general public an image of a greedy work force more concerned about the maintenance of its narrow-vested interests and
privileges than about the welfare of the province. By contrast, the
government is pictured as the defender of the people and the
protector of the public interest.

The two most powerful components of the strategy used to implement the government's plan are the increasing centralization of
authority and power, already mentioned, and the downgrading of
citizen participation which is the logical complement of a high
level of centralization. The government practices a pseudo-form of
citizen participation. Selected groups only are asked for their comments and suggestions. These suggestions are ignored if they do
not coincide with decisions contemplated or already made by the
government. There are few opportunities for genuine debates
about important issues and situations or controversies which
could be embarrassing to the government are dismissed as nonexistent when questions are raised by the press, the opposition, or
concerned citizens.

The strategy, designed with the help and guidance of expert advisors and administrative assistants, has been very successful. A
few temporary failures have occurred, but they were caused by the
mistakes of unskilled or inexperienced ministers or back benchers
and not by flaws in the strategy itself. The strategy owes some of
its success to two other factors, the election of a Conservative government in Ottawa and the opposition's apparent inability to
maintain a counter-coalition, cohesive and united. The conserva-

tive private sector unions, and the more militant public sector ones, have worked sometimes at cross-purposes and have been unable, in general, to pursue a joint defensive strategy. As well, the N.D.P., the political opposition, has been torn by internal disagreements since a leadership change which took place in 1984.

Professional groups not having previously experienced so ruthless and contemptuous a treatment on the part of an elected government have tried to learn new protective strategies and have not always fared too well. Their problems have been heightened, in some cases, by splits in the membership between those who wanted their professional associations to use all their resources on behalf of clients, and those who believed that the primary mandate of a professional association is to protect the standards and interests of the profession.

Conclusions

The problems affecting the western model of state welfare developed in the post-war period now appears to many social policy analysts to have been inevitable. The situation of economic stagnation and decline in resources facing all welfare states and other types of governments as well is global since developing nations are affected by the spillover. The situation of social development is also problematic. As more and more people want the purchasing power, social and fiscal benefit entitlements, and rights which protect them equally from economic insecurity, risk-taking, menial, or dangerous jobs, and from the burden of unpaid labour for the care of children, the elderly, and the handicapped, the social and economic resources necessary to meet the needs of a well developed and mature welfare state are becoming increasingly difficult to obtain.

The emphasis on the financial aspects of the welfare state crisis has tended to hide the problem of maldistribution of tasks, responsibilities, and contributions which is also adding to the welfare deficit because the cost of buying in the market the equivalent of unpaid contributions is extremely high. In B.C. a solution to the welfare state crisis has not been part of the official agenda of the current government but it has been integrated into the resolution of the economic crisis. Since 1983, the nature of the resolution has become bolder and more "innovative" in the sense that it has moved beyond a simple attempt at balancing the budget and curbing the deficit to an attempt to transform the socioeconomic structure of the province. Inevitably this transformation must include some transformation in the conceptualization and implementation of social welfare policies.

There are crucial distinctions between the approach chosen by the B.C. government to operate the transition from industrialism to post-industrialism and the more democratic approach which would be taken, presumably, by an opposition government. A democratic approach would encourage broad citizen participation in the development of creative ideas and community experiments and in the search for an innovative model of post-industrial society. It would rely also on the development of an ongoing process of collaboration involving the government, labour, business, and other important societal systems.

The approach chosen by the government has consisted instead of minimum citizen participation, the introduction of a preplanned model of socioeconomic change, which places little emphasis on social welfare, through state legislation and the imposition of overt, as well as subtle, controls from the top down.

In 1984, the premier described the future in the following terms:

> In the new world economy, there will be survivors and there will be casualties but there will be no social privileges. This is the new reality.[8]

This is also a description of the human condition in one version of a dismantled welfare state where families and ultimately individuals, some of whom will enjoy still the benefits of personal privileges in the form of inherited wealth or natural abilities, must take full responsibility for supporting and improving the quality of their lives. The new reality and its implications are chilling but they have attracted and will continue to attract those who know that they can, or assume that they will survive, and be able to make their way to one of the upper socioeconomic strata.

The strategies and methods used in B.C. since 1983 to install the new reality have been brutal and insensitive but questions have been raised also about the nature of the policies themselves and the ability of the government to guide the province toward an appropriate future because these policies have not been producing the economic results expected initially.

Some of the mega-projects are short lived and cannot provide permanent jobs, others have run into difficulties.[9] For example, Expo 86, the most visible of the mega projects, seems to have brought a temporary improvement in the economy but concerns have been expressed by many British Columbians that once Expo closes, in October 1986, the province will plunge into an economic recession worse than the 1981 recession.

The deficit has not vanished, the educational system is deteriorating, while the food bank tradition is becoming more firmly entrenched. One of the government's favourite dogma, free trade, suffered a blow when the U.S. government threatened to impose a high tariff on the import of cedar products, a basic B.C. export product, and the province has a yearly trade deficit with the rest of Canada estimated to be around $3 billion a year.

Unemployment, however, is still the major problem facing many British Columbians, the number of jobs created in the past three years remains smaller than the number of jobs lost and the province is facing another round of fights involving unionized labour, nonunionized labour and management.

The catalogue of visible and suspected problems has grown rapidly but the current government will not have to account for these problems. In May 1986, Premier Bennett announced suddenly that he was resigning as premier and would leave politics when the next election was called.

In July, 1986 a leadership convention selected as new party leader, William Vander Zalm, who had been a member of the B.C. cabinet but had resigned several years before because he disagreed with the premier and felt, at the time, that the government lacked the toughness and determination needed to enforce radical right-wing policy changes. Vander Zalm inherited an ailing economy, a deficit for Expo 86 estimated by its chairman to be around $311 million and a deeply troubled and divided province.

During the leadership convention there were signs of a split within the Social Credit Party between the elitists who favoured the continuation of the approaches developed by political and administrative advisors since 1981, and the populists who favoured a return to the more traditional Social Credit customs: close relationships with grass root supporters, less emphasis on administrative technology, on secrecy, and on concern for the preferences of big business.

The new party leader represents the populist orientation and was not the choice of the former cabinet. Several key cabinet members resigned within weeks of the leadership convention and quit politics. So far Vander Zalm has refrained from making statements and moves which could alienate supporters and has used his charismatic personality to pacify or win over opponents. He has been given credit for helping to settle peacefully the bitter and long standing government employees' contract dispute and for attempting to seek a solution for another labour/management dispute involving the forest industry. Another accomplishment has been a government purchase of 55 million preferred shares in Cominco which enabled the business company to create 300 temporary jobs and to resume the modernization plan of its smelter.

On September 6, 1986, one month after being sworn in as premier, Vander Zalm announced that he hoped to have an economic strategy blueprint ready within a few days. This blueprint, developed to create jobs in B.C as quickly as possible, would include a three-pronged approach consisting of the following: increased investment sought from Europe, the U.S., and the Pacific Rim; attempts to obtain a greater share of federal contracts for the province; and a commitment by the provincial government to purchase goods and services from B.C. companies. The premier has promised also to eliminate, modify, or replace many aspects of government including the possible elimination of various sales taxes, a lowering of the price of beer, and an expansion of the eastern market for B.C. products, such as coal, to reduce the dependency on Pacific Rim markets. The premier mentioned his belief that free trade between Canada and the U.S. is vital to economic recovery. In addition his comments that hospital abortion committees were too lax in their interpretation of the law earned him the approval of anti-choice groups and the disapproval of pro-choice groups. Subsequently he retracted his statement that hospital committees sometimes approved abortion as a means of birth control.

Members of the opposition have wondered whether the new Social Credit leader has more style than substance, while political
analysts have wondered where the money was to come from to pay
for the moves and official promises already made. It has been
pointed out that there has not been any clear indication of the
manner in which the economy of B.C. was to be strengthened.[10] No
specific social welfare policy directions have emerged yet although
the Ministry of Human Resources has a new minister and has been
renamed the Ministry of Social Services and Housing.

Given his views on social welfare recipients and the programs
when he was minister of Human Resources in the late 1970s, the
premier may try to proceed with a more radical and swift attempt
to dismantle state welfare in B.C. than his predecessor, if he wins
the next election. If the N.D.P. forms the next government the
socioeconomic policies of the province would change course but a
new course would not herald a return to the welfare state concepts
of the sixties and early seventies. The consequences of the transition from an industrial to post-industrial economy will have to be
faced and handled by any government in power and it is doubtful
that the ideals of the traditional welfare state could be recaptured
easily. They need to be replaced not by the new economic reality
but by a new Welfare Society reality. How to create this society is
the real challenge facing Canadians now and in the future.

Notes

1. For a comprehensive analysis of the experience with community resource boards in B.C., see Michael Elague et al., *Reforming Human
   Services* (Vancouver: University of British Columbia Press, 1984).
2. See for instance Patricia Marchak, *Green Gold: The Forest Industry,
   British Columbia* (Vancouver: University of British Columbia Press,
   1983).
3. William Schworm, *The Economic Impact of the British Columbia
   "Restraint" Budgets* (B.C. Economic Institute, U.B.C., distributed by
   Pacific Group for Policy Alternatives, May 1984), 2–3.
4. John Malcolmson, "The Hidden Agenda of 'Restraint'," in Warren
   Magnusson et al., *The New Reality* (Vancouver: New Star Books Ltd.,
   1984), 78–79.

5. Neil Nevitte and Roger Gibbins, "Neo-Conservatism: Canadian Variations on an Ideological Theme?" *Canadian Public Policy* 4 (1984): 385.

6. See Bjonn Wittrock, "Governance in Crisis and the Withering of the Welfare State, the Legacy of the Policy Sciences," *Policy Sciences* 15 (1983): 196.

7. The tendency to priorize economic factors and the need to adhere to the blueprint for change was illustrated by a 1985 decision of the Health Ministry to spend some $15 million to cover the cost of the first two phases in the purchase of experimental radiology equipment from West Germany.

   A provincial government advisory committee had advised against this purchase because the equipment was so new that part of it had yet to be invented and because no one knew whether it would be more effective than standard and cheaper equipment. From the point of view of the government, however, the fact that a substantial fragment of a potentially valuable piece of medical technology could be acquired before its price went up, combined with the potential advantages of selling coal to West Germany as part of the deal, were worth taking the risk that the purchase of relatively untested and not fully invested medical equipment could turn out to be a costly fiasco.

8. William Bennett, "What a Difference a Year Makes," *British Columbia Report* (British Columbia Solidarity Coalition, 1984), 2.

9. For instance, a major mining project developed to sell coal to Japan, did not yield the anticipated profits. In addition, one of the two mines in the project was found to have been located in the wrong place and had to be written off.

10. See *The Vancouver Sun*, September 6, 1986, articles by Keith Baldrey, A1 and A10 and Gary Mason, A10.

14 Public Policy and Social Welfare
The Ideology and Practice of Restraint in Ontario

RAMESH MISHRA

The period after the beginning of the crisis of "stagfla-tion," i.e., from about 1975 onwards, shows a range of policy responses on the part of governments, both national and provin-cial. Potentially, at least five different responses can be identified in respect of the welfare state: Dismantling, Retrenching, Restraining, Maintaining, and Transforming. These must be seen as analytical constructs, encapsulating both an ideology and a strategy in respect of social welfare in the context of the 1980s. Like all analytical constructs they are meant as aids in under-standing the untidy situations in the real world. These concepts, then, do not purport to *describe* the reality of public policy but rather help us understand the nature of public policy choices and developments in the post-crisis period.

In the literature on the welfare state there has been a tendency to see the post-crisis situation in dichotomous terms. On one side of the divide stands the old welfare state with its commitment to uni-versal and comprehensive social programs and to social rights more generally. On the other side stands its arch enemy neoconser-vatism—with its doctrine of monetarism and the gospel of the free market—hell-bent on demolishing the social welfare system built up painstakingly over many decades. A well-known Canadian formulation expresses this graphically as a contrast between "the welfare state" and "the farewell state." Similar notions abound in the literature.[1]

The problem with this dichotomy is twofold. First, it focuses on the most dramatic aspects of the New Right—represented by the monetarism of Friedman and the political agenda and rhetoric of Thatcher and Reagan. This tends to reduce the range of policy responses associated with the idea of restraint to a single policy stance, "neoconservative" and thus, quite unwittingly, tends to play down the importance of the different types and forms of restraint. Second, as we shall see below, the dichotomy of welfare state versus the New Right ignores an important form of policy response on the left connected with the strategy of maintaining and/or transforming the welfare state. This chapter seeks to move away from this dichotomy and draws attention to the wide range of policy responses—stretching politically from the radical right to the left—that can be made and are being made in different juris- dictions in the West. Moreover, the classification of policy responses presented in this chapter takes account of the fact that various precrisis formulations of the ideologies of welfare, found in the writings of George and Wilding, Djao, and others are not very helpful—at least not directly—in making sense of the recent devel- opments.[2]

What then are the main features of each of the five policy responses identified above? And how relevant is this classification for Canadian developments, especially at the provincial level? These questions are explored in this chapter and, in the final sec- tion, Ontario's social policy is briefly examined as an example of one of these responses—that of Retrenchment. One important is- sue that has been left aside is the nature of the political, economic, and social forces associated with each of these responses. For ex- ample, why does the government in British Columbia, seemingly, embrace the ideology of dismantling whilst the government in Ontario adopts a different approach? Such questions, however im- portant and interesting, are too large to be addressed in this chap- ter and must be left out.

The Policy Responses

DISMANTLING

This policy stance is associated with the ideology of the radical right. The hallmark of this approach is that at the ideological level there is a total rejection of the mixed economy and the welfare state. This rejection is important both as symbolism and as reality. The professed objective of public policy is to withdraw government from social responsibility beyond the very minimum, the so-called social safety net. In short what is envisaged is a return to the residual social policy of the prewar days. The aim is to reprivatize services on a large scale by denationalizing social welfare. The main feature of this strategy is a dramatic and frontal attack on social programs and expenditures. Typically this involves the abolition of programs, tightening up on eligibility, withdrawal, or restriction of funding, winding up of government departments, and the dismissal of public employees. The deregulation of business and industry (affecting for example health and safety, equal opportunity, and other aspects of human rights), the decertification of unions, and a more general weakening of the power and influence of employees' associations is also a part of this strategy. Thatcherite Britain, Reaganite United States, and at the provincial level the Social Credit government in British Columbia epitomise this type of public policy.[3]

However, it is one thing to profess the ideology of dismantling the welfare state, it is quite another to be able to implement policies that will realize the professed aims. For a start, there are serious political constraints. The policy of dismantling has to be formulated and carried out within the context of an electoral democracy. The governing party as a whole may be reluctant to push policy too far in the direction of ideology since public opinion as well as interest group and party sentiments have to be taken into account. Thus, the Reagan administration abandoned its plans for cutting back on security affecting senior citizens.[4] In Britain, the so-called "wets" in the Conservative Party appear to have acted as a force moderating the policy stance of the Thatcherites.[5] Beyond this, it must be noted that the New Right's strategy of discrediting government generally and lowering people's expectations of the government in respect of economic and social welfare has met with limited success. As public opinion polls almost everywhere show people remain wedded to the notion that universal social programs are a good thing.⁶ And although a majority of the people approve of the idea that social help should go to the needy in the first place, it also remains true that programs based on means test and selectivity are the ones that remain, by and large, unpopular and become targets of welfare backlash.⁷ Moreover, even if the principle of selectivity (the needy deserve to be helped most) is endorsed by the public in abstract, when it comes to parting with universal benefits most beneficiaries show a great deal of reluctance to do so. In respect of unemployment and other economic issues too, the idea that the government has general responsibility for economic management and can influence the course of the economy remains in place.⁸ In other words, the political success of the New Right can neither be seen as an endorsement of that ideology of welfare by the voters nor can it be assumed that ideology can be converted into the hard currency of policy readily.⁹

Indeed, it is no coincidence that neoconservatives (possibly with the exception of Reagan) have not campaigned on a platform of dismantling the welfare state. Rather the emphasis has been on bringing about economic growth, reducing the budget deficit, and in this sense practicing restraint. It is usually after being voted into office that neoconservative governments launch their attack on the welfare state. For example, the legislative package and budget introduced by the government in British Columbia in July 1983 showed "a glaring contradiction between vague principles of moderation on which the government had achieved its mandate in May and the draconian measures introduced within a few weeks of the election. Many people questioned the authority of a government whose claim to power seemed based on manipulation and deception."¹⁰ Brian Mulroney's declaration during the election campaign that universality of social programs was "a sacred trust" and his government's attack on universality following the elections is another case in point.¹¹

In any case, it is important to note that even where the policy of Dismantling has been tried, e.g., in the UK and USA, the results have been somewhat paradoxical. In both countries the middle class—directly or indirectly—has successfully resisted attempts on the part of the government to take away universal benefits. Despite the shibboleths of neoconservatism about the "social safety net" and concentrating resources on those who need them it is in fact the poor, the needy, the weak that have suffered most.[12] As the case of the United States has shown all too clearly, it is far easier to cut back on programs meant for the poor—food stamps, medicaid, general welfare—than to dismantle the mainstream, universal programs which benefit all.[13] Thus universal programs remain in place even if starved of funds. In sum, despite the rejection of the mixed economy and the welfare state in principle, in practice it has not been possible to dismantle the welfare state in any major way. And it is unlikely that such an attempt will succeed.

RETRENCHING

In one sense this can be considered a moderate version of the ideology of Dismantling. But it is more useful to see it as a *different* approach rather than as a watered down version of dismantling. True, the basic beliefs and ideology underlying this approach have a great deal in common with the dismantling approach. But it differs from the latter in that it does not reject outright the mixed economy and the welfare state. Rather it believes in tilting the balance away from the state towards the private sector. Its objective is to restrict the scope of the welfare state rather than abolish it. Because of the "moderate" and "reasonable" nature of this doctrine its appeal is likely to be broader. The government in Ontario can be seen as a very successful practitioner of this policy since the mid-70s. And there are plenty of indications that the new federal government will most likely develop a policy stance of this kind.[14]

Unlike the frontal assault on the welfare state characteristic of the ideology and strategy of Dismantling, here the stress is on prudent public housekeeping, on the virtues of the private sector as a creator of wealth and employment and on the need to reduce the size of government substantially. Reducing the deficit ("living within our means") is a major concern and cutting back on social expenditure a major route to this objective. What we have here is a pragmatic and generalist approach of moving in the direction of a stronger and prosperous private sector and a substantially leaner, though not apparently meaner, public sector. As we shall see below, the Ontario government has had considerable success in implementing just such a policy. It enjoys a major advantage on the frontal assault approach in that there is far less public outcry and little opposition over the restraint measures applied under this policy.

The main features of this policy then are a gradual, piecemeal but nonetheless systematic reduction in the scope of government programs and social expenditure. Government withdrawal and privatization are also the objectives here. But the privatization which takes place under the auspices of this approach tends to be of the "passive" variety—happening more by default than explicit design—compared with the aggressive privatization envisaged in the Dismantling mode. Medical underfunding and the resulting growth of user fees and extra billing is a good example of privatization by default. As the scope and effectiveness of public programs is systematically reduced the space opens up for nongovernmental activity, of both for-profit and nonprofit variety. At the same time the government claims to maintain its commitment to quality services of a broadly universal nature. Finally, if substantial tax breaks for the rich and for business generally is a hallmark of the Dismantling mode, that approach is far more muted here.[15]

RESTRAINING

This policy response is easily recognized as the one practiced by the federal government under the Liberal administration.[16] Here the principles of universality and comprehensiveness are adhered to, i.e., at least *in principle* the basic tenets of the welfare state are upheld. But *in practice* priority is accorded to the economy over social welfare. Government spending is directed at promoting economic growth—mainly through the market and the private sector but also under the public auspices—at the cost of social expenditure which therefore takes a back seat. The hallmark of this approach is pragmatism. The need to hold down public, especially social, expenditure is recognized in light of the burgeoning deficit. Social welfare is therefore to be put in cold storage until such time as the economy recovers. Tight money supply and substantial unemployment are accepted as a necessary price to pay for reducing inflation and reviving growth through the private sector. Within this policy framework elements of monetarism co-exist with the philosophy of welfarism in a state of unholy alliance.

The hiatus between the acceptance of social rights as legitimate on the one hand and the attempt at cost-cutting and tax reduction in order to provide the right "climate" for private sector growth on the other results in a variety of eclectic developments. One of these may be described as the policy of "social welfare without dollars" whereby money is taken from one program and put into another.[17] The child tax credit program funded by reducing the family allowances is a case in point. A somewhat different example is the Canada Health Act, 1984. The act imposes financial penalty for extra billing on the provinces without attending to the underlying problems of medical care funding. Indeed in one sense the Canada Health Act can be seen as a "political" measure in so far as the system of block funding (Established Programs Financing, beginning 1977) and the subsequent financial arrangements appear to have reduced the federal contribution to health costs.

As time goes on, however, the "frozen" welfare state cannot but lead to privatization at the fringes and a weakening of the principle of universality and comprehensiveness and hence a decline in the effectiveness of the social welfare system. Lacking a clear strategy for defending and maintaining the welfare state, the pragmatism of Restraint can leave the field clear for the ideologies of Retrenchment or even Dismantling to grow and flourish since these appear to have a clearer rationale and a more purposive plan of action. This is what has tended to happen in Canada in respect of federally underpinned social programs in recent years.

MAINTAINING

Here the ideological orientation is the very opposite of that associated with the policy of Dismantling. Commitment to the principle of social protection based on universality and comprehensiveness is one hundred percent. Not only universal social programs but also full employment is seen as a part of the post-war welfare state idea and maintaining high levels of employment receives top priority.

Deficit, inflation, economic growth, and the like remain important concerns but, in contrast to the other positions outlined above, full employment is not sacrificed at the altar of these. State action continues to be viewed as positive and attempts are made to harmonise economic and social objectives through various tripartite or bipartite agreements, e.g., a "social contract." Within such a policy framework it has been possible to maintain social expenditures and even to reflate the economy without running foul of the problem of inflation. In this way, the objectives of economic growth, full employment, and social welfare are all addressed, relatively successfully. Chiefly under the aegis of social democratic governments, countries such as Sweden, Norway, and Austria have developed such a policy response.[18] Could such a policy response develop at the *provincial* level in Canada, for example in British Columbia?

In the North American context the importance of this policy stance is twofold. First, it shows that neoconservatism or some variant of it which emphasizes fiscal restraint (our first three categories) is not the only plausible response to the crisis of the Keynesian welfare state. A qualitatively different response of a "post-Keynesian" variety remains a viable alternative. Moreover, it seems to be equally (if not more) effective than neoconservatism in respect of controlling inflation, generating economic growth, reducing deficit, and the like.[19] But it does so with the important difference that through effective commitment to full employment and social welfare the equity and social justice objectives are maintained. This policy approach responds to the difficulties of welfare capitalism by going "beyond" the old framework rather than retreating into the familiar terrain of economic and social laisser faire. Instead of reducing the scope of the public domain in decision-making and in seeking collective solutions to welfare it tries to extend it.[20] Second, it is arguable that in order to maintain the welfare state effectively in the post-crisis period a "post-Keynesian" approach (one that may also be called "social-corporatism") is virtually essential. Britain under the last Labour government (1974–79) and, more recently, France under the Mitterand regime has had to pay dearly for being unable to develop (France) or sustain (Britain) an adequate post-crisis response. By contrast, Austria, Norway, and Sweden and more recently Australia have, in their various ways, been relatively successful in maintaining or rebuilding (Australia) the welfare state.[21] The policy framework adopted in these countries is a form of social corporatism whose centrepiece is a working compromise or consensus arrived at between the state, the employers and the workers (unions) over major economic and social priorities. An active labour market policy, such as that followed by Sweden, enhances the effectiveness of social corporatism considerably.[22]

In the Canadian provincial context, it might be argued, the failure of social-democratic governments to seize the initiative from the New Right and to maintain the welfare states stems from their inability to develop a post-Keynesian approach. Speculatively, one might suggest that if the prospects of a social-corporatist approach at the federal level remain meagre this is not necessarily the case at the provincial level. However, this is too large a question to be pursued here.

TRANSFORMING

The project of transforming or transcending the welfare state is of mixed provenance. Moreover, it concerns largely ideas, ideals, and ideologies of a diverse kind rather than a clearly identifiable set of policies or practices of a government or even a political party.

The most venerable theory of transformation is Marxism (or some variant of it), and some of the "transition to socialism" type strategies elaborated in European countries (Alternative Economic Strategy, Eurocommunism, etc.) come under this heading. Most of these, however, do not yet belong to the realm of practical politics and in this sense tend to be somewhat short on feasibility. From the latter viewpoint, the Meidner Plan developed by LO, the Swedish trade union federation, appears promising. A modified though watered down version of the Plan has been implemented by the governing social-democratic party in Sweden.[23] One aspect of this strategy is to gain control over investment capital. Thus the Meidner Plan seeks to socialize a part of the company's profits and to place it under the control of the employees. Among its objectives are first, to ensure that if companies are profitable and workers contribute to the productivity of the companies then a part of that income would accrue to the workers themselves; this would ensure that modernization of technology and gains in productivity will not simply benefit the capitalists. Further, workers will gain control over a part of the capital funds. Second, removing a part of the profit from current appropriation, e.g., wage raises, would help keep wage inequality under check and maintain the policy of "wage solidarity."[24]

The details of the Meidner Plan need not detain us here. Suffice to say that the Plan is a part of the strategy of Swedish social democracy to maintain worker solidarity and commitment to welfare; it is also meant to enhance popular control over profits and capital ("the supply side") in order to harness capitalism to humanitarian social objectives.

Among other ideas falling under the rubric of transformation are those of decentralization and debureaucratization of the welfare state. Alternative forms of social welfare—decentralized, popular, self-managed, and participatory—are being advocated from several quarters. Drover, for example, has proposed developing a "social market" in welfare, e.g., systems of social welfare based on the workplace.[25] Tobin has suggested replacing the hierarchical mode of operation in social welfare with that of "networking."[26] At a more politicized and organized level, the Green party in West Germany, for example, has put forward some interesting models of social cooperation along similar lines. Attempts to look at the changing nature of work and employment and its interface with ongoing changes in the sphere of the family and domestic labour is another area of new thinking. The policy implications of these ideas for full employment, income maintenance, day care, parental leave, and the like could be far reaching.[27]

A major critique of the welfare state as constituted at present in the West is its sexist bias.[28] This critique and the demand to restructure the welfare state along nonsexist lines is being made everywhere. This perspective is not directly related to the economic crisis of the welfare state and the New Right. Nonetheless it points to the need to rethink the objectives and foundations of the welfare state from the viewpoint of women's equal rights and the ultimate goal of emancipation from gender ascription.

To what extent will social-democratic and other governments be willing and able to incorporate transformative objectives such as debureaucratization, democratization, and desexualization of the welfare state remains to be seen. In any case what we are dealing with here is not a unitary ideology or policy that can be identified with governing political parties. Rather it represents a clutch of ideas and ideals that seek to restructure the welfare state in a rather fundamental way or wish to go beyond its bounds altogether. True, the aspirations of the feminists or debureaucratizers could in part be realized in conjunction with some of the other policy responses we have identified. It is also true that some of the ideas and formulations identified above may be little more than interesting proposals, destined to remain peripheral to public policy in most jurisdictions. Nonetheless, it is important to recognize that there is a range of responses—at least potentially available as policy—that seek to *transform* rather than simply *maintain or uphold* the welfare state as we have known it through the postwar years.

The Social Policy of Retrenchment: The Case of Ontario

To what extent are the various policy approaches outlined above relevant to social policy in Canada, especially in the provinces? Somewhat speculatively I have suggested that Canadian social policy at the federal level, over the last ten years, may be understood as one of Restraint. Rather more speculatively I would suggest that under the Mulroney government we are edging towards Retrenchment. It is important to remember that these concepts are in the nature of "ideal types" or analytical constructs. In reality, public policy will not fall neatly into any of the analytical boxes but more likely represent a "mixed" situation. It is useful therefore to think in terms of a scale or continuum on which these policy approaches mark out a cluster of values representing the basic characteristics involved. This suggests a policy mix in terms of adjacent categories. For example, policies in both UK and USA might be seen as a mix of Dismantling and Retrenching, the social policy of the federal government in Canada during the last decade a mixture of Maintaining and Restraining, and so on.

With these caveats in place, I would suggest that all five categories outlined above seem, to a greater or lesser extent, to be relevant to the Canadian situation especially at the provincial level. Thus we now have the policy of Dismantling in operation in British Columbia. Ontario under the Progressive Conservatives offers a good example of Retrenching (1975–85). Could public policy in Quebec over the last ten years be seen as an amalgam of Maintaining and Restraining? What of the other provinces? Is Restraining the category most generally applicable? And what of the idea of

Transformation? While Transformation is unlikely to become a mainstream policy response, radical policy alternatives such as redefining work and income maintenance programs in light of un-waged labour and worklife choices, or moving towards a popular welfare state by encouraging more decentralized and self-managed social services and delivery systems, are being developed and debated in many parts of the country.[29]

The policy of Retrenching, in particular, merits attention for a number of reasons. First, compared with the Dismantling ap-proach it is far less dramatic and therefore tends to escape scru-tiny. For example, in Ontario the policy of retrenchment and the cutbacks that go with it have yet to be examined in detail.[30] More-over, the political response to policy has also been rather muted. Yet the long-term consequences of Retrenchment may turn out to be not dissimilar to those of the policy of Dismantling. Second, as noted earlier, it is plausible that the Mulroney government will de-velop a policy stance close to the Retrenching mode at the federal level. Experience might therefore be instructive in giving us some idea of the shape of things to come. Finally, from the point of view of interprovincial comparison too it is important to place Ontario's strategy alongside those of other provinces.

THE POLICY OF RETRENCHMENT IN ONTARIO: 1975–85

Long before Reaganomics and Thatcherite monetarism came to symbolize a new departure in social policy in the West, the Prov-ince of Ontario embarked on a program of reducing the size of gov-ernment that, in retrospect, appears impressive in its candor and its pioneering role. Even more impressive is the fact that the pro-vincial government achieved a good deal of what it set out to do under difficult circumstances, including the recession of 1982.

In the early 1970s Ontario was still a long way from monetarism. Its budgets tended, if anything, to be Keynesian. Government deficit had not yet acquired the evil connotation that it acquired later and was sometimes created deliberately in order to stimulate growth. Unemployment was considered a more important prob-lem than inflation.[31] By 1975, however, partly under the impact of "stagflation," rising deficits and the failure of Keynesian remedies, Ontario embraced the gospel of monetarism.[32]

From then on reducing the deficit and eventually balancing the provincial budget and therefore retrenching public expenditure became the avowed intention of the government. In his budget speech, Frank Miller, the provincial treasurer declared:

> I am convinced that one of the root causes of the current inflation problems in Canada is excessive government spending and unnecessary growth in the size and complexity of the public sector. This has shifted an increasing share of our total resources out of private production uses in the economy, and has eroded the taxpayer's hard-earned income.[33]

The treasurer spoke of "tough measures" that were required to "curb the growth of government." A Special Program Review was initiated.[34] The Review Committee was chaired by the provincial treasurer and included business leaders. The Committee's analysis of the situation was textbook monetarism and its language carried the unmistakable stamp of resurgent neoconservatism. Public spending was "out of control" and threatened the economic future of Ontario; budget deficit was fuelling inflation and pushing up interest rates, thus crowding out private investment. The deficit could not, however, be reduced by increasing taxation as that would discourage private enterprise, investment, and productivity. The urgent problem, emphasized the Review, was not simply to contain government spending but to "face up to the difficult job of cutting it back."[35] And this was precisely the agenda set by the Review for the Provincial government.

The Review made detailed recommendations (184 of them) and set specific targets. With one or two exceptions, such as day care, the recommendations were for cutting back on expenditure. "The expenditures of the Ontario government as a percentage of the Gross Provincial Product should decline," the Review declared bluntly.[36] It advocated user charges for services like health care, and more stringent means test and selectivity for income maintenance services. The government should "explore the possibility of transferring back to the private sector some of the activities that it currently undertakes."[37] The philosophy of social welfare articulated by the Review and the general thrust of its detailed recommendations have informed much of social policy development in the province since 1975. Table 14.1 quantifies the change in bold outline.

Until 1975/76 growth in public expenditure exceeded the growth

Table 14.1 Public Expenditure, Gross Provincial Product (GPP), and Consumer Prices in Ontario, 1975/76 to 1982/83

Year	Growth in Public Expenditure (%)	Growth in GPP (%)	Rise in Consumer Prices (%)
1975/76	15.1	9.4	7.5
1976/77	10.1	14.8	8.0
1977/78	8.6	10.6	9.0
1978/79	6.4	9.3	9.1
1979/80	9.8	12.0	10.1
1980/81	9.1	10.2	12.5
1981/82	18.0	5.0	10.8
1982/83	12.5	5.0	5.8

SOURCE: Ontario, Ministry of Treasury and Economics, *Ontario Budget* (1983) Toronto: Queen's Printer, 1983: 44; *Ontario Budget* (1984) Toronto: Queen's Printer, 1984: 50–51.

Table 14.2 Public Expenditure and Budget Deficit as a Percentage of the Gross Provincial Product in Ontario, 1975/76 to 1984/85

Year	Expenditure	Deficit
1975/76	17.5	2.8
1976/77	16.7	1.8
1977/78	16.5	2.1
1978/79	16.1	1.3
1979/80	15.7	0.6
1980/81	15.5	0.7
1981/82	16.0	1.2
1982/83	17.2	1.9
1983/84	17.1	1.6
1984/85	16.8	1.3

SOURCE: Ontario, Ministry of Treasury and Economics, *Ontario Budget* (1984), Toronto: Queen's Printer, 1984: 50–51.

in the Gross Provincial Product (GPP) by a substantial percentage. The figures for 1976/77 show the effect of the restraint program quite clearly. In that year public expenditure growth was held well below the growth of the GPP. It remained that way for the next four years. Even more strikingly, in 1977/78 growth in public expenditure fell below the rate of inflation and remained that way for the next three years, resulting in an absolute decline in real public spending. It was not until 1981/82, when interest rates rose to unprecedented levels and the recession hit the Canadian economy hard, sending unemployment soaring, that expenditures rose again to levels substantially higher than the rate of growth of the GPP, which after adjusting for inflation showed very little real rise in the years 1980/81 to 1982/83.

Table 14.2 charts the change in Ontario's public expenditure and budget deficit as a percentage of GPP. The effect of the policy of restraint can be seen clearly from 1975/76 onwards. There is an upward thrust, mainly due to the recession and high interest rates, in 1982 and 1983 but the figures resume their downward slide in 1983/84.

A government determined to slash public expenditure has a wide range of instruments at its disposal. Among these, reduced budgetary allocation is the most visible and also the most effective. The Province of Ontario has used this instrument quite effectively in pursuing its objective of reducing public spending. The impact of provincial budgetary reductions—the extent to which the "slack" is picked up by municipalities, voluntary and private sector and where the cutbacks ultimately fall—is less easy to chart and document.

In general, underfunding rather than the elimination of services and programs or the tightening up of eligibility and direct manpower cuts has been the preferred strategy. The fiscal squeeze, combined with inflation restraint programs such as the "6&5," has meant a reduction in the real wages and salaries of public service workers. It has also meant a relative underfunding of the voluntary social services sector and in the case of programs such as general welfare, family benefits, and Guaranteed Annual Income Supplement (GAINS) a substantial reduction in benefit rates. Increased user fees are reflected in extra billing by doctors. Between 1975 and 1982 the general welfare rates in Ontario were eroded by over

30 percent and family benefits by about 25 percent in real purchasing power.[38] More recently these rates have risen somewhat, but the "Scrooge" approach to social welfare is evident in Ontario's low per capita social expenditure. In 1975 Ontario ranked seventh among the provinces in per capita social spending. In 1981 it ranked ninth.[39] During 1975–82 provincial social security expenditures rose by 40 percent in constant dollars. In Ontario the rise was the lowest: a mere 10.2 percent compared to British Columbia's 47.1 percent, and Saskatchewan's 45.0 percent.[40] In 1982/83, Ontario's total public expenditure (provincial and local) was estimated at 19.4 percent of the GPP compared with the average of 23.9 percent in other provinces. Ontario's per capita *public* expenditure of $2,637 was the lowest among the provinces, boasted Treasurer Miller in his budget statement.[41]

In considering the impact of the policy of retrenchment on the level of services and the standard of living of Ontarians and their somewhat muted response two things have to be kept in mind. First, provincial cutbacks have been taking place within a framework of federal-provincial partnership in social welfare. Thus the universality of programs such as medicare is underwritten by federal legislation. Basic cash transfers such as Old Age Security, Guaranteed Income Supplement, unemployment insurance, family allowances, and child tax credit are also federal programs. Indexation has helped maintain the real value of many of these benefits and allowances. Moreover, under the Liberal administration, the federal government has followed a policy of Restraint rather than Retrenchment. Despite reduced funding, general commitment to the social welfare state has been maintained. Consequently, the brunt of the deficit has been borne by the federal government, ensuring that at least the major programs remain in place and receive reasonable, even if far from adequate, funding. In short, in the context of a federally underwritten framework of social welfare the impact of provincial cutbacks has tended to be marginal. This is not to deny the negative impact of underfunding on human services in general and on the standard of living of some groups in particular.

Second, the gradualism involved in the policy of Retrenchment may also have been important in the general public's acquiescence to these policies. As Tables 14.1 and 14.2 show, if the drop in expenditure has been substantial it has also been gradual. Unlike the drama and suddenness of the policy of Dismantling, the process involved here is one of erosion and gradual reduction.

What of the future? It seems likely that under a Conservative administration, Ontario's public policy would have continued to pursue the objective of reducing the state welfare sector further. Recent elections (1985) have put a minority Liberal government, supported by the NDP, in office which is likely to halt this trend. However, if federal policy moved towards Retrenchment then federal and provincial policies together could have a bigger impact on the well-being, and possibly on the social consciousness, of Ontarians. But that, for the present, must remain a matter of speculation.

Notes

1. A. G. Tobin, "Keynote Address to the Conference on Privatization and the Public Trust," (unpublished manuscript, Vancouver, B.C., 1984). See also A. G. Frank, *Crisis: In the World Economy* (London: Heinemann, 1980), 137–42; F. F. Piven and R. A. Cloward, *The New Class War: Reagan's Attack on the Welfare State and Its Consequences* (New York: Pantheon, 1982); P. Resnick, "The Ideology of Neo-Conservatism," in W. Magnusson et al., eds., *The New Reality: The Politics of Restraint in British Columbia* (Vancouver: New Star Books, 1984).

2. V. George and P. Wilding, *Ideology and Social Welfare* (London: Routledge, 1976); A. Djao, *Inequality and Social Policy* (Toronto: John Wiley, 1983).

3. R. Mishra, *The Welfare State in Crisis* (New York: St. Martin's Press, 1984), ch. 2; M. Davis, "The AFL-CIO's Second Century," *New Left Review* 136 (1982): 50–51; G. Rayner, "The Reaganomics of Welfare," *Critical Social Policy* 2, 1 (1982): 90–98; Piven and Cloward, *The New Class War*, ch. 2; P. Riddell, *The Thatcher Government* (Oxford: Martin Robertson, 1983).

4. Piven and Cloward, *The New Class War*; M. Greenberg, "A Breakdown of Consensus," *Dissent* (Fall 1982): 473; "A Debt-Threatened Dream," *Time*, 24 May 1982, 12–23.

5. Riddell, *The Thatcher Government*, 44–48.

6. P. Taylor-Gooby, "Attitudes to Welfare," *Journal of Social Policy* 14, 1 (1985): 73–82; I. McKinnon, "What Does the Public Think About Deficits? What Does Bay Street Think About Deficits?" in D. W. Con-

klin and T. J. Courchene, eds., *Deficits: How Big and How Bad?* (Ontario Economic Council, 1983), 199, 206; "Polarizing the Nation," *Newsweek*, 8 February 1982, 34.

7. E. Ladd, (Jr.) and S. M. Lipset, "Public Opinion and Public Policy" in P. Duignan and A. Rabushka, eds., *The United States in the 1980s* (California: Stanford University, 1980), 69; P. Golding and S. Middleton, *Images of Welfare: Press and Public Attitudes to Poverty* (Oxford: Martin Robertson, 1982), ch. 6; "Polarizing the Nation," 34.

8. McKinnon, "What Does the Public Think . . . ?" 190; "A Confident Nation Speaks Up," *Maclean's*, 7 January 1985, 13–15.

9. "A Confident Nation Speaks Up," 13–16.

10. W. K. Carroll, "The Solidarity Coalition," in Magnusson et al., eds., *The New Reality*, 96.

11. *Globe and Mail*, 9 November 1984; 10 November 1984.

12. N. Glazer, "The Social Policy of the Reagan Administration: A Review," *The Public Interest* 75 (1984): 80–81, 95–97; R. Lekachman, "Reagan's Joy and Misery Index," *New Society*, 3 May 1984, 175–77.

13. Glazer, "The Social Policy of the Reagan Administration: A Review."

14. So far (mid-1985) the Mulroney government, unlike its conservative counterparts in UK and USA, has proved to be "more bark than bite." After warning Canadians that a fundamental review of social programs aimed at reducing the deficit and reducing the size of government was on its way, the government seems to have got cold feet in the face of widespread support for universal social programs and protest from advocacy groups. The cuts in social programs and allied government activity (e.g., environmental protection) have so far been modest, if not marginal. In any case they do not bear comparison with the cuts in the USA or even the UK in recent years. On Canada see: Canada, Department of Finance, *A New Direction for Canada: An Agenda for Economic Renewal* (Ottawa, 1984); *Globe and Mail*, 9 and 10 November 1984; 24 May 1985; 13 June 1985.

15. Both Thatcher and Reagan governments have given very substantial tax breaks to the wealthy and to business generally. While the Ontario government has refused to raise taxes, allowed its revenue to decline, and given tax breaks to business, its fiscal policy cannot be seen as having moved significantly towards a "supply side" approach. It must be remembered, however, that as a provincial government Ontario is somewhat hamstrung in its ability to develop an independent fiscal policy. At the federal level too the Mulroney government's policies are prorich and probusiness but only mildly so. For federal budgets see *Globe and Mail*, 9 and 10 November 1984; 24 May 1985.

16. G. B. Doern, "The Liberals and the Opposition," in G. B. Doern, ed., *How Ottawa Spends* (Toronto: James Lorimer, 1983), 11–16, 29–35.

17. M. Prince, "The Liberal Record," *Perception* 8, 1 (1984): 23–25.

18. R. Kuttner, *The Economic Illusion: False Choices Between Prosperity*

and Social Justice (Boston: Houghton Mifflin, 1984), chs. 1–2, 4, 6; Mishra, *The Welfare State in Crisis*, ch. 4.

19. Ibid.
20. Mishra, *The Welfare State in Crisis*, ch. 4.
21. Ibid. See also Organization for Economic Cooperation and Development, *Economic Surveys 1983–1984: Australia* (Paris: OECD, 1984).
22. Mishra, *The Welfare State in Crisis*, ch. 4; OECD, *Integrated Social Policy: A Review of the Austrian Experience* (Paris: OECD, 1981).
23. W. Korpi, *The Democratic Class Struggle* (London: Routledge, 1983), 232–35; "The Final Fund Proposal," *Sweden Now* 4 (1983): 11; "Sweden: Survey," *The Economist*, 6 October 1984, 18.
24. Korpi, *The Democratic Class Struggle*, 232–35; U. Himmelstrand, "Sweden: Toward Economic Democracy," *Dissent* (Summer 1983): 329–36.
25. G. Drover, "Beyond the Welfare State," *The Social Worker* 51, 4 (1983): 141–44.
26. Tobin, "Keynote Address."
27. Canadian Mental Health Association. *Work and Well-Being: Changing Realities of Employment*, (Ottawa, 1984).
28. E. Wilson, *Women and the Welfare State* (London: Tavistock, 1977); M. Barrett, *Women's Oppression Today* (London: Verso, 1980); M. McIntosh, "Feminism and Social Policy," *Critical Social Policy* 1, 1 (1981): 32–42.
29. Drover, "Beyond the Welfare State"; G. Drover and P. Kerans, "Worker-Organized Welfare Schemes," in M. D. Kimberley, ed., *Beyond National Boundaries: Canadian Contributions to International Social Work and Social Welfare* (Ottawa: Canadian Association of Schools of Social Work, 1984); CMHA, *Work and Well-Being*.
30. See, however, M. R. Novick, "Social Policy: The Search for a Provincial Framework," in D. C. MacDonald, ed., *The Government and Politics of Ontario* (Toronto: Van Nostrand Reinhold, 1980); Social Planning Council of Metropolitan Toronto, *Caring for Profit: The Commercialization of Human Services in Ontario* (Toronto, 1984).
31. K. Bryden, "The Politics of the Budget," in MacDonald, ed., *The Government and Politics of Ontario*, 434–35; R. J. Drummond, "Ontario Revenue Budgets 1960–1980," *Journal of Canadian Studies* 18, 1 (1983): 83.
32. Bryden, "The Politics of the Budget," 436.
33. Ontario, Ministry of Treasury and Economics and Intergovernmental Affairs, *The Report of the Special Programme Review* (Toronto, 1975), 16.
34. Ibid.
35. Ibid., 1–6.
36. Ibid., 36.
37. Ibid., 37, 161, 189.

38. Social Planning Council of Metropolitan Toronto, *Social Infopac* 1, 3 (1982).
39. J. Patterson, *Voluntary Sector at Risk: Update 1983* (Toronto: Social Planning Council of Metropolitan Toronto, 1983).
40. Health and Welfare Canada Social Security statistics cited in A. Moscovitch, "The Welfare State Since 1975" (unpublished manuscript, Ottawa, 1984), 7.
41. Ontario, Ministry of Treasury and Economics, *Ontario Budget (1983)* (Toronto: Queen's Printer, 1983), 44–45.

V Perspectives on the Welfare State

15 Canadian Federalism and the Welfare State
Shifting Responsibilities and Sharing Costs

FRANK STRAIN

DEREK HUM

Despite significant effort, there is no agreement as to what constitutes federalism. Indeed, the only common point seems to be that a federal state occupies some middle ground between a unitary state and a loose alliance of governments. In a unitary state the national government is supreme. Other levels of authority may exist but they wield power at the pleasure of a national government wishing decentralization. In an alliance, on the other hand, member states are politically independent, and a central authority exists only at the pleasure of the component governments. In a federal state no order of government is merely an agent of another. Rather, orders of government possess some measure of constitutional sovereignty and are accountable only to their citizens.

The welfare state entails the institutional assumption by society of the legal and explicit responsibility for the basic well-being of all its members. However, the manner in which a state discharges this responsibility is sensitive to its governing structure, and the social institutions of a unitary state will differ substantially from those of a federal state. Furthermore, social welfare arrangements in a federation with tightly separated powers and financial resources may bear no resemblance to those of a federal state with much overlap, duplication, and concurrence of powers.

Given the vagueness and lack of consensus on federalism it is not surprising that there is sharp disagreement surrounding both the assignment of jurisdiction over functions associated with the welfare state and the design of intergovernmental fiscal arrangements to finance them. This is especially true in Canada where constitutional debate is a perennial feature of the political landscape and where federal-provincial fiscal arrangements are subject to regular renegotiation.

This chapter discusses the way political, economic, and constitutional forces interact to shape federal-provincial arrangements for the welfare state. Its purpose is to integrate recent literature in political economics on the topic of federalism with certain social welfare themes, while drawing particularly on Canadian historical experience. We indicate the close connection between popular views of Canadian federalism and formal models in political economics and then exploit this connection to reveal the normative underpinnings of these positions. We then discuss the implications of these alternative views for the structure of the federal welfare state.

The popular view of Canadian federalism attributed to the Founding Fathers suggests that powers entrusted to the federal government, in general, bore on subjects in which all Canadians had a common stake.[1] Of these, military defence and an integrated Canadian economy were most important. The provinces, on the other hand, were given responsibility for local and cultural matters. The intent in this arrangement was to limit conflict in areas where the policy preferences of French Catholic and English Protestant citizens were most likely to collide. Since areas associated with the welfare state are especially vulnerable to such conflict they were appropriately assigned to the provinces. Conveniently for the nonjurist, this view of Canadian federalism mirrors that prescribed by economists working with either the common market or the public choice paradigms of federalism. It is possible therefore to employ either or both of these elaborate models to discuss the structure of the welfare state and, thereby, provide normative support for this view of federalism.

However, the common market and public choice models are not immune to criticism. A serious weakness in these models is their concentration on allocative efficiency to the virtual neglect of equity questions. Our response, which underlies earlier work on Canadian fiscal federalism, is to emphasize social equity, economic redistribution, and the importance of citizenship.[2] Significantly it can lead to an alternative view of Canadian federalism.

This second view of Canadian federalism emphasizes the compromise which emerged to ensure harmony between French and English citizens and the "rights" of those citizens, qua Canadians, to minimum standards of both income and essential public services. The evolution of Canadian citizenship to include a "right" to minimum standards and how this right has, from time to time, passed from one order of government to another, can therefore be added to Guest's list of dominant themes in the history of the Canadian welfare state.[3] We will illustrate the evolution of these citizenship "rights" by tracing several major developments in the social history of Canada which shifted financial responsibility for welfare state activities from the provinces to the national government. These programs include: Old Age Security, Unemployment Insurance, Family Allowances, Equalization, the Canada (and Quebec) Pension Plans, the Canada Assistance Plan, and the EPF Programs.

Our discussion is organized as follows. We begin by considering the "classical" federal principle and discussing its implications and relevance for the welfare state today. This is followed by a discussion of several episodes illustrating Canada's evolution towards a welfare state. The next section outlines the common market and public choice models of federalism and underscores the correspondence between views of federalism on the one hand and approaches to the structure of the welfare state on the other. To intertwine these various themes will require a contrapuntal narrative tact. In the final section we show the importance of "citizenship" and the actual shift of responsibility for financing welfare state activities from provincial governments to the national government.

Classical Constitutional Federalism

The study of federalism has traditionally been dominated by constitutional scholars. As a consequence, early literature emphasized formal constitutional provisions and jurisprudence. The classic constitutional study of federalism is by the late Sir Kenneth Wheare. Wheare defined federalism as a system of general and regional governments encompassing the federal principle, by which he meant a division of powers such that both the general and regional governments are, within a sphere, coordinate and independent.[4]

One feature of this "classical" approach is the way it narrows the definition of federalism. Classical federalism is not merely a form of government lying somewhere between a unitary state and an alliance but rather a structure wherein powers are divided among orders of government so that each is supreme within its own sphere. In short, classical federalism is concerned with describing the constitutional division of powers. But although constitutional scholars like Wheare were primarily interested in taxonomy—the classification of constitutions and forms of government—others have extended "classical federalism" to encompass normative concerns over the design of government, stressing political accountability. Pierre Elliot Trudeau articulated a normative position when he argued:

> A fundamental condition of representative democracy is a clear allocation of responsibilities: a citizen who disapproves of a policy, a law, a municipal by-law, or an education system must know precisely whose work it is so he can hold someone responsible for it in the next election.[5]

For the classical federalist, the clear division of powers is more important than the assignment of specific individual legislative powers. Independence of exercise of these powers by the different orders of government is paramount. However, one might concede that powers are indeed properly divided in a federation but still hold that some functions (e.g., income security or education) are misassigned from the perspective of a welfare state. In any case, the classical approach to federalism is difficult to sustain in the Canadian context, despite valiant attempts to finesse the constitution by cost-sharing mechanisms of all sorts, intergovernmental formula transfers and endless negotiations and judicial interpretations. The recent Parliamentary Task Force on Federal-Provincial Fiscal Arrangements was eventually led to reject the classical model. They argued:

In the integrated and interdependent community of the closing years of the 20th century, the "classical" model of federalism, based on the principle of fiscal responsibility (which would assign each province the revenue sources necessary to permit it independently to provide the services allocated to it, or to discharge responsibilities assigned to it under the BNA Act) is not appropriate nor can a system of unconditional "National Adjustment Grants" be exclusively relied on for this purpose.[6]

The classical model has, nonetheless, left a deep mark on the way we think about Canadian federalism. It is still important. But since it emphasizes the division of powers rather than the allocation of legislative responsibilities, we must turn elsewhere for an understanding of the issues relevant to the appropriate assignment of powers in a federal welfare state. Putting the point sharply: if the welfare state must ultimately lead to redistribution, which order of government in a federal state ought to hold the power to redistribute, and by what reasoning?[7] Before considering the dominant economic models of federalism, we review some major episodes associated with the Canadian welfare state.

Evolving the Federal Welfare State in Canada

A close examination of the conflicts over welfare state functions in Canada ferrets out certain themes: proliferation of cost-sharing practices, transfer of responsibility through constitutional amendment, fiscal crisis and national reorientation, the federal spending power, and continual federal-provincial negotiation. With immense violence to detail, we can illustrate these themes with specific episodes.

Viewing sections 91 and 92 of the BNA Act in conjunction with the assignment of major tax powers, it is clear that the major functional responsibilities and financial resources were to reside with the Dominion government. Welfare state activities, if contemplated at all, were a municipal concern at Confederation. Consequently, the original division of legislative powers was not meant to accommodate a significant role for either the federal or provincial governments, thereby resulting in few national programs and little consistency across the country. For example, although the first significant shared-cost program, the Old Age Pension, was introduced in 1927, it was not until 1948 that revisions were made to ensure some measure of uniformity.[8]

Still, the Old Age Pensions Act of 1927 illustrates at one and the same time the question of jurisdiction, the role of conditional grants, federal-provincial differences and, finally, the process of constitutional amendment. The Act authorized the federal government to reimburse provinces for payments to residents seventy years of age or over. Administration was provincial but had to meet federal approval. The 1927 Act remained on the statute books until 1951 when a two-tier program was established by the Old Age Security Act and the Old Age Assistance Act. The Old Age Security Act established a universal pension at age seventy. Consequently, it was a demogrant; that is, a payment based solely upon demographic characteristics (in this case, age) and without regard to individual income or need. The federal government assumed full responsibility for these demogrants. The Old Age Assistance Act continued the principles of the 1927 plan; namely, cost-shared, provincially-administered, means-tested pensions for those between sixty-five and seventy years of age. As federal funds would come from a special levy, the "old age security tax," Parliament's authority to impose such a tax was questioned. The constitutional validity of an "earmarked income tax" being dubious, prudence dictated a constitutional amendment. All provinces consented, and on May 31, 1951 a new section, 94A, was inserted in the BNA Act, stating that "the Parliament of Canada may . . . make laws in relation to old age pensions in Canada, but no law made by the Parliament of Canada in relation to old age pensions shall affect the operation of any law present or future of a Provincial Legislature in relation to old age pensions." Powers with respect to old age pensions were now concurrent; and the phrasing of 94A would eventually enable Quebec to establish its own pension plan in 1966.

The idea of relating pension benefits to earnings (contributing plans) gained increasing favour and the Canada Pension Plan was enacted in 1966. A two-tier structure was introduced. A demogrant was paid to all individuals over sixty-five (Old Age Security); this universal payment was supplemented by amounts from a contributory plan (Canada Pension Plan). Old Age Assistance was phased out and disappeared in 1969; but a Guaranteed Income Supplement payment was given to those receiving Old Age Security subject to an income test.

The Canada Pension Plan does not include Quebec, which operates its own plan. In 1962 Quebec established a committee to develop proposals on private retirement plans. In reaction to federal proposals for a national pension plan adopted by the House of Commons in June 1963, Quebec quickly announced its own plans for a contributory program over which it would have full jurisdiction. At federal-provincial conferences in 1963 Quebec objected to federal proposals on the grounds that provincial jurisdiction was being encroached. Quebec's own proposals were revealed in 1964; they were generally judged superior and more comprehensive than the federal plans, and a compromise was eventually reached after renewed negotiation between Quebec and Ottawa. A new section 94A was submitted to the British Parliament and adopted as an amendment to the BNA Act after all provinces gave consent. The federal program was modified to conform with Quebec's plan and though two separate plans co-exist, they have developed in parallel.

Canada's experience with income security for the elderly is instructive. The 1927 Act was "the first significant and continuing federal intervention in the social welfare field. It was also the first significant and continuing shared-cost program."[9] The technique of conditional grants was thereby established as a flexible means of federal-provincial fiscal adjustment. Furthermore, attaching conditions to intergovernment grants is commonly held to be constitutionally proper.[10]

The 1951 reforms also point out that transfer of jurisdiction can only be achieved with certainty through constitutional amendment. The history of the Canada Pension Plan reveals the importance attached to national uniformity, the necessity of federal-provincial negotiation and compromise to ensure consistent legislation, and the concerns and precedent of Quebec in the field of social security. Finally, the development of income security for the elderly typifies changing philosophy and delivering methods. The transition from the 1927 Act to present arrangements exemplifies the passage from a totally residual conception of social welfare to an "institutional" approach, whereby benefits are conferred by right.

A second important shift in government attitudes towards social welfare culminated in the Unemployment Insurance Act of 1940. The Depression was a strong catalyst. The federal government initially provided emergency grants for direct relief and public works but made it quite clear that it had no constitutional obligation to do so. "Unemployment relief always has been, and must necessarily continue to be, primarily a municipal responsibility, and in the second instance the responsibility of the province."[11] The Liberal government which shortly replaced the Conservatives also maintained the notion of local jurisdiction: "The Minister concurs in the view that unemployment relief is fundamentally a municipal and provincial responsibility; that the abnormal economic and industrial conditions now existing and arising in a measure out of the late war alone cannot afford justification for action on the part of the federal authorities."[12]

Lack of jurisdiction for public assistance made the federal government reluctant either to formulate social policy or administer minimum standards, even though an increasing portion of the costs were being paid by the federal government. The Dominion merely undertook to assist provinces because of the "extraordinary conditions" and because the problem had "become so general . . . as to constitute a matter of national concern."[13] There was, however, growing realization that certain aspects of social assistance, such as unemployment relief, should become a national, and not merely local, responsibility.

In 1935 Parliament passed the Employment and Social Insurance Act as part of R. B. Bennett's "new deal." The Act proposed a standardized national insurance plan to provide unemployment relief and to do away with the emergency relief methods of the Depression. The constitutional validity of the Act was tested; the federal government cited its residual power to legislate for the "Peace, Order and Good Government" of the country and its authority to levy taxes. However, the Supreme Court declared the Act *ultra vires*, a decision later upheld in 1937 by the Privy Council which ruled the legislation a matter of "property and civil rights."[14] Clearly, constitutional reform would be required if the federal government were to play a significant role in unemployment relief. By 1940 all provinces agreed to amend the constitution to permit the federal government to assume control of unemployment assistance. Section 91 of the BNA Act was amended on July 10, 1940 to grant the federal government exclusive jurisdiction over unemployment insurance. In August 1940 Parliament passed the Unemployment Insurance Act, giving Canada its first nationwide income maintenance program. The plan was based upon principles of social insurance; that is, eligibility for benefits was determined on the basis of a record of contributions and the occurrence of a (social) contingency (in this case, unemployment).

The Unemployment Insurance Act finally recognized unemployment as a national problem, to be dealt with on a national level by the central government. The severity of the problem and the totally inadequate fiscal resources of the municipalities and provinces to provide relief compelled consensus on a constitutional amendment. But unlike the case of Section 94A, the federal government received exclusive jurisdiction over unemployment insurance, thereby enabling it to introduce future program changes without federal-provincial negotiation or consultation. The administration of the unemployment insurance program should also be noted. Centralized administration and policy development was adopted to ensure uniform protection to wage earners in all parts of the country; yet decentralized local offices and differentiated application of criteria could also meet regional needs. Federal jurisdiction, therefore, need not necessarily mean national uniformity nor imply provincial administration as a method for decentralizing delivery. Finally, the Unemployment Insurance Act, as in the case of Old Age Security, represented a move towards universality.

Interest in family allowances in Canada was initiated by a federal parliamentary committee as early as 1929. But not until 1944 was a bill providing for family allowances introduced in Parliament. Though there was some opposition at first reading, the second reading passed unanimously and the Family Allowances Act came into effect July 1945. Benefits were paid to all children up to sixteen years of age and attending school; there was a residency requirement and benefits were not taxed. In 1964 Youth Allowances were introduced to provide payments for children aged sixteen to seventeen in full-time attendance in educational institutions. Quebec, which had introduced its own Schooling Allowance Programme in 1961, was compensated by tax abatements. Both these programs were eventually rendered obsolete by a new Family Allowance Act (December 1973) which took effect January 1974. The new Act was part of a federal-provincial review process of social security initiated in 1973. The new Act raised the age of eligibility to eighteen, substantially increased the amount per child, indexed the payments and made them taxable. In addition, the 1973 Act permitted provinces to vary the amount of payment to families according to the number of children, the age of children, or both, subject to an overall average payment to all families being maintained by the province. Only two provinces (Alberta and Quebec) have chosen to vary payments.

Judicial interpretations of the BNA Act have construed federal powers quite narrowly, particularly the "Peace, Order and Good Government" clause. This is especially significant because social welfare falls within provincial jurisdiction. The federal government cannot levy direct taxes for social welfare programs; it can only impose direct taxes for federal purposes.[15] The federal government can, however, provide social assistance to all Canadians through its "spending power." The term "spending power" has come to have a special constitutional meaning; it refers to the power of Parliament to make payments to anyone for any purpose, even if Parliament does not have the formal power to legislate in that area.[16] Though not specifically mentioned in the BNA Act, the "spending power" and the right to give "gifts" are derived from "doctrines of the Royal Prerogative and the common law."[17] The power to grant gifts is a provincial as well as a federal one but, in the case of the federal government, such gifts must be taken from the Consolidated Revenue Fund. Governments may give gifts to individuals, institutions, or other governments. Although the federal government has not exercised its spending power to make payments directly to individuals on an extensive basis, it has made considerable use of it to make grants to provincial governments. Furthermore, conditions may be attached to these grants; individuals or governments may refuse such "gifts" if they disagree with the conditions attached; but in any case, such gifts do not appear to violate any rules of constitutional jurisdiction. "Generosity in

Canada is not unconstitutional."[18] It is generally acknowledged, however, that Quebec does not share this interpretation.[19]

Family Allowances were initially conceived in the context of extending social assistance programs such as Mother's Allowance, Workmen's Compensation, and unemployment and general relief.[20] However, the Family Allowance Act introduced a new element to the welfare state by providing the first universal social assistance program, meaning that neither eligibility to receive benefits nor the amount of benefits is tested with respect to income, means, or need.

These constitutional vignettes are sufficient to illustrate the ever-attendant tensions bound up with a federal structure in evolving towards a welfare state: the federal-provincial conflict over jurisdiction, the imbalance of resources and responsibilities, and the constraining interpretation of a constitution forged in another time. Certain themes emerged: jurisdiction shifting; constitutional amendment; proliferation of cost-sharing mechanisms; "nationalization" of certain elements of the welfare state; the emergence of standards and "equalization." We now turn to models of economic federalism for guidance concerning the functional allocation of powers.

Political Economy Models of Federalism

One view of Canadian federalism suggests that the federal government have responsibility for matters of common interests or national concern (especially defence and economic integration) while the provinces retain responsibility for matters of local interest (especially social and cultural matters). Both the common market and public choice models of federalism provide support for this view.

Common market federalism emphasizes the potential social gains which accrue from an integrated economy. The standard criterion for assessing a common market is economic efficiency; that is, the extent to which scarce resources are employed in locations and/or sectors so as to yield the maximum amount of goods and services. A common market federation involves the complete absence of restrictions on commodity movements between federal partners, a unified tariff to outsiders, and free mobility of resources such as capital and labour throughout the federation. Since each province or region will have a comparative advantage in producing certain goods, benefits accrue to all partners in a federation through the usual gains from trade. Consequently, absence of barriers to interprovincial commodity movements increases overall income and economic welfare. There may be other gains as well, arising, for example, from a more intensive exploitation of scale economies, a larger market, more competition, and so forth.

The rationale for a national tariff (clearly expressed in Canada's post-Confederation National Policy) is to "nation build" by protecting infant industries in the federation and to secure the maximum benefit at the expense of outsiders. The tariff will hopefully lead to new trade among federation members. Gains arising from this trade creation will, of course, accrue to member provinces. Although some goods might be obtained more cheaply from foreigners, the advantages of domestic production may be greater after accounting for economies of scale, or self-sufficiency objectives. Finally, further gains are available still with free factor mobility. In general terms, these result from deploying resources efficiently; for example, if unemployed labour in one province moves to accept jobs in another province, if scarce capital flows to another province where it is more productive, or if entrepreneurial talent and effort expands or develops in other regions of the country without interprovincial restraint. Consequently, in so far as mobility of labour and capital reduces unemployment and duplication by facilitating greater efficiency, there will be increased total income in the sense of an enlarged final output from given resources.

The common market model of federalism thus identifies economic benefit as the source of common interest; economic integration results in higher total income from given resources. In principle, then, all could enjoy higher incomes.[21] The common market model has two implications for the allocation of powers in a federal country. First, only the national government should be allowed to impose tariffs. Second, powers must be so arranged as to secure the benefits of integration permanently. The concern here is with uniformity of regulatory powers to ensure a minimal degree of coordination or "policy harmonization." Indeed, such has been the concern to preserve these common market benefits for Canada that many authors (but mainly economists) have argued for constitutionally guaranteeing the various free mobility provisions.[22]

The common market model indicates why an integrated economy may be in the interests of all and why the national government must have certain powers. Thus it supports one aspect of the popular view of Canadian federalism under discussion. However it sheds no light on issues such as which functions ought to reside at the provincial or subnational level. The public choice model is much better suited to this task.

Public choice theories emphasize the relationship between public institutions and the ability of individuals to choose policies most preferred by them. The analysis begins with the notion of a public good. A public or collectively-consumed good is one characterized by nonrivalry and nonexcludability. In other words, if public goods are supplied to one individual they must be simultaneously supplied to others without extra cost (nonrivalry). Furthermore, it is generally impossible to withhold the public good from other persons wishing to consume it (nonexclusion). The typical examples are national defence, lighthouses, and the like.

The focus on public (or collective) goods is not particularly restrictive. Indeed, many welfare state activities, including income redistribution, can be considered public goods. Mancur Olson, a leading public choice theorist, indicates the generality of the concept when he argues:

> The achievement of any common goal or the satisfaction of any common interest means that a public or collective good has been provided for that group. The very fact that the goal is common to a group means that no one in the group is excluded from the benefit or satisfaction brought about by its achievement. It is of the essence of any organization that it provides an inseparable, generalized benefit. It follows that the provision of public or collective goods is the fundamental function of organizations generally. A state is first of all an organization that provides public goods for its members, the citizens; and other types of organizations similarly provide collective goods for their members.[23]

Samuelson was the first to systematically explore the nonrivalry and nonexcludability characteristics of public goods.[24] One important implication of Samuelson's analysis was that the group consuming a public good should be as large as possible. The logic underlying this conclusion is straightforward. An additional consumer can always be accommodated without reducing the consumption of anyone else. Moreover, since the new member can be taxed to help finance the public good, the cost of providing it can be spread over a larger group. Accordingly, public goods such as national defence should be provided by the central government in a federal state on grounds of efficiency, and not because of the propriety or otherwise of provincial armies.

It is common, however, for the benefits of a public-type good to taper off after some point, either because benefit declines with increasing distance from the point of input (benefit variation), or because an expanding number of consumers makes it difficult to supply the same standard of service because of congestion or crowding costs (quality deterioration). Consequently, most collectively-consumed goods are actually "impure public goods," admitting spatial and cost dimensions.

Public choice theorists address the problem of multilevel government structures by focusing on the public good, noting that its technical characteristics have important implications for collective organization. When applied in a federal context, the public choice model attempts to identify those institutional arrangements most sensitive to the preferences of individual citizens. First, it is argued that collectives should be defined by spatial considerations. Geographical boundaries should be drawn so that the benefits of collective goods provision are exhausted. This would generate the "perfect mapping" solution of Breton.[25] Second, since there are many public goods, each supplied over a specific geographical area, a "federal" structure is appropriate. The case for "federalism" based on local public goods is accordingly summarized in the "decentralization theorem" of Oates:

> For a public good—the consumption of which is defined over geographical subsets of the total population, and for which the costs of providing each level of output of the goods in each juris-

diction are the same for the central or respective local government—it will always be more efficient (or at least as efficient) for local governments to provide the Pareto efficient levels of output for their respective jurisdictions than for the central government to provide any specified and uniform level of output across jurisdictions.[26]

Decentralization is therefore appropriate when considering "local" matters; that is, where the benefits of public goods taper off with distance from the point of input (e.g., fire protection services). Some localities will supply large quantities of public goods; other localities may supply small quantities. "Each community will do its own thing and everyone will be satisfied."[27] This logic applies for all collectively supplied goods and services, including welfare state services: education, health, housing, income security, social services, etc. For example, the benefits from a particular social service will taper off with distance. Thus a system of local provision is deemed best since it results in a variety of delivery institutions, each reflecting the preferences of the local communities.[28]

The public good and common market models of federalism, therefore, provide some normative support for those who believe that Canadian federalism should be centralized only in areas for which there is an unambiguous common interest. They also suggest that if provinces are to be responsible for matters where preferences are likely to conflict sharply, then a decentralized federal welfare state is best.

A Welfare State Perspective on Federalism

The common market and public choice models are not without problems. From the perspective of the welfare state, both models largely ignore the redistributive implications, focusing exclusively on allocative efficiency concerns. The common market model of federalism emphasizes free commodity and factor mobility. Distribution of individual well-being is totally ignored. The public choice models emphasize the satisfaction of preferences. Only when redistribution is viewed as a public good (redistribution benefits the donor) is it treated at all.[29] It has been argued that in both models the distribution issue is "peripheral" and, where taken into account at all, "the emphasis is on regional disparities rather than individual incomes."[30]

Most theorists acknowledge this deficiency. They argue, following Wicksell, that allocative efficiency is attractive only if the initial distribution of income is "just."[31] But, typically, public choice theorists are social contractarians and hold that a "just" distribution must be chosen at some prior (and unspecified) stage by unanimous agreement.[32]

The contractarian position is a source of difficulty, however, especially when analyzing federations. Dennis Mueller indicates the difficulty:

> If one starts with the individual before the collective can be analyzed, it must, at least conceptually, be formed. The issues of what individuals make up the collective and what questions it can resolve must be faced. If the state of anarchy is chosen as a starting point, as in much of the contractarian literature, then the issue becomes a decision on which individuals are to be joined by the social contract, and what rights assigned to the collective. . . . If primary citizenship is assigned to the local community, then individuals in a community blessed with natural advantages or simply industrious neighbours have an important property right which can allow them to sustain their natural advantage over time. If primary citizenship is vested with the inclusive polity, citizens in unfavourably endowed communities are able to tax those living in other communities.[33]

There is no easy solution to this problem if one remains a social contractarian. However, the issue of primary citizenship is still of fundamental importance in federations, and, we believe, one key to understanding the welfare state. Every federation must grapple with the primary citizenship problem.

We advocate an alternative approach to the contractarian position.[34] Recall the welfare state as the "institutional outcome of the assumption by society of the legal, and therefore formal, and explicit responsibility for the basic well-being of all its members."[35] In a federation, individuals are members of more than one society.

They can be considered citizens of a province and citizens of the country at the same time. But what of the welfare state? Which society should be entrusted with the legal and explicit responsibility for the basic well-being of its members?

To pose the issue in this manner compels two further lines of inquiry: the matter of rights and the notion of standards. The existence of a "right" with respect to access to basic requisites of well-being highlights the importance of citizenship.[36] Citizens have rights; noncitizens only have privileges. If individuals are first members of the national society (Canadians first, Manitobans second), then the national society is obliged to meet their needs. On the other hand, if individuals are first members of the provincial society (Quebecois first, Canadians second), the provincial society must assure their needs are met. Concomitantly, the issue of sovereignty in setting standards (one national standard? or many provincial standards?) also reduces to whether primary citizenship is national or subnational in a federation. Thus the position one adopts on primary citizenship is pivotal to one's orientation to the federal welfare state.

Significantly, assigning primary citizenship to the national community does not imply federal responsibility for the delivery of welfare state services. Provincial autonomy, subject only to national standards (based on a national definition of needs) and assumption of financial responsibility by the national society, is both possible and practical; hence, cost-sharing arrangements of any conceivable variety.[37] Although the federal welfare state may be construed as a problem of primary citizenship, there is no easy or unique solution. Each federation will evolve its own accommodation based on its own political, cultural, and historical circumstances.

We believe that primary citizenship with respect to the welfare state in Canada is now vested in the inclusive polity. We support this thesis by citing the evolution of Canadian citizenship "rights." All the major milestones of the Canadian welfare state—Old Age Security, Unemployment Insurance, the Family Allowance, Equalization, the Canada Assistance Plan, the EPF programs—indicate the shift in responsibility for welfare state activities from the provincial societies to the national government. However, it is important to note that this shift of primary citizenship from provincial societies to the national level is incomplete and, additionally, a relatively recent phenomenon.

The BNA Act, Sections 92(7), (8), (13) and 93, gave responsibility for social policy to the provinces. Still, the view of social welfare at Confederation was a "residual" one, meaning that charity was the responsibility, first of all, of institutions other than government.

The first public assistance programs in Canada involved financial assistance to needy mothers. Initially developed during World War One, by 1920 only five provinces had implemented the Mother's Pension.[38] Sporadic coverage simply reflected primary citizenship being vested with the provinces.

The shift in primary citizenship really began in the twenties with the federal government's Old Age Pension Act in 1927 (see our discussion above). Though administration of Old Age Pensions was a provincial responsibility, national standards limited provincial discretion (provincial plans had to receive federal approval). Further, the Act specified a cost-sharing arrangement which shifted part of the financial responsibility to the national society.

At first the Act had little immediate impact on primary citizenship of the elderly as we noted that not until 1936 were all provinces and territories participating; and not before 1948 were revisions made to assure some uniformity.[39] But by 1951, with the introduction of the Old Age Security Act and the Old Age Assistance Act, the dramatic shift in primary citizenship was completed. The Old Age Security Act established a universal demogrant payable at age seventy. A constitutional amendment enabled the federal government to finance the pension via a special "old age security" tax, and province of residence became an irrelevant factor. The "right" became a "national right."

The development of Canadian citizenship rights was not restricted to the elderly. Again, all governments agreed, in 1940, to amend the constitution to permit the federal government to assume responsibility for unemployed employables. Unlike Old Age Security, the federal government assumed exclusive jurisdiction over unemployment insurance, thereby insuring uniform protection to wage earners throughout the entire country. This "right" was also now a "national right."

The Family Allowance Act of 1945 is yet another example of an initiative which changed primary citizenship by establishing responsibility for a social program with the federal government. The current version of the Act (1973) is especially interesting since it explicitly permits provincial flexibility (by allowing provinces to vary payments according to the number of children, the age of children, or both) subject to national standards (defined as an average payment to all families). The "right" is again a "national right," and furthermore, there are national standards for these "rights" as well.

Old Age Security, Unemployment Insurance, and the Family Allowance reflect one type of movement toward national primary citizenship. The feature common to all these shifts towards national primary citizenship is their focus on individual rights, and the concomitant responsibility of the central government to fulfill its obligations. However, a second type of movement is equally important, representing those rights which either remain with the provinces or are, in some sense, concurrent matters by virtue of divided jurisdiction, decentralized delivery, or cost-sharing arrangement. The Federal Provincial Fiscal Arrangements Act reflects the compromise necessary to reconcile the primacy of national citizenship and the necessity of provincial flexibility. This Act covers the major intergovernmental transfer programs: Equalization, the EPF (Medicare, Hospital Insurance, Post Secondary Education), and the Canada Assistance Plan. Here, the focus is not upon the direct right of individuals to well-being, but upon the rights of respective governments to their "fair" share of national resources. Without the fiscal capacity to discharge their responsibilities, provincial governments proclaiming primary citizenship for their citizens are granting empty rights. Canadians, in long recognition of this, have gone so far recently as to enshrine these principles in their new constitution. It is significant to note the exact phrasing: the "right" to essential public services is one granted to "all Canadians"; and further, equalization payments are to guarantee that provincial authorities will have the wherewithal to provide these services. Therefore, whereas a welfare state must entail rights of citizenship in a state-to-individual relation, the federal welfare state must additionally consider rights in a state-to-state context; that is, intergovernmental arrangements.

We have discussed the programs covered by the Federal Provincial Fiscal Arrangements Act in detail elsewhere.⁴⁰ Space precludes a detailed summary of these programs and their significance for the federal welfare state. Here we would simply like to emphasize the importance of these arrangements in assuring Canadian governments actually fulfill the commitment formally entrenched in Section 36 of the Canadian Constitution. It is instructive to review the actual wording of the Constitution. Section 36 reads:

> 36. (1) Without altering the legislative authority of Parliament or of the provincial legislatures, or the rights of any of them with respect to the exercise of their legislative authority, Parliament and the legislatures, together with the government of Canada and the provincial governments, are committed to:
> (a) promoting equal opportunities for the well-being of all Canadians;
> (b) furthering economic development to reduce disparity in opportunity;
> (c) providing essential public services of reasonable quality to all Canadians.
> (2) Parliament and the government of Canada are committed to the principle of making equalization payments to ensure that provincial governments have sufficient revenues to provide reasonably comparable levels of public services at reasonable levels of taxation.

The entrenchment of Section 36 would appear to complete, in principle, the transformation of primary citizenship in Canada. Nonetheless, the actual fiscal arrangements do not provide for full national financial responsibility nor explicit, but flexible, national minimum standards (for a critique see our earlier work). We conclude that despite the significant shift in primary citizenship, there remain more than a few finishing touches to complete the process.

Notes

1. D. Smiley, "Two Themes of Canadian Federalism," *Canadian Journal of Economics and Political Science* 31 (1965): 82.
2. D. P. J. Hum, *Federalism and the Poor: A Review of the Canada Assistance Plan* (Toronto: Ontario Economic Council, 1983); D. P. J. Hum and F. Strain, "Redistribution and Equalization in a Federal State: A Social Welfare Approach," *Western Economic Review* 3 (1984): 49–65; F. Strain, "Fiscal Federalism and the Welfare State: A Theoretical Framework Applied in an Examination of Educational Finance in Canada" (Unpublished Ph.D. dissertation, University of Manitoba, 1985).
3. D. Guest, *The Emergence of Social Security in Canada* (Vancouver: University of British Columbia Press, 1980).
4. K. C. Wheare, *Federal Government* (Oxford: Oxford University Press, 1946), 10.
5. P. E. Trudeau, *Federalism and the French Canadians* (Toronto: McMillan, 1968), 77.
6. Parliamentary Task Force on Federal-Provincial Fiscal Arrangements, *Fiscal Federalism in Canada* (Ottawa: Minister of Supply and Services, August 1981).
7. Hum, *Federalism and the Poor.*
8. Guest, *The Emergence of Social Security in Canada,* 76–78.
9. K. Bryden, *Old Age Pensions and Policy Making in Canada* (Montreal: McGill-Queens University Press, 1974), 8.
10. W. R. Lederman, *Continuing Canadian Constitutional Dilemmas* (Toronto: Butterworth, 1981), 364.
11. Cited in A. H. Birch, *Federalism, Finance, and Social Legislation* (Oxford: Clarendon Press, 1955), 179.
12. Ibid.
13. D. Smiley, ed., *The Rowell-Sirois Report,* Book I (Toronto: McClelland and Stewart, 1963), 176.
14. Birch, *Federalism, Finance, and Social Legislation,* 160–61; P. Russell, *Leading Constitutional Decisions* (Toronto: McClelland and Stewart, 1965), 46–50.
15. F. R. Scott, *Essays on the Constitution* (Toronto: University of Toronto Press, 1977), 294.
16. For an examination of this aspect of federal government power, see Ottawa's submission to the June 1969 Constitutional Conference, *Federal-Provincial Grants and the Spending Power of Parliament,* (Ottawa: Queen's Printer, 1969).
17. Scott, *Essays on the Constitution,* 296; see also G. La Forest, *The Allocation of Taxing Powers Under the Canadian Constitution,* Second Edition (Toronto: Canadian Tax Foundation, 1981), 45–51, 196–99.
18. Scott, *Essays on the Constitution,* 26–27.
19. Quebec, *Report of the Royal Commission of Enquiry on Constitutional*

Problems, Vol. II (Quebec: Queen's Printer, 1956), 217–23.

20. Guest, *The Emergence of Social Security in Canada*, 131–33.

21. In the jargon of normative economics, the common market generates an allocation of resources which meets the "hypothetical compensation" test. All need not be better off, however. We deal with this important detail later.

22. A. E. Safarian, *Canadian Federalism and Economic Integration*, a study prepared for the Government of Canada (Ottawa: Information Canada, 1974); J. A. Hayes, *Economic Mobility in Canada: A Comparative Study* (Ottawa: Ministry of Supply and Services, 1982); F. Flatters and R. G. Lipsey, *Common Ground for the Canadian Common Market* (Montreal: Institute for Research on Public Policy, 1983).

23. M. Olson, *The Logic of Collective Action* (Cambridge: Harvard University Press, 1965), 15.

24. P. A. Samuelson, "The Pure Theory of Public Expenditure," *Review of Economics and Statistics* 36 (1954): 387–89; "Diagrammatic Exposition of a Theory of Public Expenditure," *Review of Economics and Statistics* 37 (1955): 350–56; "Aspects of Public Expenditure Theories," *Review of Economics and Statistics* 40 (1958): 332–38.

25. A. Breton, "A Theory of Government Grants," *Canadian Journal of Economics and Political Science* 31 (1965): 175–87.

26. W. Oates, *Fiscal Federalism* (New York: Harcourt Brace Jovanovich, 1972), 35.

27. R. A. Musgrave and P. B. Musgrave, *Public Finance in Theory and Practice* (New York: McGraw-Hill, 1976), 619.

28. On the income redistribution case see J. M. Buchanan, "Who Should Distribute What in a Federal State?" in H. M. Hochman and G. E. Peterson, eds., *Redistribution Through Public Choice* (New York: Columbia University Press, 1974); and M. V. Pauly, "Income Distribution as a Local Public Good," *Journal of Public Economics* 2 (1973): 35–58. On social services as a public good see D. P. J. Hum, *Federalism and the Poor;* and "The Nature and Role of Social Services: An Economist's Perspective," *The Social Worker/Le Travailleur Social* 52 (1984): 52–56.

29. The benefit of redistribution to the donor may be a consequence of the donor's altruism, the donor's concern that the poor are a threat to his or her property, social stability, or the like. In essence, donors must gain a benefit by voluntarily transferring some of their resources to others.

30. Hum, *Federalism and the Poor*, 7.

31. K. Wicksell, "A New Principle of Just Taxation," *Finanztheoretische Unfersuchungen* (1896). Reprinted in *Classics in the Theory of Public Finance*, R. T. Musgrave and A. T. Peacock, eds., (New York: St. Martins Press, 1967).

32. J. Rawls, *A Theory of Justice* (Cambridge: Harvard University Press, 1973); J. M. Buchanan and G. Tullock, *The Calculus of Consent* (Ann

Arbour: University of Michigan Press, 1962). Contractarians such as Rawls are interested in "rules of the game" that would command universal support. They employ the social contract as an analytical device merely to stimulate rational discourse on redistributive issues.

33. D. Mueller, *Public Choice* (Cambridge: Cambridge University Press, 1979), 267.

34. The focus on redistribution and individual well-being within the context of federalism was first developed in Hum (1983) who called it a social welfare perspective. Hum was concerned to show the practicality of such an approach by applying it to the Canada Assistance Plan. The discussion here provides a more explicitly normative framework based upon a notion of rights. See Hum, *Federalism and the Poor*.

35. H. K. Girvetz, "Welfare State," in *The International Encyclopedia of Social Sciences*, Vol. 16 (New York: MacMillan, 1968), 512–21.

36. See Strain, "Fiscal Federalism and the Welfare State," for a detailed discussion of the definition of "rights" used here. Rights, as we define them, are not "natural"; rather they evolve in actual societies according to the views of citizens with respect to the "rules of the game."

37. See Hum, *Federalism and the Poor*, for a detailed discussion of this point with respect to the Canada Assistance Plan.

38. Guest, *The Emergence of Social Security in Canada*, 63.

39. Ibid., 76–78.

40. See Hum, *Federalism and the Poor;* Hum and Strain, "Redistribution and Equalization in a Federal State: A Social Welfare Approach"; Strain, "Fiscal Federalism and the Welfare State."

16 Controlling the Deficit and a Private Sector Led Recovery
Contemporary Themes of the Welfare State

GORDON W. TERNOWETSKY

The Canadian Federal election of September 1984 produced a landslide victory for Brian Mulroney and his Conservative Party. The results signalled that Canadians were ready for a change. People had tired of Liberal rule and, from Newfoundland to British Columbia, Canadians fell under the spell of Brian Mulroney's new directions for change and his promise of "jobs, jobs, jobs." Without any clear indication of specifically how these would be accomplished, the electorate gave the Conservatives a huge majority and ensured that they would have sufficient power to implement their plans for economic renewal.

Left behind in the Conservative sweep was a decimated Liberal Party and, because of its numerically small number, a seemingly ineffectual parliamentary opposition. Like the rest of us, the opposition parties may have little choice but to accept the course the Conservatives chart over the next few years. From the beginning we were forewarned. The choices ahead may be tough and hard, but firm and decisive action is necessary to pull us out from the legacies of unemployment, debt, and economic stagnation inherited from fifteen years of Liberal Party mismanagement.

This paper explores selected themes and concepts running through the public economic and policy statements made by the Conservatives as they shape new pathways for economic renewal.

372

It is argued below that the "consultative," "consensus" style of political decision-making put forth by the government may be more a matter of appearance than fact. Caution seems to be in order for, at this stage of their political ascendancy, the Conservatives have been able to masterfully control and shape the framework of the debate on the changes required in this country. A major problem in the Conservative agenda is that it overlooks key elements in its effort to lower the deficit and create favourable conditions for a private sector led recovery. Unless the framework, in which we are invited to participate, is challenged and broadened, the future course of social policies in this country may undermine many of the gains we have come to accept and take for granted.

The Conservative Course

The first objective indication of what lies ahead came in Finance Minister Wilson's economic statement of November 1984. In this address and the supplementary budget papers, a range of strategies for improving economic growth and creating employment were outlined.[1] The scenario presented rests on the basic assumption that the motor of economic growth is the private sector, which will reinvest its profits and create jobs for Canadians. Before growth and employment can reach their potential it is, however, forcefully argued that the deficit must be reduced and controlled. The source of Canada's problems, we are told, lies in the deficit and its adverse impact on the private sectors' investment and job creation decisions. It is these two pillars of lowering the deficit and creating conditions for a private sector led recovery that hold the key to economic renewal in Canada.

Repeatedly we read about the harmful effects of the deficit in the Government's "Agenda for Economic Renewal."

> The magnitude of the debt problem, if not managed prudently, will clearly have increasing adverse impacts on investor confidence....
>
> The growing public debt has become a severe handicap to economic progress and the most serious obstacle to economic growth....

If the projected pattern of deficits were allowed to materialize, confidence would be further depressed, producing adverse
effects on investment, growth and jobs.[2]

Over the last decade the negative influence of deficit spending on
growth, investment, and job creation has been used by different
levels of Canadian governments and governments in other countries to support cutbacks in the name of fiscal responsibility. Without an economic surplus, it is argued, the demands of labour can
no longer be placated and income support services need to be
checked. Governments can no longer continue the ambitious level
of social spending initiated in earlier, more prosperous years.

There is another twist to this fiscal crisis. In the sixties and early
seventies, "deficit spending" under the guise of Keynesian interventionism was a normative solution to the growing demand for
state assistance. Such a strategy is unacceptable to the
neomonetarist assumptions of our new government. Under conditions of slow growth, welfare state expenditures exacerbate the
deficit and push up interest rates and thereby erode activity in the
private sector.

What should concern us is the growing support for parties that
follow this doctrine. Not only are we facing a fiscal crisis, but the
political success of these parties suggests that the legitimacy of
what we have come to accept as the welfare state may be increasingly under threat.

The private market assumptions guiding the Conservatives are
no different from Reaganomics in the United States, Thatcherism
in the United Kingdom, or Bennettism in British Columbia. There
is, however, a significant shift in the way these market policies are
being presented and implemented. Gone are the days of "union
bashing," draconian welfare cuts and open confrontation. In its
place is a style of consensus, openness, cooperation, consultation,
and the appearance of responsiveness. As witnessed in the current
review of family allowances and universality, we are encouraged
to participate and work together in charting the course for the necessary changes in social policy.

Is the government building bridges, mending fences, and making allies in an effort to include the Canadian people in the
decision-making process? This is unlikely. To devise policies that
reflect a range of competing interests is not only difficult but also

touches on the problem of excessive expectations and ungovern-ability.[3] What is more likely happening is that the Conservatives are being tactful. They are selling a set of priorities in a manner that precludes consideration of other credible alternatives. In the review of universality, for example, the guidelines set by our leaders contain the twin goals of saving money and ensuring that those in greatest need are the main recipients of assistance. In the context of our current debt crisis these objectives appear to be rea-sonable. Indeed, Mr. Wilson's argument that the deficit is a matter of fact, not ideology, has been persuasive.[4] What we have to be aware of, however, is that by making deficit control a central issue, the government has skillfully set the boundaries for the debate on the policy choices available.

A good deal can be accomplished in the name of consensus and consultation. Already there is a tendency for people and groups in the community to acquiesce to the government's "inescapable reality" of lowering the deficit and to the methods by which this can be attained. The best example is illustrated in the Canadian Council of Social Development's (CCSD) response to the invitation to participate in the review of family allowances.[5] While there are several attractive aspects in the CCSD's proposed changes to the distribution of child benefits, it should concern us that the CCSD has, in its draft proposal, accepted both the deficit framework and the government's operational definition of how the deficit is created. The CCSD knows better. In a special edition on income security issues in Canada, which was distributed simultaneously with its Child Benefit proposals, the CCSD demonstrates that the approach to the deficit taken by the government selectively ig-nores crucial deficit-producing elements in its review of the deficit and universality.[6] These other elements were not, however, in-cluded in the draft proposal on changes in child benefits outlined by the CCSD.

There are also signs that under the guise of consensus, the pro-cess of consultation is being "perverted into authoritarianism."[7] Despite the much heralded consensus-building approach to social policy changes, the government has quietly and without consulta-tion implemented several cost-saving measures in unemployment insurance. By tightening up eligibility criteria and rationalizing the administration of Unemployment Insurance some $300 million will be saved at the expense of the unemployed.[8] Curiously there has been little public response to these punitive cost-saving exercises. Might it be that people have already accepted the importance of cutting expenditures to control the deficit?[9] Do they view such steps as difficult, but necessary?

An affirmative answer seems in order, for—as illustrated above—there appears to be a willingness to endorse the options presented by the government. This is not surprising as the government has been careful in its use and salesmanship of terms and concepts that bolster its approach. Concepts such as the "deficit" and a "private sector led recovery" are treated as "moral" and "sacred" recipes. To question their truth and the noble outcomes they point to is to question the self-evident. As the CCSD points out, it is already taken for granted that the deficit needs to be reduced.[10]

The strong electoral support received by the Conservatives is also being used judiciously as evidence that the policies of the government reflect the "collective will" of the Canadian people.

> Canadians looked back on a decade of soaring government deficits and sluggish uncertain economic growth. They voted for a change in policies and in the approach of a government to making these policies. This is our mandate and our challenge.[11]

As policy analysts we also have a "mandate." This is to engage conventional wisdom and the prescriptions associated with the "private sector" and "deficit" concepts. Are these symbols of liberation, renewal, and change, as the Conservatives would have us believe? Or are they symbols of social control and legitimation? Will they open the door of opportunity or further exacerbate and reinforce the structure of Canadian inequality? One way to answer these questions is to assess whether these concepts tend to "divert our attention" from other issues and outcomes that need to be placed on the public agenda.

The Deficit

The federal government's approach to the deficit is a cause for concern because we are being conditioned to equate deficits with excessive spending.[12] Witness Mr. Wilson in the November 1984 Economic Statement: "Our immediate goal is to reduce the deficit through expenditure reduction not through major tax increases." This theme was recently repeated both in his opening and closing comments in the March 1985 economic summit between government, business, labour, and different interest groups.

Lowering the deficit by spending restraint is, however, a tactic that holds little credence in a recent report of the Economic Council of Canada. The Council notes that over the last ten years government expenditures have been relatively restrained. The national debt continues to mount because successive governments continue to forego revenue they were once able to collect. According to Council estimates, between 1975 and 1983 the federal government lost some $99 billion through the indexation of taxation and the proliferation of tax expenditures. In 1979 alone, the provincial and federal governments lost more than $20 billion through tax breaks to individuals.[13]

Those benefiting the most from these "administrative tax decisions" are individuals who already have substantial incomes. In 1981, for example, more than a billion dollars in foregone tax revenue was redistributed amongst the richest 9,000 Canadians earning about $200,000. In Saskatchewan, some $20 million in lost tax revenue went to 241 residents with pre-tax incomes above $200,000.[14]

Under the Joe Clark Conservative administration information on the amount of revenue the Canadian government lost, through preferential tax treatment for corporations and individuals, was published for 1979 and 1980.[15] Why has the current government chosen to exclude these Tax Expenditure Accounts in its deficit estimates? Why does it underplay and even ignore the Economic Council of Canada's forceful conclusion that traces the deficit to the government's decisions to forego revenue? One can, of course, only speculate on a number of reasons. However, what is clear is that by turning the deficit debate into a problem of direct spending, the government has presented a one-sided and selective perspective of the issues and types of policies and programs that need to be reviewed.

It needs to be noted that the impact of tax expenditures on the deficit is partially outlined by the government in the November

1984 Economic Agenda. This, however, is done in a very restricted way, in the context of tax exemptions as they apply to family allowances and elderly benefits. Care is taken to show that a lot of revenue is lost and that most of this ends up in the hands of the richest Canadians. But one searches the Agenda in vain to find similar, thorough documentation of the money the government loses through the total spectrum of tax expenditures. While this information could be estimated, it is excluded from the discussion on spending choices. Perhaps we need to remind the government of the advice of one of its own bodies, the National Council on Welfare:

> Just because the Tax Act disguises its spending as tax deductions, no one should be deceived into thinking that tax expenditures are anything other than real spending—every bit as real, in fact . . . as direct spending which attracts so much attention.[16]

Another area in which the government's Agenda offers few details is on the financial assistance provided to corporations. To work these out we are forced to consult independent sources. The figures are staggering. In 1984, $18 billion in financial aid was turned over to corporations operating in this country. Seven and a half billion dollars was in the form of direct income transfers and $11 billion through special tax concessions.[17]

In place of these hard data we find in the Agenda a review of the different methods of assisting corporations. It appears that the preferred avenue for such assistance is shifting away from direct subsidies to special tax concessions. The advantage of this method is that, unlike income subsidies, governments are removed from direct involvement and interference in market place decisions. Again this fits well with Conservative philosophy that "[g]overnment has become too big. It intrudes too much into the market place and inhibits or distorts the entrepreneurial process."[18] The other important outcome of the tax assistance route is that the level of corporate income transfers is usually hidden, less easily traceable and therefore more difficult to debate publicly.

The general omission and understating of the cost of corporate assistance does not permit a creative examination of the impact of these transfers on the deficit. Some examples may illustrate the need to know and debate this information.

The current review of universal programs and their impact on the deficit was legitimated, for some, by the prime minister's question, "Should a bank president earning over $500,000 a year receive the Family Allowance?" Well, the response of at least one prominent banker is on record. The chairman of the Royal Bank of Canada, Mr. Rowland Frazee, said "no," stating that "universality should be scrapped" in order to reduce the deficit.[19] During the March 1985 economic summit, Mr. Frazee continued to champion this view as chairperson of the "blue-chip" lobby group, The Business Council on National Issues. To realize economic renewal Frazee argued that a " 'gradual' reduction in the deficit of five billion a year for the next several years is 'imperative'."[20]

But there is another revealing part of this story that does not appear in the Business Council's chairperson's concern with the deficit or in the spending/deficit framework set by the government. In 1982, the Royal had profits in excess of $358 million. However, through corporate tax breaks it is reported that the Royal Bank did not pay one cent in taxes.[21] Here we have a bank with assets above $85 billion and annual profits in the hundreds of millions quite legally avoiding the payment of income tax.

How can we be expected to debate the deficit and consult on government cutbacks without knowing the impact that foregone corporate corporate tax revenue has on the deficit? We cannot. Yet, the government has chosen not to table this information. Instead, the deficit is treated as an outcome of direct spending, which diverts our attention from other crucial questions on the way the deficit is formed by handouts to corporations.

It is not that this information is unknown. In 1982 a government standing committee on Trade, Finance and Public Affairs looked carefully into the taxation of Canadian banks. Of concern was the "sharp decline in the effective tax rate for Canadian chartered banks."[22]

Theoretically, the Chartered Banks have a tax rate of 48.3 percent to 51.0 percent, depending upon provincial tax rate variations. Some examples of the bank profit and taxation data examined by the Standing Committee are given in Table 16.1. After

Table 16.1 Canadian Chartered Banks: Taxation and Foregone Revenue ($millions)

| | Years Ended October 31 | | | | | | | | | | | | | |
	1971	1972	1973	1974	1975	1976	1977	1978	1979	1980	1981	1982	1983	Total
Pre-Tax Balance of Revenue	556.0	668.8	778.5	874.6	1,234.3	1,199.6	1,243.0	1,495.4	1,346.5	1,452.1	2,178.8	1,630.2	2,721.0	17,379.8
Taxes Paid	277.7	313.4	376.5	433.6	591.0	536.3	512.4	518.4	227.2	209.6	458.8	104.8	826.3	5,386.0
After-Tax Balance of Revenue	278.3	355.4	402.0	440.9	663.3	663.3	730.6	977.0	1,119.2	1,242.5	1,720.0	1,525.4	1,894.7	12,012.6
Effective Tax Rate	49.9%	46.9%	48.4%	49.6%	44.7%	44.7%	41.2%	34.7%	16.9%	14.4%	21.1%	6.4%	30.4%	
Foregone Revenue	—	20.3	12.0	2.8	24.9	62.3	107.8	227.8	444.7	514.9	628.4	708.7	531.5	3,286.1

SOURCE: Parliamentary Standing Committee, Finance, Trade and Economic Affairs, *Bank Profits* (Ottawa: Queen's Printer, 1982); J. Calvert, *Government Limited: The Corporate Takeover of the Public Sector in Canada* (Ottawa: Canadian Centre for Policy Alternatives, 1984). Foregone revenue is calculated at a "statutory tax rate" of 49.8%.

1974, the effective tax rate of banks begins to fall, at first slowly and then dramatically. Profits, on the other hand, rise markedly as do after-tax bank revenues. Comparing profits and taxes paid in the early years with the later years in this table illustrate the magnitudes of these incongruities. In 1977, banks paid taxes of $277.7 million on $566 million in profits. Their effective tax rate was 49.9 percent. This closely approximates the "statutory income-tax rate" for banks. By 1982, however, the effective tax rate fell to 6 percent. Only $104.8 million in taxes was paid on $1.6 billion in pre-tax profits. Over $700 million was lost by the federal government through tax concessions to the banking industry in 1982 alone.

By failing to collect their tax complement, governments contribute to their own fiscal crises. If the legal, statutory tax rate is applied throughout this period to pre-tax profits, the shortfall in government tax income exceeds $3.2 billion. This figure is larger than the 1984–85 budget outlays of Saskatchewan and a number of other Canadian provinces.[23] What is clear is that, if the advice Mr. Frazee gave to the March summit is acted upon, the deficit could quite easily be reduced "gradually" if the government collected the full complement of taxes owed by the banks.

This revenue that is lost to Canadians is channeled to a very profitable sector in the Canadian economy. A select few benefit while Canadians on the whole lose out. Revenue shortfalls, on the other hand, are being made up by less than progressive increases in personal taxes, regressive "special recovery sales taxes" of the type the government implemented in October 1984, and by deficit spending that is now being used to justify cuts in social expenditure.

A series of 1984 articles in the *Globe and Mail* further underscores our right to know and debate the dollar value of corporate assistance. It is shown, for example, that Shell Canada with assets over $4.7 billion and recorded profits of $302 million in 1982 paid no tax. Consolidated Bathurst also escaped tax with 1982 profits above $78 million. Over the last few years, Bell Canada, one of the largest and most profitable corporations operating in Canada, has attained public assistance, through just one type of tax break, to the tune of $1.2 billion.[24]

These examples are only the tip of the massive levels of government aid available to corporations in Canada. What has evolved is

Figure 16.1 Federal Government Revenue From Personal and
Corporate Income Tax

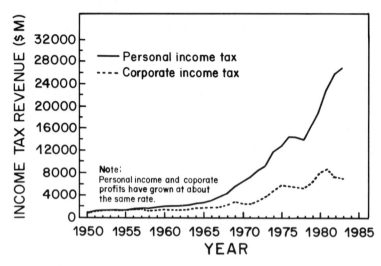

SOURCE: Canadian Council on Social Development, "Special Issue on Income
Security," *Social Development Overview* 2, 3 (Winter 1985).

a system of tax concessions which transfer the burden of government fund-raising to individuals from corporations. Figure 16.1
shows that in 1954, 54 percent of government income tax revenue
came from individuals. This increased to 76 percent or $26 billion
by 1982. Corporations by contrast, contributed 24 percent of government revenue in 1982, a decline of some 23 percent compared
to their portion of 47 percent in 1954. This occurs because the corporate sector is able to quite legally avoid paying its statutory tax
rate. It is estimated that corporations operating in this country
pay less than one-quarter of their tax bill.[25] Clearly the money lost
through these tax expenditures places an enormous drain on revenue and contributes substantially to the deficit.

This shifting burden of taxation is clearly illustrated in the February 1983 update of the Government of Canada Budgetary Revenue (see Table 16.2). In percentage terms, personal income tax revenue grew by 21.2 percent in 1981–82 and 8.5 percent in 1982–83.
Direct corporate income tax in the last year reported in Table 16.2
fell, however, by some 31.3 percent.[26]

One area where governments gained considerable income from

Table 16.2 Government of Canada Budgetary Revenue, February
1983 Update

| | Millions | | % Change | |
	1981–82	*1982–83*	*1981–82*	*1982–83*
Personal Income Tax	24,046	26,100	21.2	8.5
Corporate Income Tax	8,118	5,580	0.1	-31.3
Petroleum & Gas Revenue Tax & Incremental Oil Revenue Tax	864	1,500	–	73.6
Nonresident Tax	1,018	1,015	17.4	-0.3
Sales Tax	6,185	5,850	13.9	-5.4
Customs Import Duties	3,439	2,750	7.9	-20.0
Excise Duties	1,175	1,300	12.8	10.6
Other Excise Taxes	564	660	-1.6	17.0
Gasoline Excise Tax	436	405	-3.8	-7.1
Oil Export Charge	519	355	-38.4	-31.6
Natural Gas & Gas Liquids Tax	998	1,295	433.7	29.8
Net Petroleum Compensation Revenue	0	360	0.0	0.0
Special Petroleum Compensation Charge	473	0	0.0	0.0
Miscellaneous Tax	120	130	21.2	8.3
Total Tax Revenue	47,955	47,300	18.0	-1.4
Return on Investments	5,095	5,145	23.4	1.0
Other Nontax Revenue	1,018	765	64.7	-24.9
Total Nontax Revenue	6,113	5,910	28.7	-3.3
Total Budgetary Revenue	54,068	53,210	19.1	-1.6

SOURCE: Parliamentary Standing Committee on Finance, Trade and Economic
Affairs, *Budget Review* (Ottawa: Queen's Printer, 1983).

corporate taxation was through the Petroleum and Gas Revenue
Tax (see Table 16.2). This, however, has now been shelved in the
1985 energy pact signed by Pat Carney, the western oil producing
provinces, and the major oil companies. At the signing it was
estimated that some $300–500 million would be lost in federal tax
revenue. A few days later these estimates were publicly scrutinized
and quickly revised to somewhere in the vicinity of $2 billion dol-
lars. This latter figure should not come as a surprise. It was public
knowledge in November 1984. Only then it was argued that the
government was unlikely to end this tax because without the revenue it generated there would be a sharp jump in the deficit.[27]

A Private Sector Recovery

Through the years successive Canadian governments have assisted the private sector with direct grants and tax write-offs on the assumption that investments will result and jobs will be produced. Many people would agree there is some room for this type of assistance. However, in the present economic climate, when the cost and benefit of universality and other public expenditure programs are being reviewed in relation to their impact on the deficit we also need to know the cost of corporate assistance, its effect on the deficit, and whether the Canadian people benefit from these transfers of public funds. What is required is a public, cost benefit analysis of the type being used to examine universality.

One way to look at the issue of corporate accountability is to see if jobs are produced when profits grow.[28] The cornerstone of the Conservative government's economic philosophy is that the private sector will invest, stimulate economic activity, and create jobs once profits are secure. It is this noble assumption that justifies the outlay of public funds to private corporations.

Canadian Business's annual publication on "Getting the most out of the Top 500" indicates, however, that the number of corporate employees seems to be declining regardless of profit levels. The Royal Bank with profits of $492 million in 1981, $358 million in 1982 and $480 million in 1983 had fewer employees in 1983 than in 1981. Profit increases of $310.2 million and $314.8 million in 1981 and 1983 have resulted in a decline of 3,140 employees at the Canadian Imperial Bank of Commerce. Jobs at Shell Canada have also fallen, although Shell reported annual profits in the hundreds of millions during this same time frame. Between 1981 and 1983 those employed by Bell Canada are down by 4,200 while Bell's profits during this period rose from $550.7 million to $745.2 million.[29]

The assumption that profits and government assistance to corporations will translate into jobs does not seem to be warranted. Yet governments continue to transfer huge sums of public money to corporations. Even with the 1985 energy agreement Pat Carney and Michael Wilson are unable to be precise about the number of jobs that will result from the concessions given over to the oil companies. Instead it is assumed that thousands of jobs will result.

Table 16.3   Profits, Assets, and Employees for Selected Canadian Chartered Banks and Major Oil Companies, 1981 and 1983

Company	MAJOR OIL COMPANIES Profits ($ Million)		Assets ($ Billion)		Employees	
	1981	1983	1981	1983	1981	1983
Imperial	465.0	290.0	7.096	8.049	16,029	14,732
Texaco	316.3	344.0	2.879	3,288	4,522	3,900
Shell	236.0	102.0	4.751	5.240	8,822	7,975
Gulf	299.0	218.0	4.583	5.112	11,367	9,700
Dome	199.1	105.0	2.238	8.178	9,500	7,500
Husky	43.6	47.6	2.074	2.386	2,895	1,627
Mobil	N/A	160.5	1.164	1.529	1,228	1,140

Bank	MAJOR BANKS Profits ($ Million)		Assets ($ Billion)		Employees	
	1981	1983	1981	1983	1981	1983
Royal Bank	492.5	479.9	87,516	84,681	38,783	38,687
Canadian Imperial Bank of Commerce	310.2	314.8	66,884	68,112	36,665	33,525
Bank of Montreal	358.5	282.5	63,779	63,194	28,582	29,125
Nova Scotia	224.1	347.7	50,138	54,808	23,910	25,537
Toronto-Dominion	255.3	325.1	44,862	42,488	18,925	17,575

SOURCE: "Canada's Top 500 Companies," *Canadian Business*, Special Issue (1982); (1984).

N.B.: See note 31.

More than faith is required to justify this huge outlay of public money. Instead, the facts suggest extreme caution is required. For example, the deputy energy minister in Ontario predicts that deregulation of the oil industry will "cost the province 60,000 jobs." Manitoba's Energy minister estimates a job loss of 1,500.[30]

The findings presented in Table 16.3 indicate there are good reasons for insisting on corporate accountability for public funds.[31]

On the whole, among the larger corporations, employees decrease as profits grow and stabilize. Business health does not appear to be compatible with social health. A private sector led recovery seems to mean that while corporations increase their assets and profits and attain public assistance, few benefits are transferred back to the Canadian people.

This is not the noble outcome we are led to believe will flow from predictable profits in the private sector. Instead of permitting governments to bankrupt our economy at the expense of wishful assumptions we need to force the debate back to empirically verifiable patterns. Profits do not now automatically lead to expanded employment opportunities.

Conclusions

Social policy is about choices. Unfortunately, the options given to us by the government are limited by both its concern with the deficit and its one-sided, very selective operational definition of the deficit. Likewise, the promise of jobs through the private sector seems to have little redeeming value. Among some of the largest corporations looked at in this paper, profits do not result in the expansion of job opportunities. If the course chosen by the Conservatives is allowed to go unchecked the future of social policy and the conditions under which we exercise our crafts will be difficult indeed.

In the name of fiscal responsibility cuts have started and we have been asked to participate in the process of consulting on ways and means of further rationalizing expenditures on social programs. Under the guise of equating social health with business health we are also asked to believe that our future for recovery lies in promoting the interests of the private sector. The facts suggest otherwise.

Our role is to divulge the real consequences of the mystical concepts used by the Conservatives to disarm effective opposition. It is important we enter the debate prepared, with our eyes open and aware of what lies behind the style and rhetoric of our new leaders. We need to shift the gaze of our research and policy concerns from traditional areas of expenditure to those more or less hidden forms of public transfers that go unnoticed, benefit powerful corporations and the rich, and offer little return to the Canadian people. It is important that the concepts and prescriptions of the government are not allowed to "divert our attention" and become, as Mills correctly argues, "symbols of legitimation."[32] Symbols that leave the "winners" or masters of men untouched.[33] Symbols that lead us to think about residual categories and prescriptions and hold little potential for meaningful change.

Notes

1. Canada, Department of Finance, *A New Direction for Canada: An Agenda for Economic Renewal,* Presented by the Honourable Michael Wilson (Ottawa: Department of Finance, 1984); *Supplementary Information,* Tabled in the House of Commons by the Honourable Michael H. Wilson, 8 November 1984, (Ottawa: Department of Finance, 1984); and Treasury Board of Canada, *Expenditure and Program Review,* Statement by the Honourable R. de Cotret, president of the Treasury Board (Ottawa, November 1984).
2. Department of Finance, *An Agenda for Economic Renewal,* 13, 15, 21.
3. P. Resnick, "The Ideology of Neo-Conservatism," in Warren Magnusson et al., eds., *The New Reality* (Vancouver: New Star Books, 1984), 133.
4. H. Chorney, *The Deficit: Hysteria and the Current Economic Crisis,* Publication 13 (Ottawa: Canadian Centre for Policy Alternatives, 1985), 2.
5. CCSD, *CCSD Discussion Paper on Social Security* (Ottawa: CCSD, February 1985).
6. CCSD, "Special Issue on Income Security," *Social Development Overview* 2, 3 (Winter 1985).
7. L. Mardsen, "After 1984: Controlling the Agenda," *Canadian Forum* (January 1984): 6–9.
8. Treasury Board, *Expenditure and Program Review,* B2–B3.
9. An illustration that this may be occurring is found in the deficit reduction campaign currently being run by the National Citizens Coalition. The major aim of this group is to enlist the people of Canada in a broader coalition to bring pressure on the government to reduce the deficit. In the Coalition's view the deficit is a direct outcome of excessive spending, not inadequate revenue. Its message is that spending must be cut. This is illustrated with an example of how much could be saved if universal, family allowances (the baby bonus)

and old age pension payments were made selective and given to "only those that really need them." According to the Coalition "this alone will save billions." This aspect of the advertisement fits right into the government's concern that universal payments unnecessarily put strain on government resources. Like the government, however, the Coalition's approach also ignores very important aspects of foregone tax revenue and who benefits from these forms of public expenditure. The Citizens Coalition could have tremendous public appeal. At the least it does seem to suggest that the spending/deficit debate framed by the government is enjoying and gaining widespread public acceptance. National Citizens Coalition, "The Deficit, It's Your Move," *Globe and Mail*, 20 April 1985, 1–3.

10. C. W. Mills, *The Sociological Imagination* (Don Mills, Ont.: Oxford University Press, 1959), 32–36; CCSD, "Special Issue on Income Security," *Social Development Overview* 2, no. 3 (Winter 1985).

11. Department of Finance, *An Agenda for Economic Renewal*, 1.

12. It is beyond the scope of this paper to thoroughly disentangle the competing views of how the deficit is calculated and its impact on growth, investment and unemployment. The Conservatives present one view. Deficits are harmful. Other perspectives which present alternatives need to be brought into this debate. See Chorney, *The Deficit*; A. Redish, *Is There a Social Policy in British Columbia? Who Has Been Hurt and Why?* (British Columbia Economic Policy Institute, Paper P84–87, May 1984).

13. Economic Council of Canada, *Steering the Course* (Minister of Supply and Services, 1984); L. McQuaig, "Rich Rewards," *Globe and Mail*, 21 April 1984, 1.

14. G. Ternowetsky, "It's Time to Implement Tax Reform," *Canadian Review of Social Policy/Revue Canadienne de Politique Sociale* 12 (December 1984): 23–24.

15. The publication of these tax expenditures data permitted, for the first time, public scrutiny of hidden government spending on the rich and powerful corporations in Canada. This exercise in dissemination was short-lived. The Tax Expenditure Accounts were discontinued after the Liberals returned to power. How this was permitted to happen should concern us. We might also expect that, in this period of concern with the deficit and openness in decision-making, these data will once again be published. Part of our mandate is to force this issue if a realistic debate on the deficit is to be entertained.

16. National Council of Welfare, *The Hidden Welfare System Revisited* (Ottawa 1979), 4.

17. L. McQuaig, "The Ottawa Albatross," *Globe and Mail*, 7 November 1984, 3.

18. Department of Finance, *An Agenda for Economic Renewal*, 23, 35–41.
19. C. Rachlis, "The Right Wing Threat to Universality," *Our Times* 4, 1 (1985): 27–29.

20. *Regina Leader Post*, "Conference told that jobs, people should be a priority," 27 March 1985, 1.

21. Rachlis, "The Right Wing Threat to Universality," 27–29. Not only did the Royal not pay taxes, but it received a tax credit of $28 million from the Federal government (Royal Bank of Canada, Annual Report 1985, p. 52).

22. Canada, House of Commons, Standing Committee on Finance, Trade and Economic Affairs, *Bank Profits* (Ottawa: Queen's Printer, 1982), 112.

23. Saskatchewan, *Estimates for the Fiscal Year Ending March 31, 1985* (Regina, 1984).

24. L. McQuaig, "How Big Corporations Beat the Taxman for Billions," *Globe and Mail*, 10 March 1984, 1; "Companies Pay Only 24% of Tax Bill" (30 March); "Rich Rewards" (21 April); "The Ottawa Albatross" (7 November).

25. McQuaig, "Companies Pay Only 24% of Tax Bill," 1.

26. Canada, House of Commons, Standing Committee on Trade, Finance and Economic Affairs, *Budget Review* (Ottawa: Queen's Printer, 1983).

27. McQuaig, "How Big Corporations Beat Taxman for Billions," 1. Another interesting aspect to this agreement needs to be noted. Tax breaks are used to encourage investment. Through deregulation, however, the price of "old oil" (oil discovered prior to 1974) will rise and "new oil" will fall. Companies like Texaco which invested little in new oil ventures will gain about $77 million from the new oil price structure. All of the major oil companies will attain windfall profits, but those that invested little in new projects will gain the most. (McQuaig, "Deregulation is Bonanza for Texaco," *Globe and Mail*, 15 April 1985, B1).

    Under deregulation alone (not including tax breaks) the following windfall profits from the sale of "old oil" will accrue to the four most profitable oil companies:

Imperial Oil	$54.9 million
Texaco	$76.8 million
Gulf Oil	$58.9 million
Shell Oil	$43.7 million

    There is little wonder that the executive director of the Canadian Petroleum Association stated he was "delighted with the result" (J. Gallagher, "Tory Oil Policy Points to Bias Towards the Rich," *The Commonwealth* 45, 7 (April 1985): 8).

28. Another way to assess corporate accountability is to see if tax concessions result in increased investments. From a theoretical perspective one role of tax breaks is to help the economy by generating private investments. However, there is now widespread agreement that tax concessions have little bearing on investment decisions. It is even being suggested that "the proliferation of tax breaks in recent years has more to do with the government's desire to appease the business com

munity than with its interest in fixing the economy," McQuaig, "How Big Corporations Beat the Taxman for Billions," 1.

29. "Canada's Top 500 Companies," Special Issue, *Canadian Business* (1982); (1984).

30. Gallagher, "Tory Oil Policy Points to Bias Towards the Rich," 8. In a recent, national advertising campaign, Gulf Oil pointed out that the large corporations no longer create jobs. As they prosper, however, the local market is stimulated and jobs in the small business sector are created. These indirect jobs are welcome. However, if corporations like Gulf do not create jobs as they accumulate and accept public funds, it is important that we raise for public debate the policy of corporate assistance and corporate accountability.

31. The following profit increases for 1984 are reported: Imperial Oil, $533 million; Texaco, $423 million; Gulf Oil, $308 million; Shell Oil, $158 million. See Gallagher, "Tory Oil Policy Points to Bias Towards the Rich," 8.

32. L. Bryson, "Poverty Research in Australia: Unmasking Noble Terms," *Australian and New Zealand Journal of Sociology* 17, 3 (1977): 196–202; Mills, *The Sociological Imagination.*

33. A. Gouldner, "The Sociologist as Partisan: Sociology and the Welfare State," in L. Reynolds and J. Reynolds, eds., *The Sociology of Sociology* (New York: David-McKay Co., 1970), 204–17.